ELIZABETHAN
JOURNA

ELIZABETHAN AND JACOBEAN JOURNALS 1591–1610

G. B. Harrison

VOLUME I
An Elizabethan Journal
being a record of those things most talked of during the years 1591–1594

VOLUME II
A Second Elizabethan Journal
being a record of those things most talked of during the years 1595–1598

VOLUME III
A Last Elizabethan Journal
being a record of those things most talked of during the years 1599–1603

VOLUME IV
A Jacobean Journal
being a record of those things most talked of during the years 1603–1606

VOLUME V
A Second Jacobean Journal
being a record of those things most talked of during the years 1607–1610

ELIZABETHAN AND JACOBEAN JOURNALS 1591–1610

Volume II

A Second Elizabethan Journal

G. B. Harrison

LONDON AND NEW YORK

First published 1931 by Constable & Co. Ltd

Reprinted by Routledge 1999
2 Park Square, Milton Park,
Abingdon, Oxon, OX14 4RN

Simultaneously published in the USA and Canada
by Routledge
711 Third Avenue, New York, NY 10017

Reprinted 2001

Transferred to Digital Printing 2007

Routledge is an imprint of the Taylor & Francis Group

First issued in paperback 2012

Publisher's note
The publisher has gone to great lengths to ensure the quality of this reprint but points out that some imperfections in the original book may be apparent.

British Library Cataloguing in Publication Data
A CIP record of this set is available from the British Library

Library of Congress Cataloging in Publication Data
A catalogue record for this book has been requested

ISBN 978-0-415-322145-0 (hbk)
ISBN 978-0-415-84575-5 (pbk)
5 Volumes: ISBN 978-0-415-22143-6 (set)

A SECOND
ELIZABETHAN
JOURNAL

A SECOND ELIZABETHAN JOURNAL

BEING A RECORD
OF THOSE THINGS MOST TALKED OF
DURING THE YEARS
1595—1598

G. B. Harrison

LONDON AND NEW YORK

First published in 1931
by Constable & Co. Ltd
Reprinted in 1974
by Routledge
2 Park Square, Milton Park,
Abingdon, Oxon, OX14 4RN
270 Madison Ave, New York NY 10016

ISBN 0 7100 7882 X

CONTENTS

1595

3rd January. THE REVELS AT GRAY'S INN.

The revels at Gray's Inn were this night continued and because of the tumults on the 'Night of Errors' good watch was kept with whifflers, so that all had good places to their liking and contentment. There were present many great and noble personages, as the Lord Keeper, the Earls of Shrewsbury, Cumberland, Northumberland, Southampton and Essex, the Lords Buckhurst, Windsor, Mountjoy, Burleigh, Mounteagle, Thomas Howard; Sir Thomas Heneage, Sir Robert Cecil; and a great number of Knights, Ladies and very worshipful persons.

When all were placed, the Prince of Purpool came into the Hall with his wonted state and ascended his throne at the high end of the Hall, and after him the Ambassador of Templaria with his train; who, after variety of music, were presented with this device. At the side of the Hall within a curtain was erected an altar to the Goddess of Amity, her arch-flamen ready to attend the sacrifice that should be offered, and round about nymphs and fairies with instruments of music. Then issued forth of another room, the first pair of friends, being Theseus and Perithous. They came arm in arm, and offered incense upon the altar, which shined and burned very clear without blemish, and so departed; and in like manner came Achilles and Patroclus, Pilades and Orestes, then Scipio and Lelius. But when Graius and Templarius came lovingly to the altar and offered their incense, the Goddess did not accept of their service, for the flame was choked by a troubled smoke and dark vapour. Hereat the arch-flamen, willing to pacify the angry goddess, preferred certain mystical ceremonies and commanded the nymphs to sing some hymns of pacification, so that when the friends again proffered their devotion the flame burnt more clear than at any time before: and so they departed. Whereupon the arch-flamen pronounced Graius and Templarius to be friends, and denounced a heavy curse upon them that in any way go about to break the bond and league of sincere amity.

Then the Prince, in token of their amity, offered the Ambassador of the Templarians and some of his retinue the Knighthood of the Helmet, an order of his own institution. So the King at Arms placed the Ambassador and some of his followers, and also some of the Templarians, that they might receive the dignity at his hands; which done, the Prince came down from his chair of state, and put a Collar about the Ambassador's neck, he kneeling on his left knee, and said to him, '*Sois Chevalier*'; and so was done to the rest, to the number of twenty-four. Then the King at Arms stood forth, and after a speech read out the Articles of the Order, being of this nature:

Item, No knight shall be inquisitive towards any lady or gentleman, whether her beauty be English or Italian, or whether with care taking she have added half a foot to her stature, but take all to the best. Neither shall any knight presume to affirm that faces were better twenty years ago than they are at this present time, except such knight have passed three climacterical years.

Item, No knight shall put out any money upon strange returns or performances to be made by his own person, as to hop up the stairs to the top of St. Paul's without intermission, or any such like agilities or endurances, except it may appear that the same practices do enable him to some service or employment; as if he do undertake to go a journey backward, the same shall be thought to enable him to be an Ambassador unto Turkey.

Item, No knight, that hath licence to travel, be it by map, card, sea or land, and hath returned, shall presume upon the warrant of a traveller to report any extraordinary varieties; as that he hath ridden through Venice on horseback post, or travelled over the most part of the countries of Geneva.

Item, Every knight shall endeavour to be much in the books of the worshipful citizens next adjoining to the territories of Purpool; and none shall unlearnedly, or without looking, pay ready money for any wares, to the ill example of others, and utter suppression of credit betwixt man and man.

Item, Every knight shall endeavour to add conference and experience by reading; and therefore shall not only read and peruse Guizo, *The French Academy*, Galiatho, *The Courtier*, Plutarch, the *Arcadia*, and the Neoterical writers from time to time; but also frequent the Theatre, and such like places of experience; and resort to the better sort of ordinaries for conference, whereby they may not only become accomplished with civil conversations, and able to govern a table with discourse; but also sufficient, if need be, to make epigrams, emblems, and other devices appertaining to his Honour's learned revels.

Item, No knight that weareth fustian, cloth, or such statute stuff for necessity shall pretend to wear the same for the new fashion's sake.

Item, No knight in walking the streets or other places of resort shall bear his hands in the pockets of his great rolled hose with the Spanish wheel, if it be not either to defend his hands from the cold or else to guard forty shillings sterling, being in the same pockets.

Item, That no knight shall take upon him the person of a Malcontent, in going with a more private retinue than appertaineth to his degree, and using but certain special, obscure company, and commending none but men disgraced and out of office; and smiling at good news, as if he knew something that were not true, and making odd notes of his Highness's reign, and former governments, and the like.

When all these Articles of Knighthood had been read and the ceremonies finished, there was variety of consort music; and in the meanwhile the Knights of the Order, which were not strangers, brought into the Hall a running banquet in very good order, and gave it to the Prince, the Lords and other strangers. This done the Prince held a Council of six of his Privy Councillors, to whom he gave charge that they should advise him in general of the scope and end whereunto the government of the State might best be directed.

Then the first Councillor made a speech advising the exercise of war whereby in later years he should find a sweet respect into the adventures of youth, enjoy his reputation, eternize his name, and leave deep footsteps of his power in the world.

The second Councillor would have him study philosophy, commending four principal works to the Prince. The first was the collecting of a most perfect and general library, wherein whatsoever the wit of man hath heretofore committed to books of worth, be they ancient or modern, printed or manuscript,

European or of other parts, of one or other language, might be made contributory to his wisdom. Next a spacious wonderful garden wherein whatsoever plant the earth bringeth forth may be set and cherished: this garden to be built about with rooms to stake in all rare beasts, and to cage in all rare birds, with two lakes adjoining, the one of fresh water, the other of salt, for like variety of fishes; and so he might have in small compass a model of Universal Nature made private. The third, a goodly huge cabinet wherein shall be stored whatsoever the hand of man by exquisite art or engine hath made rare in stuff, form, or motion. The fourth, such a still house so furnished with mills, instruments, furnaces and vessels as may be a palace fit for a philosopher's stone.

The third Councillor, confuting those that had gone before, would have the Prince's fame eternized by the magnificence of goodly and royal buildings and foundations, and the new institutions of orders, ordinances and societies.

The fourth Councillor advised absoluteness of state and treasure, for he had needs conquer at home the overgrowing of his grandees in factions and too great liberties of the people, the great reverence given to laws and customs in derogation of his absolute prerogatives.

The fifth Councillor advised virtue and gracious government, but the sixth would have him take counsel only of his five senses and follow his pleasures.

To all of which the Prince said he must take his time to consider. Then rising from his seat, he made choice of a lady to dance withal, and so likewise did the Ambassador and the courtiers attending on the Prince. So the rest of the night is spent in these pastimes, being so carefully and orderly handled that the former disgrace is now quite taken away.

4th January. GRAY'S INN REVELS.

To-day the Prince of Purpool, accompanied with the Ambassador of Templaria and attended by both trains, took a progress from Gray's Inn to Crosby's Place, the Lord Mayor's house in Bishopsgate Street, having before been invited to dine with him. This show was very stately and orderly performed, and everyone had his feather in his cap to distinguish of what state he was, the

Grayans using white and the Templarians ash-coloured. Thus they rode very gallantly from Gray's Inn, through Chancery Lane, Fleet Street, so through Cheapside, Cornhill and to Crosby's Place, where was a very sumptuous and costly dinner. Dinner being ended, the Prince and his company having revelled awhile returned the same way, the streets being thronged with people to see the gentlemen as they passed by, who thought there had been some great prince in very deed passing through the City.

10*th January*. A NOTABLE CASE OF COSENAGE.

A certain widow, by name Mrs. Mascall, hath been notably cosened by one Judith Phillips, otherwise known as Doll Pope. Two men, the one called Peters, the other Vaughan, dealt with this Judith to be a means to procure Peters' favour with the widow. Thereupon Vaughan devised a letter in the name of one Mr. Grace, a near friend of the widow's, to the effect that she should make much of Judith, for she was one that could do her great good. Peters and Vaughan also told Judith what suitors the widow had and where they dwelt, also of many accidents which they knew to be true, to the intent that she might seem to be a wise woman.

Whereupon Judith going to the widow was well entertained and had into her chamber. After some speeches past Judith looked into her hand, and then began to tell her what suitors she had. Also she asked of the widow whether she was not troubled in the night with sights and noises in her house; to which the widow answered yea.

'Yea,' said Judith, 'hath there not been lights seen in your house?'

'How know you that?' said the widow.

'I know it well,' quoth Judith, 'and the cause too; for there is money hid in your house.'

The widow therefore being more persuaded of Judith's great skill began to speak of her suitors and prayed that she would get the money hid in the house. Judith then told her that first she must have such gold as the widow had, which she would not carry away but leave in the house; and within two days the gold hid in the house should be found in the place which she appointed for this gold to be. So the widow brought forth certain gold, a chain of gold, seven rings and a whistle, all of which were put in a purse and delivered to Judith. Judith wrapped this purse up in yarn, and having before wound two stones in other yarn, closely conveyed the yarn with the two stones to the widow, which she took and laid up in the appointed place with charge from Judith not to look at it until three days were past. She also told the widow that she must have a turkey and a capon to give to the Queen of the Fairy, which the widow provided. Also she made the widow say certain prayers in sundry places of the house, and then departed. Judith then departed with the gold and the chain, which she divided with Peters and Vaughan, but the rings she took out secretly and kept them to herself.

The next morning, intending to cosen the widow of her plate also, Judith brought the head and legs of the turkey in a basket to the window, and began to tell the widow that she must lay one leg under the bed and the rest in other places; but the widow having by this discovered the stones in the yarn knew herself to be cosened and caused Judith to be apprehended.

This Judith hath long used her trade of cosenage, wandering about the country in company with divers persons that call themselves Egyptians. For that kind of life she was condemned to die at Salisbury, but afterwards had her pardon.

13th January. GOSSON'S 'PLEASANT QUIPS.'

Mr. Stephen Gosson, parson of Great Wigborough in Essex, hath written very invectively against the fantastical foreign toys daily used in our women's apparel, which he entitleth *Pleasant Quips for Upstart New fangled Gentlewomen.*

Complaineth that masks were once to hide the face from wantons bold:

> But on each wight now are they seen,
> The tallow-pale, the browning-bay,
> The swarthy-black, the grassy-green,
> The pudding-red, the dapple-grey,
> So might we judge them toys aright
> To keep sweet beauty still in plight.

What else do masks but masquers show,
And masquers can both dance and play:
Our masking dames can sport, you know,
Sometime by night, sometime by day:
'Can you hit it' is oft their dance,
Deuce-ace falls still to be their chance.

17th January. BARNFIELD'S 'CYNTHIA' AND 'CASSANDRA.'

Mr. Richard Barnfield hath written two poems, the one in praise of Cynthia, the other of the life and death of Cassandra. Of Cynthia, he saith that the gods and goddesses all promised her wealth, wisdom and beauty, but that between the goddess and her Gracious Majesty there is this difference:

She shines by night; but thou by day dost shine;
She monthly changes; thou dost ne'er decline.
And as the sun to her doth lend his light,
So he by thee is only made so bright:
Yet neither sun, nor moon, thou canst be named,
Because thy lights have both their beauties shamed.
Then since an heavenly name doth thee befall,
Thou Virgo art, if any sign at all.

Of Cassandra, telleth the story of her lamentable life; how the god Apollo loved her so that, encouraging his love, she caused him solemnly to promise her the gift of prophecy, which promise being made she chastely counterchecked his approaches. Hereat the god, being greatly enraged, cursed her that she should indeed foretell truly of things to come, but for her falsehood no man should believe her; and moreover, for a penance on that sex, a constant woman should be hard to find; which prophecy (saith the author) hath proved true for that their 'sex are subject to inconstancy as other creatures are to destiny.'

23rd January. COMPLAINTS AGAINST PATENTS.

The leather sellers in the City send a petition to her Majesty concerning the enormities of Mr. Darcy's patent for stamping of leather which the Lord Mayor upholdeth; for, saith he, the exactions and other inconveniences of Mr. Darcy's patent cause great grief and murmur of the people throughout the land, and Mr. Darcy's violent manner of proceeding is very unmeet in this time of dearth when great numbers of poor people are grieved already and exasperate enough by their own misery and great want of food. There are at this present time seven such patents, being, for leather to Mr. Darcy; for brushes, bottles and stone pots; for soap and barrel butter; for cards; for vinegar, alliger, *aqua vitae*, *aqua composita*; and for steel to a stranger.

'THE ESTATE OF THE ENGLISH FUGITIVES.'

There is entered a work entitled *The Estate of the English fugitives*, being the true copy of that book which, contrary to the author's intention, was lately printed in Paul's Churchyard, but corruptly and ignorantly intermixed with fictions of the publisher. Herein our unexperienced gentlemen and credulous Catholics are warned by many examples of the monstrous cruelty and treacheries of the Spaniard towards those who have entered into his service.

Of the Jesuits it is written that there is not any man's business but they must have an oar in it; they never plant themselves in any places but in the midst of goodly cities where they wring themselves into the fairest palaces. Their churches are rich and sumptuous, their movables and household stuff magnificent rather than decent, their gardens fine and comely, their fare plentiful and of the best; nor are they tied to any risings in the night, or any the like hardness to which other religious houses are subjected. Their first mass doth never at any time begin before 8 of the clock. They are accounted the greatest intelligences and statesmen of the world. They may not receive any higher office or dignity, but they take the name of a Jesuit not to be any whit inferior to the title of a bishop; nor are they subject to any controlment but only the Provincial of their order. But the best is to see how busy and diligent they are when they hear of a wealthy man that lieth sick and in danger of death.

As a proof of the affection of the subjects for the Queen in England, note the behaviour of the people when a traitor is carried to his arraignment or execution; which though it should move the minds of men to commiserate the calamitous estate of those unfortunate wretches, yet are the people, in jealousy of her Majesty's safety and hatred of her enemies, many times hardly restrained by the officers from doing violence to the prisoners on the way. Then do they curse, ban and revile them with the most opprobrious speeches they can invent; and commonly applaud the instant of their deaths with a general shout of joy, and cries of ‘God save the Queen and confound all traitors’; whereas they do usually accompany all other kinds to their deaths with a kind of feeling of sorrow and compassion.

24th January. THE SCOTTISH AMBASSADOR GIVEN AUDIENCE.

To-day the Lord Wemyss was given audience by the Queen who taxed the King of Scots with unkindness in that he goes about to make a new league with the French King, to which he answereth that it is but the renewing of the old. When he had drawn to an end the Queen willed him to assure the King, his master, that when he had tried all his new friends, he should find that her kindness overweighted all theirs; to which he replied, ‘As you have, madam, proved his love and fidelity to have been above that which you can expect at the rest of your kind friends' hands.’ Coming forth from the Privy Chamber he asked the Lord Chamberlain for Sir Robert Cecil. ‘Why, sir,’ said he, ‘he was within.’

‘By my soul,’ said Lord Wemyss, ‘I could not see him.’

‘No marvel,’ said Sir George Carey, ‘being so little.’ Whereat the Lord Wemyss burst out of laughing.

25th January. THE IRISH REBELLION.

Rebellion is now broken out in Ireland and if forces be not sent both Enniskillen and all the North will be lost. Such is the strong combination of the Earl of Tyrone that there is not any dare show himself a dutiful subject.

THE VACANT SOLICITORSHIP.

Mr. Francis Bacon's friends at Court now deal with the Queen for his advancement to the Solicitorship; for if he get not promotion, he declareth that he will travel. But my Lord of Essex carrying the matter somewhat too far, her Majesty sweareth that if Mr. Bacon continue in this manner, she will seek all England for a Solicitor rather than take him. She hath never, saith she, dealt so with any as with him ; she hath pulled him over the Bar and used him in her greatest causes.

27th January. HURAULT'S DISCOURSES.

Mr. Arthur Golding hath translated into English the politic moral and martial discourses written in French by M. Jaques Hurault, one of the French King's Council, wherein in three parts he treateth firstly of the office, duties, and necessary qualities of a king ; in the second, of wisdom and discretion, fortitude, prowess, diligence, continence and other virtues ; in the third, of leagues, and governors, of the leading of an army, of divers policies and sleights necessary in war.

28th January. GRAY'S INN REVELS.

The revels at Gray's Inn have been discontinued these three weeks past by reason that the Prince of Purpool made a pretended voyage to Russia ; and at his return it was intended to have performed certain good inventions wherewith his reign should have been very conceitedly determined. But the purpose of the gentlemen was frustrated by the Readers and Governors who caused the scaffolds to be taken away from the Hall and would not have them built again by reason of the term. This night there came into the Hall the King at Arms to announce the Prince's return from Russia and summon his subjects to meet him on the 1st February.

31st January. THE JESUITS AT WISBEACH CASTLE.

The state of the seminary priests and Jesuits that are confined in Wisbeach Castle is reported to be grown as dangerous as a seminary college by liberty and favour of their keeper. There are about twenty-eight of them who have compounded with their keeper for their diet, provision and servants as if they were in a free college. They send abroad their servants into the town to the market where they buy up the best victuals. Great resort is daily made there of gentlemen and gentlewomen and others who dine and sup with them, walk with them in the castle yard, and confer in their chambers, whereby they receive and send intelligence. They want no money, and by giving alms and devotions at the gate the poor esteem them for godly men. They keep eight poor townsborn children and two strangers of good wit and choice, beside their cooks, and those recusants. They are all young and lusty people, disposed to mirth and viciousness with women, and attempt them, as the keeper's maid and two daughters have been, in whorish manner. Most of these men were banished and have returned, some were men condemned for treason. Hereby scholars of the Universities and priests beyond the sea hold that if they be taken and so entertained the worst is but good cheer, and great hopes of bishoprics and preferments hereafter.

1st February. THE GRAY'S INN REVELS.

This day the Prince of Purpool with his train came up the Thames in fifteen barges, bravely furnished with flags and streamers from Blackwall, and so to Greenwich where a letter is despatched to Sir Thomas Heneage, praying that the Prince may pay his homage on Shrove Tuesday. To which the Queen returned answer that she liked well his shows that were made at his triumphant return, and that if he come at Shrovetide, he and his followers shall have entertainment according to his dignity. Then the Prince and his company continued their course until they came to the Tower where, by the Queen's commandment, he was welcomed with a volley of great ordnance by the Lieutenant of the Tower. At Tower Hill there waited for the Prince's landing men with horses, very bravely furnished, to the number of a hundred, whereon they rode very gallantly through Tower Street, Fenchurch Street, Grace Church Street, Cornhill, Cheapside, and so through St. Paul's Churchyard where at St. Paul's School his Highness was entertained with an oration made by one of the scholars, whom the Prince rewarded very bountifully before continuing on his way by Ludgate and Fleet Street to Gray's Inn.

3rd February. GRAY'S INN REVELS AT COURT.

This night the Prince of Purpool and some of his followers performed a masque of Proteus before the Queen at Court, who is much pleased by the good performance of all that was done and wished the sports might continue longer, which might well appear by her answer to the courtier who danced a measure immediately after the masque was ended. 'What,' said she, 'shall we have bread and cheese after a banquet?' Her

Majesty willeth the Lord Chamberlain that the gentlemen shall be invited to-morrow, and presented unto her.

4th February. SIR JOHN NORRIS'S RETURN.

Sir John Norris is now returned from Brittany having been delayed for want of shipping, and by ill weather. The soldiers that were employed in those parts are at Paimpol, waiting for their return.

THE GRAY'S INN REVELS ENDED.

The gentlemen of Gray's Inn were presented to her Majesty this evening, and she gave them her hand to kiss with most gracious words of commendation, and particularly of Gray's Inn, as an House she was much beholding unto for it doth always study for some sports to present unto her. And afterwards there was fighting at the barriers, the Earl of Essex and others challengers, and the Earl of Cumberland and his company defenders ; into which number the Prince of Purpool was taken and behaved so valiantly and skilfully that he had the prize adjudged due unto him, which it pleased the Queen to deliver with her own hands, telling him that it was not her gift, for if it had been it should have been better. The prize is a jewel set with seventeen diamonds and four rubies, in value accounted worth 100 marks.

Thus are these sports and revels ended at the Court, and the principality of Purpool determined in the greater brightness of the royal presence of her Majesty.

7th February. AN ALARM AT OSTEND.

There is new alarm of an attack at Ostend for that a prisoner from the garrison, to save his life, is reported to have promised to show some places in the defences which would be easily battered and entered by reason of the new fortifications not half perfected. Wherefore the enemy sent men to discover the places, but nothing is yet come of it.

8th February. SIR WALTER RALEGH'S VOYAGE.

Sir Walter Ralegh set out with his fleet from Plymouth two days ago.

9th February. THE QUEEN'S LETTER TO THE GRAND SIGNIOR.

The Queen writeth to the Emperor of Turkey at the importunity of Sigismund, the Vayrod of Transylvania, that she should intercede on his behalf. Wherefore the Queen, by reason of her old friendship with Sigismund, and for that he followeth the same form of Christianity as we, (having rejected the superstition of the Pope of Rome and the worshipping of images), now urgeth the Grand Signor that the Vayrod's complaints may be heard and remedied according to law.

11th February. BISHOP FLETCHER'S MARRIAGE.

Dr. Fletcher that was made Bishop of London at the end of last year hath of late married a gallant lady and widow, sister to Sir George Gifford the pensioner, (the Bishop himself also being a widower), who if she be virtuous is the more unhappy in that the world believeth it not. Hereat the Queen is so greatly displeased that she sendeth the Lord Buckhurst to confer with the Archbishop about sequestrating him from his function of Bishop.

15th February. FLESH PROHIBITED DURING LENT.

As in former years orders are published for the restraint of killing and eating of flesh during this coming season of Lent. Six butchers are to be licensed for the City and the sums so paid to be for the relief of maimed soldiers and mariners.

18th February. MOSSE'S 'ARRAIGNMENT AND CONVICTION OF USURY.'

There is a book of sermons called *The Arraignment and conviction of usury*, by Miles Mosse, Minister of the Word, dedicated to the Archbishop of Canterbury, wherein are handled four principal points, namely: usury, what it is and what are the kinds and branches thereof; proof that it is manifestly forbidden by the Word of God, and sundry reasons alleged why it is justly and worthily condemned; the objections answered which are usually made out of the Scriptures for the defence of some kind of usury and towards some kind of persons; divers causes why usury should not be practised of a Christian, especially not of an Englishman, though it could be proved that it is not simply forbidden in the Scriptures.

20th February. THE TRIAL OF FR. SOUTHWELL.

Robert Southwell, the Jesuit, was arraigned at the King's Bench before Lord Chief Justice Popham, having been removed from the Tower to Newgate some days since. Being brought along with halberts and bills, and his arms tied with a cord, at length he came through the press to the bar, and there, having his hands loosed, he put off his hat and made obeisance. The Chief Justice, casting his eyes upon him, asked him his age, who answered that he was about the age of Christ when he was brought before Pilate. 'Why then,' quoth he, 'you make yourself Christ, his companion?' 'No,' saith Southwell, 'but a poor worm created for to serve him.'

Then was the indictment read, to which Southwell after some pause answered, 'I confess I am a Catholic priest and, I thank God for it, no traitor: neither can any law make it treason to be a priest.' The Chief Justice importuned him to answer according to form of law, and his answer was 'Not guilty of treason.'.

Then Mr. Coke, the Attorney-General, began to open the indictment. 'I had not thought,' quoth he, 'to have spoken anything this day; but that the prisoner let fall a word, *videlicet*, that no law could make his case treason. I have occupied this room but three years, and there have been divers high points of treason practised by Jebusites, I should say Jesuits'; and drawing upon recent examples, concluded that the statute upon which the prisoner was arraigned was not made but upon some urgent cause. 'They pretend conscience,' saith he, 'but you shall see how far they are from it.'

One Bellamy's daughter was then brought in that had betrayed Southwell to Topcliffe. Her deposition was that Southwell told them that if any should inquire for him and propose to them an oath whether they had seen him, they might deny it by oath though they had seen him that same day, reserving this intention—'not with a purpose to tell you.'

Hereupon the Attorney exclaimed that the rotten Chair would down which maintained a doctrine by which all judgments, all giving of testimonies, should be perverted.

Southwell answered that his words were not altogether as she reported; 'but I told them,' said he, 'that to an oath were required justice, judgment and truth.' Some few words he spake more; but his utterance was somewhat unready, and they always cut him off when he began to speak.

And now Topcliffe began to question him, and as he answered, he was often interrupted so that he could seldom or never end one sentence when he did begin. Then said he, 'I am decayed in memory with long and close imprisonment, and I have been tortured ten times. I had rather have endured ten executions. I speak not this for myself but for others; that they may not be handled so inhumanely, to drive men to desperation if it were possible.'

To this Topcliffe answered, 'If he were racked, let me die for it.'

'No,' quoth Southwell, 'but it was as evil a torture, of late device.'

'I did but set him against a wall,' quoth Topcliffe.

To which Southwell answered, 'Thou art a bad man.'

'I would blow you all to dust, if I could,' said Topcliffe.

'What, all?' asked Southwell.

'Ay, all,' said Topcliffe.

'What, soul and body too?' said Southwell.

Hereupon Topcliffe exclaimed that he found him in a corner treading upon books, and also having letters directed to him from Parsons the Jesuit; which letters Topcliffe showed, but nothing was read of them, nor of other papers nor books which he poured out of a bag.

The jury staying not above a quarter of an hour, returned saying 'Guilty'; so he is condemned to death.

21st February. New Plays at the Rose.

New plays by the Lord Admiral's men this month at the Rose are *The French Comedy* and *The Mack.*

22nd February. The Execution of Fr. Southwell.

This day Southwell was haled upon a draw from Newgate, laid upon straw, to the place of execution by Tyburn, having a cord fastened about his wrists. All the way he prayed, with his countenance and eyes lifted towards Heaven, and used not any speech.

When he was come to the place, as they were taking him off the draw, the minister of the Tower came to him and used these words: 'You hold the decrees of the Council of Trent for authentical?'

'I do,' said Southwell.

'Therein,' said he, 'is decreed that no man shall presume to believe that he is sure to be saved, but is to doubt. If you believe to be saved, you contradict the Council; if you doubt, being about to die, your case is hard; and you doubting, we must needs doubt.'

Southwell replied, 'I hope to be saved by the merits of my Saviour; but I pray you trouble me not.'

So he was lifted into the cart, at which time his countenance appeared very modest, yet cheerful, like the sun when it breaketh out after that it hath dispersed the clouds. The minister began to speak to him again, to whom he answered, 'I pray you Master Minister, give me leave.' So turning himself to the under-sheriff, he asked him whether he might speak; who answered that he might, so that he would confess his fault. 'I will,' said he, 'speak nothing against the State.'

His beginning to pray had entrance with this place of the apostle, '*Siue viuimus Domino viuimus, siue morimur Domino morimur; siue viuimus siue morimur, Domini sumus*'; at which words the sheriff interrupted him, so where it seemed he would have made some speech, being cut off, he desired all Catholics to join with him in prayer to Almighty God, that it would please Him to forgive him all his sins which he had committed in this miserable life; miserable not for that he died a reproachful death, ignominious in the sight of the world, but honourable before God, for that it was for the testimony of His cause; but miserable for that he had sinned so often against so merciful and gracious a God. He then prayed for the Queen, that she might enjoy all gifts of nature and grace, all helps of friends and faithful councillors, whereby she might reign to God's glory, and after this life be inheritor of the Kingdom of Heaven, and wished that she would pardon him for that he had come into her kingdom without licence. He prayed that God would be merciful to the whole land and vouchsafe to convert them which were out of the way of truth.

And so protesting that he died a Catholic priest and in the Roman faith, standing in his shirt, often repeating these words, '*In manus tuas, Domine,*' the cart was removed. When he had hanged a while, the sheriff made a sign to the sergeants to cut the rope, at which there was a great confused cry in the company that he prayed for the Queen; 'And therefore let him hang till he be dead,' said they. So he was not cut down till he was senseless as far as could be perceived. A man might perceive by the countenances of the beholders that there was almost a general commiseration; none railed against him. The Lord Mountjoy was present, who is said, having beheld the mild and godly end of this man, to have uttered these words: 'I cannot judge of his religion; but pray God, whensoever I die, that my soul may be in no worse case than his.'

26th February. THE FORT AT BLACKWATER TAKEN.

Ten days ago the rebels in Ireland assaulted and took the fort and castle of Blackwater. Some forty or fifty of Tyrone's men, having passed through the town and within the stone castle, made sudden assault against the door of the inner castle which was made of wood; there being within only Henry Marche, the warder, and four others, whereof two were straightway sore wounded. These killed and galled thirteen of the rebels. When the assault had continued for a quarter of an hour, the warder and three others came out of the castle and drave them away with their swords. But afterward learning from the other Englishmen in the place that their munition was gone, and that the rebels would burn the castle, they were forced to yield.

4th March. A FATAL MISCHANCE.

Yesterday evening two youths called Goldstone and Carpenter were playing together in the house of one William Harrison when they found in the hall a dag and a fowling piece, and not knowing them to be loaded Carpenter by mischance shot Goldstone in the face, whereof he died instantly.

5th March. A NEW PLAY.

There is a new play at the Rose entitled *Selio and Olimpo.*

6th March. THE WIDOW OF DR. LOPEZ.

The Queen hath granted to the widow and children of Lopez, that was executed for his treasonable practices in June last year, the leases that he held in London, and of his goods, forfeit by his attainder, not exceeding £100, but excepting a jewel set with a diamond and a ruby that was sent to Lopez by some minister of the King of Spain.

15th March. THE EARL OF CUMBERLAND'S SHIP.

My Lord of Cumberland, not liking his ill partage with the Great Carrack in '92 nor the unhappier loss of two carracks last year for want of sufficient strength to take them, now buildeth a ship of his own of 900 tons at Deptford; which the Queen at her launching named the *Scourge of Malice*, the best ship that hath ever been built by any subject.

26th March. MR. CHAMPERNOUN'S CHOIRBOYS.

It hath been reported about the Court that Mr. Richard Champernoun, the music master, to satisfy his own humour doth use boys otherwise than were fit for one that professeth Christianity, gelding them to preserve their voices; which report he vehemently denieth.

1st April. NEWS OF SIR WALTER RALEGH.

A ship of Portugal is lately come into Plymouth, of 80 tons burden, laden with fish, a prize that was taken near Cape St. Vincent. The Portugals of this ship declare that they with five others were taken by Sir Walter Ralegh on the 28th February; and that he had some of the principal men aboard him for two days, and finding their lading to be but fish, took some small quantity out of every ship, also a pipe of wine and a pipe of water, and thus let them pass. They say that he was merry and in good health.

2nd April. THE LEWDNESS OF DOLL PHILLIPS.

There is a pamphlet written by one calling himself 'Oliver Oatmeal' concerning the knaveries of Judith or Doll Phillips and the beguiling of Mrs. Mascall, the tripe-wife. This old woman, being much sought after in marriage for her goods, was at last beguiled to the house of one of her sisters, where the wine walking lustily about and many merry matters familiarly disputed on, it was set down that the tripe-wife must dine next day at her suitor's house. Next day thither she comes, where the time being wasted in conference, home he would not let her go that night, and then they so whittled her with wine that he drew a promise of marriage from her. Shortly after, the widow sitting asleep by the fire, he valiantly coming behind her pulled the stool from her, when down fell she, and he by (or upon) her, with that learned and witty adverb in his mouth, 'Keep the widow waking.' Small rest had she that night, for before it was daylight, they made her pass through his cellar, enter a boat lying ready for her, and to sail so far as Pepper Alley and thence to St. George's Church, where she is married at two o'clock in the morning. But now the wooer, being a grocer by trade, made such a brag of his tricking the tripe-wife, and she such lamentations and complaints, that the matter is not only come to the law but also is sung abroad by the ballad makers.

4th April. A STRANGE MANNER OF DEATH.

Last night one William Saxton slew his wife in strange manner. The woman was in her bedroom preparing herself to go to bed with her husband, but he, having a quarrel with her and not wishing her to lie with him, threw a metal chamberpot at her, striking her so violently in the belly that her breath was taken away and she died instantly.

5th April. SOUTHWELL'S 'ST. PETER'S COMPLAINT.'

A poetical book by Southwell, the Jesuit, is entered for the press, entitled *St. Peter's Complaint*, wherein the author saith, 'Poets by abusing their talent, and making the follies and feignings of love the customary subject of their base endeavours, have so discredited this faculty, that a poet, a lover and a liar are by many reckoned but three words of one signification.' In his complaint Saint Peter mourneth his betraying of Christ, and the griefs arising therefrom, together with loss of sleep:

> Sleep, Death's ally, oblivion of tears,
> Silence of passions, balm of angry sore,
> Suspense of loves, security of fears,
> Wrath's lenitive, heart's ease, storm's calmest shore,
> Senses and souls, reprival from all cumbers,
> Benumbing sense of ill, with quiet slumbers.

There is added *Mary Magdalene's Blush* with her *Complaint at Christ's death*, '*Look home*,' *Fortune's Falsehood*, *At home in Heaven*, *Lewd Love is loss*, and other short poems.

12th April. DRAYTON'S 'ENDIMION AND PHOEBE.'

Mr. Michael Drayton hath written a poem of *Endimion and Phoebe : Idea's Latmus*, wherein is told that fable of the love of the goddess Phoebe for the shepherd Endimion whom she found upon Latmus ; and when he had declared his love for her she revealed herself to him, and transported him from earth to heaven.

THE DESCRIPTION OF ENDIMION.

Endimion, the lovely Shepherd's boy,
Endimion, great Phoebus' only joy,
Endimion, in whose pure-shining eyes
The naked fairies danced the hey-de-geys.
The shag-haired satyrs, mountain climbing race,
Have been made tame by gazing in his face.
For this boy's love, the water Nymphs have wept,
Stealing ofttimes to kiss him whilst he slept :
And tasting once the nectar of his breath,
Surfeit with love and languish unto death ;
And Jove ofttimes bent to lascivious sport,
And coming where Endimion did resort,
Hath courted him, inflamed with desire,
Thinking some nymph was clok'd in boy's attire.
And often-times the simple rural swains,
Beholding him in crossing o'er the plains,
Imagined Apollo from above
Put on this shape to win some maiden's love.

SIR PHILIP SIDNEY'S 'DEFENCE OF POESY.'

Last November Mr. Ponsonby entered his copy of that treatise of poetry written by Sir Philip Sidney, but without printing it ; now Mr. Olney, ignorant of the former entry, hath entered another copy and published the same. Hereupon Mr. Ponsonby claimeth his prior entry, and agreement is made between them that Mr. Ponsonby shall have it.

In this treatise, entitled *The Defence of Poesy*, Sir Philip went about to defend poetry against those that speak against it, saying that it is not only a divine art, but greater than either history or philosophy. 'The poet,' quoth he, 'beginneth not with obscure definitions, which must blur the margent with interpretations and load the memory with doubtfulness; but he cometh to you with words set in delightful proportion, either accompanied with, or prepared for, the well inchanting skill of music; and with a tale forsooth he cometh unto you, with a tale which holdeth children from play and old men from the chimney corner.'

THE BENEFITS OF FISH DAYS.

There is set forth in print by the Lord Mayor a brief note of the benefits that grow by fish days, very necessary to be placed in the houses of all men and especially common victuallers. Firstly, forasmuch as our country is for the most part compassed with the seas, so by a certain expense of fish fishermen are the better maintained and men at all times held in readiness for her Majesty's navy. Secondly, because of the decay of many towns and villages upon the sea coast that in times past were not only replenished with fishermen, but also with shipwrights, ropemakers, sailmakers and divers other trades. Furthermore the trade of grazing cattle, through unlawful expense of flesh, is so much increased that many farm houses and villages are entirely decayed. Showeth also that by one day's abstinence in a week 13,500 beeves might be saved yearly in this City of London.

15*th April.* DR. FLETCHER'S DISGRACE.

The Bishop of London that was to have had the place of the Queen's Almoner at the Maundy is now commanded not to deal it. It is said that both he himself and his wife have used insolent speeches and words to be wondered at concerning her Majesty.

16*th April.* 'THE OLD WIVES' TALE.'

There is entered for printing that play written by George Peele entitled *The Old Wives' Tale* which was played by the Queen's Players about five years since.

17*th April.* SPANISH PREPARATIONS IN BRITTANY.

It is reported that there are many men of war of the Spaniards come to the coast of Brittany. Of late the Spaniards took a bark of Guernsey, and sent all the men home saving four ancient men and good pilots for that coast, which putteth the people of that place in great fear of some attempt of the Spaniard. At Blavet are seventeen flyboats and three galleys.

23rd April. THE FEAST OF ST. GEORGE.

This year at the feast there were present thirteen of the Knights of the Garter. The Communion in the Chapel being ended, the Knights of the Order proceeded into the castle yard before her Majesty, who walked beneath a canopy of cloth of gold, lined with red, and held up by four. There were present many noblemen and ladies and gentlemen of the Court; who passed three times round the yard that all might take a good view of them. At the feast my Lord Cobham represented her Majesty, being honoured as if she herself had been present, the guards serving him on the knee, and the Earls (who handed the water to him before and after) on both knees. The feast began at one o'clock and continued for over three hours, many foreign gentlemen being present, among them the envoy of the Duke of Wirtenberg who would remind her Majesty of her pretended promise to bestow the Order on his master.

26th April. THE DUKE OF WIRTENBERG'S ENVOY.

To-day the Queen gave audience to the envoy of the Duke of Wirtenberg that would importune her of a promise that he should be admitted to the Order of St. George; to whom the Queen returned answer that no such promise had been made nor could be, seeing that the Garter is not yet despatched to certain Kings that were a long time past elected by the Order. She added that the Duke should suffer our merchants to carry on their trade in his realms with all security, and put down those that slander her person.

30th April. TROOPS IN THE LOW COUNTRIES.

Her Majesty hath now in her pay in the Low Countries 50 foot companies, being 4 of 200 men, 44 of 150, and 2 of 100 each, making in all 7,600, which men with their winter and summer apparel, victuals, pay and other expenses cost annually £109,600.

6th May. LODGE'S 'FIG FOR MOMUS.'

There is a new book of Mr. Thomas Lodge entitled *A Fig for Momus*, dedicated to my Lord of Derby, being sundry satires, eclogues, and epistles. Of these, the satires are here published to prepare the ear of the reader ; because if they pass well, the whole *centon* of them, already written, shall suddenly be published. Treateth in this book of the necessity for parents to set good examples in their lives before their children ; of dreams ; of covetousness and the folly of ambition ; of saving and spending. Concludeth with an Anatomy of Alchemy, very invectively condemning the professors of that science, yet, saith he, unto artists there is a certain quality that can be perceived :

> It feeds the ear, it amplifies the thought,
> Except to those that know it, it is nought.

There is also an epistle to a lady that wrote to him asking both the cause and the remedy of pursiness and fat. Giveth this remedy :

> Much sitting, and long abstinence from care,
> Drinking of oily wines our fat prepare ;
> Eggs, white meat, pottage, do increase the same
> And bring the waxing body out of frame.
> Let therefore men grown fat by gluttony
> (For to the rest no medicine I apply)
> Open a vein ; or if that seem too sore,
> Use cuppings, and oft rubbings evermore,
> Live in that air which is both hot and dry,
> Watch much, and sleeping little, hardly lie.
> Walk much, and toss, and tumble in the sun,
> Delight to ride, to hawk, to hunt, to run ;
> Drink little, gargarize, fly grosser food,
> Or if some deem a hare or partridge good,
> Feed modestly thereon, and if he hath
> Some crowns to spend, go often to the Bath.

Nevertheless he is of an opinion that fatness is no deformity, for

> fat, slick, fair and full
> Is better lik'd than lean, lank, spare and dull.

8th May. A CATALOGUE OF ENGLISH PRINTED BOOKS.

A catalogue of English printed books is to be printed by Mr. Andrew Maunsell, bookseller, whereof the first part treateth of such matters of divinity as have been either written in our own tongue or translated out of other languages; the second of books concerning the sciences mathematical, arithmetic, geometry, astronomy, astrology, music, the art of war, navigation, physic, and surgery.

9th May. THE EARL OF CUMBERLAND'S COMMISSION.

The Earl of Cumberland is granted special commission to attack the powers of the King of Spain or any of his subjects and adherents with his ships, which shall not exceed the number of six. He shall also have full power to distribute all merchandises and prizes taken as he will, saving the usual customs and duties due upon all goods brought into the realm.

15th May. BANKS' HORSE.

There is one Banks hath a bay gelding, called Morocco, of wondrous quality, that can fight, and dance and lie; and find your purse and tell you what money you have.

22nd May. 'CERTAIN VERY PROPER SIMILES.'

Mr. Anthony Fletcher, a minister, hath collected more than two hundred and thirty godly similes and set them forth in a book with this title: *Certain very proper and most profitable similes, wherein sundry, and very many, most foul vices, and dangerous sins of all sorts are so plainly laid open, and displayed in their kinds, and so pointed at with the finger of God, in his sacred and holy Scriptures, to signify his wrath and indignation belonging unto them, that the Christian Reader, being seasoned with the spirit of grace, and having God before his eyes, will be very fearful, even in love that he beareth to God, to pollute and to defile his heart, his mind, his mouth or hands, with any such forbidden things. And also many very notable virtues, with their due commendations, so lively and truly expressed, according to the holy word, that the godly Reader, being of a Christian inclination, will be mightily inflamed with a love unto them.* Addeth thereto the cut of an idle tree.

23rd May. NEW PLAYS.

At the Rose this month the Admiral's men played a new play called *The first and second part of Hercules.*

25th May. THE NEGOTIATIONS WITH THE STATES.

These past weeks Mr. Thomas Bodley, her Majesty's Agent in those parts, hath urged her demands to the States that they should ease her of the great charge of maintaining garrisons and repay some part of her expenses, appointing commissioners to settle a course how the whole sum disbursed upon their account and due to Sir Horatio Palavicino, to whom she payeth great sums in interest. Mr. Bodley is now come over with the answer of the States, which is that they acknowledge themselves infinitely bound to the Queen, and would pay according to their ability as may be brought to pass with liking of the inhabitants; but as for the demand made by the Lord Treasurer for £100,000 they are destitute of means to satisfy it, or even a far lesser sum. These proposals have greatly moved the Queen, who was even heard to say in Court that she wished Mr. Bodley had been hanged; whereat he stirs not abroad these ten days.

27th May. DR. JOHN DEE PROMOTED.

The Queen hath granted to Dr. John Dee the wardenship of Christ's College in Manchester.

'THE WORLD'S HYDROGRAPHICAL DESCRIPTION.'

To-day is published a little book entitled *The World's Hydrographical Description*, written by Captain John Davis, wherein is shown, not only by authority of writers, but also by late experience of travellers, and reasons of substantial probability, that the world in all his zones, climates and places is habitable and inhabited; and the seas likewise universally navigable, whereby it appears that from England there is a short and speedy passage by northerly navigation into the South Seas to China, Molucca, Philippine and India. In his book Captain Davis writeth much of his own travels into the frozen parts of the north. Noteth that, being deserted of his consort, in one small bark of thirty tons without further comfort or consort he proceeded northward until he came to a great strait which he followed for eighty leagues until he came to many islands, whence he concludeth the north part of America to be all islands.

28th May. THE IRISH REBELLION.

The rebels, being led in those parts by a notable traitor called Feogh MacHugh, have taken the fort at Enniskillen, that was held by some thirteen or fourteen with the constable. The rebels allowed them to come out of the castle with bag and baggage and promise of life, and then put them to the sword. Thirty-six heads of MacHugh's men have been brought to Dublin where Tyrone shall shortly be proclaimed traitor.

THE CRUELTY OF THE TURKISH EMPEROR.

The Turk hath lately caused to be executed his brother-in-law for having discovered some matter of state. He caused a butcher to be quartered on his own stool, and a baker to be burnt in his own oven for false weights.

30th May. MR. ROBERT DUDLEY'S RETURN.

Mr. Robert Dudley is returned to England, having set out last November in the *Bear* as admiral, with the *Bear's Whelp*, vice-admiral, and two small pinnaces, the *Frisking* and the *Earwig*. The vice-admiral and one of the pinnaces being separated from him in a storm at their starting, he went on alone with the other, sailing along the coast of Spain, and thence to the Canaries. Thereafter shaping his course to Trinidad in the West Indies, he came at length to Waliame, the first kingdom of the Empire of Guiana.

Here he was told by an Indian, his interpreter, of a golden mine in a town called Orocoa in the river of Owrinoicke, but his men being utterly unwilling that he should go himself, Mr. Dudley sent forward a company of his discreetest men. These went forward up the river, and there they were met by the Captain of the town of Orocoa and of the mine, who told them that by force they should have nothing but blows, yet if they would bring him hatchets, knives and jews-harps he would trade in gold with Mr. Dudley. Also he told them of another rich nation that sprinkle their bodies with powder of gold and seem to be gilt, and far beyond them a great town called El Dorado.

The men being satisfied returned, having been absent sixteen days, but in pitiful case, almost dead with thirst, for they had not drunk in three days before they recovered the ship, so long were they out of the fresh rivers. Hereupon Mr. Dudley attempted his company to go with them again but they flat refused.

On his return he came to the Isles of Flores and Cuervo, hoping to meet with some great fleet from England, but finding none and his victuals being almost spent, he directed his course alone for England. Soon after he met with a great armada of 600 tons (the *Bear* being but of 200 tons), and fought with her for two days, till his powder being all spent, he left her 300 leagues from land and in miserable state so that in short space she sank.

In this voyage have been taken, sunk or burnt nine Spanish ships, which is a great loss to the enemy, though Mr. Dudley himself hath gained nothing.

3rd June. A NEW PLAY.

There is a new play at the Rose called *The Seven days of the week.*

5th June. A RIOT IN LONDON.

To-day a certain citizen, being a silkweaver, came to the Lord Mayor's house, using some hard speeches concerning him and in dispraise of his government. The Lord Mayor said he was mad and so committed him to Bedlam as a madman, but not having his officers about him sent him thither by some of his own servants; but without Bishopsgate he was rescued by prentices and divers other to the number of two or three hundred persons.

9th June. NEWS FROM LISBON.

One lately come from Lisbon reporteth that eight ships of the Indian fleet have come in, bringing two English Captains, Captain John Middleton, and Captain Goddard, the Earl of Cumberland's man, and nine or ten mariners, who report that in the South Seas the *Dainty* is captured with Captain Hawkins who had taken great treasure. In March and April on a report that Sir Francis Drake was coming with a fleet of English, French and Hollanders' ships, about 8,000 fled; and now the coast is replenished with soldiers. The Canaries and the Azores are also being fortified.

0th June. A SKIRMISH WITH TYRONE.

On 27th May it was determined to revictual the garrison in Monaghan, our soldiers set out from Newry, under Sir Henry Bagnal, being 1500 foot and 250 horse. On the way 1500 horse of the enemy appeared on a hill and would have drawn our horse after them, but the General would not. Next morning Tyrone brought all his forces to a straight which our men were to pass and turned off seven or eight companies to skirmish which annoyed them much, the passage being between a bog and a wood. They passed through this straight and reached Monaghan, having lost twelve slain and thirty hurt, the enemy's loss being 100 slain and many hurt. Having put victual into Monaghan and changed the ward, our men dislodged and marched back, being harassed by the rebels in the straights and passages, but at length they reached Newry, where our losses were found to be thirty-one slain, 109 hurt, but none hurt of account except Sir Henry Duke, Captain Cunye, five lieutenants, an ensign and a sergeant.

In this fight Tyrone had 14,000 foot, and 300 shot in red coats, like our English soldiers.

MacHugh is reported to be shot in the thigh and hurt with a skeyne in the body, flying from our men so fast that he threw away his helmet, target and sword, which are brought in.

13th June. DISORDERS IN THE CITY.

Divers prentices this day being pinched in their victuals took butter from the market people in Southwark, paying them but 3d. the pound, though they demanded 5d. Certain of these prentices are apprehended.

15th June. FURTHER RIOTING IN THE CITY.

Some prentices being to-day committed to the Counter by the constable for certain misdemeanours, others congregating themselves came to the Counter, and said they would have them forth again, using very hard speeches against the Lord Mayor; but the gates being shut against them, they tarried not long but departed away.

Not long after a serving man, whose brother, being a prentice, had complained of his master's hard dealing, came to the master, and quarrelled with him; and in the multiplying of words the master's head was broken. By this brawl the people gathered together and much hurly-burly followed so that Sir Richard Martin hearing thereof came into the street, apprehended the serving man and sent him to the Counter by the constable. As they were going, the prentices that had already resorted to the Counter met them, rescued the serving man from the Counter, and brought him back to Cheapside. Whereupon Sir Richard Martin came forth suddenly with such company as he had of his own servants and forthwith he apprehended the serving man again, reprehended the prentices for their so great disorder, took six of the principal offenders, and so by the constable sent them all to the Counter, causing irons to be laid upon them.

About an hour afterwards, when all was quiet, the Lord Mayor cometh into Cheapside and commandeth Sir Richard Martin and Sir John Hart to take order for the safe keeping of these prentices. On his return, about London Wall, a prentice meeting him will not put off his cap; whereupon he also is sent to the Counter, which is done quietly and without opposition of any.

16th June. THE RIOTOUS PRENTICES.

Certain prentices and soldiers or masterless men are said to have met together in Paul's, and there had conferences, wherein the soldiers said to the prentices, 'You know not your strength.' Then the prentices asked the soldiers if they would assist them; and the soldiers answered that they would within an hour after be ready to aid them and be their leader; and that they would play an Irish trick with the Lord Mayor, who should not have his head upon his shoulders within an hour after.

The causes of these present inconveniences are said to be the great number of loose and masterless men about the City, pretending to be soldiers; the great dearth of victual; and the remiss care of the magistrates in time to have remedied the same. The Lord Mayor also is blamed for his insatiable avarice; for his selling and converting of offices to his own gain and then suffering those officers to be negligent; and for his refusing to bear or join with his brethren.

17th June. SLIGO TAKEN BY THE REBELS.

From Ireland comes news that as Captain George Bingham sat writing in his chamber in Sligo Castle, his ensign, one Burke, and twenty of his men, all Clanricarde men, fell upon him suddenly and slew him.

20th June. 'THE TRUMPET OF FAME.'

There is published by one H. R. a poem of encouragement to all sailors and soldiers that are minded to go with Sir Francis Drake and Sir John Hawkins, wherein are related the names of the ships and their former actions against the enemy, ending thus:

Thus valiant hearts, which now to seas are bound
To cheer you on, that erst hath been renown'd,
I have explain'd the names of your brave fleet,
That careth not with what foes they shall meet.
What other ships of foreign sail there go,
I do omit, because I do not know.
Nor what they be, you need not much to care,
God and your generals doth for you prepare.
Then frolic hearts! and to your healths one can,
Let love united be firm with every man:
And love and duty in each one so abound,
That faithful subjects you may still be found.
'Tis England's honour that you have in hand;
Then think thereof if you do love your land.
The gain is yours, if millions home you bring;
Then courage take to gain so sweet a thing.
The time calls on, which causeth me to end;
Wherefore to God I do you all commend.
For whom all subjects that do love our Queen,
Shall truly pray to send you safe again.
And, for my part, I wish you always health
With quick return; and so much store of wealth
That Philip's regions may not more be stor'd
With pearl and jewels, and the purest gold.

23rd June. DISORDERS IN SOUTHWARK.

About 4 o'clock this afternoon certain prentices and other servants, being sent to Billingsgate by their masters to buy mackerels and finding none there, were informed that divers fishwives a little before had gone on board the fisherboats and bought up the whole share and carried it with them to Southwark. Hereupon the prentices, in number sixty or eighty, pursued after them without any weapons, having only baskets under their arms; and coming to the fishwives they took their mackerels from some of them, giving them money 4 for the groat (which is the rate formerly set by the Lord Mayor). Then one of the fishwives began to lay about her, and offered to strike some of the prentices with her fish basket; but when the constable, seeing the disorder, commanded these rude and unruly persons to surcease their strife then without any further unkindness or breach of the peace they departed.

27th June. Riotous Prentices Whipped.

The riotous prentices that took from the market people at Southwark their butter were this day punished with whipping, setting in the pillory, and long imprisonment.

29th June. Unruly Youths on Tower Hill.

This Sunday afternoon a number of unruly youths on Tower Hill being blamed by the warders of Tower Street ward, drave them back with stones, being heartened thereunto by the sound of a trumpet. The trumpeter, one that formerly was a soldier, and many of the company are taken by the Sheriffs and in prison. About 7 o'clock this evening, Sir John Spencer, the Lord Mayor, with his officers rode to Tower Hill to see the hill cleared of tumultuous persons; and here some warders of the Tower and men of the Lieutenant told the Lord Mayor that the Sword ought not to be borne up in that place; and thereupon two or three of them catching hold of the Sword, there was some bickering and the sword-bearer hurt. But the Lord Mayor by his discretion and by proclamation in the Queen's name in short time cleared the hill of all trouble and rode back, the sword-bearer bearing up the Sword before him.

Sir John Hawkins' Agreement with the Queen.

It is agreed between the Queen and Sir John Hawkins concerning the voyage that he purposeth to the southward, that she shall at her own charges put in order and furnish six ships, for which she shall have a third part of any booty taken from the enemy; and Sir John at his own charge shall victual the same ships for four months, for which he shall have another third; the remaining third shall be to the sailors and servitors in those ships. If her Majesty shall stay the journey, the charges disbursed by Sir John shall be refunded.

A Seditious Pamphlet.

The Lord Mayor, being required to advertise the Council concerning the printing of a certain pamphlet by the Company of Weavers, hath discovered that fifteen of them were privy to it. The pamphlet was printed by one Gabriel Simpson, and the proof of the first print was then read in the house of a certain Muggins in the hearing of the whole number. Twelve of them showed their dislike to have the pamphlet proceed into print, but the other three continued in their purpose and required the printer to print for them some 40 copies, which they would have delivered to the French Church, the Dutch Church, and one apiece to the Lord Mayor and Aldermen; but only 22 were printed, whereof 19 are taken. The principal doers in this business are one Millington, Muggins and Deloney, who with the printer are committed to Newgate.

2nd July. A Case in the Star Chamber.

This day was begun the hearing of the suit for slander brought against one Wood by Mr. Edward Talbot, brother to my Lord of Shrewsbury. This Wood had charged Mr. Talbot that he secretly intended the poisoning of the Earl by means of himself, and to this end had given him an annuity of £100 per annum. Mr. Talbot's counsel enforced the impeachment of Wood's credit by sundry deceitful practices in physic (he practising physic, being neither licensed nor graduate in any University), of ministering oil of stag's blood to the Countess of Shrewsbury for the gout, and divers other sophisticated oils, receipts and compositions, as oil of wax, butter, antimony, liquor of pearl and such like. Moreover he would show that this Wood had treacherously concealed this practice from my Lord for two years and a half, and had manifestly forged the deed of annuity. For the credit of the defendant, it was argued that things done in his youth should not be brought forward; gentlemen of Inns of Court and others have done many worse practices, and as for sophisticated drugs, many apothecaries in the town are in like fault. But the case is left unfinished.

4th July. A Proclamation against Unlawful Assemblies.

Because of the great disorders lately committed in and about the City there is now issued a proclamation straitly charging all her Majesty's officers, that have authority to preserve the peace, more diligently to punish offenders, and especially to suppress all unlawful assemblies, upon pain to be not only removed from their offices but to be also punished as persons maintaining or rather comforting the offenders. And because the late unlawful assemblies and riots are compounded of sundry sorts of base people, some known prentices, such as are of base manual occupation, some others, wandering idle persons of condition of rogues and vagabonds, and some colouring their wandering by the name of soldiers returned from the wars, therefore certain special orders are to be prescribed and published in and about the City. These her Majesty will have strictly observed, and for that purpose meaneth to have a Provost Marshal, with sufficient authority to apprehend all such as shall not readily be reformed and corrected by the ordinary Officers of Justice, and without delay to execute them upon the gallows by order of martial law.

ORDERS PRESCRIBED BY THE COUNCIL IN THIS TIME OF TUMULT.

The Council have prescribed and caused to be published these and other orders for the preservation of peace.

No persons but such as be officers for preservation of peace or such as be of known honest conversation shall walk up and down the streets or fields after sunset or nine o'clock at night; nor assemble themselves in a company at any time or in any place, other than in churches for prayers or sermons, or for appearances before Officers of Justice or by their commandment, or in common Halls of Companies.

That no householder nor any that keepeth inns or lodging for strangers do suffer his servants or guests (not being gentlemen) to go out into the streets in the evening; and if they cannot be restrained then to inform the officers speedily.

That no person do write or be privy to any seditious bills to be dispersed or set up, upon pain to be executed by martial law. And any person who shall reveal an offender, the information being found true and the party taken, the revealer shall have £20 or a better reward.

All persons arrested by any officer shall obey him, and if any make resistance, every other person there present if required by the Officers shall assist to the best of his power. If any shall attempt to aid the party that should be arrested to be rescued, he and all those accompanying him shall be apprehended and executed by the Provost Marshal by martial law.

THE CASE OF MR. EDWARD TALBOT CONCLUDED.

Mr. Talbot's case against Wood is concluded, the Lords condemning Wood for a most palpable machiavellian, but deferring their sentence till they had heard the next suit, of the Earl of Shrewsbury against his brother, Mr. Edward Talbot, for that by practice of Wood he should have poisoned the Earl, first by gloves, and then by potion or plaster. This charge my Lord essayed to prove by no direct witnesses save Wood (who was not allowed but taken as infamous), and by circumstances that at the first seemed somewhat probable. My Lord's Counsel endeavoured to discredit the defendant for his haughtiness of mind, his prodigality and the like, showing that he had spent 10,000 marks in three years since the death of his father: and for his religion, for defending one John Baldwin who questioned whether there was a God; if there were, how He should be known; if by His Word, who wrote the same; and if the prophets and the apostles, they were but men, and *humanum est errare*; and such like most damnable doubts, which were not suffered to be read in the hearing of the court. Then the plaintiff argued that Mr. Talbot practised and agreed with Sir Edward Stapleton for effecting of the poisoning, and Sir Edward had suborned a man of his, of his own name, to buy the gloves.

At this the Court seemed dubious for a long time. The milliner therefore was summoned, and his man that sold the gloves, who denied upon the sight of Stapleton that he could be the man. So after long hearing (for this day the Lords sat from 9 in the morning until 6), Wood is herein condemned as a palpable ass, a very villain, and of Satan's brood, being called *Diabolos* for that he is an accuser.

After the Counsel had argued very learnedly, the Queen's Attorney craved that his silence might not prejudice the defendant's cause, for whom he spake in the former action wherein he was plaintiff, but could not now speak for him seeing that he was defendant. Whereupon he proved Wood to be no scholar for he used false orthography, for 'process' writing '*prossus*,' whereas every scholar knoweth 'process' to come of *procedendo*.

The sentence of the whole court, excepting only my Lord of Essex and the Archbishop of Canterbury, is that Wood shall ride from the Fleet to Westminster with his face to the horse's tail, and there stand upon the pillory, and so ride to the Fleet again; and another day from thence to Cheapside to the pillory there; and be fined to the Queen £500 and to be imprisoned at her pleasure. But the Lord Treasurer moved that if Wood should confess his fault and submit himself to Mr. Talbot at the next assizes, then the £500 should be released.

16th July. THE EXPEDITION FROM PLYMOUTH.

Sir Thomas Gorges that hath been sent down to Plymouth to join with Sir John Hawkins and Sir Francis Drake reporteth that the ships are in very good sort, for that Sir John is an excellent man in those things and sees all things done properly. Sir Thomas's coming at first greatly amazed them, they fearing that he had been sent to stay them; but when they knew the contrary they were very joyful that her Majesty had sent down someone to see their bravery. Their expedition cannot depart for fourteen days at least as some pinnaces are not yet ready.

17th July. THREE NOTABLE OUTRAGES.

This past month there have been three notable crimes committed, whereof two of the doers are already hanged and the other shortly shall be.

The first, in the parish of Upmaster in Essex, where dwelt one Thomas Chambers with his mother and his step-father, a certain John Wright. This Chambers, being a young man of great towardness, was by his father left heir to £30 a year and a portion of £200 and upwards in money, which money and land were to come to him at Christmas next; but if he should die under age, then a great part of it to fall into the hands of his sister, that was married to one John Graygoose. For this cause Graygoose and Wright plotted to murder him in the Whitsun holidays.

On 6th June therefore between the hours of 10 and 12 Wright

waited for him at a place called Rushy Green near Barrow Hill in the parish of Hornchurch ; and there, with a stake taken out of a stile, he assaulted the unmistrusting young man and at one blow given on the right side of the head struck out his brains. Which done he dragged him into a bush and there hid the murdered body ; then with a bold face he returned home. The youth being well beloved was in sundry places sought for, and at length on Whitsun Monday (being the 9th June) a greyhound found the murdered body and never left baying until it was drawn forth.

When Chambers' body was thus found a rueful sight it was to look upon ; his fair countenance was discoloured, worms crawled in his mouth, nose and ears, and his whole body was putrefied. The missing of Wright that evening the deed was done, some suspicious words, but chief God's will, made Wright suspected ; and albeit at the first he sought to face it out, yet before a Justice he confessed it, for which he worthily suffered death last Monday (14th) at Romford in Essex. Graygoose abideth his trial in Chelmsford.

The second felony was acted at Ruislip in Middlesex, in which parish dwelt two neighbours, Murdox, the one, an honest wealthy farmer, Pets, the other, a carpenter, though not rich yet of honest reputation. Murdox had among divers children a young man to his youngest son, of body well proportioned, of face lovely, a great company keeper, given over to much riot. This youth, being persuaded Pets was very rich, on Sunday, 22nd June, after his own father was rid to Hounslow, entered the house (Pets and his wife being at church), and there found a son of Pets, about ten years old. The child knowing young Murdox had no fear, albeit Murdox in his sight did rifle the house, but missed £4 that was tied in the corner of a sheet, taking only a little purse wherein 14d. was. Finding no more, he called the boy : 'Jack,' saith he, 'wilt thou not tell ?' 'No, indeed,' saith the child. 'Then come and bring a knife,' quoth Murdox, 'and we will into the grove to cut whipstocks.'

The simple child took a knife and followed him ; and being come through a close into the grove, he, with the knife the child brought, gashed him about the throat but missed the weazand ;

and so thinking the child to be dead left him. But hearing the boy cry, he returned and stabbed him into the right breast. Then listening a second time he returned and stabbed him again: and the third time coming back, stopping the child's mouth with moss, and thinking him to be surely dead, he went toward the church. By which time, morning prayer being done, he with his mother returned home, where being but newly entered they heard an outcry at their neighbour Pets'. Thither the mother and her eldest son came to see the cause; the young son would not go.

When Murdox's wife came there, they saw the house rifled, but the woeful mother cried only for her son, her son. Some neighbours spied a footing towards the grove, followed it, and found the boy all-to-beweltered in gore; and perceiving life to be in him, two laid him on a cloak and between them brought him home, where, when he had recovered speech, Murdox's mother most of any other sought to have him tell who did the deed. At last with great fear he told, and forthwith young Murdox was apprehended, but found bail, denying the deed with many bitter curses. That day he carelessly followed his pleasures; but the child's constancy in his accusation made the parents to bring him before Sir Edmund Anderson, Lord Chief Justice, who so sifted him that he confessed the fact; for which he was condemned at the Sessions at Newgate and executed on the 14th July. The moan he made, the grief he had of his mis-spent life, too late, too helpless, was lamentable. The child (by God's power) is recovered and at the bar gave evidence against him.

The third is the murder of one William Randolph, a grazier dwelling about Cardiff and having much dealing about London. This Randolph being very open with one Dernley, a man of the same profession, told him that he was to ride through Aylesbury to Wales with above £300. Hereupon Dernley acquainted two men, called Parry and Richardson, of the matter, who fell in company with Randolph and very court-eously bare him company to Aylesbury. By the way one Tayler of Aylesbury chanced among them, and noting by Randolph's talk that he concealed not his charge of money, besides observing how Parry and Richardson were horsed and weaponed, warned Randolph against them ; but the good old man refused to believe him. These speeches came to the ears of Parry and Richardson. Whereupon making show of displeasure, in the morning they went before him out of town. Randolph hearing they were gone greatly blamed the chamberlain of the inn, and posted after, overtaking them near a wood side where the way was hollow.

Then these hollow hearted companions, under colour of kind salutation, turned their horses' heads to bid him welcome, and Parry first with a Judas-like welcome discharged his pistol in his bosom, while Richardson with the second bullet shot him through hand and belly. So he fell down and they doubling in his death wound upon wound mangled his face with inhuman cruelty. Then drew they him into a thicket and rifled his dead body, where Richardson yet unsatisfied with cruelty stabbed him into the neck with such violence that in pulling back his hand, the pummel and handle of his dagger came off, but the blade he left sticking in his neck ; which blade was one witness against him.

This done they turned his horse into the wood and hovered about the country some two days and more after, for it was the second day before the body was found by a fellow that sought cattle. When the hue-and-cry came to Aylesbury, Tayler among others went to see the body, and by the apparel better than the face knew it was the wretched man that had refused his counsel at Aylesbury. He described the murderers' apparel, proportions, horses and all such marks as he advisedly had taken while he rid in their company. To London, toward Wales, and every way the hue-and-cry went. Parry was taken in Wales, and confessed the fact ; Richardson at his own house in London. A while he denied the deed, but long he stood not on it, both of them accused Dernley ; and to Aylesbury are they all gone to suffer deserved death.

18th July. THE PROVOST MARSHAL APPOINTED.

Sir Thomas Wyllford is appointed a provost marshal for these times of tumult, with power to attach notable and incorrigible offenders upon signification of the justices of peace and by justice of martial law to execute them openly. Likewise he shall repair with a convenient company to all common highways near London to apprehend all vagrant and suspected persons.

23rd July. An Englishman burnt in Rome.

About five weeks ago during a procession in Rome a young Englishman smote the Sacrament out of the hands of an archbishop that was carrying it in procession with such force that it fell to the ground, the crystal of the monstrance being broken and his hand cut withal. Whereon a crowd collected and thrusting burning torches in his face would have killed him had not the archbishop restrained them. The Englishman was then thrown into prison and tried by the Inquisition. A week afterwards he was handed over to magistrates; and the next day he was bound to a cart and his right hand cut off. Then he was taken through the City, being frequently smitten by the executioner with burning brands, and at last burnt alive in the Piazza del Capitolio.

24th July. The Unruly Youths Condemned.

Five of the unruly youths apprehended for the disorder on Tower Hill on 29th June were arraigned in the Guildhall and condemned of high treason two days since, and to-day were drawn from Newgate to Tower Hill, where they were hanged and bowelled as traitors.

25th July. Excessive Prices.

This year by reason of the transportation of grain into foreign countries, the same is grown into an excessive price, as in some places from 14s. to 4 marks the quarter, and more. In London, such is the scarcity of victual, that an hen's egg is sold for a penny, or three eggs at the most for 2d., a pound of sweet butter for 7d., and the like of flesh and fish, exceeding measure in price, such are our sins in deserving it.

26th July. The Spaniards Land in Cornwall.

From Cornwall it is reported that four hundred Spanish soldiers were landed from four galleys who have burnt Moldsey, a small village, and Newlin, with Penzance, a very good town. The town of Penzance had been saved if the people had stood with Sir Francis Godolphin, but the common sort utterly forsook him, saving for some four or five gentlemen.

This landing of the Spaniards hath bred in the Court diversity of passions; but the most part take courage against them in such sort as they that have heretofore seemed abated in spirit do now lift up the crest. This night Sir Roger Williams hath, in presence of all the Court, received of her Majesty a friendly public welcome. This afternoon the Lord Admiral rode to Chatham to put order to the navy; and in effect it is a stirring world.

27th July. THE IRISH REBELLION.

This past month the army in Ireland under Sir William Russell, the Lord Deputy, and Sir John Norris, have made a journey through the rebels' country, setting forth from Dundalk on the 18th June and returning on the 17th July.

28th July. THE SPANISH LANDING.

Certain Englishmen that were landed by the Spaniards in Mount Bay say that after they had burned Penzance and other villages they had mass the next day on the Western Hill by a friar, and there they vow to build a friary when they shall have conquered England.

7th August. A NEW SPANISH ARMADA.

It is reported that a new armada is preparing by the King of Spain at Lisbon. There are ten Biscayan ships and thirty others, and some not yet come in; and enough biscuit prepared for 10,000 men.

11th August. THE SPANISH SHIPS.

From Portsmouth it is reported that fifteen or sixteen Spanish sail, whereof six are very great ships, were sighted off Scilly, and as many ride the other side of the Scillys.

13th August. IRISH NEWS.

The Council in Ireland meeting to consider the measures to be taken to bring the rebels into obedience, it was concluded to send 1600 men under Sir John Norris through the Pale, and to this end pioneers, masons, carpenters, boats and carriages are being prepared. From the borders daily come the complaints of the soldiers, who have neither money, victuals, nor clothes, so that they grow into desperate terms and spare not to say to their officers that they will run away and steal rather than famish. There is considerable sickness, as much as twenty in every band, amongst the men from Brittany who, though they made no good impression on the Lord Deputy when they first came, are in proof found very good, though they like so ill of the country that they run away as fast as they can by any means escape; which to prevent some have been hanged for an example to the rest. Sir John Norris himself declareth that if there were good order and good provision made, not only these rebels might be in short time extirpated, but the country reduced into such terms as they should never be able to lift up their heads; but no other success than an unprofitable expense and a lasting rebellion can be looked for so long as those that have the chiefest disposition of things there care not how long the war last so they may make their profit, whilst in England the chiefest hope of the good event is reposed upon accidents, whereby timely provisions are neglected and time lost. In Ardes 4000 Scots are landed to succour Tyrone, who offereth to give in marriage to the bachelors of them the daughters of his gentlemen and freeholders, every one a wife of degree proportionable to the man that is to marry her.

17th August. The Death of Don Antonio.

Don Antonio, that is called King of Portugal, is dead in Paris five days since. He died in great poverty, and frequent collections were made for him at the French Court. The King appointed for him certain revenues yet these were not paid regularly, wherefore Don Antonio had to throw himself on the charity of others.

22nd August. Rumours.

There is a most certain expectation of the enemy attempting us next year, either directly here at home or by the way of Scotland; and these fears are grounded not on apprehension only but upon the sure knowledge that the preparations in Spain be far greater than in '88. Whereupon there is great diversity of opinions of the proceeding of this sea voyage; some would have it stayed, alleging the impossibility of their return in small time, should need require; the hazard of loss of so many mariners going into hot countries; the absence of ships and ordnance. The other party alleging the loss of the Queen and the adventurers if it break off; the dishonour, and the probability that the return might be timely enough, besides the hope of treasure, which is our greatest desire and want. Some there be that propose to convert this fleet to an offensive course upon the ports of Spain; but this is checked above, or crossed under hand, not without great distemperature of humours on both sides for a few days; yet in most men's judgments this is likeliest to succeed.

23rd August. THE LANDING IN CORNWALL.

From Fowey in Cornwall comes news that the four Spanish galleys which made spoil of the west parts about four weeks ago encountered a fleet of hulks of seventy sail and gave chase to fourteen of them that were severed from the company. In that fight they lost 140 of their men and had one of the galleys so torn that they could not carry her to Blavet; one of the hulks laden with salt was sunk.

26th August. 'ORPHEUS HIS JOURNEY TO HELL.'

There is entered a poem of *Orpheus his journey to Hell* written by one R. B., telling the story of Orpheus, how his bride Eurydice being slain by a serpent on her wedding day, he went down to Hades with his harp to charm Pluto into giving her back again; but on his return looking back on his beloved, she was snatched away from him, and thereafter Orpheus would sit complaining in invective ditties of the uncertain pleasures of unconstant love, until the women fell upon him in their rage and slew him.

A BOOK OF MERRY TALES.

A book of merry tales from the Spanish entitled *Wits, Fits and Fancies*, by Antony Copley, being a general collection of sententious speeches, answers, jests and behaviours of all sorts of estates, from the throne to the cottage, is to be printed.

MR. BARNES' 'DIVINE CENTURY OF SPIRITUAL SONNETS.'

Mr. Barnabe Barnes hath published *A Divine Century of Spiritual Sonnets*, which he dedicateth to Dr. Toby Matthew, Bishop of Durham.

THE LXIX SONNET.

Who to the golden Sun's long restless race
  Can limits set ? What vessel can comprise
  The swelling winds ? What cunning can devise,
With quaint arithmetic, in steadfast place
To number all the stars in heaven's palace ?
  What cunning artist ever was so wise
  Who by the stars and planets could advise
Of all adventures the just course and case ?
  Who measur'd hath the waters of the seas ?
Who ever, in just balance, pois'd the air ?
  As no man ever could the least of these
Perform with human labour, strength and care :
  So who shall strive in volumes to contain
  God's praise ineffable contends in vain.

TWO TALES OF MR. BARNABE BARNES.

Of this Mr. Barnabe Barnes Nashe hath these two tales. The first of his French service four years ago, when, having followed the camp for a week or two, and seeing there was no care had of keeping the Queen's peace, but a man might have his brains knocked out, and no justice or constable near at hand to make hue-and-cry after the murderers, he went to the General and told him he did not like of this quarrelling kind of life and common occupation of murdering, wherein, without any jury or trial or giving them so much leave as to say their prayers, men were run through and had their throats cut, both against God's laws, her Majesty's laws, and the laws of all nations ; wherefore he desired leave to depart, for he stood every hour in fear and dread of his person. Upon this motion there were divers warlike knights and principal captains who offered to pick out a strong guard amongst them for the safe engarrisoning and better shielding him from peril. Two stepped forth and presented themselves as musketeers before him, a third and fourth as targeteers behind him, a fifth and sixth vowed to try it out at the push of the pike before the malicious foe should invade him. But home he would and nothing could stay him.

The second of how he got him a strange pair of Babylonian breeches, with a codpiece as large as a Bolognian sausage, and so went up and down town and showed himself in the Presence at Court where he was generally laughed out by the noblemen and ladies.

29th August. A NEW PLAY.

Since the end of June till five days ago there was no playing at the Rose, but now they begin afresh and to-day they play a new play called *Long Shanks.*

31st August. DRAKE AND HAWKINS SAIL.

The fleet of Sir Francis Drake and Sir John Hawkins are sailed from Plymouth, being the *Defiance*, *Garland*, *Hope*, *Bonaventure*, *Foresight* and *Adventure*, the Queen's ships, together with twenty other ships and barks, and containing 2500 men and boys. With them is gone Sir Thomas Baskerville as commander by land.

5th September. THE EARL OF ESSEX'S ADVICE ON TRAVEL.

Now that the Earl of Rutland hath a purpose to travel, my Lord of Essex hath composed for him sundry letters of advice for his guidance. In the first, setteth down the purposes of travel; to see the beauty of many cities, to know the manners of the people of many countries, and to learn the language of many nations. Some of these may serve for ornaments and all of them for delights. By travel men reach of study, conference, and observation which is knowledge; and the true end of knowledge is clearness and strength of judgment, and not ostentation or ability to discourse. The second letter giveth more exact particularities for the traveller. He shall restrain his affection and participation of his own countrymen and seek the acquaintance of the best sort of strangers, who will instruct him in their abilities, dispositions and humours. Nor should his aim be, like an intelligencer, to fish after the present news, humours, graces or disgraces of the Court, which may haply change before he come home, but to know the consanguinities and alliance of Princes, the proportion between the nobility and the magistracy, the constitution of the courts of justice, the state of their laws; how the sovereignty of the King infuseth itself into all acts and ordinances; how many ways they lay down impositions and taxes, and gather revenues to the Crown; what be the liberties and servitudes of all degrees; what discipline and preparation for wars; what inventions for increase of traffic at home, for multiplying their commodities, encouraging arts or manufactures of worth of any kind: also what good establishments to prevent the necessities and discontents of the people, to cut off suits at law and quarrels, to suppress thieves and all disorders. In the last letter noteth other matters worthy of observation, concluding that if they be too many to remember then should he rather trust his notebook than his memory.

13th September. A PETITION AGAINST PLAYS.

Since the commission of the provost marshal was revoked the masterless and vagabond persons that had retired out of his precinct are returning to their old haunt and frequent the plays at the Theatre and Bankside. Wherefore the Lord Mayor petitioneth the Council for the suppressing of stage plays, declaring that they contain nothing but profane fables, lascivious matters, cozening devices, and other unseemly and scurrilous behaviours which are so set forth that they move wholly to imitation. Moreover he verily thinketh them to be the chief cause of the late stir and mutinous attempt of those few apprentices and other servants, who no doubt drew their infection from these and like places, and also of many other disorders and lewd demeanours which appear of late in young people of all degrees.

14th September. ABUSES IN THE CITY.

Mr. Richard Carmarden that was lately appointed to be Surveyor of the port of London seeketh to reform the abuses caused through the blindness and impotency of the late surveyor. Whereupon the better sort of the merchants yield, but some four or five most frowardly resist him. When by his command some packs belonging to one Leveson were stayed, this man on Wednesday last, with wild words despising the Queen's authority, beat Mr. Carmarden's substitutes and arrested one of them in an action of £200. The sheriffs' sergeants carried Leveson violently to prison, and the Clerks of the Court refused bail, Leveson saying that the Queen's letters patents, the order of the Exchequer and the Lord Treasurer's letters were all without the law.

CAPTAIN AMYAS PRESTON'S VOYAGE.

Captain Amyas Preston that set forth in the *Ascension* six months since is returned, being arrived in safety at Milford Haven in Wales. On his outward passage he surprised the Isle of Porto Santo to the northward of Madeira which is inhabited by old soldiers of the Kings of Portugal. Here after some skirmishes, our men possessed themselves of the town, though the inhabitants had conveyed their wives and children and the rest of their goods into a high hill. Nor would Captain Preston allow them to redeem their town, because of their cruelty and treachery offered beforetime to some of ours, but caused the town and villages to be utterly burned.

Thence having joined with Captain Somers and his ship the *Gift* and three other ships they sailed westward to the Island of Dominica and from there to Margarita where the Indians fish for pearls. In the end of May they took the city of S. Iago de Leon, a very strong place, surrounded by high mountains, which they reached by a path used by the Indians. And here they had conference with the Spaniards for the ransoming of the town, Captain Preston demanding 30,000 ducats but the Spaniard refusing more than 4000, so the town was set on fire and consumed.

In July, off Cape St. Anthony, they met with Sir Walter Ralegh returning from his discovery of Guiana, with his fleet of three ships, but lost them in the night.

15th September. A GREAT FIRE AT WOBURN.

Last Saturday (13th) there was a great fire at Woburn in the County of Bedford, whereby houses and buildings to the number of one hundred and thirty are consumed, as well as barns, stables and the rest, with the goods and provisions therein, besides what was carried out into the streets and there purloined and embezzled. This fire started in a poor cottage at the further end of the town towards Brookhill where dwelt a single old woman, slow in speech, deaf in hearing, and very dull of understanding. She had shifted her bed straw and put new therein, laying the old in the chimney, supposing that there had been no fire therein, and afterwards going abroad upon her business. In the meanwhile the cinders in the chimney took hold of the straw and so set on fire this thatched house and others adjoining, which by the wind was soon driven from place to place. And so fierce did it wax that it made as it were a glade from the end of the town to the church; where by the violence of the wind a flake of burning thatch, as broad as it were a sheet, was carried clean over the chancel of the church, the school house and other buildings, and fell on the east side of the town. Moreover the confusion was much increased by those that came in to help from the country, many of them leaving their own labours, and freeing their hired workmen from their tasks (and paying them notwithstanding their day's wages), who in their hurly-burly increased rather than lessened the desolation and waste.

19th September. NEWS FROM IRELAND.

This morning there comes from Ireland advertisement that Tyrone hath drawn our force to fight of necessity; that Sir John Norris is shot in the belly, Sir Thomas Norris shot in the thigh, and Capt. Richard Wingfield in the elbow with a musket and likely to lose life or arm, but the others not in danger of life. The hope of a peace is now turned to an assured war for 'twere much dishonour to dally longer.

BEGGING IN THE CITY.

There continue to be erected great numbers of poor tenements, which they call 'pennyrents,' in Southwark and Kentish Street, wherein are placed a great company of very poor people. These having no trade nor honest endeavour to maintain themselves, nor to pay their rent (which must usually be done at the week's end), make it their daily occupation to beg in the streets of the City. At this time one Mr. Sawyer hath given leave to a bricklayer to build a great number of tenements upon his ground within Kentish Street whereby he hath encroached three feet upon the common street.

20th September. FRENCH NEWS.

Because of the constant rumours concerning affairs in France, Sir Roger Williams was sent over to the French King some days since and arrived at Paris, all unexpected, on the 9th. The next day the King himself came to Paris, preparing to depart immediately to the succour of Cambray; but on the 14th he received advertisement that the enemy were in the town, and the soldiers forced to retire to the Castle. At Paris news is received that the Pope in public, with great solemnity, hath given absolution to the King in the person of the Bishop of Evreux, and that the greatest ceremony of joy was performed there in applause of it.

BRETON'S 'SOLEMN PASSION.'

Mr. Nicholas Breton hath written a poem called *A Solemn Passion of the Soul's Love*, setting forth the great love of God for man in this high strain:

Confess thyself unworthy of the sense
To learn the least of the supernal Will;
Beseech the heavens in strength of their defence,
To save and keep thee from infernal ill:
  Then fall to work, that all the world may see
  The joyful love betwixt thy God and thee.

Tell of His goodness how He did create thee,
And in His justice how He doth correct thee,
And in His love how He will never hate thee,
And that His mercy never will reject thee,
  And how He helped thee when the world distressed thee,
  And with His graces how He sweetly blessed thee.

MARKHAM'S 'MOST HONOURABLE TRAGEDY OF SIR RICHARD GRENVILLE.'

There is also Mr. Gervase Markham's poem of *The Tragedy of Sir Richard Grenville* that was slain in her Majesty's ship *Revenge* off the Azores in '91.

THE DEATH OF GRENVILLE.

They took him up, and to their General brought
His mangled carcase, but unmaimed mind.
Three days he breathed, yet never spake he ought,
Albe his foes were humble, sad, and kind;
The fourth came down the Lamb that all souls bought,
And his pure part, from worser parts refin'd;
  Bearing his spirit up to the lofty skies,
  Leaving his body, wonder to wonder's eyes.

22nd September. LYLY'S 'WOMAN IN THE MOON.'

Mr. John Lyly's comedy of *The Woman in the Moon*, that was formerly presented before the Queen, is to be printed.

23rd September. THE EARL OF SOUTHAMPTON.

It is said at Court that my Lord of Southampton doth with too much familiarity court the fair Mistress Vernon, while his friends observing the Queen's humours to my Lord of Essex do what they can to bring her to favour him, but it is yet in vain.

27th September. THE FIGHT IN IRELAND.

The conflict between Sir John Norris and the Earl of Tyrone happened on the return of Sir John to Newry from victualling the fort by Blackwater, wherein he was assailed by 500 horse and 2000 foot of the enemy, Sir John having only 1000 foot and 120 horse. In this encounter Sir John was hurt with two musket shots, the one through the left arm, the other athwart the belly, but neither of them dangerous. Few of ours were slain but 400 of the enemy left dead in the field.

Notwithstanding there is an expectation of the Earl of Tyrone coming in upon pardon for himself, O'Donnell and Macguire; and to that end authority is given to the Lord Deputy.

SIR WALTER RALEGH'S RETURN.

Now that Sir Walter Ralegh is come back to England from his voyage to Guiana there are not wanting many to traduce him, saying that his going to sea was but a bravado or even that he went not to sea but lay hidden in Cornwall or elsewhere. Others, at his setting out, prejudged that he would rather become a servant of the King of Spain than return to England, and that he was too easeful and sensual to undertake a journey of so great travail. Nor hath he returned with riches, for, saith he, it became not his former fortune to go journeys of picory, to run from cape to cape and place to place for pillage of ordinary prizes.

But Sir Walter's friends do tell her Majesty what great service he hath done unto her in discovering the way to bring home the wealth of India and in making known to that nation her virtues and her justice. He hath brought hither a supposed prince and left hostages in his place. The Queen gives good ear unto them.

30th September. NEW PLAYS.

There were two new plays by the Lord Admiral's men this month, the one called *Crack me this Nut*, and the other *The World's Tragedy*.

2nd October. THE HIGH PRICE OF CORN.

In the county of Leicester is great complaint of the high price of all corn and grain, to the grief of the poor people whose want is increased by the evil custom of the farmers and graziers in those parts that feed their sheep with pease, which in time of scarcity is the best relief that the poor find for their bread.

6th October. THE SOLDIERS FURNISHED BY THE CLERGY.

Her Majesty being desirous to be truly informed of the state of the whole forces of the realm, the Lords Lieutenant have been directed to have the enrolled soldiers viewed, mustered, and trained. The clergy also who in '88 found certain able men as well of horse as of foot are now to review and supply the like number; and where there is defect in their armour, horse or furniture, to cause the same to be amended or supplied, and perfect rolls to be made of the names and surnames of the soldiers and of those that set them forth which shall be sent to the Council.

TROUBLE OVER THE STARCH MONOPOLY.

Of late certain apprentices of London violently took away a 1000 lbs. weight of starch that had been seized on for her Majesty's use by Mr. James Anton, her patentee, and not only carried the same to a warehouse but did grievously beat and wound Mr. Anton's deputies. The Lord Mayor shall examine this foul outrage and not only commit the offenders to prison, but certify the manner of the outrage to the Council.

9th October. M. LOMENIE'S STOUT SPEECHES.

Sir Roger Williams is returned from the French King, and with him one Monsieur de Lomenie, a secretary of the King's Chamber, who both by the King's letters and his own speech hath dealt so roundly with the Queen and the Council that there is great offence at Court; for, not concealing that Cambray is lost to the Spaniard, yet he would urge that some auxiliary forces might forthwith be sent over into Picardy; and that afterwards commissioners appointed to treat about the managing of the war. These things appearing preposterous to the Queen and the Council, he grew impatient, imputing the loss of Cambray to the Queen, saying that she rejoiceth in the King's misery. Moreover the King declareth that he hath his absolution from the Pope and that there are deputed four cardinals to give him the solemnity thereof; but that their chief errand is to draw him to a peace with Spain and to unite against all that are divided from the Church. He saith that the King is assured to receive for himself honourable conditions, but knowing that he shall be sought to be divided from the Queen and the Low Countries, desireth by her to be enabled by a common concurrency of both their forces that he be not compelled to such a peace as willingly he would not make, but such as may comprehend them all in such terms, as holding always together, they might be a balance against Spanish greatness. That if she refuse him in it, he must provide for himself as he may. These letters delivered with very stout speeches have greatly offended the Queen who loveth not to be terrified, so the gentleman is despatched without any hope of obtaining relief from hence.

14th October. WHEAT SPENT WEEKLY.

The Lord Mayor complaineth to the Lord Treasurer how hard is this restraint on the City from buying wheat from Kent and Essex, for great quantities of wheat are required in the City, and by reason of the restraint the prices are enhanced in more remote counties. There is consumed weekly in the City, brown bread, 535 qrs.; white bread, 1317 qrs.; in markets, 600 qrs.; in houses providing for themselves, 40 qrs.; in all 2492 qrs.; besides Hackney and Stepney.

15th October. MR. HUGH PLATT'S INVENTIONS.

Mr. Hugh Platt that last year put forth a book of inventions called the *Jewel House of Art and Nature* hath caused to be printed a little pamphlet, being *A Discovery of certain English wants*, wherein he complaineth that in his own experience it is an easier matter to devise many and very profitable inventions than to dispose of one of them to the good of the author himself; and because there are many gentlemen that be always ready and willing to entertain good suits, he giveth them to understand that he is still well furnished with inventions for them if they come in time, and whilst his small store lasteth, *videlicet* ;—a means to prepare flesh without any salt, and fit to be laid up in storehouses for many years or to furnish ships withal ; a defensative in the highest kind of all armour and artillery whatsoever from rusting in seven years after one preparation ; some English secrets whereby we may be less beholding either unto France or Spain in some of their best commodities ; an excellent oily composition defending all iron works from rust wherewith Sir Francis Drake is furnished in this last voyage ; a pump not weighing 20 pounds in weight and yet sufficient to deliver five tuns of water in one hour, being an excellent engine to water all houses that are near the river Thames or any river, also for ships of war ; a liquor to keep either boot, shoe or buskin made of dry leather both black in wearing and defensible against all rain, dew or moisture, to be had of the author in several kinds.

All those that are desirous to have any conference with the author may be advertised of his abode by William Ponsonby, stationer in Paul's Churchyard.

SIR WALTER RALEGH.

Sir Walter Ralegh is now in London and goes daily to hear sermons, because he hath seen the wonders of the Lord in the deep ; 'tis much commended and spoken of.

27th October. HIGH PRICES.

Notwithstanding the seasonable harvest this summer, the price of corn and of white meat is of late greatly risen in many counties, which is thought due to the want of care of the Justices to seek reformation, and to the covetous dispositions of farmers that, not acknowledging God's goodness, seek immoderate gain by enhancing the price of corn to the great oppression of the poor. The Council recommend that the Justices should bestow their pains that the orders set down and published last year with certain new additions be carefully looked unto for the relief of the poor. The Justices moreover should contribute amongst themselves and by their good example induce others of the richer sort to do the like, whereby a good sum of money might be collected to make a stock to be employed in corn, out of which a proportion might be sent weekly to the markets to be uttered to the poor at reasonable rates.

Likewise in London the price of sea coals standeth at a very high rate to the great oppression of the poor that are not able to furnish themselves with wood ; the occasion whereof is that some of the richer sort of the town of Newcastle, having a lease of the Bishop of Durham of twelve coal pits, forbear to work the same but work in certain coal pits of their own which yield a worse sort of coal and less quantity. Moreover these owners outbid and hire from the rest all the coal wains that bring coals to the waterside. Another reason of raising the price of coals is that great quantities are transported to Rouen and other places beyond the seas. The Mayor of Newcastle is ordered to cause one or two of the chief coalmasters to be sent before the Council who shall bring with them the covenant wherein they are bound not to exceed a certain limit imposed on them : and in the mean season to take order that less quantity be transported out of the realm.

29th October. AN ATTACK ON IRELAND FEARED.

A Spanish pilot, taken by a captain of the Earl of Cumberland's upon the south coast of Spain, confesseth that there are a number of Levant ships of war of great burden come to Lisbon this month, where there are also eight or nine great ships of war and others expected : of these the Adelantado is to take charge and to come with them upon some parts in the West of Ireland. If the Lord Deputy shall find the Spaniard to attempt any landing in any place of the South as Waterford or Cork, he shall leave the prosecution of the rebellion in Ireland and march against them, leaving the forts of Armagh and Monaghan well guarded ; and to encourage the great towns to stand fast, 1000 footmen are to be put in readiness to be sent thither from Chester upon a day's warning.

30th October. NEW PLAYS AT THE ROSE.

At the Rose this month were three new plays, being *The Disguises*, *The Wonder of a Woman* and *Barnardo and Fiametta.*

1st November. THE ACCOUNT OF SIR WALTER RALEGH'S VOYAGE.

Sir Walter Ralegh hath now brought to completion and sent the account of his voyage to Guiana to the Lord Admiral.

After leaving Plymouth last February, he reached the island of Trinidad on 22nd March, where there is an abundance of stone pitch at a point called Tierra de Brea or Piche, wherewith he made trial in trimming the ships, for this pitch melteth not with the heat of the sun as the pitch of Norway. Thence by night he attacked a Spanish city called St. Joseph which they took, together with a Spanish gentleman called Berreo who was the governor there and hath travelled in Guiana, whom Sir Walter used very courteously as his prisoner. When this Berreo learned that Sir Walter would make his way up the river to see Guiana he was stricken with great melancholy and sadness, using all the arguments he could to dissuade him, and saying that they could not enter any of the rivers with their barks or pinnaces, it was so low and sandy. Further, none of the country would come to speak with them, but would all fly, and if followed would burn their dwellings; and besides, that winter was at hand when the rivers begin to swell, and that the kings and lords of all the borders of Guiana had decreed that none of them should trade with any Christians for gold, because the same would be their overthrow, and that for love of gold the Christians meant to conquer and dispossess them of all together.

When Sir Walter had by experiment found Berreo's words to be true he resolved to go on with the boats, and a galego boat, cut down and fitted with banks to row on. Into the galego were thrust sixty men, in three other boats and in Sir Walter's own barge ten a piece, making 100 in all. With this company, having passed over some twenty miles of rough sea, they entered one of the rivers which their guide declared would take them into the great river of Orenoque; and there might they have been lost in the labyrinth of rivers but by chance they met with a canoa with three Indians, one of them an old man; and him they took for guide. Up these rivers they sailed westward for many days often in great distress for lack of victuals.

At length they reached a port called Morequito where they were visited by the old King of that place called Topiawari, to whom Sir Walter made known the cause of his coming thither, of her Majesty's greatness, her justice, her charity to all oppressed nations, with many other of her beauties and virtues, and that her pleasure was to deliver them from the tyranny of the Spaniards; all which being with great admiration attentively heard and marvellously admired, he began to sound the old man concerning Guiana.

The next day they sailed westward up to the river called Caroli, as well because it was marvellous of itself as also because it led to the strongest nations of all the frontiers; these are enemies of the Epuremi, that abound in gold, being subjects to Inga, Emperor of Guiana and Manoa. But when they came to this river, they could not row one stone's cast in an hour by reason of the force of the stream. Sir Walter therefore sent his guide to the people of those parts and there came down a lord or casique called Wanuretona, with many people and much store of provision. Of them he learnt that all who were either against the Spaniards or the Epuremi would join with him, and that if he entered the land over the mountains of Curaa he should satisfy himself with gold and all other good things.

Here they landed to go by foot to view the great river, and to see if they could find any mineral stone alongst the river side; and when they came to the tops of the hills adjoining to the rivers they beheld that wonderful breach of waters which ran down Caroli, and might from that mountain see the river how it ran in three parts over twenty miles off; and there appeared some ten or twelve overfalls in sight, every one as high over the other as a church tower. For his own part Sir Walter would have returned from thence, but the rest were all so desirous to go near the strange thunder of waters that they drew him on by little and little, till they came into the next valley where they might better discern it. 'I never saw,' saith he, 'a more beautiful country, nor more lively prospects, hills so raised here and there over the valleys, the river winding into divers branches, the plain adjoining without bush or stubble, all fair green grass, the ground hard sand, easy to march on either for horse or foot, the deer crossing in every path, the birds towards the evening singing on every tree with a thousand several tunes, cranes and herons of white, crimson, and carnation, perching in the river's side, the air fresh with a gentle easterly wind, and every stone that we stooped to take up promised either gold or silver by his complexion.'

But now the fury of the river Orenoque began daily to threaten them with dangers on their return, for no half day passed but the river began to rage and overflow very fearfully, and the rains came down in terrible showers, and gusts in great abundance. Having for well near a month passed westward farther and farther from their ships, at length they turned eastward. Returning therefore to the country of Topiawari, Sir Walter again had conference with the old man, who told him that four days' journey from his town was Macureguarai, and that those were the next and nearest subjects of Inga and of the Epuremi, and the first town of apparelled and rich people, and that all those plates of gold which were carried to other nations came from the Macureguarai and were there made; but that those of the land within were far finer, and fashioned after the images of men, beasts, birds and fishes. The old King would indeed have had Sir Walter stay and attempt this people, but he, knowing that Berreo did daily expect a succour out of Spain and from Granada, was unwilling to attempt the enterprise at that season but promised to return next year.

Of marvels in those parts, noteth that in the parts south of the river there be a race of Amazons, and they accompany with men but for one month in the year, and at that time all the Kings of the borders assemble and the Queens of the Amazons, and, after the Queens have chosen, the rest cast lots for their valentines. If they conceive and be delivered of a son, they return him to the father ; if of a daughter, they nourish it and retain it ; and as many as have daughters send a present to the begetters. At the port of Morequito one gave him a beast called by the Spaniards ' armadilla,' which seemeth to be barred all over with small plates somewhat like to a rhinoceros, with a white horn growing in his hinder parts as big as a great hunting horn, which they use to wind instead of a trumpet. In those parts there be a people called Ewaipanoma ; they are reported to have their eyes in their shoulders, and their mouths in the middle of their breasts, and a long train of hair groweth backward between their shoulders : these Sir Walter saw not, but so many of the inhabitants declare the truth of the matter that he is fain to believe. Moreover such a relation was written of by Mandeville whose reports were many years holden for fables, and yet since the Indes were discovered we find his relations true of such things as heretofore were held incredible. A Spaniard also, a man in all things else esteemed a man of his word, declareth that he hath seen many of them.

Sir Walter urgeth very vehemently the advantages of this country of Guiana, being a country that hath yet her maidenhead, never sacked, turned nor wrought, the face of the earth not torn, nor the virtue and salt of the soil spent by manurance, the graves not opened for gold, the mines not broken with sledges, nor the images pulled down out of the temples. It is besides so defensible that it could be held by two forts built on a channel by which all ships must pass ; nor is there other way of entry.

5th November. COURT NEWS.

On Monday last the Queen showed the Earl of Essex a printed book, which was that *Conference about the Succession to the Crown of England*, written two years since (as is supposed) by Parsons the Jesuit and dedicated to my Lord ; than whom, he saith, no man is in more high and eminent place at this day in the realm, whether we respect his nobility, or calling, or favour with the Queen, or high liking of the people ; and consequently no man like to have a greater part or sway in deciding of this great affair, when the time shall come for determination.

At his coming from Court the Earl was observed to look wan and pale, being exceedingly troubled at this great piece of villainy done unto him. He is sick and continues very ill. Yesterday in the afternoon the Queen visited him ; but the Earl is mightily crossed in all things, for Mr. Bacon is gone without the place of Solicitor. The Lord Treasurer is come to London and lies in bed so ill of the gout in his hands, arms, knees and toes that his pains make him pitifully groan.

6th November. MR. BACON DISAPPOINTED OF THE SOLICITORSHIP.

Mr. Sergeant Fleming was yesterday made Solicitor, so my Lord of Essex and Mr. Bacon are finally disappointed. When the matter was concluded, my Lord came over from Richmond to Twickenham Park, where Mr. Bacon was, to break it with him, in these words: 'Master Bacon, the Queen hath denied me yon place for you, and hath placed another. I know you are the least part of your own matter, but you fare ill because you have chosen me for your mean and dependence. You have spent your time and your thoughts in my matters; I die if I do not somewhat towards your fortune; you shall not deny to accept a piece of land which I will bestow upon you.'

At first Mr. Bacon was somewhat unwilling to accept of the gift lest he should be too much bound to my Lord by this obligation. But my Lord bade him take no care for that, and pressed it. Whereupon Mr. Bacon saith, 'My Lord, I see I must be your homager and hold land of your gift: but do you know the manner of doing homage in law? Always it is with a saving of his faith to the King and his other Lords. And therefore, my Lord,' quoth he, 'I can be no more yours than I was, and it must be with the ancient savings, and if I grow to be a rich man, you will give me leave to give it back to some of your unrewarded followers.'

MR. DARCY'S PATENT.

Mr. Darcy in pursuit of his patent hath caused divers of the leather sellers to be committed to prison, notwithstanding they gave attendance in the cause three times at the Star Chamber and once at the Court at Richmond; whereat the Lord Mayor petitioneth the Council for a trial at law touching the validity of this and other patents made by her Majesty.

9th November. A TRUCE WITH TYRONE.

The Earl of Tyrone hath now made submission, complaining he was led into these courses chiefly from the bad usage of him by Sir John Perrot. Now he would have pardon and declares that he will not join with any foreign prince. A truce is therefore made until the 1st January.

12th November. THE EARL OF HERTFORD COMMITTED.

The Earl of Hertford was committed to the Tower six days ago. The cause is said to be a record secretly put into the Court of Arches to prove his first marriage lawful and his children legitimate. 'Tis said he is one of the wealthiest subjects of England. It is since given out that by commandment his son shall no more be called Lord Beauchamp but Seymour; and it is credibly said that my Lady Hertford is become stark mad. Note that my Lord is the son of the Duke of Somerset that was Lord Protector to King Edward the Sixth; his first wife was the Lady Catherine Grey (sister to the Lady Jane), whom he married after she had been divorced by the Earl of Pembroke; and for whose sake he was nine years in the Tower. This lady died in 1567.

My Lord of Essex hath put off the melancholy he fell unto by reason of the printed book delivered to the Queen, wherein by her Majesty's gracious favour and wisdom the harm meant to him is turned to his good and strengthens her love towards him. Within these last days many letters sent to her from foreign countries are delivered to my Lord, and he to answer them.

EXTRAORDINARY MEASURES AGAINST INVASION.

The Lords Lieutenant of counties on the sea coast are specially warned to have all men that are apt for the wars in readiness to withstand any invasion of the enemy. These men shall be put into bands under principal leaders, and held in readiness with all necessary furniture to be sent to such landing places where the enemy hath a purpose to land. To every thousand men are appointed one hundred pioneers, with their necessary instruments, and provision made of carts and carriages with some small nags for the more speedy conveyance of the men, who shall take with them a convenient proportion of victual and some overplus of powder, lead and match to supply any want. It is further ordained by the Council that the Lords Lieutenant shall succour each other should the enemy land in other counties than their own. They shall also warn all persons having habitations near the sea coast to attend with all their forces for the defence of the coast and of their land and habitations, as by the law of nature and of the land they are bound to do upon pain of forfeiture of their livelihoods and further punishment. The sum total of men to be put in readiness by fifteen counties and the towns of Southampton and London is 61,800.

An Impudent Cook.

One Owen Saintpire, a cook in the City, a very perverse and obstinate fellow, was lately committed to prison by the Lord Mayor for refusing to pay such contribution as by his own company was proportioned upon him for the Queen's service, and for other misdemeanours and parts of disobedience. Hereupon he hath entered an action of wrong imprisonment against the Chamberlain and other officers of the City.

17th November. The Queen's Accession Day.

This day was held as a day of great triumph at London for her Majesty's long and prosperous reign. The pulpit cross in Paul's Churchyard is now newly repaired, painted and partly inclosed with a wall of brick; here Dr. Richard Fletcher, the Bishop of London, preached in praise of the Queen before the Lord Mayor, Aldermen, and citizens in their best liveries, and the sermon being ended, upon the church leads the trumpets sounded, the cornets winded, and the choristers sang an anthem. On the steeple many lights were burned, the Tower shot off her ordnance, and bonfires were made.

At the Tilt there was a device of my Lord of Essex which is much commended. Some pretty while before he came in himself, he sent his page with some speed to the Queen, who returned with her Majesty's glove. When my Lord himself came in, he was met with an old hermit, a secretary of state, a brave soldier, and an esquire. The first presented him with a book of meditations, the second with political discourses, the third with orations of brave fought battles, the fourth was but his own follower, to whom the other three imparted much of their purpose before his coming in. Each devised with him, persuading him to this and that course of life, according to their inclinations. Then comes there into the Tiltyard unthought on the ordinary post boy of London, a ragged villain all bemired, upon a poor lean jade, galloping and blowing for life, and delivered the secretary a packet of letters which he straightway offered to my Lord of Essex.

In the after-supper before the Queen they first delivered a well-penned speech to move this worthy Knight to leave his vain following of Love and to betake him to heavenly meditation; the secretary's speech tending to have him follow matters of state; the soldier's persuading him to the war; but the esquire answered them all, and concluded with an excellent, but too plain English speech that his Knight would never forsake his Mistress's love, whose virtue made all his thoughts divine, whose wisdom taught him all true policy, whose beauty and worth were at all times able to make him fit to command armies. He showed all the defects and imperfections of all their times, and therefore thought his course of life to be best in serving his Mistress. Hereupon many constructions are made of these speeches, comparing the hermit and the secretary to two of the Lords, and the soldier to Sir Roger Williams; but the Queen said that if she had thought there would have been so much said of her, she would not have been there that night; and so went to bed.

20th November. SOUTHWELL'S 'TRIUMPH OVER DEATH.'

Mr. John Trussell hath sent to the press that consolatory epistle written by Southwell the Jesuit on the death of the Lady Margaret Sackville, Countess of Dorset. 'Our life,' saith he, 'is but lent, a good to make thereof during the loan our best commodity. It is a due debt to a more certain owner than ourselves, and therefore so long as we have it, we receive a benefit. When we are deprived of it, we have no wrong; we are tenants at will of this clayey farm, not for term of years. When we are warned out we must be ready to remove, having no other title but the owner's pleasure. It is but an inn, not a home; we came but to bait, not to dwell, and the condition of our entrance was in fine to depart.'

'Nature's debt is sooner exacted of some than of others, yet is there no fault in the creditor that exacteth but his own, but in the greediness of our eager hopes, either repining that their wishes fail, or willingly forgetting their mortality whom they are unwilling by experience to see mortal. Yet the general tide washeth all passengers to the same shore, some sooner, some later, but all at the last: and we must settle our minds to take our course as it cometh, never fearing a thing so necessary, yet ever expecting a thing so uncertain.'

22nd November. COURT NEWS.

We wait to hear what the French King's countenance will be on the return of Monsieur Lomenie, who went hence discontented and speaks lewdly of us wherever he goes. The King has not yet seen him, but the answers thence to our excuses of our usage of Monsieur Lomenie are sour and savouring of an alienate mind. Sir Henry Unton is named as the man to be sent over but would stand upon terms. Then Sir Arthur Gorges had vogue one week; now it is Sir Henry again, who is warned on his allegiance and let to understand that Princes will not be capitulated with by their servants.

23rd November. IRISH NEWS.

Letters are come from Ireland with good news of Tyrone's submission which brought the Lord Treasurer to Court from his sick bed. The Council have been three days about this Irish peace, and a formal pardon, according to our Law, is now a drawing. Sir George Carew is presently to be sent over to take his oath and to be Commissioner in the business with the Lord Deputy, to whom small countenance or trust is committed in this or anything else; and the credit of all things given to Sir John Norris.

26th November. AN INQUISITION CONCERNING RECUSANTS.

Because of the increase of recusants at this time which may infect others and also cause a diminution of the forces for the defence of the realm, in the present dangers extraordinary care must be taken for their reformation. The Archbishops shall now cause the Bishops and ordinaries to make exact and diligent inquisition into the number of recusants, their state, degree and value, and how many be vagrants and fugitives, and what means are used to reform them by instruction and teaching, and how many are indicted by form of law.

30th November. New Plays.

This month there were two new plays at the Rose, *A Toy to please chaste ladies* and *Harry the Fifth.*

1st December. French Opinions.

Mr. Edmondes who is the English Resident in France reporteth that Monsieur de Lomenie (that came over with Sir Roger Williams about three weeks since) is returned to the King who is now besieging La Fere. The King by Monsieur de Lomenie's relation is reduced from ill satisfaction and weak hope into strange despair of the English Court, so that he is resolved not to send Monsieur de Sancy here as he had intended, being persuaded that it would serve no other purpose than to give him more discontent, and to heap more indignity on him. The French say that they see clearly into our dispositions toward them by our demand for Calais, which, they allege, doth much touch the heart of France : by our refusing to join in treaty with them ; and this last proceeding with Monsieur de Lomenie. They declare that they are in so hard a condition that they know not how to subsist against the great forces wherewith the enemy doth threaten them ; but that they see their apparent ruin before their eyes if, seeing they are abandoned by those who are interested in common fortune with them, they do not otherwise provide for themselves. These be their discourses ; and to anything we can allege of former merit and future hope, they answer that past remedies do not cure present diseases ; and that we pay them with words, and not with deeds, seeking nothing more than to keep them still miserable. The Spaniard so constantly seeking a truce in Brittany giveth great suspicion of further consequence, either of some attempt elsewhere, or else to extend it to a further treaty.

Mr. Edmondes much lamenteth his own miserable estate and inability to serve longer by reason of his great debts, and earnestly petitioneth that her Majesty would have compassion on him and grant his revocation.

5th December. The Lieutenant of the Tower Committed.

Sir Michael Blount, the Lieutenant of the Tower, is put out of his place. It is said that he grew very familiar with Mr. Neville, *alias* Latimer, and Captain Wainman, and in discourse with them, they began to talk of the dangers of the time; from that to argue of the town, how it might be made defensible, what provision, what men would serve the turn, what a brave command it was in a change. Then they grew madder as to talk of titles, and it is reported that the Lieutenant delivered his mind how he was affected; that he and his friends would keep the place till he saw great reason to yield it. But when they had waded so far, 'Masters,' said he, 'these matters we speak of are perilous, and therefore I will have nothing to do with them.' But the other two found means to discover it first to the Queen, whereupon the Lieutenant was examined by the Lords and is now committed to the Tower. Sir Drue Drury is sworn in his place.

6th December. WOOD IN THE PILLORY.

Wood that was condemned in the Star Chamber last July hath now confessed. To-day on a pillory in Cheapside he had an ear cut off, and three letters burned in his forehead. He made an oration, declaring his confession is voluntary: in his examination he charges Lady Shrewsbury very deeply with the matter; but she denies it.

7th December. THE QUEEN'S LETTER TO THE KING.

On the 30th November Mr. Edmondes read before the French King a letter from her Majesty answering those complaints of Monsieur de Lomenie, and his demand for succours. Mr. Edmondes reminded the King of the great services which her Majesty had rendered him for a long space of time, and lastly at Brest when the Queen, though she had in hand several other designs both of honour and advantage, had consented for the King's service to employ her forces by land and sea to drive the enemy from thence. As for the declaration that the King might be obliged to agree with the common enemy without comprehending her Majesty in the treaty, she would not suffer herself to be disturbed with the thought that the King's honour and so many vows on his part and so many services on hers could admit so odious and dangerous a resolution.

After the letter had been read, the King answered that he was not alone able to sustain the burden of the war for such reasons as are too true and too well known to all men; and that he would consult with the princes and officers of his crown, what he was to resolve on; wherein if necessity shall force him to change course, as the fault thereof shall not be his, so her Majesty on her part, instead of excuses and justifications, shall have only cause afterwards of sorrow.

12th December. THE QUEEN DINES WITH THE LORD KEEPER.

Her Majesty in these days cometh much abroad. Yesterday she dined at Kew, at the Lord Keeper's house, where her entertainment was great and exceeding costly. At her first alighting she had a fine fan, with a handle garnished with diamonds. When she was in the middle way, between the garden gate and the house, there came one running towards her with a nosegay in his hand, and delivered it to her with a short, well-penned speech; it had in it a very rich jewel, with many pendants of diamonds, valued at £400 at least. After dinner in her privy chamber, the Lord Keeper gave her a fine gown and juppin, which things were pleasing to her Highness; and to grace his Lordship the more, she of herself took from him a salt, a spoon, and a fork of fine agate.

13th December. THE NAVY TO BE SET OUT.

The Queen hath now given order for the speedy setting forth of the Navy to the seas and hath appointed the same to be victualled for five months for 12,000 men; the victuals to be delivered aboard the ships by the last of March next.

THE DEATH OF SIR ROGER WILLIAMS.

Sir Roger Williams died of a surfeit in Baynard's Castle yesterday at 3 o'clock after midnight. He gave all he had to my Lord of Essex, who indeed saved his soul, for none but he could make him take a feeling of his end; but he died well, and very repentant. His jewels are valued at £1,000; 'tis said he had £1,200 out at interest; in ready gold £200; and £60 in silver. His plate is worth £60, his garments £30, his horses £60, and this is his end. He desired to be buried in Paul's, and my Lord of Essex means to have it done in very martial sort.

14th December. MR. DARCY'S GRANT.

Some days since three of the Company of the Leathersellers, having disobeyed her Majesty's grant made to Mr. Edward Darcy for viewing and sealing of leather, were committed to the

Marshalsea. To-day being at their own request admitted to make their excuse before the Council, there was relation made of the whole proceedings since the grant was first made; but their Lordships, finding their obstinacy to proceed without due regard, return them to prison, there to remain until they shall submit themselves and permit Mr. Darcy to enjoy the benefit of his grant. Moreover the Lord Mayor shall inhibit the rest of the Leathersellers from putting on sale any leather until they have submitted themselves.

17th December. 'MAROCCUS EXTATICUS.'

There is a pamphlet called *Maroccus Extaticus*, or *Banks' Bay Horse in a trance*, set down in the form of a dialogue between Banks and his beast and anatomising some abuses and bad tricks of this age, and especially of those landlords who for raising of their rents will turn their houses into brothels.

19th December. THE LORD PRESIDENT OF THE NORTH DEAD.

The Lord Huntingdon, Lord President of the North, died on Sunday last past, the 14th of this month, having been sick for nine days. The Archbishop of York being with him desired two things of his hands; to prepare himself to die, which he did, not using many words but such as did give good assurance he died a good Christian; the second, to dispose of his estate, which by no means he would hearken unto, and said little to that, only that it was a wild world, which he would not think upon. This was at first kept from my Lady Huntingdon, but the Queen came to Whitehall very suddenly of purpose to break it to her herself.

When the news was brought on Wednesday morning, the Lord Keeper was sent to her from the Queen that my Lord was sick. In the afternoon he came again unto her to let her know the Queen was advertised he was in some danger and therefore besought her to consider what should be done about his estate. This morning my Lady Puckering came to see her, and finding her so disquieted, she told her by circumstances that his danger was great, and small hope of recovery. Being desired by my Lady to tell her the very truth, she then told her that indeed assured word was come he was dead. This evening, at 4 o'clock, the Queen herself came in a litter to visit her.

21st December. PRIVATE SHIPS FOR THE NAVY.

Letters are being sent to the mayors and principal officers of sundry port towns to the effect that upon advertisement made of some attempt against this kingdom by way of invasion this next spring, the Queen hath given order to put the Navy Royal in readiness and to have the same assisted with some reasonable number of good ships of her subjects. Wherefore ships of good burden shall be prepared, manned and furnished, provided with munition and victual for five months, by the same that did contribute in '88 ; these ships to be ready by the end of March.

SIR HENRY UNTON SENT TO THE FRENCH KING.

Sir Henry Unton is sent ambassador to France to discover how the French King standeth affected, and hoping to divert him from a course with Spain which by his own answers and Mr. Edmondes and other conjectures, it seemeth he is like to enter into, the Pope working earnestly to bring it to pass, and almost all his Council discovering no good conceit of our amity.

THE INVASION IN CORNWALL.

After the sudden incursion of the enemy in Cornwall last summer, a collection was made both in Cornwall and some other counties for the relief of the inhabitants of those villages that suffered spoil. Now it appeareth that this money was neither well ordered nor distributed, for the licence to gather was sold by the parties that undertook the collection, and the villages most spoiled like to be defrauded of it.

25th December. NEWS OF SIR FRANCIS DRAKE.

At Plymouth an Irish captain new come from Lisbon declareth that Sir Francis Drake and Sir John Hawkins have taken great treasure at St. John de Porto Rico, besides other pillage of great value, and that the fleet will speedily return to England.

28th December. SMUGGLING OF CORN.

From the Isle of Ely it is reported that divers boats come up in the night time and convey much grain by water from the inland counties to Lynne whence it is transported overseas.

OTHER BOOKS ALSO SET FORTH ANNO 1595

'CHURCHYARD'S CHARITY' AND 'A PRAISE OF POETRY.'

A musical consort of heavenly harmony called *Churchyard's Charity*, by Mr. Thomas Churchyard, which he dedicateth to the Earl of Essex, noting that now, by reason of great age, his wits and inventions are almost wearied with writing of books, this being one of the last. In this poem, he lamenteth that great lack of charity in our days. Machievel, saith he, is now made an Englishman :

> Fine Machievel, is now from Florence flown
> To England where, his welcome is too great ;
> His busy books, are here so read and known
> That charity, thereby hath lost her meat.
> Who doth for debt, in danger long remain
> Must fall down flat, and seldom rise again.

Also, he hath written *A Praise of Poetry*, some notes whereof are drawn out of the *Apology* made by Sir Philip Sidney that was published this last spring.

HUNNIS' 'RECREATIONS.'

A book of godly verses entitled *Hunnis' Recreations*, written by Mr. William Hunnis, the Master of the Children of the Queen's Chapel, being Adam's Banishment, Christ his Crib, The Lost Sheep, The Complaint of Old Age, published together with The Life and Death of Joseph. Noteth in the Complaint of Old Age that he will speak the best of the dead :

> The common custom is,
> to flatter them that live ;
> And of the dead reproachful words
> and ill reports to give.
> But sure the fault is great,
> to speak ill of the dead,
> Who harm them not, but quietly
> do rest within their bed.

‘ POLIMANTEIA.’

From Cambridge a book called *Polimanteia* showing the means lawful and unlawful to judge of the fall of a commonwealth by signs astronomical and the like, being put forward against frivolous and foolish conjectures. To this is added a letter of England to her three daughters, being the two Universities and the Inns of Court, exhorting their children to write of the worthies of our time ; England to all her inhabitants exhorting them to stand together for that England cannot perish but by Englishmen ; Religion's speech to England's children ; and lastly Loyalty's speech.

PLUTARCH'S LIVES.

A new edition of that translation which Sir Thomas North published in 1579, made from the French of James Amyot out of the original Greek of *The Lives of the Noble Grecians and Romans, compared together* by that grave, learned philosopher and historiographer Plutarch of Chaeronea.

1596

3rd January. THE LADY HUNTINGDON.

My Lady of Huntingdon continues so ill of grief that many doubt she cannot live. She is so much weakened by sorrow that no officers of hers dare go to her sight to know her pleasure, either in her own private fortune or to know what shall be done with the dead body of my Lord.

8th January. 'THE BLACK DOG OF NEWGATE.'

There is entered a book called *The Black Dog of Newgate* by one Luke Hutton, dedicated to Sir John Popham, the Lord Chief Justice, and containing a poem of the Black Dog, being the jailor of Newgate, whom for his cruelty he likeneth to a dog; also a discourse between the author and one Zawny, a prisoner, discovering the ways of certain connycatchers, E. N. or N. S., that prey especially upon their fellows.

THE CONDEMNED.

The sermon ended, the men condemned to die,
  Taking their leaves of their acquainted friends,
With sorry looks paysing their steps they ply,
  Down to a hall where for them there attends
A man of office, who to daunt life's hopes,
  Doth cord their hands and scarf their necks with ropes.

Thus roped and corded they descend the stairs;
  Newgate's Black Dog bestirs to play his part,
And doth not cease for to augment their cares,
  Willing the carman to set near his cart;
Which done, these men with fear of death o'erpanged,
  Bound in the cart are carried to be hanged.

Noteth that the rats be so many that they will take a candle from a man's hand, and when one dieth in the common ward they will prey upon his face ere he be fully dead.

18th January. VICTUALS FOR THE NAVY.

The Council having ordained the proportion of victuals of wheat, malt, pease, oxen, porks, bacon and cheese to be rendered by the several counties for the service of the navy, complaints are now being made by most of them that the charge is too heavy; so that in some cases the demand is abated.

The cities of New Sarum and Winchester, being cities near to the port of Southampton and taking special benefit from it, are required to consider of some contribution from such as exercise merchandize towards the setting forth of ships.

19th January. 'A WATCHWORD FOR WAR.'

There is from Cambridge a godly book called *A Watchword for War*, by one C. G., published by reason of the dispersed rumours amongst us and the suspected coming of the Spaniard. Noteth and confuteth these fearful objections which make against us; as that the power of the enemy is great, and it may be he shall have the aid of the Indians, the assistance of the Pope, and perhaps the help of such as have greater cause to gratify us than be against us. Or some sinister civil practice; yet this is the common saying: 'If we be true within ourselves, we need not care or fear the enemy.' Many suspect the papists, yet, albeit they jar about matters of religion, when they see the Spaniard, they will join with us against him, if it were but to save their lives.

20th January. 'THE SECOND PART OF THE FAERY QUEEN.'

The second part of Mr. Edmund Spenser's *Faery Queen* is now entered for the press, containing the fourth, fifth and sixth books, being the Legend of Cambel and Telamond, or of Friendship; the Legend of Artegal, or of Justice; and the Legend of S. Calidore, or of Courtesy.

23rd January. COPLEY'S 'FIG FOR FORTUNE.'

There is a poem entered by Mr. Anthony Copley, dedicated to the Lord Viscount Montague and entitled *A Fig for Fortune*, whereof the author giveth this argument:

An Elizian outcast of Fortune, ranging on his jade Melancholy through the desert of his affliction, in hope to find out somewhere either ease or end of the same, hapneth first upon Cato's ghost, a spirit of despair and self-misdoom, which would persuade him to kill himself. But for that she endeth her oratory with a sulphur vanish from his sight, he misdoubted both her and her tale. Then posting onward through the residue of the night, he chanceth next on the spirit of Revenge ; she persuadeth him blood and treachery against all his enemies as the only means to remount to pristine bliss in despite of Fortune. But she likewise manifesting in the end the treason of her tale by a sudden whip away from his eye at the sight of break of day in the east, left him also conceited of her danger. Thirdly, rapt from off his Melancholy, which now began to faint under him at the light of a new day of Grace, he was suddenly mounted upon the steed of Good Desire, and by him brought to Mount Sion, the Temple of Peace ; where by Catechrysius, an hermit (who greatly wondered to see a distressed Elizian in those parts under so happy days of Eliza), he was by him in the house of Devotion catechized, and there also celestially armed by an angel, and within a while after in-denized by the high Sacrificator a Champion of that Temple against the insults of Fortune, who is titled by the name of Doblessa in respect of the double danger both of her luring and lowering inconstancy. She, whiles the Sionites were all in peaceful adoration of Almighty God in the Temple, came with her Babellonian rout to assault the place, but was eftsoons by the nature of those Templars shamefully repulsed. Feast and thanks was made to God therefor throughout all the region ; in which solemnity the Grace of God, hovering over the multitude in the procession time (like a virgin attended upon with all the Court of heaven), showered down roses amongst them, leaving them there a scrambling for the same. The Elizian was one that scrambled his lapful among the rest ; and for he thought it was his sovereign Lady Eliza, and those roses hers, he was suddenly in joy thereof rapt home again to Elizium.

24th January. SIR HENRY UNTON AND THE FRENCH KING.

Sir Henry Unton reached La Fere, which the French King besiegeth, on the 7th, the King then being absent. On the 9th the King returned, and the next day gave audience to Sir Henry, who after due compliments delivered unto him the

Queen's salutations and her letters; next he declared that he was come over according to the Queen's promise given to Monsieur Lomenie to send one by whom she could more particularly express herself than by letters. Then, entering into particularities, he related why her Majesty was forced to withdraw her forces out of Brittany; why she could not assent to Monsieur Lomenie's demands for succour for Picardy, and therewithal Monsieur Lomenie's insolent carriage towards her Majesty; and lastly acquainted him with an Italian pamphlet wherein it was pretended that the King would make peace with Spain.

The King gave patient hearing, and after the ambassador's speech was ended asked whether that was all the satisfaction he brought; for he was little favoured and the ambassador little honoured to be employed in so fruitless a message of words. Time no longer permitted him to trust words, for he looked daily to be assailed by a mighty enemy, which he had sufficiently and often made known to the Queen; which seeing it will nothing prevail, he must, saith he, otherwise provide for his safety by such means as he may.

MR. DARCY'S PATENT IS ANNULLED.

The patent for searching and sealing of leather granted to Mr. Darcy is now revoked upon the leather sellers paying unto him the sum of £4,000.

25th January. CONDEMNED PRISONERS TO BE PARDONED.

Her Majesty hath resolved that those prisoners condemned to death at the late gaol delivery and meet to be favoured of their lives shall be pardoned and bestowed in the service of the wars with hope of their good demeanour hereafter.

26th January. NEWS FROM FRANCE.

Sir Henry Unton the ambassador is much cast down at his ill success, which had been much worse but for the King's special favour, who took some pity on him for his former merit; the French term his message '*un discours du foin*' among themselves, and both the King and his Council take great scorn thereat. The King gave him private audience in his cabinet, saying that it was for Sir Henry's particular satisfaction, being loath to discontent one who had so well deserved of him, reputing him his soldier after the old manner howsoever he was now qualified with the title of the Queen's ambassador.

It is believed that this general truce between France and Spain is likely to ensue, whereof the grounds are these: the King's reconciliation with Rome; his being given to pleasures and desire of repose; the necessity of his estate, wanting treasure and forces to maintain the wars; his subjects being harried and wearied out with the former wars, which cry out for peace; the zeal of all his Catholics in their religion; the forwardness of his choice Councillors to sway the King to the amity of Spain; the threats of the King of Spain's intended invasion of Picardy upon the arrival of the Cardinal of Austria in the Low Countries, who bringeth war and peace with him; and lastly the small comfort which the King expecteth from his confederates' association and aid.

30th January. A SECOND VOYAGE TO GUIANA.

Four days since Mr. Laurence Keymis set forth from Portland in the *Darling* of London to make a further voyage of discovery at the charges of Sir Walter Ralegh.

31st January. NEW PLAYS BY THE LORD ADMIRAL'S MEN.

The Lord Admiral's men have played three new plays this month, *Chinon of England*, *Pythagoras*, and *The Second Week*.

THE MILD WEATHER.

This month there hath been notable mild weather, and so like the spring time that the sparrows have been seen to build their nests.

1st February. FLESH PROHIBITED DURING LENT.

The customary orders against killing and eating of flesh during Lent are published. This year eight butchers are to be licensed within the City without paying anything for their licence,but being bound in reasonable sums of money to observe the orders prescribed to them.

2nd February. PROCEEDINGS WITH TYRONE.

Sir Henry Wallop and Sir Robert Gardiner, appointed commissioners to treat with Tyrone under the Great Seal of Ireland, have met with the Earl, O'Donnell, and others. The commissioners at first would have him come to Dundalk but he refused, and on the 20th January they with three others met Tyrone and O'Donnell a mile out of the town, none of either side having any other weapons than swords. The forces of either side stood a quarter of a mile distant from them, and whilst they parleyed (which was on horseback) two horsemen of the commissioners stood firm in the midway between Tyrone's troops and them, likewise two horsemen of Tyrone's were placed between them and the English forces; which were to give warning if any treacherous attempt were made on either side. This treaty continued for three hours but without conclusion. The next day they met again, at which time the Irish behaved as men exceeding fearful, continually gazing about, their spies riding near, and themselves less attentive than at first. At the conclusion of this parley it was agreed that they should set down dividedly all the causes of their grievances, their demands and offers, and thereupon the commissioners would answer them so reasonably as they hoped would be to their satisfaction.

3rd February. CONTRIBUTIONS TO THE FLEET.

The inhabitants of certain ports and coast towns in Essex having made complaint that the setting forth of three hoys laid upon them is too great, the Council give order that the inhabitants of the county in general being as much interested as the parts maritime shall confer and resolve of some good proportion to be given in this behalf.

4th February. FRENCH NEWS.

It is said in the French King's camp that the Cardinal of Austria hath power from the King of Spain to conclude a peace between France and Spain for certain years; but the Spanish King doth rather affect a long truce than a peace, whereby he might retain what he now possesseth in France. The Cardinal is now at Namur; he intendeth (as appeareth from certain letters taken) to draw out all the old soldiers into the field, being resolved to besiege Calais or Boulogne to divert thereby the siege of La Fere.

5th February. NEWS OF DRAKE.

A carvel from Havannah bringeth news that Sir Francis Drake has taken the castle there and landed 4000 men.

7th February. MR. THOMAS ARUNDEL'S RETURN.

Mr. Thomas Arundel that some months since went to take service under the Emperor against the Turk is now returned, having gotten an extreme cold by tumbling into the sea for safety of his life, when his ship was wrecked, and thereby his apparel, linen, horses, money, and whatsoever else all lost. So honourably hath he carried himself in the wars that the Emperor made him an Earl of the Empire. But when it was carried to the Queen that he hath presumed to a dignity from the Emperor without her privity he is to be committed to his lodging or to the Fleet until her pleasure be known.

11th February. FORGERS SENTENCED.

Five men called Nixen, Pepper, Ellis, Johnson and Anglesey, that had counterfeited the hands of the Lord Treasurer and others of the Council, were sentenced to-day in the Star Chamber. The first three are condemned to stand on the pillory and lose their ears, and be branded on the forehead with an F, and condemned perpetually to the galleys. Johnson suffereth the same; but Anglesey, inasmuch as he wrote the names fearing lest Johnson would stab him, to the pillory and imprisonment only. The Lord Treasurer moved that since such burnings die out in a short time, they should be scarified on the cheeks with the letter F by a surgeon, and that some powder be put there to colour so it would never vanish; but the others made no reply to this.

12th February. 'THE BLIND BEGGAR OF ALEXANDRIA.'

To-day there is a new play at the Rose by Chapman called *The Blind Beggar of Alexandria.* Herein one Irus, supposed a blind beggar, disguising himself as an humorous Count (one that maketh much of his pistol), an usurer, and a nobleman, marrieth several ladies to enjoy their love, and in the end, pretending that the Count and the usurer are suddenly slain, becometh King.

THE HUMOURS OF COUNT HERMES.

Come, gird this pistol closely to my side,
By which I make men fear my humour still,
And have slain two or three as 'twere my mood,

When I have done it most advisedly
To rid them as they were my heavy foes.
Now am I known to be the mad-brain Count,
Whose humours twice five summers I have held,
And said at first I came from stately Rome,
Calling myself Count Hermes, and assuming
The humour of a wild and frantic man,
Careless of what I say or what I do;
And so such faults as I of purpose do
Is buried in my humour and this gown I wear
In rain or snow, or in the hottest summer,
And never go nor ride without a gown,
Which humour does not fit my frenzy well,
But hides my person's form from being known.

13th February. FRENCH NEWS.

The Governors in Picardy take such alarm of the preparations of the Cardinal of Austria that upon the fear thereof they come to the French King to solicit his care of their preservation and to furnish them with money and means, and especially the Governor of Calais; but they are all returned home only with good words. It is feared that Calais is not very well furnished with means to endure a siege, and that the town is not so well fortified nor so strong for defence as it is in opinion.

COLSE'S 'PENELOPE'S COMPLAINT.'

There is entered a book called *Penelope's Complaint* or a mirror for wanton minions, by Peter Colse, dedicated to the Lady Edith, wife of Sir Ralph Horsey, Lord Lieutenant of the County of Dorset; which poem is committed to her Ladyship because an unknown author hath of late published a pamphlet called *Avisa*, overslipping so many praiseworthy matrons to praise the meanest. The book telleth of the complaint of Penelope at the departure of Ulysses, of the wooers' misrule, and of their slaughter at Ulysses' return.

14th February. THE FRENCH KING AND HER MAJESTY'S PICTURE.

The French King of late gave audience to Sir Henry Unton on the presenting to him of certain letters from the Queen.

After which the King sent for Madame Gabrielle, and at her coming he drew near to her with great reverence, holding his hat at first in his hand, and declaring that the ambassador was so well known unto them both as he doubted not that she would welcome him; which she did, unmasking herself, and gracing the ambassador with her best favours. The King after these ceremonies passed took her on his left hand and the ambassador on his right hand, and so continued almost an hour walking together in the Park. Afterwards the King asked whether Sir Henry found his mistress anything changed, who answered sparingly in her praise and told him that, if without offence he might speak it, he had the picture of a far more excellent mistress and yet did her picture come far short of her perfection of beauty. 'As you love me,' said the King, 'show it me if you have it about you.' Sir Henry made some difficulties; yet upon his importunity offered it to his view very secretly, holding it in his hand. The King beheld it with passion and admiration, saying 'You are right; *je me rends*'; protesting he had never seen the like; so with great reverence he kissed it twice or thrice, the ambassador still retaining it in his hand. In the end, after some kind of contention, he took it away vowing that the ambassador might take leave of it, for he would not forgo it for any treasure; and that to possess the favour of the lively picture, he would forsake all the world and hold himself most happy, with many other most passionate words.

23rd February. THE SUBURBS.

Great abuses continue to grow by the multitude of base tenements and disorderly houses erected in the suburbs of London, and though the Council from time to time have given direction to stay or suppress such buildings, yet they have found not such success and effect of their directions as was expected. For there is an increase of dissolute, loose and insolent people harboured in noisome and disorderly houses, such as be poor cottages and habitations of beggars and people without trade, stables, inns, alehouses, taverns, garden houses, bowling alleys and brothels; all pestering these parts of the City with disorder and uncleanness, apt to breed contagion and sickness and serve for the resort of masterless men, and the cause of cosenages, thefts and other dishonest conversations; and which may also be used to cover dangerous practices. The magistrates in the County of Middlesex are now ordered to suppress such places and the unlawful games or exercises used therein.

25th February. THE CONDEMNED PRISONERS.

The Lord Mayor, Recorder and Sheriff having now prepared a certificate of those condemned prisoners meet to be pardoned for service in the wars, the rest are to be executed, lest by overmuch toleration and evil example others be encouraged to like offences.

28th February. MASTERLESS MEN TO BE TAKEN UP.

For the defence of the new fort at Plymouth the Council require the Lord Mayor of London to take up fifty able men of such as are masterless and can best be spared, and to despatch them to Sir Ferdinando Gorges.

RELUCTANT SEAMEN.

Sundry mariners, carried with the desire of gain above the duty they owe to Her Highness and the love each man ought to have unto his country, have conveyed themselves into remote parts of the shires away from the port towns and seaside, to the end that they may absent themselves from the press and stay at home till her Majesty's Navy be at sea, and then to go on merchant voyages. Proclamation is to be made in market towns that all mariners shall, on pain of death, repair to the port towns and there remain until the commissioners and presters shall take view of them and choose such as be fit for the service.

1st March. A HORRIBLE MURDER.

Two days since there was one executed at Grinsted in Sussex for the murder of his wife at Mayfield. This man, by name Raph Meaphon, whose trade was to dig in the iron mines and to make coals, coming home, his wife with her son of 5 years of age being abed, he knocked and was let in, whereon he fell to railing and chiding with her; and in the end, whether it were a matter pretended or otherwise, he drew out his knife and cut her throat, and so leaving her weltering in her own gore went again to his work. Soon after, the house was seen to be on fire, which the neighbours and the whole town came to quench, marvelling where the good man and his wife was. The child was recovered from the fire and the body found, but they could not save the goods. Then was the child examined and required to tell when his father came home, and without any blushing fear (as commonly is seen in children) told them his father came home when his mother was in bed and first used some churlish speech unto her, then he drew out his knife, cut her throat and so left her ; describing in good order the bigness of the knife and the colour of the haft, but wherefore his father did this wicked deed he could not say anything.

Hereupon they sent for the father from his work and strictly examined him of the same, who stoutly and most audaciously denied the fact. But his tale not agreeing with the words of his fellow workmen, he was for that night committed to the stocks. The next day being more thoroughly again examined in the cause, though the evidences were found too apparent, yet he still denied it. The coroner therefore committed him to the jail at Lewes, whence on the 24th February he was arraigned at Grinsted ; where on the evidence of his son he was found guilty and on the 27th executed.

4th March. Soldiers for Ireland.

The Council have given order that 300 horsemen and 1500 footmen shall be sent over into Ireland at the beginning of next month, with another thousand to be held in readiness. Of these one half shall be shot, whereof a fourth part to be muskets, the other half to be armed with corselets and pikes saving some few halberts ; all to be furnished with coats of good cloth well lined and of blue colour.

8th March. The Soldiers' Coats.

The men levied in the County of Kent for Ireland having been already provided with coats of marble colour, the Council allow the coats to serve at this time.

11th March. Tyrone's Grievances.

Sir Robert Gardiner, Lord Chief Justice of Ireland, is come over from Ireland with the grievances and demands of Tyrone and the rest, which were laid before the Queen, whereof for some part she findeth great cause of mislike that the commissioners should receive or give ear to any such presumptuous and disloyal petitions and answers. As for their petition for free liberty of conscience, this request is deemed disloyal, for her Majesty will never grant to any subject of any degree the liberty to break laws, though heretofore she has acted mercifully. Nevertheless, rather than that the purpose of pacification should fail upon some private demands, not being dishonourable, nor not much disprofitable to her Majesty, it shall be lawful to yield thereto.

Abuses in Play.

There is of late great abuse in play arising especially by people of base quality dwelling in the City of London and the suburbs who make false dice and dice of advantage to the undoing of many, and against whom there is no statute law. The Lord Mayor is required to assist Mr. Cornwallis, her Majesty's Groom Porter, in his travail to suppress these abuses by providing some remedy for the stopping of such lewd people from uttering false dice, and that neither haberdashers nor any other shall sell any but such as are square and good.

13*th March*. The Queen and Lord Burleigh.

'Tis said in Court that the Queen purposeth to make a progress of some fifteen days to consume the Lent, and to return to Greenwich eight days before the solemn feast which she will keep there ; for she seemeth weary of Surrey and would go over into Middlesex, from thence to Osterley, Highgate and Hackney. The old Lord Treasurer, upon some pet, would needs away against her will on Thursday last, saying that her business was ended ; and that he would for ten days go take physic. When the Queen saw it booted not to stay him, she said he was a froward old fool.

15*th March*. The Late Earl of Huntingdon.

By order of the Council the corpse of the late Lord President was embowelled, embalmed and closed in cerecloth and lead, but still lies unburied, attended nightly by four servants, for the Countess will neither accept administration nor give order for the funeral, to the great inconvenience of the Council in those parts.

17th March. A SPANISH RAID NEAR PLYMOUTH.

Three nights since a Spanish pinnace came into Cawsand Bay with twenty-five men in her, who landed armed with muskets, and fixed barrels of powder and brimstone to the doors of five several houses and to two boats, and set them on fire, whereby the whole village would have been burned had not force arrived. A man having fired one shot at them, they all fled to their pinnace and put to sea.

20th March. MR. THOMAS ARUNDEL.

Mr. Arundel being still restrained because of his Earldom from the Emperor complaineth that he is more straitly treated than was Sir Anthony Shirley. Moreover, saith he, this will be a slender satisfaction to the Emperor and a certain breaking off of all well-hoped-for proceedings of amity with the Queen, for the princes of Germany cannot but take it very ill when they shall see the Queen attempt to infringe their privileges by taking on her the unmaking of an Earl Imperial; all Italy and Germany will think her not willing to offend the Turk. Besides, though a King can make an Earl, yet cannot an Earl be unmade but being tried and convicted by his peers.

21st March. EVASION OF COMMON CHARGES.

Sundry persons of good ability in the county of Middlesex are refusing to contribute the reasonable taxation at which they are assessed by their neighbours, some alleging that they are merchants and have their habitations in London, others pretending that they are mint men, moneyers, or have their living in other counties, or privileged by reason of her Majesty's service. The Council require that all manner of persons, under the degree of Lord of Parliament or of the Privy Council, that inhabit or hold any houses or land in the county shall henceforth pay these sums; wherein, if any refuse to contribute, then shall the commissioners for musters require them friendly to contribute as good and dutiful subjects ought to do with their neighbours in this public service. And if any of them persist, then to inform the Council, who will take such further order with them as may be convenient.

To the like effect complaints are being made by inhabitants of the liberties of Salisbury Court and Ely Rents, alleging that it may in after times be drawn in argument against their liberties ; to the avoiding of which the Council have commanded an order to be entered in the register of Council, and also enregistered as an Act by the Lord Mayor of London.

In the counties also many are unwilling to contribute to the charges of the Navy.

25th March. Sir Henry Unton Sick.

Sir Henry Unton is reported to be very sick, being visited for several days with a violent burning fever so that he hath no benefit of sleep, which redoubleth oftentimes with so extraordinary accidents (being as the physicians declare a malignant fever and accompanied with the purples) that he is in all opinion abandoned by them. The King hath visited him, although his own physicians would have dissuaded him, to whom he answered that he had not hitherto feared the harquebus shot and did not now apprehend the purples.

27th March. The Death of Sir John Hawkins reported.

A certain mariner, one of the company of Sir Francis Drake and Sir John Hawkins, that was taken by the Spanish and hath escaped to Plymouth, reporteth that his ship having lost company was taken by the Spaniards and the crew imprisoned in the Isle of St. John de Porto Rico. The Spaniards sunk ships in the harbour to hinder the entrance, but Sir Francis summoned the town, and when they refused to yield sent fifteen vessels to burn the frigates. Two were fired, but by the light thus made the Spaniards fired on the English ships and drove them away. The English attacked the fort and Sir John Hawkins was killed. Sir Francis then went to the south of the island to get provisions and thence sailed to Carthagena, but meanwhile the treasure ships in Porto Rico sailed and are come safe to St. Lucar.

28th March. Counterfeiting of Passports.

Certain vagrants, that have been taken with counterfeit licences and passports, being strictly examined have confessed the names of divers lewd persons about the City of London that not only counterfeit the names of the Generals of her Majesty's forces beyond the seas but affix seals of arms to the same. These persons are now to be apprehended and very straitly examined what passports and licences they have made.

A SCARCITY OF GAME.

The purveyors of poultry for her Majesty's household complain of the scarcity of rabbits and conies, also of partridges and pheasants wherewith the Queen is served daily throughout the year; wherefore it is required by the Council that bonds shall be taken of all victuallers and poulterers that no rabbits be bought or uttered before the first of June or any partridges or pheasants sold hereafter.

29th March. CALVIN'S 'APHORISMS.'

Mr. Henry Holland hath translated Calvin's *Aphorisms of Christian Religion*, a very compendious abridgment of his *Institutions* that were set forth in short sentences methodically by M. Piscator. Herein are handled twenty-eight commonplaces, as, Of knowledge of God, Of Faith, Of Christian liberty, Of Predestination, Of the Civil Magistrate, and the like. Noteth of predestination that it is the eternal decree of God, wherein He determined with Himself what He would have done with every man, as concerning their eternal salvation or damnation. Which doctrine hath two notable fruits; the one, that we may with humble adoration acknowledge how much we are bound unto God that hath vouchsafed to choose us, so unworthy, out of the company of the damned and to advance us to the state of heavenly glory; the other, that we may with good assurance rest ourselves on the unchangeable purpose of God touching our salvation, and therefore be fully persuaded and assured thereof in Jesus Christ.

30th March. A BOOK OF SURGERY.

Mr. William Clowes, one of the Queen's surgeons, hath written a profitable and necessary *Book of Observations*, for all those that are burned with the flame of gunpowder or wounded by musket or caliver shot, and such like accidents, relating the cases and cures of many of his own patients; also added thereto a treatise of *lues venerea*.

2nd April. CALAIS ASSAULTED.

Sudden news is come that the Cardinal Albert of Austria that was threatening the French King's siege of La Fere hath suddenly turned his course and is seated round Calais.

4th April. THE ATTACK ON CALAIS.

The Earl of Essex is now at Dover, whence he hath sent Sir Conyers Clifford to see whether he can get into Calais and view the state of the town, but the wind was so scant that he could not stem the tide; and another gentleman to Boulogne to find out what is become of the King and his army, and what means they propose on that side to succour Calais.

5th April. CALAIS.

My Lord of Essex, on his way from Dover yesterday to Court, met the Lord Admiral's packet between Canterbury and Sittingbourne, and seeing that the Queen had resolved to save Calais, he is returned to Dover to have all things ready. The enemy is now battering a ravelin to the east of the haven, which if taken will impede the succours; but the garrison promise to hold out two days.

SIR HENRY UNTON DEAD.

Sir Henry Unton is dead in the French camp, having been ill more than three weeks, although tended by the King's physicians. When the purple spots appeared above his heart they gave him *Confectio Alcarmas* compounded of musk, amber, gold, pearl, and unicorn's horn, with pigeons applied to his side, and all other means that art could devise to expel the strongest poison if he were not bewitched withal; notwithstanding he died shortly afterwards.

MR. NORDEN'S 'CHRISTIAN COMFORT.'

Mr. John Norden hath written *A Christian familiar comfort and encouragement unto all English subjects* not to dismay at the Spanish threats; to which is added an admonition to all English papists who openly or covertly desire a change, also to all inferior magistrates and loyal subjects to show themselves watchful in these dangers which may move sudden and indiscreet hurly burlies. Noteth especially the policy of the enemy that by sudden reports, dangerous bruits and open hoobubs would move indiscreet tumult, that factious people might draw the rest to violate their sworn obedience and under colour of some public good for them or of some imminent danger, working their own confusion, may yield the more ease to the enemies' purpose.

6th April. CALAIS.

My Lord of Essex makes all preparation for transport of the troops at Dover, hoping to embark them to-day, and to-morrow to send word that they are entered. All yesterday forenoon the enemy's battery played.

7th April. A MUTINY AT CHESTER.

From Chester is reported the lewd and mutinous carriage of the soldiers sent from North Wales for the Irish service, some of them running away from their conductors; and the conductors appointed by the counties themselves refusing to see the soldiers conducted beyond Chester to the ports.

9th April THE BISHOP OF ST. DAVID'S UNHAPPY SERMON BEFORE THE QUEEN.

The Bishop of St. David's lately preached before the Court at Richmond, taking his text out of Psalm xc., verse 12, 'O teach us to number our days, that we incline our hearts unto wisdom,' and therein began to speak of some sacred and mystical numbers as 3 for the Trinity, 3 times 3 for the Heavenly Hierarchy, 7 for the Sabbath, 7 times 7 for a Jubilee, and lastly 7 times 9 for the Grand Climacterical. The Queen perceiving whereto it tended began to be troubled with it. The Bishop discovering all was not well (for the pulpit standeth *vis-à-vis* to her closet), he fell to treat of some more plausible numbers as of the number 666, making 'Latinus,' with which, said he, he could prove the Pope to be Antichrist; also of that fatal number 88, which being so long before spoken of for a dangerous year, yet it had pleased God not only to preserve her but to give her a famous victory against the united forces of Rome and Spain. He ended with an excellent prayer, as if in her Majesty's person, in which there occurred these words:

'Oh Lord, I am now entered a good way into the climacterical year of mine age, which mine enemies wish and hope to be fatal unto me. But thou, Lord, which by Thy prophet Jeremy commanded the House of Israel not to learn the way of the heathen, nor to be afraid of the signs of heaven, and who by Thy Almighty hand and outstretched arm, madest the year of the greatest expectation, even '88, marvellous by the overthrow of Thine and mine enemies, now, for Thy Gospel's sake, which hath long had sanctuary in this land, make likewise '96 as prosperous unto me and my loyal subjects.' And again: 'Lord, I have now put foot within the doors of that age in the which the almond tree flourisheth, wherein men begin to carry a calendar in their bones, the senses begin to fail, the strength to diminish, yea all the powers of the body daily to decay. Now therefore grant me grace that though mine outward man thus perish, yet my inner man may be renewed daily. So direct me with Thy Holy Spirit that I may daily wax elder in godliness, wisdom being my grey hairs and undefiled life mine old age.'

The sermon being ended, the Queen, as is her manner, opened the window of her closet, but she was so far from giving him thanks or good countenance that she said plainly he should have kept his arithmetic for himself; 'but I see,' said she, 'the greatest clerks are not the wisest men.' With that the Queen went away discontented, and since by the Lord Keeper's command he has kept to his house.

SUDDEN LEVIES CALLED FOR.

Because of the news from Calais, the commissioners of musters are ordered with all speed to levy out of the trained bands 6,000 men furnished with their armour to be sent to Dover with their captains, and to be at the port of Dover by Sunday night at the farthest. This afternoon the Lord Mayor and Aldermen being in Paul's Churchyard hearing the sermon at the Cross were suddenly called from thence and forthwith by a precept from her Majesty and Council are ordered to press 1,000. By eight of the clock the men are ready and their furnishing will be complete ere morning.

10th April. THE LEVIES DISMISSED.

Further news having been received that the forces cannot reach Calais in time, those already impressed are now to be dismissed.

THE QUEEN AND THE BISHOP OF ST. DAVID'S.

The Queen being displeased at the restraint of the Bishop of St. David's hath now caused him to be released. Moreover she rebuked one of her ladies that spake scornfully of him and his sermon. And to show that the Bishop is deceived in supposing her to be so decayed in her limbs and senses as he, perhaps, and others are wont to be, she said she thanked God that neither her stomach nor strength, nor her voice for singing, nor fingering for instruments, nor lastly her sight was any whit decayed. And to prove the last before the courtiers, she produced a little jewel that hath an inscription of very small letters. She offered it first to my Lord of Worcester and then to Sir James Crofts to read, and both protested *bona fide* they could not. Yet the Queen herself did find out the posy and made herself merry with the standers-by upon it.

11*th April* (*Easter Sunday*). THE LEVIES AGAIN REQUIRED.

Fresh advertisement now being received from the French King that the citadel of Calais will hold out longer than was before reported, the soldiers are required with all speed to be sent to Dover by to-morrow night. Wherefore this morning, being Easter Sunday, about ten of the clock, comes there a new charge from the Council that the soldiers shall again be levied, so that, all men being in their parish churches ready to have received the Communion, the aldermen, their deputies and the constables are fain to close up the church doors till they have pressed so many men to be soldiers. By noon they have in the City 1,000 men and these, being furnished forthwith of armour, weapons, and all things necessary, are for the most part sent towards Dover to-night; and the rest follow in the morning.

THE SERVICE OF POSTS.

All mayors, sheriffs and other officers are commanded at their uttermost peril by the Council to assist in the service of posts, providing ten or twenty able and sufficient horses with furniture convenient to be ready at the town or stage where the post abideth. The owners to have such rates as the post from time to time payeth for his own horses.

13th April. THE EARL OF ESSEX'S COMMISSION FOR CALAIS.

The commission for my Lord of Essex is now drawn, making him Lieutenant-General of an army of 6,000 men for the relief of the citadel of Calais. But withal he is instructed not to carry over the forces unless the King signify his compliance with the condition of delivering the town to her Majesty until she is assured of her great expenses, and he better able to defend it without driving her still to these unsupportable burdens; not to take over more than the 6,000, and not to embark them unless he is likely to arrive in time to save the town; not to employ them unless the French King has such strength of horse and foot that the burden may not fall upon the Queen's subjects, but they be used as auxiliaries; not to attempt anything of importance without consulting the principal officers, and especially Sir George Carew and Sir Thomas Wilkes; to take with him only such nobles as have leave to go, namely, my Lords Sussex, Rich, Herbert and Burgh, but not Derby, Southampton, Mountjoy, Compton, Windsor, nor Sheffield, who shall return.

14th April. THE QUEEN'S LETTER TO THE EARL OF ESSEX.

This day the Queen went on board the ship *Due Repulse* and there with her own hand she wrote these words to the Earl of Essex. 'As distant as I am from your abode, yet my ears serve me too well to hear that terrible battery that methinks sounds for relief at my hands; wherefore, rather than for lack of timely aid it should be wholly lost, go you, in God's Blessed Name, as far as that place where you may soonest relieve it, with as much caution as so great a trust requires. But I charge you, without the mere loss of it, do in no wise peril so fair an army for another Prince's town. God cover you under His safest wings, and let all peril go without your compass."

CALAIS.

Yesterday hard shooting was heard about Calais, so the truce is broken. The French think that Monsieur Vidazon will hold out to the uttermost, and the King has sent him word that he shall hang him if he gives it up by composition.

15th April. MR. ARUNDEL RELEASED.

Mr. Thomas Arundel is now released. To-day he was with the Lord Treasurer, from whom he received his discharge and leave to go into the country or anywhere else, the Court excepted. The Lord Treasurer said that it was the Queen's pleasure to forbid his honour, and gave two reasons why he should satisfy himself that he had no wrong; the one, *nemo potest duobus dominis inservire*; the other, that stranger Earls have by courtesy a place above the Earls of this land, which to be granted to one that was but a squire were a great inconvenience.

A MURDER AT OXFORD.

Of late Robert Lingard, servant to Dr. Colepepper, Warden of New College, was murdered by one Winckle (or Wrincle), a townsman. Whereupon the Mayor and Recorder of Oxford, by virtue of their commission of Oyer and Terminer, purposed to have brought the man before them for his trial; but the Council, knowing that partiality is not unknown to be used in such cases concerning a townsman, advise that this Winckle receive his trial before the Justices of Assize for the avoiding of suspicion and other inconveniences.

16th April. CALAIS TAKEN.

My Lord of Essex and the Lord Admiral were very passionate at the delays in setting forth, but yesterday the whole afternoon was spent in embarking the army troop by troop with all their necessaries. In the evening as my Lord and the other noblemen were at supper on board the *Rainbow* with Captain Monson news was brought that the citadel of Calais was fallen.

17th April. THE TROOPS FOR CALAIS DISMISSED.

Now that the intended expedition for Calais is countermanded, the soldiers are to be returned under their captains to their own counties, and strict charge taken that the armour, weapons and furniture be well and truly delivered back. Notice also is to be given to the counties that her Majesty levied this force upon very special advertisement from the French King, which afterwards proving very variable and not agreeable to her intent hath been the cause of the alteration of her purpose. Howbeit the readiness of the country to do her service her Majesty very graciously accepteth and commandeth that knowledge be given thereof.

18th April. THE FRENCH TREACHERY.

Shortly before the Spaniards took the citadel of Calais the States sent 400 resolute old soldiers, who in despite of the Cardinal's forces attained the walls and parleyed with the French within to give them entertainment, but though these soldiers had come only to their aid they would not receive them within the walls, so that, not being able to make long resistance without the walls, they were all slain by the Spaniards. For the French were all in one mind, being willinger that the Spaniards shall possess Calais than to permit either the English or other their friends to relieve it, saying, 'If the Spaniards win it, yet there is good hope by mediation of the Church to regain it ; but if the English repossess it, they will never restore it.'

20th April. ANOTHER ORDER CONCERNING POST-HORSES.

The Council have again very straitly required that their former order concerning the service of horses for the posts shall be obeyed.

22nd April. A DECLARATION OF THE CAUSES OF THE PRESENT NAVY.

There is published a *Declaration* showing the causes why the Queen's Majesty of England is moved to send a navy to the seas. Herein is shown how the Spanish King hath purpose to invade Ireland, and this last winter having amassed a great number of ships and men many of these same were destroyed. Nevertheless, not being warned by this just punishment by God's ordinance, and forgetting how by the favour of Almighty God his proud navy in the year '88 was overthrown, and his loss at Cadiz, yet still he pursueth his former purpose to animate the rebels in Ireland. Wherefore her Majesty doth appeal to all the world whether she be not necessarily enforced to send out this army to the seas. This declaration is printed also in the Latin, French, Dutch, Italian, Spanish and German tongues.

24th April. INSTRUCTIONS FOR THE FLEET.

It is ordained by the two generals that certain articles for the discipline of the fleet shall be read openly at service twice a week. Prayers are to be had twice a day, except urgent cause enforce the contrary, and no man shall dispute of matters of religion, unless to be resolved of some doubts, when he shall confer with the minister of the army; as it is not fit that unlearned men should openly argue of such high and mystical matters. Swearing, brawling and dicing are forbidden as they breed contentions and discords; picking and stealing shall be severely punished. Great care to be taken to preserve victuals, and every captain shall receive an account once a week how his victuals are spent, and what remains. Special charges shall be given for the avoiding danger by fire, and no candle to be carried without a lantern. The powder to be carefully preserved from spoil and waste, as without it there cannot be any great service; and care also taken not to bear too high a sail when going by the wind, and especially in a high sea, lest the spoil of masts endanger the enterprise. No spoil is to be made of any prizes, and whoever goes on board one to give an account for anything taken. No person shall land in any country without orders until his return to England upon pain of death. No person to strike any superior officer upon pain of death, nor any inferior under other severe punishment, and no report to be made which touches the reputation of any officer without producing the author, who will also be severely punished.

25th April. SIR ANTHONY SHIRLEY'S VOYAGE.

Sir Antony Shirley departed from Southampton two days since with nine ships and a galley, being the *Bevice*, admiral, 300 tons; the *Galleon*, vice-admiral, 240 tons; the *George*, rear-admiral, 160 tons; the *Archangel*, 250 tons; the *Swan*, 200 tons; the *George Noble*, 140 tons; the *Wolf*, 70 tons; the *Mermaid*, 120 tons; the *Little John*, 40 tons; together with the galley and a pinnace; all of which ships are furnished for ten months, and manned with soldiers and sailors, exceedingly well appointed, to the full number of 900 men.

26th April. THE RETURN OF DRAKE'S FLEET.

It is daily expected that the fleet of Sir Francis Drake and Sir John Hawkins will return to Plymouth, which may cause confusion since the place is appointed as the *rendezvous* of the army about to set out. The Council have ordered that a pinnace shall continually lie out to command any ships to forbear to come into Plymouth except in case of necessity, but to come directly to Portsmouth. A messenger of the Chamber is also to be despatched to the Mayors and Customers of all ports from Portsmouth to Penzance, St. Ives and Padstow that they suffer none to come to land until he has been diligently searched for Spanish money, pearls, jewels or any other thing of value, lest her Majesty or any of the adventurers in the voyage be defrauded of the benefit that ought to come to them. The messenger shall leave a copy of his warrant with every Mayor and receive from him a certificate.

27th April. THE DEATH OF DRAKE AND HAWKINS.

Several of Sir Francis Drake's fleet have now come in to Falmouth, but he and Sir John Hawkins, and many men of worth are dead. They have brought back some things but not enough to countervail the charge of the journey. They bring news that a very great fleet is preparing at Ferrol, by the Groyne.

29th April. ONE CONDEMNED FOR SPREADING FALSE RUMOURS.

One Smith, being a base fellow, a peasant and a boy, was this day sentenced in the Star Chamber to lose one of his ears upon the pillory at Westminster, the other at Windsor, to be whipped, and to have a paper on his head containing his slanderous words, to be imprisoned during pleasure, and fined £20. This fellow being recently one of the pressed men at Dover reported when he was dismissed that the news throughout the soldiers was that the Lord Admiral's ship being searched by the Earl of Essex, and he, opening divers barrels wherein he supposed to have been gunpowder, found ashes, dust and sand; and thereupon he called the Lord Admiral traitor. And so they came both to Court, and there the Earl of Essex and the Earl of Cumberland before the Queen took the Lord Admiral by the beard, saying, 'Ah, thou traitor.'

A New Play.

To-day the Admiral's men play for the first time *Julian the Apostate.*

1st May. Recusants in Sussex.

At the outside of Battle Park, Mr. Edmund Pelham, the chiefest justice of peace in that part and chief of Lord Montague's Council, is reported to be a man very backward in religion, and his wife a professed recusant. Many recusants resort to his house.

At the time of the siege of Calais one Mr. Dorel, a notable recusant, lay there hovering about toward the sea coast; and when the men were to be shipped from Rye and Dover to Calais, a servant of his, mounted upon a gelding and well appointed with a case of pistols, rid to Sussex and a great part of the Weald of Kent with an alarm that the Spaniards were landed at three places in Sussex and had burnt Bourne and Pevensey. He could not be stayed but fled, leaving his cloak in the constable's hand. Upon that false alarm there was the greatest hurly burly and woeful outcries of the people; the soldiers at Rye ready to march out of the town, and the Calais service greatly hindered.

At the same time the Lady Montague's people seeing the town of Battle in that uproar and miserable state, rejoiced and showed signs of joy; insomuch that the people fell into great exclamation and cursings of them openly in the streets. When news was brought that Calais was lost, they gave out these speeches: 'God be thanked, we shall have better neighbours.'

Drake's Fleet Return.

The remainder of the fleet that set sail with Sir Francis Drake and Sir John Hawkins are returned to Plymouth, the last to come in being the *Defiance*, the *Garland*, the *Adventure*, and the *Phoenix*.

The Last Voyage of Drake and Hawkins.

The first intent of this voyage was to land at Nombre de Dios and thence to march to Panama to possess the treasure that comes from Pene, and, if they saw reason, to inhabit and keep it; but a few days before they left Plymouth they received letters from her Majesty of an advertisement had out of Spain that the Indian fleet was arrived and that one of them with loss of her mast was put into Porto Rico. She commanded them therefore, seeing the weakness of Porto Rico, to possess themselves of that treasure and the rather for that it was not much out of the way to Nombre de Dios.

On 27th September of last year by break of day the fleet reached the chief town of Grand Canaria and by nine were at anchor before the fort to the eastward of the town. At one o'clock they offered to land 1,400 men in the sandy bay betwixt the fort and the town, but by this time the Spaniards had made a bulwark and planted ordnance so that our men could not land without endangering the whole force, which the General would not do. Then they went to the west end of the island and there watered; and here Captain Grimston going up the hill with six or seven in his company was set upon by the herdsmen, who with their dogs and staves killed him and most of his company. Moreover the *Solomon's* surgeon was taken prisoner, who also disclosed the purpose of the voyage so that the Viceroy sent a carvel into the Indies to all places where our fleet had intended to go. Howbeit they had previously received intelligence from the King of all our voyages the 8th August, which was three weeks before the fleet set forth from England; as also by a Fleming that had seen all their provision in London.

Thence the fleet stood away S.W. and S.S.W. some two hundred leagues until they came in the height of the islands of Cape Verde and so to Dominica and Guadalupe, where Sir John Hawkins who had been separated came up to them again. Here they watered, washed the ships, set up the pinnaces and refreshed the soldiers on shore. On 30th October Captain Wignol in the *Francis*, a bark of 35 tons, was chased by five of the King of Spain's frigates or zabras, ships of 200 tons apiece, which came of purpose with three other zabras for the treasure of St. John de Porto Rico. The *Francis* going room with them, supposing they had been our own fleet, was taken; but they left her driving with four or five sick men in her, taking the rest into their ships, as was afterwards learnt of prisoners.

In November they reached certain broken islands called Las Virgines but could find no fresh water there, though much fish was to be taken with nets and hooks, and fowls on shore. Here Sir John Hawkins grew extreme sick, which began upon news of the taking of the *Francis*. The 12th they set sail in the morning and that night came up to the easternmost end of St. John de Porto Rico, where Sir John Hawkins departed this life; whereupon Sir Thomas Baskerville went into the *Garland*.

Thence in the following afternoon they came to anchor in a sandy bay at the easternmost end of the chief town called Porto Rico, where they received twenty-eight shot from the forts and ordnance, of the which the last struck the admiral's mizzen, and the last but one, passing through her quarter into the steerage, struck the stool from under the General who was at supper; the shot hurt him not but wounded several who were at the same table, of whom Sir Nicholas Clifford and Mr. Browne died. Next day, shifting their anchorage to the west, they rode till night, when twenty-five pinnaces and small boats, manned and furnished with fireworks and small shot, went into the road within the great castles, and in despite of them fired the five zabras, quite burning the rear-admiral to the water, which was the greatest ship of them all, and also mightily spoiling the admiral and vice-admiral. But the treasure which the zabras had come to fetch had been conveyed into the strongest and surest castle of defence, being, as one of the prisoners confessed, 3,000,000 ducats or thirty-five tons of silver. The fight on our side was resolute, hot and dangerous, wherein 40 or 50 men were lost and as many hurt. There was also great death of the Spaniards aboard the frigates with burning, drowning and killing, besides some taken prisoners.

Some days being spent there, the fleet weighed anchor and came to Cape de la Vela, and in the morning of 1st December all the soldiers were embarked for Rio de la Hacha, which town our men took by ten o'clock at night. The 6th December the Spaniards came in to talk about the ransom, but not to the General's liking; and that night Sir Thomas Baskerville marched up into the country to overrun those parts, and the General the same night with some hundred and fifty men went by water six leagues to the eastward and took the Rancheria, a fisher town where they drag for pearl. The people all fled except some sixteen or twenty soldiers which fought a little but were taken prisoners, besides many negroes, with some pearls and other pillage. Next day Mr. York, captain of the *Hope*, died, and then Mr. Thomas Drake, the General's brother, was made captain. On the 10th the Spaniards concluded for the ransom of the town for 24,000 ducats, and one prisoner promised to pay for his ransom 4,000 ducats, and four days afterward they brought in the town's ransom in pearls, but rated so dear that the General misliking it sent it back again, giving them four hours to clear. The 16th December the Governor came into the town about dinner and after conference with the General told him plainly that he cared not for the town, neither would he ransom it; that the pearl was brought in without his consent; and that his detracting of time so long was only to send the other towns word that they were not of force to withstand our men that they might convey all their goods, cattle, and wealth into the woods out of danger. So the General gave him leave to depart according to promise, having two hours to withdraw himself in safety.

On the next day Sir Thomas Baskerville with the *Elizabeth and Constance*, the *Phoenix*, the carvel and four or five pinnaces went some five leagues to the westward, and landing, marched four leagues up into the country to a place called Tapia, which he took, and burned certain villages and farm houses about it. The 18th the General caused the Rancheria and the town of Rio de la Hacha to be burnt clean down to the ground, the churches and the house of a lady, who had written to the General, only excepted. On the day following they weighed and took the town of Santa Martha, the people all being fled except a few Spaniards, negroes and Indians which in a bravado gave them forty shot at their landing and so ran away. This town was burnt two days later, but that night the *Phoenix*, Captain Austin, Mr. Peter Lemond, and the *Garland's* pinnace which stood along the shore were chased by galleys out of Carthagena, and Mr. Lemond and nine men taken; the rest came back safe.

They took Nombre de Dios on the 27th, all the people being fled except some hundred Spaniards which kept the fort and played upon them, but seeing the resolution of our men in running upon them, they all fled and took to the woods. The town was big but nothing left of value, though there was a show in their shops of a great store of merchandise that had been there. There was a mill above the town, and upon the top of another hill in the woods stood a little watch house where was taken twenty sows of silver, two bars of gold, some money in coin and other pillage. The soil in this place is subject to much rain and very unhealthy, having great store of oranges, plaintains, cassavy roots and other such fruits, but very dangerous to be eaten for breeding of diseases.

On the 29th Sir Thomas Baskerville with 750 armed men, besides surgeons and provand-boys, went for Panama, but returned four days later, with his soldiers weary and hungry, having marched more than half way to the South Sea. This march was so sore as never Englishman marched before, the way being cut out of the woods and rocks, both very narrow and full of mire and water ; and the Spaniards played upon them divers times from the woods. Having marched ten leagues, upon the top of a hill they came on a fort which the Spaniards had set up and kept with 80 or 90 men who played upon our men as they came up before they were aware of it, and so killed more than twenty, amongst them, Captain Marchant, Quartermaster-General, Ensign Sampson, Maurice Williams, one of her Majesty's guard, besides divers others hurt. When Sir Thomas learnt that he must pass two such forts more, if he got that, and besides that Panama was very strong, the enemy knowing of their coming, also that the soldiers had no victuals left nor any means to get more, these considerations caused him to return and give over his attempt.

In the meanwhile the General had burned Nombre de Dios, half on the 31st December and the rest on 1st January, with all the frigates, barks and galliots which were in the harbour and on the beach. On the 5th they again set sail, and on the 15th, the fleet being anchored at an island called Esendo, Captain Platt died of sickness, and then the General began to keep his cabin and to complain of a scouring or flux. The 23rd they set sail for Puerto Bello.

On 28th January at 4 o'clock of the morning the General, Sir Francis Drake, departed this life, having been extremely sick of the flux which began the night before to stop on him. He used some speeches at or a little before his death, rising and apparelling himself, but being brought to bed again within an hour died. He made his brother, Mr. Thomas Drake, and Captain Jonas Bodenham executors, and Mr. Thomas Drake's son his heir to all his lands, except one manor which he gave to Captain Bodenham.

That same day they anchored at Puerto Bello, where after the solemn burial of Sir Francis Drake in the sea, Sir Thomas Baskerville being aboard the *Defiance*, Mr. Bride made a sermon, having to his audience all the captains in the fleet. Then Sir Thomas commanded all aboard the *Garland* where he held a council, and there, showing his commission, he was accepted as General, and Captain Bodenham made Captain of the *Defiance* and Mr. Saville Captain of the *Adventure*. At that time also died Captain Josias of the *Delight*, Captain Egerton, a gentleman of the *Foresight*, James Wood, chief surgeon out of the *Garland*, and Abraham Kendall out of the *Saker*. Here they watered, washed the ships and made new sails, it being by the General and all the Captains agreed that if they could by any means turn up again for Santa Martha, they should; but if not, to go directly for England. Then the *Elizabeth* of Mr. Watts, the *Delight* and Captain Eden's frigate were discharged and sunk; and being mustered, there were left, sick and whole, 2,000. Thence they set sail on the 8th February.

On the 26th being off Cuba they espied twenty sail about one in the afternoon. This was a third part of the fleet which the King sent for Carthagena, the rest being gone for Honduras; they were in all sixty sails sent only to meet the fleet, being commanded wheresoever they heard our fleet to be that they should come upon them with all their forces. As soon as they descried our fleet they kept close upon a tack, thinking to get the wind; and when the admiral with all the rest of our fleet were right in the wind's eye of them, Sir Thomas Baskerville, putting out the Queen's arms, and all the rest of the fleet their bravery, bare room with them, and commanded the *Defiance* not to shoot but to keep close by to second him. The vice-admiral of the Spaniards being a greater ship than any of ours and the best sailor in all their fleet luffed by and gave the *Concord* the two first great shot, which she repaid again, and thus the fight began. The *Bonaventure* bare full with her, ringing her such a peal of ordnance and small shot that he left her with torn sides. The admiral also made no spare of powder and shot. But the *Defiance* in the midst of the Spanish fleet, thundering of her ordnance and small shot continued the fight to the end, so that the vice-admiral with three or four of her consorts were forced to tack to the eastward, leaving their admiral and the rest of the fleet who came not so hotly into the fight as they did. The fight continued two hours and better. At sunset all their fleet tacked about to eastward, but ours continued the course to lie westward for Cape de los Corrientes. In this conflict in the *Defiance* were slain five men, three Englishmen, a Greek and a negro. That night, some half hour after, their fleet keeping upon their weather quarter, our men saw a mighty smoke rise out of one of their great ships which stayed behind, and presently after she was all on a light fire, and so was consumed and all burnt.

The next day the Spanish fleet kept still upon the weather quarter but dared not come room with ours, although the admiral stayed for them, and not long afterward began to fall away astern. Thereafter they met with none of the enemy and on 9th April came to anchor on the south side of Flores in the Azores, where the *Defiance* was watered. Here they bartered with the Portugals for some fresh victuals and set on shore their two Portugal pilots which Sir Francis Drake had carried out of England with him. And so are they come back to Plymouth.

2nd May. SIR ANTHONY SHIRLEY'S VOYAGE.

The fleet which sailed from Southampton with Sir Anthony Shirley some days since is anchored at Plymouth. Three ships and 500 soldiers now go with the Earl of Essex.

3rd May. A PROCLAMATION AGAINST COUNTERFEIT MESSENGERS.

There have of late been divers dissolute and audacious persons that falsely take upon themselves to be messengers of her Majesty's chamber, and for that purpose undutifully wear boxes or escutcheons of arms as messengers are wont to do. These men go up and down the country with warrants wherein are counterfeited the names of the Lords of the Council or of the Ecclesiastical Commissioners, and by colour thereof they warn gentlemen, ministers of the church, women, yeomen and others to appear before the Council, and exact fees of them for their labour and travel. By this slanderous practice divers gentlemen and other honest persons have, to their further charge and hindrance, been caused to repair from counties far distant from the court. And although divers of these shameless counterfeit persons have been apprehended and brought into the Star Chamber, where some of them have been condemned and set on the pillory, lost their ears, and some also marked in the face, yet these notable abuses continue more and more.

Proclamation is now made that if any person so warned shall have any suspicion of the messenger or of the warrant to be counterfeit, he may cause the constable or the officer of the place to bring the supposed messenger before the next Justice of Peace, where the warrant may be viewed and the party thoroughly examined.

Moreover there are another sort of vagabond persons that bear counterfeit licences to beg and gather alms, pretending that they have been maimed in her Majesty's service or received some great loss or hindrance by casualty. All parsons and vicars, churchwardens, and other officers are ordered to consider well such licences, and those men that are suspected shall be strictly examined, and upon further cause of suspicion committed to prison till more certain information be known. The Justices of the Peace are likewise ordered to use all possible means to apprehend such vagabonds, for that they often assemble in great numbers together and commit robberies, spoils and other outrages.

11th May. SIR THOMAS EGERTON MADE LORD KEEPER.

Five days since Sir Thomas Egerton, Master of the Rolls, was made Lord Keeper and had delivered unto him the Great Seal. To-day accompanied of the nobility and great numbers, he rode to Westminster and there took his place.

16th May. THE DISPUTE BETWEEN YARMOUTH AND LOWESTOFT.

There hath of long time been dispute between the towns of Yarmouth and Lowestoft concerning the trade of buying and selling herrings, the town of Yarmouth claiming by virtue of their charter which giveth to the inhabitants privilege within the space of seven miles during the time of the fair. This dispute ariseth particularly touching the measuring of the seven miles, the one party saying that it should begin at the haven's mouth, the other at the quay where the fair useth to be kept. By the agreement of the parties before the Council there are now to be appointed commissioners to undertake the measuring and at the end of the seven miles to set down apparent marks.

18th May. A MISCHANCE AT LONDON BRIDGE.

Monsieur de la Fontaine that is to be the Duke de Bouillon's agent in London hath suffered a mischance like to have been very dangerous, being carried by the violence of the stream into the water mill at London Bridge through the negligence of a young waterman. To save himself the better he leapt out of the boat before he came to the fall of the water, and was carried through under the wheel and divers lighters as far as Billingsgate before he was recovered; and here he was miraculously preserved. He is very sorely bruised upon the forehead, but without any danger of loss of life, the skull being sound.

19th May. A NEW PLAY.

A new play of the *Tragedy of Phocas* was played at the Rose.

23rd May. SIR ANTHONY SHIRLEY'S VOYAGE.

Sir Anthony Shirley hath again put to sea from Plymouth with five ships, a galley and a pinnace.

31st May. CERTAIN MAYORS COMMENDED.

The Council have written letters commending and thanking the Mayors of Chester, Beaumaris and Liverpool, and the Sheriffs of Chester, for their care and diligence shown in her Majesty's service, and especially in their well ordering of the passage of the horse and foot lately sent over to Ireland.

1st June. THE ARMY AT PLYMOUTH.

Matters at Plymouth now grow to a ripeness, and the Generals have begun to embark their regiments, and will be gone when the wind is favourable. There are three hundred green headed youths, covered with feathers, gold and silver lace, and at least 10,000 soldiers, as tall handsome men as can ever be seen; in the navy, at least 150 ships, besides hoys and flyboats, whereof 18 of her Majesty's own, and since her reign never so many before. The States have sent 18 large ships of war and six others for the carrying of munition, but to be subject to our generals; they land 1000 men.

There have been some differences among the principal leaders at Plymouth, for it hath pleased my Lord of Essex to give Sir Francis Vere much countenance and to have him always near at hand, which draweth upon him no small envy; insomuch as open jars have fallen out betwixt Sir Francis and Sir Walter Ralegh and Sir Conyers Clifford. These my Lord hath qualified for this time, ordering that at all meetings at land Sir Francis shall have the precedence of Sir Walter, and he to have precedence at sea. Wherefore by Sir Francis' proposition are set down in writing the several duties that properly belong to every office in the field.

3rd June. THE FLEET SAILS.

The great fleet sailed from Plymouth on the 1st. All the soldiers and mariners being embarked, and the wind coming round to the N.W. and by N., the Lord Admiral being aboard the *Ark* commanded his master-gunner to shoot off a piece to give warning to all the fleet, which they did incontinently.

While they lay at Plymouth the Lords Generals governed their charge with very good justice and martial discipline. Two soldiers were hanged upon the Hoe with papers upon them showing their offences: upon the one was written, 'For drawing his sword and raising mutiny against his commander'; upon the other, 'For running away from his colours.' A lieutenant that had taken £60 to discharge men pressed in Wales was disarmed by proclamation, adjudged to repay the money, and banished the army. A soldier also in a Dutch regiment that had killed one of his companions was, by order of martial law, tied to the party murdered and so thrown both into the sea.

THE STATE OF THE MIDDLE MARCHES.

The state of the Middle Marches towards Scotland of late years is so negligently ordered that the Council have commanded the Lord Evre, the Lord Warden in those parts, to take a view of all the serviceable horses, armour and furniture of those chargeable before the end of the present month or some short time after. They shall supply all defects and wants, and a certificate of the musters shall be sent up ; which done the Lord Warden shall enjoin everyone to keep their tenants so furnished upon pain of forfeiture.

5th June. THE FLEET.

After setting sail on the 1st, the fleet reached Dodman's Point in Cornwall, but the wind scanting they were fain return again, the greater ships into the Sound of Plymouth, and the lesser into Cawsand Bay, lest any of the mariners should return again into Plymouth ; but on the 3rd they set sail again and are gone with a favourable wind.

6th June. SUPERFLUOUS ALEHOUSES.

Many of the alehouses in London and the county of Middlesex that were suppressed some months since are again restored so that the rogues and vagabonds, which the Provost Marshals do by day drive from about the City, keep the fields and commit pilferies in the country in the night season, and then stealthily return to the alehouses. The Council again require the alehouses to be suppressed, and no strong drink to be used or made in them.

DEFENCE OF THE REALM.

Seeing that the army and ships under the Earl of Essex and the Lord Admiral are to pass out of the Narrow Seas from the coasts of England to the Spanish Seas, it may be doubted that the enemy may make some particular attempts upon the coasts. The Lords Lieutenant of the counties by the sea are commanded to warn the inhabitants to put themselves in readiness, with continuance of watchings of beacons. Certain bands both of horsemen and footmen under meet conductors are to be ready upon convenient warning to repair to places subject to the danger of sudden landings. Furthermore, because there are reports that in divers places near the sea coast some have shown a disposition to withdraw inland, they shall be straitly warned in no wise to depart or to diminish their families that may serve for defence. If any shall attempt to do so they shall be warned on their allegiance to return, otherwise they shall be not only severely punished but have their houses and lands seized. All captains and constables in forts shall be resident with their retinues upon pain of forfeiture of their places.

In Kent where there are many foreigners, especially in Canterbury, Sandwich and Maidstone, the Lord Cobham is to take order that the exact number may be known, and that as they are partakers of the benefits of the realm in like sort as her Majesty's natural subjects, so they shall be contributory to the charges of the places where they remain. Furthermore, that the enemy may find less booty if any attempt be made perchance for spoil, the inhabitants by the coasts shall be warned that upon any probable alarum the herdsmen and shepherds shall withdraw their cattle to the more inward parts.

7th June. A Scottish Lord's Inventions.

One Lord Neper (or Napier), a Scottish lord, hath made some secret and profitable inventions for the defence of this island, being a burning mirror that receiveth the dispersed beams of the sun and doth reflect them, united and concurring, in one mathematical point where it must necessarily engender fire; a piece of artillery which being shot passeth not lineally through an army but rangeth abroad superficially within an appointed place. There is also a round chariot of metal made of proof of double musket, which motion shall be by those that be within more easy, light and speedy than so many armed men would otherwise be, and of use in moving to break the array of the enemy's battle and to making passage. By staying and abiding within the enemy's battle, it serveth to destroy the environed enemy by continual shot of harquebus through small holes, the enemy being thereby abased and altogether uncertain what defence or pursuit to use against a moving mouth of metal. Besides these inventions, divers of sailing under water and the like.

11th June. Sir John Smythe's Misdemeanour.

Very traitorous words are reported of Sir John Smythe that he uttered at a mustering of the train bands in the Windmill Field at Colchester. He rode on horseback with Mr. Seymour, the second son to my Lord of Hertford, and two other gentlemen into the field where Sir Thomas Lucas was training his band; and, coming in front of the pikemen as they stood in square with two wings of bowmen standing in flank, he said, 'My masters, if you will go with me, you shall not go out of the land, but I will spend my life with you.' The pikemen asked if they should go with him then, to which Sir John replied, 'You shall go with a better man than myself or Sir Thomas Lucas; here is a nobleman of the blood royal, brother to the Earl of Beauchamp, to whom I am assistant.' He said also that there was a press out for 1,000 men, but those who followed him should go no further than he went, that there were traitors about the Court, and that the Lord Treasurer was a traitor of traitors; the common people had been a long time oppressed and should have redress if they would go with him.

The two gentlemen held up their hands and said they would go with him; and some of the soldiers stepping out of their ranks would have followed him, but through the persuasion of those standing by, being gentlemen, constables and men of the wiser sort, who asked them if they would be hanged, they returned to their ranks and made a condition that if their captains would go, they would; whereupon Sir John and his company went away greatly discontented.

13th June. SIR JOHN SMYTHE.

The Council, being informed of the matter concerning Sir John Smythe, upon this offensive and unexpected accident send Sir Henry Gray to command him upon his allegiance to appear before them at Court forthwith; and if he shall make any extraordinary delay or attempt to escape, Sir Henry hath full authority to call unto him any forces which he may think necessary.

15th June. THE DEATH OF DR. FLETCHER.

Dr. Fletcher, the Bishop of London, is dead upon the sudden. He was taking tobacco in his chair (wherewith since his unfortunate marriage he hath sought to smother his cares), when he cried out to his man that stood by him, 'Oh boy, I die.' Hereat one hath written this epitaph upon him:

> 'Here lies the first prelate made Christendom see
> A bishop a husband unto a lady;
> The cause of his death was secret and hid,
> He cried out, "I die"; and e'en so he did.'

Before he was made Bishop of London (coming hither by way of Bristol and Worcester) he was Dean of Peterborough when Mary, Queen of Scots, was beheaded at Fotheringhay; to whom he made a wordy oration of her past, present and future condition, wherein he took more pains than he received thanks from her who therein was most concerned.

Once when there were two Councillors sworn within compass of one year, and neither of them had a grey hair, he glanced at it in his sermon with a sentence of Seneca against *iuvenile consilium, priuatum commodum, inuestum odium*. The Queen found no fault with this liberal speech, but the friends of the Councillors taxing him for it, he had the pretty shift to tell the friends of either that he meant it by the other.

Sir John Smythe before the Council.

To-day Sir John Smythe made his appearance before the Council, and, being charged to answer what he did and said to the company of pikemen to follow him, he answered very unwillingly and uncertainly. Whereupon the Council charged him with his manner of coming to the field where his pikemen were standing in order and his lewd speeches then uttered. To these charges he answered very uncertainly, confessing part of the words, alleging that he meant no harm towards her Majesty; and in some parts he sought to excuse himself by forgetfulness of what he said, colouring also certain words that he used of the Lord Treasurer with oversight by reason of his drinking in the morning of a great deal of white wine and sack. And yet in the end, finding himself charged with a multitude of witnesses, he began to defend his speeches, pretending that by the laws of the realm no subject ought to be commanded to go out of the realm in her Majesty's service, and concluding that he might lawfully advise the people not to go in service out of the realm at this time, and therefore he had just cause to use those kind of speeches. Moreover, saith he, he had been so informed by two lawyers, named Ridgeley and Wiseman.

The Council now require further examinations and in the meanwhile Sir John is committed to the Tower.

16th June. The Treatment of Spanish Prisoners.

Divers of our Englishmen that have been taken prisoners and

carried into Spain are used there with great rigour and cruelty, some in Seville and other places condemned to death, others put into the galleys or afflicted with great extremities which is far otherwise than any of the Spanish prisoners are used here in England. Her Majesty, lest her favourable usage to her enemies may be taken for a neglect of her own subjects or a kind of awe of the King of Spain, now commandeth that such Spanish prisoners as yet remain in England shall be restrained from their gentle usage. Mr. Nicholas Owsley that hath heretofore brought prisoners from Spain and carried Spanish prisoners back is now appointed to search out all Spaniards that yet remain here and to carry them to Bridewell or some such prison of severe punishment; and all that have in their keeping any Spaniards shall deliver them to Mr. Owsley. Nevertheless any man that holdeth any prisoners for ransom is assured that no prisoner shall be sent out of the realm without the knowledge and satisfaction of the party whose lawful prisoner he is.

20th June. AN ALIEN BANISHED.

There is one Cornelius Waters, a stranger of the County of Brabant, that is now a prisoner in the King's Bench for certain unlawful and seditious books that he brought into the realm. This man, albeit deserving more punishment, having lived so many years in the realm that he could not be ignorant of his offence, is not to be further proceeded with than to be sent away out of the country in the vessel of some Fleming or Low Countryman and straitly charged not to return again.

22nd June. A NEW PLAY.

There is a new play at the Rose called *Troy*.

27th June. THE CASE OF SIR JOHN SMYTHE.

The Council suspecting Sir John Smythe's late misdemeanour to proceed not from mere rashness but some farther ground of practice and conspiracy have directed the High Sheriff of Essex to repair to all houses of Sir John and to make diligent search for all letters, writings, books and any other things appertaining to any disloyal purpose and to have the same sealed and kept in a place of safe custody. The Attorney General and Solicitor General are now to examine Sir John and the charges made against him with a view to his speedy trial.

4th July. SERVICE WITHOUT THE REALM.

Mr. Nicholas Ridgeley of the Inner Temple that was committed to the Fleet for his opinions to Sir John Smythe is now to be released on his humble submission to the Council. He protesteth that he had no evil intent but doth indeed hold that her Majesty both by the common law and statute laws of the realm may lawfully compel her subjects to serve her beyond the seas in any parts wheresoever it shall please her Highness, and that the experience of all time hath been so.

5th July. SIR ROBERT CECIL MADE SECRETARY.

This day is Sir Robert Cecil, second son to the Lord Treasurer, sworn Principal Secretary to her Majesty; which being done in the absence of my Lord of Essex is like to cause him much discontent. Before his going he recommended Mr. Thomas Bodley with extraordinary praise of him as the fittest man, detracting at the same time from Sir Robert Cecil with such odious comparisons that neither is the Queen pleased to admit Mr. Bodley for Secretary (for now she showeth less favour to those whom my Lord most commendeth); nor doth the Lord Treasurer think good to join as colleague and partner to his son (which they had determined to do) one that they now suspect to be drawn to my Lord of Essex's party by reason of the immoderate praises given him by my Lord.

11th July. BLACKAMOORS IN LONDON.

Divers blackamoors have lately been brought into the realm, of which kind of people there are already here too many, considering how God hath blessed this land with as great increase of people of our own nation as any country in the world; whereof many for want of service and means to set them on to work fall to idleness and great extremity. By order of the Council the ten blackamoors that were brought in by Sir Thomas Baskerville in his last voyage shall be transported out of the realm.

15th July. THE EARL OF NORTHUMBERLAND NAMED AS AMBASSADOR.

My Lord of Northumberland being named as ambassador to the French King hath craved her Highness's dispensation from the embassage, alleging two reasons in especial; the imperfection of his hearing and the poorness of his estate. Imperfection of hearing, saith he, must of necessity beget absurdities, as of trouble to the King who shall be forced to speak with often repetitions and to strain his voice above the ordinary. Further, my Lord protesteth that seeing the scoffing and scornful humours of the French to all of other nations in whom they discover the least imperfections they will lay upon him the reputation of a fool and grace him with some such disgrace which would nothing fit with her Majesty's honour or his contentment. As for his state, his debts are so great and for want of payments his credit for money matters so shaken that he knoweth not which way or by what means he may satisfy his desire to do her Majesty service.

17th July. IRISH NEWS.

The rebels led by O'Donnell now overrun the whole of Connaught; in Roscommon more than forty strong castles, besides forts, are lost without striking one blow, whereat Sir Richard Bingham the governor (whom some name *Improvido*) is greatly blamed. Nor is it yet concluded whether there should be a continuance of war or a pacification. A great occasion of the continuance of these troubles is the difference between Sir William Russell and Sir John Norris, Sir John blaming the Lord Deputy for hindering the service, for he provideth insufficiency of victual and carriage.

18th July. NEW PLAYS.

The two new plays this month at the Rose are *The Paradox* and *The Tinker of Totnes.*

ROGUES IN MIDDLESEX.

The Provost Marshals having lately ceased to go abroad, the rogues and vagabonds that for a time were driven out of the City and suburbs are again returned in greater numbers than heretofore. The justices of peace for Middlesex are requested to take present order that the Provost Marshals may be continued; and likewise the petty constables strictly charged in the several parishes to apprehend all masterless men, vagabonds, and suspected persons that beg or wander abroad, and bring them to the justices.

BLACKAMOORS IN ENGLAND.

Mr. Casper van Sanden, a merchant of Lubec, that at his own charges brought back eighty-nine of the Queen's subjects that were detained as prisoners in Spain and Portugal, hath desired licence to take up so many blackamoors and to transport them into Spain and Portugal; which her Majesty thinketh a very good exchange and that those kind of people may well be spared in the realm. The Lord Mayor of London and other mayors and public officers are required to aid Mr. Sanden to take up the blackamoors with the consent of their masters.

19th July. GREAT GOOD NEWS FROM SPAIN.

News is come that on 19th June, 8 of the Queen's ships entered the bay of Cadiz and fought with 22 galleys and 8 armadoes, whereof they took 18 galleys, sunk 4 and burnt the *St. Philip*, a great ship of war, with 4 others; that the next day the army arrived and took 40 sail richly laden; the 21st they took the town of Cadiz, and it is thought that they have taken St. Mary Port as the Flemings that bring the news saw a great fire which burnt all night.

22nd July. PLAYING INHIBITED.

The players are forbidden to use any plays about the City of London for that by drawing of much people together increase of sickness is to be feared.

25th July. THE SECOND VOYAGE TO GUIANA.

Captain Lawrence Keymis is returned from his voyage of discovery to Guiana and reporteth much of the rivers, nations, towns and casiques (or captains) of those parts. Of Berreo, that Spaniard whom Sir Walter Ralegh took in his voyage, he reporteth that after Sir Walter's departure he returned to Trinidad with but fifteen men, but being attacked by the natives and two or three of his men killed, fled away towards the River Caroli, where the Spaniards have made a fort to defend the passage of the river. Captain Keymis was told that the old King Topiawari is dead, and the boy Hugh Goldwin, that was left behind, eaten by a tiger. They returned therefore from Topiarimacko, that was Topiawari's port, by another branch of the main river to the port of Carapana. He himself came not, but sent one of his aged followers to say that he was sick, old and weak. This old man declared that Carapana had repented him of his ambition ever to have sought by the Spaniard's means to have enlarged his countries and people, for now that the plenty of gold in that country is known, there can be no greater misery than if the Spaniards prevail; who perforce do take all things from them, using them as their slaves, and (that which is worst of all) they must be content to leave their women if a Spaniard chance but set his eye on any of them to fancy her. On the other side they could hope for no better state and usage than her Majesty's gracious government; 'for,' said the old man, 'the other year when we fled into the mountains, and measured your doings by the Spaniards in like case, we made no other account but that your commander being able, as he was, would doubtless have persecuted us to the uttermost. We found it far otherwise, and that none of your well governed company durst offer any of us wrong and violence; no, not by stealth, when unknown they might have done it.' Wherefore Carapana doth crave of her Majesty for himself and his people that they may enjoy her protection.

Hereby Captain Keymis would give this caveat to our English (who to steal the first blessing of an untraded place will perhaps secretly hasten thither) that they may be assured that these people, as they no way sought to harm but rather used our men with all kindness, so are they impatient of such a wrong as to have any of their people perforce taken from them, and will doubtless seek revenge. He concludeth that it will be blindness and deafness in those that spend their days in serving the commonwealth to seek either to forslow so fit an occasion or to forsake so general a blessing. This country of Guiana doth not only propose some hope of gold mines, and certain pieces of made gold, but also in the trade of these rivers brasil-wood, honey, cotton, balsamum, and drugs to help to defray the charges. 'The case then so standing,' saith he, 'is it not mere wretchedness in us to spend our time, break our sleep, and waste our brains, in contriving a cavilling false title to defraud a neighbour of half an acre of ground; whereas here whole shires of fruitful rich grounds, lying now waste for want of people, do prostitute themselves unto us like a fair and beautiful woman, in the pride and flower of desired years.'

26th July. THE DUNKIRK PIRATES.

Of late divers Newcastle men have been taken on the coasts of Norfolk and Suffolk by the Dunkirkers for that those hoys of Newcastle go so slenderly armed that they give occasion to the enemy to set upon them. The Mayor and others of Newcastle are now to require these ships to be furnished with iron ordnance, powder and some calivers or muskets, and to see them properly manned. Moreover, they shall go together in consort.

A PRESUMPTUOUS BALLAD.

There is a certain ballad published, written by Deloney, containing a complaint of the great want and scarcity of corn within the realm; and because it containeth vain and presumptuous matter that thereby the poor may aggravate their grief and take occasion of some discontent, the Lord Mayor hath called before him the printer and the party by whom it was put to print, who pretended a licence; but finding it untrue the Lord Mayor hath committed him. In the matter complained of, the Queen is brought in to speak with her people in very fond and undecent sort, and prescribeth orders for the remedying of the dearth of corn, extracted (as it seemeth) out of the book published last year.

27th July. THE POSSESSION OF THOMAS DARLING.

At the late assizes held at Derby by Sir Edmund Anderson, the Lord Chief Justice, there is condemned a certain witch called Alse Gooderidge that very grievously bewitched a boy, one Thomas Darling.

This Darling at the end of February last went hunting the hare with his uncle, one Robert Toone, dwelling in Burton upon Trent; but his uncle being earnest in following his game was parted from the boy, who returned home alone, and afterward waxing heavy, and growing very sick, was got to bed. The next morning he had some fits with extreme vomitings, and would many times point with his hands, saying, 'Look where green angels stand in the window,' and complaining of a green cat that would trouble him. Moreover the use of his legs was taken from him. Many and strange fits he had, which being ended, he would fall upon his knees suddenly to prayer and that so pithily that the standers-by wondered thereat; and between the fits he requested them to read the scriptures. Wherefore they sent for one Jesse Bee, who read the 9th chapter according to St. John till he came to the 4th verse, at which time the boy was overthrown into a fit like the former, which fits lasted commonly about a quarter of an hour. Jesse continued reading the 11th, 12th and 13th of St. John's Gospel, and the 1st and 2nd of Revelations; during which time the fits continued one in the neck of another; and ending with a vomit he used to say, 'The Lord's name be praised.' When Jesse either ceased to speak of any comfortable matter, or to read the scriptures, the boy was quiet; but when he was so religiously occupied the fits came thick upon him, which Jesse Bee observing told the boy's aunt that he suspected the boy was bewitched.

The next morning the boy said unto the maid that made him ready, 'I heard my aunt tell Jesse Bee that I was bewitched: the same Saturday that my sickness took me, I lost my uncle in the wood, and in a coppice I met a little old woman; she had a grey gown with a black fringe about the cape, a broad thrummed hat, and three warts on her face. I have seen her begging at our door; as for her name I know it not, but by sight I can know her again. As I passed by her in the coppice, I chanced against my will to let fall a scape; which she taking in anger said, "Gyp with a mischief, and fart with a bell: I will go to heaven and thou shalt go to hell"; and forthwith she stooped to the ground.' Hereupon a more vehement suspicion arising, some judged it to be the witch of Stapenhill; others, because she was old and went little abroad, rather thought it to be Alse Gooderidge, her daughter, who was had in great suspicion of many as a doer of devilish practices.

The fits continuing thus by the space of five weeks, at length the boy's grandmother sent for Alse Gooderidge, and when, with much ado, she was brought into the chamber where the boy was, he fell suddenly into a marvellous sore fit.

Some days later Alse Gooderidge, together with her mother, was again brought into the boy's presence by order of Sir Humphrey Ferrers, and seeing that the boy straightway had fits at their presence, Sir Humphrey ordered them to be searched for those marks which are usually found upon witches. Whereupon behind the right shoulder of the old woman they found a thing like the udder of an ewe that giveth suck with two teats. So they bade her say the Lord's Prayer, which she huddled up after her manner, always leaving out the words 'Lead us not into temptation.' Then they searched Alse Gooderidge and found upon her belly a hole of the bigness of two pence, fresh and bloody, as though some great wart had been cut out of the place, which she declared to have been caused by a knife recently on a time when her foot slipped; but a surgeon judged it to be an old wound, for it was not festered and seemed to be sucken.

Sir Humphrey charged her with witchcraft about one Michael's cow, which brake all things that they tied her in and ran to Alse Gooderidge's house, scraping at the walls and windows to have come in: whereat her old mother Elizabeth Wright took upon her to help, upon condition that she might have a penny to bestow on her god. So she came to the man's house, kneeled down before the cow, crossed her with a stick in the forehead, and prayed to her god, since which time the cow continued well. Wherefore after further examination Alse Gooderidge was committed to Derby gaol, but her mother dismissed.

Next day the boy had very grievous fits, his eyes closed up, his legs lifted up as stiff as stakes, and all his senses taken from him, at which times he uttered very strange sayings. In the mean season others wishing to be eye witnesses of these strange reports, Jesse Bee would read the Bible, and when he came to the 4th verse of 1st chapter of St. John's Gospel, 'In it was life, and the life was the light of the world,' the boy was overthrown into a fit. Many and grievous torments did the boy suffer in the days following, and when the fits ended, Jesse Bee would say, 'Thomas, shall we take the sword with two edges and bid Satan the battle?' To whom the child answered, 'Yes, very willingly'; but as Jesse would read in the 1st chapter of St. John's Gospel, so the fits would come upon him again.

At length a cunning man declared that he would make the witch confess and within a sennight after cure the boy. So he sent for her from the Town Hall to the house of Mr. Robert Toone, where many worshipful persons were ready to see proof of his skill. Being brought, they laboured to make her confess;

to which she answered that it was the first that ever she committed and if they would give her liberty she would confess all the truth freely; whereat her speech was interrupted so that she could not speak, but she prayed them to forgive her. The cunning man seeing this would not prevail fell to trial of his conclusion. He put a pair of new shoes on her feet, setting her close to the fire till the shoes being extreme hot might constrain her through pain to confess. She, being thoroughly heated, desired a release and she would disclose all; which granted she confessed nothing. Being therefore threatened more sharply, she confessed to reveal all privately to Mistress Dethick, but when she began to speak her breath was stopped, so that she could say nothing but 'I pray you forgive me.' The company continued threatening and persuading her but she would say nothing to the purpose, and so she was sent again to the Town Hall, and the company departed; after which the boy had eight fits.

These torments having endured for nearly ten weeks, very grievously, on the 6th May the boy had twelve fits in the forenoon and ten in the afternoon. After one of them taking the chamberpot, he started suddenly saying, 'Look, where a man cometh out of the chamberpot'; in another fit he cried out, 'Flames of fire, flames of fire'; in another he said, 'I see the heavens open.' In most of these fits he bleared out his tongue, having his face wry turned towards his back, groaning and shrieking lamentably.

At length, the fits having in the meanwhile increased, there came one Mr. John Darrell, a preacher, who seeing the boy in divers of his fits, assured his friends that he was possessed with an unclean spirit, and exhorted both the boy and his parents and friends to resist Satan and to prepare themselves against the next day to that holy exercise of prayer and fasting.

The next day therefore the family with some others being assembled, the holy exercise of prayer and fasting was taken in hand, in the midst whereof the boy was taken with his fits but after a while fell into a trance, and there came from him a small voice saying, 'Brother Glassap, we cannot prevail; his faith is so strong, and they fast and pray, and a preacher prayeth as fast as they'; and, 'Brother Radulphus, I will go unto my master

Belzebub and he shall double their tongues'; and later, 'Radulphus, Belzebub can do no good, his head is stroken off with a word; but I will go fetch the flying eagle and his flock.' At this time the boy declared that he saw an angel in the window, like a milk white dove, sent from the Lord to be with him and assist him. Then the voice said, 'We cannot prevail, let us go out of him, and enter into some of these here.' This voice came twice, and it made the standers-by afraid. And after other sayings, 'We cannot prevail, we cannot prevail, their Church increaseth'; at which time there came in two to join in prayer with the company. Then the voice said, 'Here cometh one of my people'; with that they looked back, and were ware of a man of bad life coming into the parlour, and albeit the boy was in one of his trances, yet he made signs to the company to get him away, which one of them perceiving did so.

About two in the afternoon he had a marvellous strange fit, at which time, if he were possessed with two spirits (as it is probable he was), one of them went out of him. All day the fits continued, but decreasing in strength; and at last, being laid upon his bed, he began to heave and lift vehemently at his stomach; and getting up some phlegm and choler, pointing with his finger and following with his eyes, he said, 'Look, look, see you not the mouse that is gone out of my mouth?' Then he fell into a quiet trance; which ended, he was well until 7 o'clock, when he with two or three others went to supper. And as he sat at the table he fell into a trance and was thence carried to bed. As he lay there a voice was heard, saying, 'My son, arise up and walk, the evil spirit is gone from thee; arise and walk.' Upon this his keeper said, 'Let us see if he can go betwixt us'; for indeed he had lost the use of his legs since the beginning of his sickness. But he answered, 'No, I can go of myself, I thank God,' and so standing on his feet straightway he went forward without any difficulty.

The next day Mr. Darrell came again to him, and counselled him to be now most heedful, lest the unclean spirit returning, and his heart empty of faith, bring seven worse than himself with him. He did indeed again fall into his trances, but the Lord being with him, he was soon well both in mind and body, and so hath remained ever since.

28th July. THE SPANISH PRISONERS.

The Spanish prisoners that are in the City having had notice of the late order keep themselves close in secret places so that they may not be taken going abroad. The Lord Mayor is now to make diligent inquiry where any Spaniards or professed subjects of the King of Spain are harboured and to cause them to be apprehended and carried to Bridewell to receive at least some part of that usage whereof our countrymen do taste in more extremity in the King's dominions.

30th July. THE QUEEN'S PICTURE.

All public officers shall yield their assistance to the Queen's Sergeant Painter touching the abuse committed by divers unskilled artisans in unseemly and improper painting, graving and printing of her Majesty's person and visage, to her great offence and disgrace of that beautiful and magnanimous Majesty wherewith God hath blessed her. All such to be defaced and none allowed but such as the Sergeant Painter shall first have sight of.

31st July. A PROCLAMATION FOR THE DEARTH OF CORN.

In divers counties rich farmers and ingrossers pretending the unseasonableness of this summer are increasing the price of the old corn, of mere covetousness. The Justices are forthwith to peruse diligently the orders made last year and to consider such points as may tend to the reformation of those that by their disorder and covetousness cause the prices of grain to be increased in this lamentable sort beyond reason. Moreover the Sheriffs, Justices and principal officers shall certify monthly to the Council the names of those Justices of Peace who dutifully towards her Majesty and charitably towards their neighbours perform the charge committed to them that her Majesty may be informed, and contrariwise to mislike those that shall neglect the execution of this commandant.

It is also forbidden at this time of scarcity that starch be made of corn of the realm.

1st August. NEWS FROM THE FLEET.

To-day, being Sunday, Sir Anthony Ashley came to Court from the Fleet and made relation of all the action first at the Council table, and after dinner to the Queen.

2nd August. PREPARATIONS FOR THE RETURN OF THE FLEET.

Sir Ferdinando Gorges, Mr. William Killigrew, and Mr. Richard Carmarden, the surveyor of the custom-house in London, are appointed commissioners to Plymouth to view the prizes as the ships return from Spain. As formerly merchants of London or residents in the ports have bought from the soldiers and mariners goods of great value but small bulk and carried them away secretly, inquisition is to be made, and merchants suspected of any such intentions to be ordered to depart on pain of imprisonment.

4th August. 'THE METAMORPHOSIS OF AJAX.'

Mr. John Harington, that hath lain almost buried in the country these three or four years, thinking to give some occasion to be talked of hath written and caused to be printed a very foul book entitled *A New Discourse of a Stale Subject called the Metamorphosis of Ajax*, treating of a new way to make a jakes that shall be rid of stink; but intermixed with many other unsavoury matters. The device is this: You shall make a false bottom to that privy that you are annoyed with, either of lead or stone, the which bottom shall have a sluice of brass to let out all the filth, which if it be close plastered all about it and rinsed with water as oft as occasion serves, but especially at noon and at night, will keep your privy as sweet as your parlour.

MR. HARINGTON'S MERRY JEST OF MR. JAQUES WINGFIELD.

Mr. Jaques Wingfield coming one day either of business or kindness to visit a great Lady in the Court, the Lady bade her gentlewoman ask which of the Wingfields it was. He told her 'Jaques Wingfield.' The modest gentlewoman, that was not so well seen in the French to know that 'Jaques' was but 'James' in English, was so bashful that to mend the matter, as she thought, she brought her lady word, not without blushing, that it was 'Mr. Privy Wingfield.'

5th August. CHURCHYARD'S POEM ON SIR F. KNOLLYS.

Mr. Churchyard hath written *A sad and solemn funeral* of Sir Francis Knollys that died a few days since. Quoth he:

> The lords and knights that at thy table fed,
> And all good guests that thither did repair,

Shall honour thee and thine, though thou be dead;
Make of thy praise an echo in the air.
Yea, drum and fife, and all the martial crew
In warlike guise shall wait upon thy hearse;
Fine writers too, and laureate poets new,
On thy farewell shall pen out many a verse;
And garlands gay shall vestal virgins fling
On thy cold grave, whiles clampering bells do ring.

8th August. A DAY OF TRIUMPH.

To-day, being Sunday, great triumph is made at London for the good success of the two Generals and their company in Spain, the winning, sacking, and burning of the famous town of Cadiz, and the overthrow and burning of the Spanish Navy.

THE TAKING OF CADIZ.

On the 20th June, being Sunday, early in the morning the fleet came to anchor within half a league of St. Sebastian, a friary at the west end of Cadiz; and here the Generals attempted to land straightway. They filled many boats and barges with soldiers, but the weather was very foul and the water went so high that two boats with some eighty soldiers armed sank, whereof some were drowned, the others saved by the other boats and set on board their own ships. This mischance did not happen as any token that God was angry with the enterprise, but that they had mischosen the day for attempting so great a work upon the Day of Rest. It was also a mercy of Almighty God, for they could not have landed there without great difficulty and much loss.

The next day, early in the morning, the Spanish fleet, which had ridden before the town under the forts and bulwarks, shot with the tide within the point of the mainland, and immediately after the English fleet weighed and came to anchor near the place where the Spanish fleet rode before; and there the fort St. Philip and the rest played upon our ships with their great ordnance, and the galleys were very busy. But, by the Generals' commandment Sir John Wingfield in the *Vauntguard*, having some lesser ships, took them to task, and so lamed them that they were glad to seek to save themselves. These crept by the shore, first to the Puntal, and from thence into the Bay, and so to a bridge called Puente de Suazo, where striking their masts and by help of certain engines upon the bridge, they went round about the Isle of Leon and came to Rota.

But the eye and care of the two Generals was chiefly fixed upon the galleons and other great ships. Whereupon they resolved to send the Lord Thomas Howard to encounter with them in the *Nonpareil*, adjoining with him some few ships of the Queen's, for the place was so narrow that hardly ten ships could come to fight. With the Lord Thomas went Sir Walter Ralegh, Sir Francis Vere, Captain Robert Cross (with whom was the Earl of Sussex) and others. And although it had been agreed in council that the Generals should not hazard their ships of greatest burden in those shoals, yet the Earl of Essex could not endure to be only a looker-on in so honourable an action, but he put in amongst the thickest of them and fought very gallantly; which the Lord Admiral seeing, and not being able to bring in his own ship, took his long boat and went aboard the *Miranore*. With him into the fight went his young son Lord William, being at these young years very desirous to seek and share honour with the oldest captains.

This fight lasted till noon, by which time the galleons were cruelly rent and torn, and so much slaughter in them that the blood gushed out at the scuppet holes. Whereupon some of the Spaniards resolved to fly to Porto Real, some to burn their ships, some to run them aground; and divers of them leapt into the water, whereof some swam ashore, some were drowned, some taken, some slain. The Lord Admiral, beholding this miserable spectacle, had compassion of them, and took his boat and rowed up and down amongst them, forbidding these cruelties and preventing the firing of the Spanish ships so much as was possible; but they first fired and burnt the *St. Philip*, a ship of 1,500 tons, the *St. Thomas*, and the *S. Juan*. The other two apostles, *St. Matthew* and *St. Andrew*, ships of 1,200 tons apiece, were saved and are now brought back to England.

The battle by sea being thus happily fought and victory obtained, the Lords Generals straightway set in hand the landing of the soldiers, and in very little space there was such diligence shown that the Earl of Essex was on land near Puntal, about a league from Cadiz, with 8,000 shot and pikes; with him was the Earl of Sussex, the Earl Lodowick of Nassau, the Lord Burke of Ireland, and divers other gentlemen adventurers. So soon as he was landed, the Earl of Essex despatched the Sergeant Major, Sir Christopher Blount, and Sir Thomas Gerrard with their regiments to the Puente de Suazo, with charge to impeach the passage so that no succours might come to the Spaniards into the Isle of Leon; to break down that engine by help whereof the galleys might pass; and to surprise or force the castle at the head of the bridge, called by the Dutch 'Herod's house.'

Meanwhile the Earl of Essex, having for his guide Captain William Morgan, marched apace with his army toward the town, although in no hope to lodge therein that night. Upon the way he was encountered with 400 or 500 cavalleros of Xeres and 600 or 700 footmen, but without any great difficulty they were beaten back and ran into the town, offering to shut the gates. But my Lord made such haste that he entered with his troops pell-mell with them; and some made such shift to get into the town that they climbed over the walls.

By this time the Lord Admiral had landed his battle of some 1,200 or 1,500 men and followed the Earl with a very round march, being accompanied with all the chief commanders of sea and captains of ships with their retinue, among them the Lord Thomas Howard and Sir Walter Ralegh, who was not able to march so fast as the rest by reason that he was hurt in the leg with a splinter in the fight with the galleons. When the Lord Admiral came into the town, he found the Earl of Essex skirmishing and fighting with the Spaniards, who fought and fled still before him. Others threw down stones from the battlements of houses which annoyed much our soldiers. But after the forces of both the Generals were joined together, the fight and resistance of the Spaniards continued not long, for they fled into the Castle and into the Town-house in the market place, and other strong places. And here Sir John Wingfield riding upon a nag unarmed, having been hurt before in the thigh, was shot in the head from a loop in the Castle, whereof he instantly died. Before night the Town-house was taken, and therein the Generals lodged, being now masters of the whole town, except for the Castle and the fort St. Philip, both which were rendered in the morning.

The Corrigidor and the rest of the town yielded on condition that they should have their lives saved and only their wearing clothes permitted them ; all the rest of their goods and wealth should be spoil and pillage to the soldiers, and besides for their ransom they should pay to the Generals 120,000 ducats, and for payment thereof forty of the chief men are to be held in England as pledges till the money be paid.

And now proclamation was made that no Englishman should offer violence to any religious person, to any woman or child, or any other of the Spanish nation ; and the Generals sent away boats, barges and pinnaces first with the ladies and religious, and then the men and all other of the inhabitants of Cadiz (except the pledges and certain prisoners of the captains) to Porto Santa Maria. The women were suffered by the Generals to wear so much apparel as they were able to bear upon them and all their jewels, and because none of them should be spoiled by our ruder soldiers and mariners, the Lords Generals themselves stood at the water gates and saw to their embarking.

In this interim the Lord Admiral appointed the Rear-admiral to take some of the lesser Queen's ships and merchant ships that drew but little water to go after the Spanish ships which were fled to Porto Real, and there either to take them or to sink or fire them if they would not yield. While this was determined, offer was made of two millions to the Earl of Essex for the ransoming of the ships and their merchandise. The Lord Admiral would by no means agree to the ransoming of the ships but only of the merchandise. But the Duke of Medina Sidonia, the Admiral of Spain, decided this controversy ; for he, being at Porto Santa Maria and always ill affected to them of Cadiz, gave order that the next morning before day the whole fleet at Porto Real should be fired. This was put in execution ; nevertheless our men made such haste thither that they recovered much merchandise and divers pieces of ordnance, but none of the ships could be saved.

Thus is the whole fleet of the Spaniards, valued by some of them at ten or twelve million ducats, all either taken, sunk or burned in a short space ; together with much rich merchandise in Cadiz, and that which pincheth the King of Spain most (his ships excepted) are the 1,200 pieces of ordnance taken or sunk in his ships. The Spaniards' losses in all are reckoned to be worth 20,000,000 ducats at the least.

These things being happily achieved, Sir John Wingfield was very honourably buried in Santa Cruz, the chief church of Cadiz, with all the funeral solemnities of war; the drums and trumpets sounding dolefully, the shot bearing the noses of their pieces downward, the pikes trailed. His body was borne by six knights, and the Generals threw their handkerchiefs wet from their eyes into the grave; and at that instant the most part of all the shot, great and small, aboard and ashore, were discharged.

The 27th June being Sunday the Lords Generals, with all the chiefs and gentlemen of the army, heard a sermon at S. Francisco, where after dinner they made a great many knights, even all almost that did deserve it, or affect it, or not neglect it and refuse it, as some did. In this prodigality of honour fifty-seven Englishmen are knighted, and as with the Count Lodowick of Nassau, Don Christopher (son to Don Antonio that was called King of Portugal) and four Dutch gentlemen are knighted; but Sir Samuel Bagnal and Sir Arthur Savage had been knighted before the town was taken for their bravery in the field.

The next day being Monday the 28th the Lord Admiral went aboard to set things in order in the fleet and to make ready for a new enterprise; and by his example also to draw the seamen and mariners to their ships that were loath to come out of the town.

About this time the Lord Admiral received from the Duke of Medina Sidonia, his old acquaintance since '88, two very honourable answers to two letters which he had written about the exchange of prisoners, Spanish for English, in the galleys. The Duke's answer was that he liked well of the motion and would do it so much as lay in him, but the charge was more particularly in the Adelantado of the galleys. To whom he wrote so effectually that within a day the Adelantado sent a principal captain to the Lord Admiral, who made full agreement for the exchange.

Upon the 1st July about forty of our English prisoners were

delivered aboard the *Ark* by the galley called *La Fama*, and promise made for the rest, which was afterwards performed. This galley *La Fama*, whereof Don Julian Hurtado was captain, came from Rota to the English Fleet with a white flag of safe conduct according to the order of war, but an ignorant sea captain made a shot at her as she passed by him and hurt and killed three men in her. Whereat the Lord Admiral was much grieved, and greatly offended with the captain and threatened to have hanged him, but the Captain of the galley and Don Pavo Patin, one of the pledges, made earnest suit to the Lord Admiral, which they obtained.

The Earl of Essex stayed all this while in the town with the rest of the commanders and captains, and companies of the army by land, which he suffered not to be idle. On the 28th June the ordnance was taken from the walls, castles and forts. Upon the 30th he made a road into the Isle and burned, razed, and spoiled all that might serve the enemy to any strength or relief. The next day he set pioneers a work, to raze and deface the forts and castle in the town. The 1st July the tower of the Town-house was battered down, and lastly upon the 4th July, he set the whole town on fire (the churches excepted) and saw all his men embarked, himself coming on board last. The next day the whole fleet set sail.

The Taking of Ferrol.

After sailing from Cadiz the fleet sailed along the coasts of Spain until they came before Ferrol where the Generals resolved to land. First Sir Amyas Preston and Sir William Monson and Captain William Morgan were sent in the evening to discover the passage in their pinnaces, and to view the place, to espy the forces, and to seek for fresh water and victuals. They brought answer next morning that the people were fled and had carried away their goods, and that they could not yet find any fresh water or victuals. For all this in the afternoon the Lords Generals landed with all their forces; but the Lord Admiral being not well, and having little hope of any relief there for their wants, at the earnest desire of the Earl of Essex, returned aboard his ship taking Sir Edward Wingfield with him, who was lame of a hurt which he had received at Cadiz.

The Earl of Essex being landed marched some two leagues with his army that night to Ferrol. He took the town with ease for the inhabitants had abandoned it and carried away most of their goods, but there was in the Nunnery some stuff, and in the palace of Bishop Ossorius a library of books, valued at 1,000 marks. There was also in the town some fruits and wines and a few hens; and in the Fort four pieces of great ordnance whereof one was the fairest and longest culverin which the King of Spain hath. Here the Earl appointed Captain Brett to march into the country with 800 soldiers of the strongest, chosen out of divers bands. He marched some two or three leagues to a town called Lotha, which he took and burnt, without any resistance; but if any of his troops straggled or were left sick upon the way, as many were, he found them at his return pitifully mangled, some with their hands chopped off, some their nostrils slit, and others killed. In this journey he got above a hundred cows and oxen and some swine for victual, and so returned to the Lord General who, after he had sacked and fired the town, the third day returned to the fleet.

All being now come on board again the Generals with their council held a new consultation on what was else to be done and how victuals and fresh water might be supplied. Some had great desire to go for Lagos; but ere anything was done the fleet was past the Cape St. Vincent, where a strong northerly wind took them and forced them to haul off into the sea and towards the Isles of the Azores. Here they called a council again and resolved to go for those islands, assuring themselves to have plenty of fresh water and victuals, and there to lie for the carracks and West Indian fleet and to encounter with the twenty-five Spanish men-of-war which lay at the Islands, as the Generals were advertised. But neither did this purpose hold, for the winds coming contrary, they held a new consultation and that was to bear with the coast of Spain and Portugal, and to search what shipping was in the harbours as they passed. This course was thought best, and kept for the most part until they came before the Groin on the 1st August.

Now lastly the Lords Generals resolved to come for England, and the rather by reason of the general wants of victuals and fresh water, and for that there were many sick men in the

Warspite and divers others of the fleet, and for a great leak that was sprung in the *Vauntguard*, and principally for her Majesty's straight command that they should stay forth but five months in this voyage. Whereupon the Lords Generals shaped their course for England.

8th August. THE SCARCITY OF CORN.

In spite of the orders formerly made the price of grain is still increased, and it is most evident that the ingrossing of corn and forestalling of markets by covetous men in buying great quantities of corn out of the market at farmers' houses hath been the cause of the dearth lately grown. The high sheriffs and justices of peace are required, even for conscience' sake, to have regard hereunto and speedily to deal severely with owners of corn that have any plenty thereof; and not only by assessment to compel them upon pain of imprisonment to bring weekly to the markets some proportions, but to overrule them in their prices so as the same may not be sold at any dearer rates than, at the least, these last two months. And if any shall murmur and repine against these orders in such a time of necessity, he shall be committed to prison until he conform.

Moreover the Council think it not amiss that the Archbishop of Canterbury should take order for the preachers generally in their sermons and exhortations to admonish farmers and owners of corn of this unchristian kind of seeking gain, recommending to the richer sort keeping of hospitality for relief of the poor and avoiding of excess. And therefore that housekeepers of wealth would be contented with a more sober diet and fewer dishes of meat in this time of dearth, and to forbear to have suppers in their houses on Wednesdays, Fridays and fasting days. Gentlemen and others of meaner sort might forbear the keeping of hounds. These and other charitable deeds would be earnestly commended by the preachers and ministers; and special order taken that beneficed clergy should reside upon their benefices to give good example to others in using hospitality.

To the like effect the Lord Mayor of London is advised to use all care to provide corn for the relief of the City, and that the citizens and especially the City Companies should use a more moderate and spare diet, leaving great feastings and superfluous fare. Moreover the order taken for inmates should be more carefully executed whereby many that have their dwellings in the country might be sent to their places of usual abode and the City disburdened of a great number.

LADY UNTON.

It is reported that Lady Unton abideth at Broad Histon, there beautifying her sorrow with all the ornaments of an honourable widow, her voice tuned with a mournful accent and her cupboard, instead of casting bottles, adorned with prayer books and epitaphs.

9th August. THE CADIZ FORCES.

The Council have written to the Generals that it is greatly to her Majesty's misliking that she should now be solicited to be put to further expense to defray the wages of the soldiers and mariners, remembering their earnest protestations that she should not only be eased of that burden but assured of great profit to defray these and all other incident charges and precedent expenses, whereby she was by their persuasions drawn, very hardly, to disburse aforehand the sum of above £50,000, apart from the great burden of charges to which the port towns and City of London were put unto in setting forth the ships.

As for the disposing of the soldiers, those drawn from the Low Countries to the number of 2,200 are to be sent back thither, as was promised through Sir Francis Vere. Of the rest, being about 3,000, 1,500 or 1,000 at the least are speedily to be sent to Ireland with their captains. All these soldiers shall be searched before they depart.

11th August. THE CADIZ VOYAGE.

Commissioners are appointed for the City of London to search the ships which are come up the Thames for all goods, money, jewels or other commodities taken in the spoil of Cadiz to be reserved towards defraying the charge of voyage; notwithstanding there may be allowed to the soldiers and mariners that which is fit for them.

12th August. THE EARL OF ESSEX AT COURT.

The Earl of Essex came to Court to-day about twelve, being a little lame by reason of a fall in his posting journey. My Lord hath now a beard which he began to grow on this voyage. The fleet is at the Downs and the greatest part of the army dispersed, many with leave, the rest without license, moreover there is infection among them.

When Sir Anthony Ashley brought the account of the action to the Court it was the Earl's intention to have it printed, but when his friends made a motion to the printers to have it published, they answered that they had received an inhibition from the Council by the Archbishop of Canterbury not to print any discourse of that kind without their special allowance. Moreover, the next day Mr. Fulke Greville was charged by the Queen to command Mr. Cuffe, my Lord's Secretary, upon pain of death not to set forth any discourse of this service without her privity. Hereupon Mr. Anthony Bacon resolved to send copies of it abroad, and his Lordship's friends would do the like.

The Queen these last few days hath been wholly possessed with discontented humours, which my Lord's backward friends nourish by all means possible. One great man being asked news of the expedition answered that there were many knights made; and that the Queen should not hereafter be troubled with beggars, all were become so rich; but where is the £50,000 she hath bestowed in the setting forth her navy and army to perform that service?

14th August. An Italian Gentleman presented at Court.

One Signor Francesco Gradenigo, the son of a great man in Venice, was of late presented to her Majesty at Court with letters of commendation from the French King. No sooner had he kissed hands than she said to him in Italian: 'My brother, the King of France, writes to me that I am to show you the most beautiful things in this Kingdom, and the first thing you see is myself, the ugliest.' To which Signor Gradenigo replied that the splendour of her virtues was so great that the whole universe knew how excellent she must be, being their source; and now that he had satisfied his eyes and fed his soul with the sight of her person, he cared to see naught else, being right well aware that the rest could not compare with her. Whereat the Queen smiled and said, 'Once on a time when I was a princess, I was more esteemed by your Lords than now that I am a Queen ; but you are afraid of that old fellow' —meaning the Pope.

16th August. THE FALL OF A HOUSE.

Last night between the hours of eight and nine o'clock at night, near to St. Bride's Church in Fleet Street, a house of timber, lately set up very high and not fully finished, suddenly fell down and with it an old house adjoining ; by the fall the goodman, his servant, and a child are killed.

18th August. THE QUEEN'S TOUCH.

This year at the touching the Queen touched ten, and then washed her hands, being served by the Lord Treasurer, the Lord Chancellor and my Lord of Essex, all three on their knees ; the Treasurer in the middle, opposite the Queen holding a basin, the Chancellor on his right with a ewer of water, and on the left the Earl of Essex with a napkin which the Queen used to wipe her hands.

19th August. THE CADIZ PLUNDER.

It is reported that certain ships followed the fleet not to do service but only to make private gain by buying from captains and soldiers commodities which they had got by spoils. By this means a great quantity of merchandise was taken into these ships and great store bought at an undervalue. Moreover, notwithstanding the order to the contrary, there hath been sale of goods both in Plymouth and other places. Gentlemen of those parts are appointed to take strict examination of such as can give any notice of commodity thus brought to land by these ships, and upon view of the nature and quality of the goods, the parties, if they shall be thought things fit to be sold, may have them again paying half so much again as they first gave. If any persons shall refuse to deliver up such goods, they shall break open their warehouses or chests, and commit the parties to prison.

THE ADVANTAGES OF THE CADIZ EXPEDITION.

By these late voyages much honour and profit has accrued to her Majesty. Being threatened with an invasion, she like a mighty and magnanimous prince, sent her army and navy to offer her enemies battle at their own doors, defeated and destroyed the best fleet the King of Spain had, and carried home in triumph two of his principal galleons, whereof one called the *St. Matthew* is thought to be equal with the *St. Philip* which was burnt. She hath defeated his fleet of galleys with so few of her ships, and when his galleys had such advantage, that their captain confessed on board the *Due Repulse* that forty galleys were not able to encounter one of her ships. She hath forced the Spaniards to deliver her poor subjects who were captives in the galleys, and in mercy has given up thousands of Spaniards who were captives under her. She has taken the fairest and strongest town the King of Spain had in those parts, and carried it as soon as her army was brought to look upon it. Her army was thirteen days on land, and no army of the King's dared look upon it.

She hath got two good ships to strengthen her navy, which were never built for £14,000 or £15,000, and her soldiers and mariners are made rich, and fit to go into any action or service, as well with more ability as greater courage.

As for the enemy, he hath lost thirteen of his best ships of war, two of which may serve to fight against himself. Of his Indian fleet he has lost forty merchantmen, all well appointed ships, as also four others that were in his harbour and bound for the Levant Seas. He has lost a town of greater importance than any especially for traffic with the West Indies; and therein his infinite sea provisions, the which will not be got together again for many years. His merchants have lost in the fleet that was burned twelve millions, and so much in the town that almost all the great traders in the Indies will be bankrupt. Above all, he has lost most in now being half disarmed at sea, and in being discovered so weak at home.

20th August. DISORDER ON THE BORDERS.

Proclamation is made straitly charging the Wardens and those that live within the Marches towards Scotland in no wise to make any incursion into Scotland publicly or privately. Great disorders have been committed by Scottishmen on the Borders, sundry murders, taking of prisoners, burning of houses, and taking of goods and cattle. Wherefore for the maintenance of the common peace between the Queen and the King of Scots, commissioners of both sides are appointed, amicably and peaceably to hear the complaints both of our nation and of the Scots, and to give speedy redress and satisfaction according to the laws and customs of the Borders.

22nd August. CAPTIVES IN ALGIERS.

There are yet eight Englishmen captives in Algiers that were left there by Captain Glemham three or four years since, still detained in very miserable sort until their ransoms be paid, for which a great sum is demanded for some piracy committed by Captain Glemham, who is since dead with very poor estate. The Archbishop of Canterbury is now moved to recommend a collection for these men, not only to relieve them out of thraldom, but lest they follow the example of others and turn Turk.

23rd August. MR. PLATT'S SUNDRY REMEDIES AGAINST THE FAMINE.

Mr. Hugh Platt hath written a little book of remedies against famine upon the occasion of this present dearth, compiled partly from his reading and partly from observation. Saith that an excellent bread can be made of the roots of aaron, called cuckoopit, or starch roots, also of pompions. If parsnip roots be sliced into thin slices, dried and beaten into a thin powder, of which one part be kneaded with two parts of fine flour and made into cakes, then you shall find them to taste very daintily. Travellers may make a speedy or present drink for themselves when they are distressed for want of beer or ale at their inn if they take a quart of fair water and put thereto five or six spoonfuls of good *aqua composita*, which is strong of annis seeds, and one ounce of sugar and a branch of rosemary, and brew them a pretty while out of one pot into another ; and then is your drink prepared.

29th August. THE TREATY WITH FRANCE SWORN.

The league offensive and defensive against the Spaniards between her Majesty and the French King was this day solemnly sworn by the Queen in the Chapel at Greenwich, before the Duke of Bouillon, and Viscount Turenne, Marshal of France, the Bishop of Chichester holding to her the book of the Gospel, and a great multitude of noblemen standing round about.

The principal terms of this treaty are that an army shall be raised as soon as may be to invade the Spaniard. Neither the King nor the Queen shall treat of either peace or truce separately without the consent of the other. Because the Spaniard at present infesteth the dominions of France that lie next to the Netherlands the Queen shall send 4,000 foot to serve for six months, and likewise for the same space in the years following if the state of England permit it; touching which the King shall stand to the Queen's affirmation and conscience. If the Queen be invaded and shall demand the King's assistance, he shall within two months raise 4,000 foot, which shall be sent into England at the King's charges. Each shall supply the other with all sort of munition and provision for war so far as may be done without prejudice to their own state. They shall reciprocally defend the merchants that are subjects of either prince in both their Kingdoms.

30th August. TWO NEW PRIVY COUNCILLORS.

This day, Sir Roger North, Lord North, was by the Queen's express commandment sworn of the Privy Council as Treasurer of her Majesty's Household; and at the same time Sir William Knollys as Controller of the Household.

THE QUEEN'S EXPENSES ON BEHALF OF THE FRENCH KING.

For 8 ships employed 3 months in the succour of Brest - - - - - - - -	£14,173
Bonds of the Duke of Bouillon to M. Sancy for £6,000 payable in 12 months - - -	6,000
Bonds, Sept. 1589 to Sept. 1590 - - -	50,233
Before he was King of France - - -	50,000
In Normandy, 1589 and 1591 - - -	48,502
In Brittany, 1591 and 1594 - - -	195,404
	£364,312

Since the year '89 there have been sent out of England to foreign parts 17,800 pressed men, and to Ireland nearly 3,300.

1st September. SPENSER'S 'FOUR HYMNS.'

Mr. Spenser hath written four hymns, of love and beauty, and of heavenly love and heavenly beauty, which he dedicateth to the Countess of Cumberland and the Countess of Warwick.

Noteth that he composed the two former hymns in the praise of love and beauty in the greener times of his youth, and finding that they too much pleased those of like age and disposition, he was persuaded by one of these Ladies to call in the same; but being unable so to do by reason that many copies were scattered abroad, he resolved at least to amend and by way of retractation to reform them, making instead of those two hymns of earthly or natural love and beauty, two others of heavenly and celestial.

5th September. VOLUNTEERS FOR THE LOW COUNTRIES.

There are needed 400 or 500 men to fill up the companies in the Low Countries under Sir Francis Vere. The Lord Mayor is therefore required to take up and imprest such soldiers or other voluntary men as shall be willing to serve, but not to take any man by force.

10th September. SOLDIERS FOR IRELAND.

For Ireland a force of 1,000 men is to be levied out of eighteen counties, and special choice to be made of able men of good behaviour, and not vagrant nor of the baser sort, which commonly run away from their captains as soon as they can find the means. They shall be assembled at Chester by the last of the month.

12th September. COMPLAINTS AGAINST LORD CHIEF JUSTICE ANDERSON.

Many complaints are made of the Lord Chief Justice Anderson this last circuit that he carrieth himself with so much wrath, so many oaths and reproachful words, that there is offence taken at it by persons of principal credit and note.

At Lincoln, Mr. Allen, sometime the preacher at Louth, a man well accepted, by occasion of a variance with a justice of the peace concerning a lease was indicted by this justice for not reading all the prayers at once. Mr. Allen was caused to go to the bar and commanded to hold up his hand there: and my Lord Anderson standing up, bent himself towards him with strange fierceness of countenance. After he had insinuated some grievous faults (but not named) against Mr. Allen, he called him 'one of the great distempers,' putting him out of countenance, and not suffering him to speak for himself. He called him 'knave' oftentimes, and 'rebellious knave' with manifold reproaches besides. The simple people rejoiced in their return homeward saying that a minister's cause could not be so much as heard at the assizes and gathered that all preaching was now cried down.

At Northampton he showed himself greatly grieved at the preacher at the assizes ; and at Leicester likewise, where he also fell out with the high sheriff and showed himself displeased with the grand jury. At Nottingham there was offensive variance between him and one of the justices about such matters.

16th September. THE DEPARTURE OF THE EARL OF SHREWSBURY.

The Earl of Shrewsbury and his company, together with Sir Anthony Mildmay that is the new ambassador to the French King, is departed on his way to France to take the oath of the King for the confirmation of this new league, and also to invest him with the Order of the Garter.

22nd September. THE QUEEN DISPLEASED WITH THE LORD TREASURER.

The Queen is highly displeased with the Lord Treasurer, with words of indignity, reproach, and rejecting of him as a miscreant and a coward for that he would not assent to her opinion that the Earl of Essex should not have the profit of the Spanish prisoners. The Treasurer wished that the Earl should first be heard that, upon the conditions with which the Earl received them, so her Majesty should direct the compt. But herewith the Queen increased her ireful speeches that the Treasurer either for fear or favour regarded the Earl more than herself. Coming from the presence the Lord Treasurer received a letter from the Earl of Essex, misliking him for the contrary reason that he would offend my Lord for pleasing of the Queen. The Lord Treasurer is now gone to Theobalds.

MONSIEUR DE REAULX'S UNFORTUNATE BREATH.

Monsieur de Reaulx that was about the Court on the French King's business is returned into France, and, as he gave out, to be married : but he was much troubled with a speech her Majesty did use of him which came to his ears. 'Good God,' said she, 'what shall I do if this man stay here ? for I smell him an hour after he is gone from me.' It is indeed confirmed by divers at Court that the gentleman hath a loathsome breath.

Sir Walter Ralegh is not pleased that the Queen doth not esteem his services worth thanks, and protests that he will go to the plough and never hearken after employments any more.

23rd September. AN AID TO THE FRENCH KING.

A force of 2,000, chosen from thirteen counties or towns, is to be sent to France to the port of St. Valery in Picardy for the defence of Boulogne and to be ready by the 8th October. The men chosen shall be able and sufficient who are not to be taken out of the select or trained companies. Of these soldiers half shall be pikes and of the remainder half muskets, and provided with good strong cloth of a russet colour and lined. Sir Thomas Baskerville is to be their commander.

25th September. ROGUES IN SOMERSETSHIRE.

The rapines and thefts by rogues and vagabonds in the county of Somerset are greatly increased, yet through slackness of the magistrates many when brought for trial escape because no evidence is offered against them. In the two assizes this year in all 40 were executed, 35 burnt in the hand, 37 whipped and 112 were acquitted. These persons have their sinews so benumbed and stiff through idleness that they will rather hazard their lives than work, insomuch that they confess felony to the magistrate that they may not be sent to a house of correction where they should be forced to work. Nor will the parties robbed willingly give evidence to the jury, for the simple country man or woman looking no further than to the loss of their own goods are of opinion that they would not procure any man's death for all the goods in the world.

Hence are arisen infinite numbers of wandering idle people. This year there assembled sixty in a company and took a whole cartload of cheese from one driving it to a fair, and dispersed it among themselves. Which things may grow dangerous by the means of such numbers as are abroad, especially at this time of dearth, who animate them to all contempt of noblemen and gentlemen, continually buzzing their ears that the rich have gotten all into their hands and will starve the poor. Of late a thief confessed that he with two others lay in an alehouse three weeks, in which time they eat twenty fat sheep, whereof every night they had one.

The Egyptians that had been cut off by the law again spring up; but they are never so dangerous as these wandering soldiers, for the Egyptians went visibly in one company, and never above thirty or forty of them in one shire. But of these wandering idle people there are 300 or 400 in a shire, and grown so strong that the constables dare not apprehend them. At a late sessions a tall man, a sturdy and an ancient traveller, was committed, and being brought to the sessions had judgment to be whipped; but he in the face and hearing of the whole bench swore a great oath that if he were whipped, it would be the dearest whipping to some that ever was. It strake such a fear into the justice that had committed him as he prayed the man might be deferred until the assizes, when he was delivered without any whipping or other harm, and the justice glad to have so pacified his wrath.

28th September. Sir Richard Bingham's Flight.

Sir Richard Bingham, the Governor of Connaught, that was commanded to Athlone to stand his trial because of the many complaints against him, is fled away secretly to England; whereat his enemies in Ireland say that he hath sought to shun this trial, being either overcarried by the greatness of his stomach to answer before the commissioners or stricken with the guiltiness of his conscience that he could not justify. But Sir Richard himself declareth that he is constrained to avoid the hard measure of his adversaries against him who work to the utmost his overthrow by indirect proceedings contrary to the rules of law and justice. He complaineth also that Sir John Norris put his brother Sir Thomas in his charge before the Queen's pleasure that he should be sequestrated was known; and moreover when he was summoned to Athlone, Sir John gave orders that he should not come through to Athlone but be stayed some five miles short, and have none of his friends near him, being used as a man utterly disgraced in the eyes of those base traitors which he had governed twelve years, and be at the mercy of the Irish to be murdered; none of his own horsemen or footmen to be permitted to come to meet him for his safety in passing through the country or himself suffered to lodge in the castle.

29th September. THE SCHEDULE OF DAILY PAY FOR THE SOLDIERS IN FRANCE.

The first and chief colonel for his ordinary wages 10s., and 30s. more for his diet and extraordinary charges. The second colonel at 10s., with an augmentation of 10s.

The paymaster at 10s.

To his clerks, 3s. 4d.

The commissary for musters at 6s. 8d.

	Daily pay.	Weekly imprest for victuals.
In a band of 200 men—		
The captain - - -	8s.	56s.
The lieutenant - - -	4s.	28s.
The ensign - - - -	2s.	14s.
The sergeants - - -	2s.	14s.
Two drums - - -	2s.	14s.
One chirugeon - - -	12d.	7s.
180 men, with 20 dead pays at 8d. each man		3s. 4d.
In a band of 150 men—		
The captain hath - -	6s.	42s.
The lieutenant - - -	3s.	21s.
The ensign - - - -	18d.	10s. 6d.

30th September. 'ULYSSES UPON AJAX.'

There is one calling himself Misodiaboles hath written against *The Metamorphosis of Ajax* (that Mr John Harington wrote) a libel called *Ulysses upon Ajax*, roundly rebuking the author for his immodesty therein. 'It is an affectation of singularity,' saith he, 'a fruit of discontent, a superfluity of wanton wit, a madding with reason, a diligence without judgment, a work fit for Volumnius the jester not Misacmos the courtier. In form contrary to all rules of science; in matter undecent, filthy and immodest: and touching the authorities, they are so weak and so wrested, as no chaste or Christian ear may in reason endure them.' He declareth that Misacmos hath no judgment to find a law of reason against the law of reverence, for many necessities, of nature to be done, are not plainly to be talked of; a circumlocution and a blush is sufficient to interpret a filthy necessity.

3rd October. HIGHWAY ROBBERS.

At the Sessions Richard Weekes, alias Hartrow, gentleman, and Thomas Simpson, a yeoman, were found guilty of assaulting one Kidwell in the highway, when they robbed him of £46 9s. 9d. in money. Simpson is found guilty and to hang; but Weekes stood silent and is committed to the *peine dure.* On the same day at Hampstead in company with one Hurford, known also as Marvyn or Browne, Simpson shot a labourer in the head with a dag. Hurford also is condemned for being present and encouraging Simpson to shoot the man.

4th October. ADVICE FOR MY LORD OF ESSEX.

There is one of his followers that hath written to my Lord of Essex very familiarly warning him of the danger of his present courses and advising him how he should carry himself for the future. The Queen, saith he, will see in my Lord a man of a nature not to be ruled; that hath the advantage of her affection and knoweth it; of an estate not grounded to his greatness; of a popular reputation; of a military dependence; nor can there be presented a more dangerous image than this to any monarch living, much more to a lady, and of her Majesty's apprehension. So long as this impression continueth in her breast, my Lord will find no other condition than inventions to keep his estate bare and low; crossing and disgracing his actions; carping at his nature and fashions; repulses and scorns of his friends and dependants; thrusting him into odious employments and offices to supplant his reputation. As for my Lord's particular disposition, when he happeneth to speak with compliment to her Majesty, he doth it with formality and not as if he feeleth it, whereas he should do it familiarly.

To win her Majesty's favour he ought never to be without some particulars afoot which he should seem to pursue with earnestness and affection, and then let them fall upon taking knowledge of her Majesty's opposition and dislike; such as to favour for void places some whom the Queen is likely to oppose unto; or to pretend a journey to see his living and estate in Wales. Nor should he neglect, as he doth, the lightest particularities in his habits, apparel, wearings, gestures and the like.

But that which breedeth to my Lord greatest prejudice is

that of a military dependence; he should keep his greatness in substance, yet abolish it in shows to the Queen; for she loveth peace; she loveth not charge; and that kind of dependence maketh a suspected greatness. He should not therefore at this time seek the Earl Marshal's place, or the place of Master of the Ordnance, because of their affinity with a martial greatness; but rather that of Lord Privy Seal, for it is the third person of the great officers of the Crown; hath a kind of superintendence over the Secretary; and it is a fine honour, quiet place, and with its fees worth £1,000 by year. And if my Lord shall pretend to be as bookish and contemplative as ever he was, it should serve his purposes also.

Another impression is of a popular reputation. It is a good thing being obtained as my Lord obtaineth it, that is, *bonis artibus*; but would be handled tenderly. Therefore he should take all occasions to the Queen to speak against popularity and popular courses vehemently; to tax it in others; but nevertheless to go on his commonwealth courses. There is also the inequality of his estate of means and his greatness of respects; for till the Queen find him careful of his estate, she will not only think him more like to continue chargeable to her but also to have a conceit that he hath higher imaginations; and nothing can make the Queen or the world think so much that he is come to a provident care of his estate as the altering of some of his officers; who though they may be as true to him as one hand to the other, yet *opinio veritate maior*.

6th October. RYE FROM THE EAST COUNTRIES.

There is a ship of the East Countries come to Harwich having on board 800 quarters of rye for use in the present great scarcity of grain. This ship has been stayed, but the Council order it to be transported to London without any delay lest by keeping the rye on shipboard it become corrupt and unserviceable.

7th October. MY LORD OF LINCOLN'S RETURN.

My Lord of Lincoln is returned from his embassage to the Landgrave of Hessen that he undertook to present her Majesty's gift for the baptizing of the Princess Elizabeth, where he was most princely entertained both at the time of the solemnity and in going and coming. Upon his parting, the Landgrave presented my Lord with princely gifts, as cups of ivory, amber and crystal, and to fit his humour with Turks and jennets. But 'tis said that my Lord hath left behind him dishonours, clamours, and curses for his base miserliness and insupportable fancies or rather furies.

9th October. MR. MORLEY'S INTRODUCTION TO PRACTICAL MUSIC.

Mr. Thomas Morley hath written *A plain and easy introduction to practical music* (which he dedicateth to Mr. William Byrd, another of the gentlemen of her Majesty's Chapel), set down in form of a dialogue; whereof the first part teacheth to sing, with all things necessary for the knowledge of pricksong ; the second treateth of descant and to sing two parts in one upon a plainsong or ground, with other things necessary for a descanter ; the third of composition of three, four, five or more parts, with many profitable rules to that effect. To the reader Mr. Morley writeth of the great travail and difficulty of this book, and if any in friendship shall make him acquainted with ought they mislike or understand not, he will think himself highly beholding to them. 'But,' saith he, 'if any man, either upon malice or for ostentation of his own knowledge, or for ignorance (as which is more bold than blind Bayerd) do either in hugger-mugger or openly calumniate that which either he understandeth not, or then maliciously wresteth to his own sense, he (as Augustus said by one who had spoken evil of him) shall find that I have a tongue also: and that *me remorsurum petit*, he snarleth at one who will bite again, because I have said nothing without reason, or at least confirmed by the authorities of the best, both scholars and practitioners.'

10th October. THE FRENCH KING'S ENTRY INTO ROUEN.

From Rouen comes news of the French King's royal entry on the 5th of this month, which was on this manner.

In the suburbs of the town on the further side of the river was erected a most stately room of plaster of Paris where the King stood to behold the companies, and to receive the townsmen's submissions as they passed. First the order of the Friars Capuchins followed their cross, their habit russet, all be-patched, girt with hempen cords, shirted with haircloth, wearing sandals only. This order may have but one habit for a man during his life; they feed standing and sleep sitting, they live by alms and are much esteemed of the people. Secondly came the Grey Friars; which order hath a library in their house containing six and fifty paces in length with three rows of desks all along, replenished with many excellent books both of philosophy and of the Fathers, the most part manuscript. Thirdly followed the Carmelites and Celestins, the Jacobins, the Augustines. Then proceeded the priests and chantries of the town in their surplices, singing, bearing forty-two crosses of silver, and every cross with the great banner of a Saint.

Then followed the mint-masters of Normandy, the merchants, receivers, customers, treasurers, advocates, procurators, and other officers of the palace. Then came Bachelors and Masters of Art, Doctors of Physic, Civil Law and Divinity, clothed in very fair and reverent garments of damask, satin and black velvet, and for the most part riding upon mules.

Then followed the officers and chancellors of the Chamber of Normandy; Judges and officers of estate in scarlet, to the number of forty; and the four Presidents of Normandy in robes of scarlet furred, wearing on their heads great caps of maintenance.

Then proceeded the several bands of the town, containing four regiments of foot and three cornets of horse, suited in green, russet and carnation satin and velvet, garnished with silver lace; their hats, plumes, scarfs and shoes white. After upon great coursers rode forty *enfants d'honneur* or henchmen, the properest and choicest young men of the town. Then came all the gallants and young gentlemen of the French Court, corvetting and fetching up their great horse, accompanied with divers of the nobility, Barons, Viscounts, Earls; the Knights of the Holy Ghost, being known by their blue ribbons and white crosses hanging thereat.

Then marched the King's three guards after their drums and fifes; the Swissers with shot and pikes, the Scots and French with halberds, the King's trumpets in horsemen's coats of green velvet and very well mounted.

At last came the King himself, mounted on a white courser, his own apparel, plumes and horses white, wearing the order of the Holy Ghost at a broad blue ribbon about his neck.

Sundry gates of triumph had been erected, whereof one at the bridge; where as the King passed, from over his head certain clouds opened and a voice was heard as from God, declaring His love for the King. Then there descended upon him the similitude of the Holy Ghost, and an angel presented unto him a sword called 'the Sword of Peace'; and the angel ascending declared that peace was returned again. Having passed over the bridge, he went up the street called *Rue du Pont*, where was set up a very stately pyramid, about a hundred feet high, and painted with the labours of Hercules, and inscribed with French verses, thus to be Englished:

'Hercules and Henry are semblable,
In virtues, words and acts;
But that Hercules is in the fable;
And Henry in the facts.'

Having passed by these and several others the King entered the Cathedral Church of Notre Dame with all the ecclesiastical pomp that might be, whence after certain ceremonies he returned more privately to his Court by coach.

13th October. SIR THOMAS BASKERVILLE'S INSTRUCTIONS.

Sir Thomas Baskerville, being appointed to command the two thousand English soldiers sent to France, hath received instructions to this effect:

Of the 2,000 soldiers, 1,000 shall be under his rule, and 1,000 under Sir Arthur Savage who shall be at his commandment when he shall have cause to require their service. The English soldiers are to join with a like number of French, sufficiently armed, in the towns of Boulogne and Muttrell and no otherwhere, except when the King shall be personally in Picardy. Further it is covenanted that the English soldiers shall enter into wages from the time they arrive at St. Valery until their return, which shall be at farthest at the end of six months; in which time they shall make their musters every month and give their oaths to the King's commissioners faithfully to serve the French King, saving all fidelity and allegiance due to her Majesty.

The soldiers shall for all faults against the order of their own colonels and their discipline be corrected by their own chief

Colonel, and if any other offences shall be committed against the King's orders general then the offenders to be ordered by the King's army, so as the colonels and captains of the Englishmen be called thereto for the assistance of the King's officers in their judgments.

The Captain General shall take care that the soldiers be preserved in good estate and provided of victual, lodging and other furniture whereby they may be continued without danger, and specially to have great care how to avoid the repair of any soldiers to any houses infected with the plague. And if he shall be required to serve in places where he knoweth the plague to reign, he shall in all dutiful manner protest against the same, and shall utterly refuse to put her Majesty's people in such evident danger, affirming that her Majesty hath sent her people to aid the French King against their common enemies but not to endanger their lives wilfully by infection of the plague.

He shall take care not to be drawn to hazard himself farther than the French are ready to accompany him, neither shall he put the people in any manifest hazard nor direct them to assault where the places are not likely to be recovered without danger of life and expense of blood. Moreover he shall use the best means he may that the whole forces of 2,000 may serve together.

Also, considering that they are in a strange country, the captains and officers of bands shall be charged to keep their people severely in good order without suffering them to quarrel with the French, or to spoil any houses or persons of the French, or to take any goods without payment; and especially that none of her Majesty's subjects enter disorderedly into any church or religious house, or use violence to any monuments. In both regiments the usual prayers shall be made, as near as may be, according to the use of this realm of England.

For the martial discipline of the forces there shall be used the same orders as were established for the army in Spain, which shall be published by proclamation immediately upon landing.

14th October. A THIRD VOYAGE TO GUIANA.

Sir Walter Ralegh hath set out his pinnace called the ***Wat*** under Mr. William Dowle to make further exploration of Guiana; and to-day the company sail from Limehouse.

15th October THE LEAGUE WITH FRANCE.

On the 9th of this month the oath of confederation between the King and the Queen's Majesty was very solemnly taken in the Church of St. Owen in Rouen, in the presence of the French nobility, who that day took the right of the choir.

On the next day the Order of the Garter was most royally performed in the same Church, where both Princes had their estates and arms erected. The Queen's Majesty being Sovereign of the Order had that day the right hand of the choir and so had the Earl of Shrewsbury (the Lord Ambassador) with his arms, style and stall accordingly. Before the Queen's estate sat Mr. William Dethick, Garter, Principal King of Arms, in his robe of the Order. Before the Earl stood Mr. William Segar, Somerset Herald. Next to the Earl, the Lord Ambassador Lieger; then the Lord Cromwell, the Lord Rich, and all other knights and gentlemen according to their quality. On the left side sat the King between the Bishops of Anjou and Evreux, and attended by his nobility.

All things being accomplished with much honour, the King's Majesty invested and sworn, the vespers ended, and the benediction given by a bishop in his *pontificalibus*, the King took the Earl by the hand and they returned as they came, attended upon by the nobility, who two and two preceded before them. That night the King and the Earl supped together under one estate in the house of the Duke of Montpensier, where also was a general feast for all the English.

17th October. THE FORCES FOR FRANCE STAYED.

The forces to be sent for France that await passage are to be stayed, the Queen having thought good to enter into deliberation again touching the sending or staying of them.

18th October. THE FORCES TO BE SENT TO FRANCE.

The Queen being again resolved that the forces for France shall be despatched and sent away with speed, the officers at London, Harwich, Gravesend and Southampton are forthwith to proceed to their embarking with as much expedition as may be.

20th October. THE CONTRIBUTIONS TOWARDS SHIPPING.

Although the Council have written several letters concerning the contributions to the charge of shipping in the voyage to Cadiz in some counties the money is still unpaid. In Somerset it is alleged that there is dearth of corn and victual and loss of cattle. Likewise in Dorset, Poole and Lyme Regis the contribution is unpaid.

23rd October. NASHE'S 'HAVE WITH YOU TO SAFFRON WALDEN.'

Nashe hath now published an answer to that book of Dr. Harvey written three years since and called *Pierce's Supererogation*, to which he giveth this title: *Have with you to Saffron Walden, or Gabriel Harvey's Hunt is up; Containing a full answer to the eldest son of the haltermaker: Or, Nashe his confutation of the sinful Doctor.* He speaketh very invectively of Dr. Harvey and of his family, saying that it is bruited up and down that Harvey pissed ink as soon as he was born, and haply some would conclude that he was begotten of an incubus in the shape of an ink bottle that had carnal intercourse with his mother. Dr. Harvey he declareth to be so enamoured of his own beauty, that he useth every night to walk on the Market Hill in Cambridge, holding his gown up to his middle to show himself, that the wenches may see what a fine leg and a dainty foot he hath in pump and pantofles; and if they give him never so little an amorous regard, he boards them with a set speech of the first gathering together of societies, and the distinction of *amor* and *amicitia* out of Tully's *Offices*. During the late plague the doctor lived upon Wolfe the printer, and thence passed into the country with Wolfe's boy as his servant, still owing £36; till at last Mr. Wolfe, perceiving himself to be palpably flouted, went and fee'd bailiffs who arrested him in the Queen's name, and without more pause hurried him away, making believe that they were taking him into the City. But when they came to Newgate, they thrust him in there, bidding the keeper take charge of him. Here after fuming for some time, at length the keeper's wife (the keeper himself being absent) came up to him. Whereupon he runs and swaps to the door, and draws his dagger upon her, with 'O, I will kill thee too: what could I do to thee now?' and so extremely terrified her that she screeched out to her servants, who burst in in heaps thinking he would have ravished her. From this Castle Dolorous he was at length relieved by the charity of the minister of St. Alban's, then living in Wood Street, who entered bond for him : and many like stories.

To Dr. Harvey's objecting to his beardless state, answereth that the doctor hath a beard like a crow with two or three dirty straws in her mouth, going to build her nest. In the latter part of the book refuteth some of Dr. Harvey's former sayings.

28th October. A GREAT ALARM FROM SPAIN.

Three pinnaces or carvels are to be despatched with all speed from Plymouth to discover the intentions of the Spaniard, for there is some very credible intelligence that there are great and speedy preparations making in Spain.

31st October. GREAT PREPARATIONS FOR DEFENCE.

Because of this news out of Spain many preparations are being made for the defence of the realm. Certain knights and gentlemen residing about London are by the Queen's special command to return for the defence of their counties. Three or four ships with all diligence to be put in readiness and sent towards Tilbury hope to give intelligence. From Hampshire and Wiltshire 900 men are to be sent to the Isle of Wight. At Plymouth and other ports along the south coasts the fireworks to be in readiness. In the counties the men formerly held in readiness are to be mustered in bands, and for every 100 footmen shall be provided 10 pioneers with instruments to entrench and fortify, and carts and small nags to carry their armour and weapons, with good supply of powder, lead and match, weapons for store and victuals. The watching of beacons to be continued or renewed with all diligence. The numbers to be put in readiness are 69,000; from the maritime counties 41,000 men and from the inland 28,000.

CORN SHIPS IN LONDON.

There are come into the Thames twenty sail of ships laden with corn from the East Countries. The Lord Mayor is required to take special order that this corn may be sold in such sort as the poor may be relieved thereby, and not ingrossed by such as use to buy great quantities to sell the same after at excessive prices.

2nd November. THE EARL OF SHREWSBURY RETURNS.

My Lord of Shrewsbury and those that accompanied him to Rouen are returned.

A PROCLAMATION CONCERNING THE DEARTH.

Because of the great dearth of corn this year proclamation is made against those ingrossers, forestallers and ingraters of corn that increase the price of corn by spreading a false report that much quantity of corn is being carried out of the realm by sea and thereby occasion given of want. Likewise it is straitly forbidden to carry any corn by sea out of the realm. Moreover sundry persons of ability that had intended to save their charges by living privately in London or towns corporate, thereby leaving their hospitality and the relief of their poor neighbours, are charged not to break up their households ; and all others that have of late time broken up their households to return to their houses again without delay. Likewise those that have charge of any castle or forts upon the sea coasts shall presently repair to their charges and there reside in their own person during all this winter season, and to have care how the forts are furnished, and to make petition for their defects.

4th November. VARIOUS OPINIONS CONCERNING THE SPANISH DANGER.

There are many advertisements from Spain of these great preparations and a purpose to come for England. It is said that every fifth man in Spain is taken for service, and that 40,000 soldiers are appointed, but most of them simple ill-apparelled boys. Mariners of all nations are constrained to serve, but there are great stirs among them for want of pay and victuals, and a great dearth both in Portugal and Spain. Wherefor some hold that an invasion is meant, others only some spoiling on the sea coast in revenge for Cadiz. Many think that they will invade the Isle of Wight, Portsmouth and Southampton or attack London from the Thames ; but all that this attack will be in winter when unlooked for and the Queen's navy not ready.

5th November. LODGE'S 'WITS' MISERY.'

Mr. Thomas Lodge hath written a book called *Wits' Misery, and the World's Madness, discovering the devils incarnate of this age.* As of Vain-glory: he walketh in Paul's like a gallant courtier, where if he meet some rich choughs worth the gulling, at every word he speaketh, he makes a mouse of an elephant; he telleth them of wonders done in Spain by his ancestors, where if the matter were well examined, his father was but a swabber in the ship where Seville oranges were the best merchandise.

Or of Superfluous Invention, who infecteth all kinds so that the ploughman who in times past was content in russet must nowadays have his doublet of the fashion with wide cuts, his garters of fine silk of Granado to meet his Sis on Sunday: the farmer that was contented in times past with his russet frock and mockado sleeves now sells a cow against Easter to buy him silken gear for his credit.

Or of Scandal and Detraction; that is a right malcontent devil. He weareth his hat without a band, his hose ungartered, his rapier *punto reverso*, his looks suspicious and heavy, his left hand continually on his dagger; if he walk in Paul's, he skulks in the back aisles. Well spoken he is, and hath some languages, and hath read over the conjuration of Machiavel; in belief he is an Atheist or a counterfeit Catholic; hath been long a traveller and seen many countries, but bringeth home nothing but corruptions to disturb the peace of his own country.

Another devil is Adulation, who generally goes jetting in noblemen's cast apparel: he hath all the sonnets and wanton rhymes the world of our wanton wit can afford him; he can dance, leap, sing, drink upsee freeze, attend his friend to a bawdy house, court a harlot for him, take him up commodities, feed him in humours. If he meet with a wealthy young heir worth the clawing, 'Oh rare,' cries he, do he never so filthily. He pulls feathers from his cloak if he walk in the street, kisseth his hand with a courtesy at every nod of the younker. If he be with a martial man, or employed in some courtly tilt or tourney, 'Mark my Lord,' quoth he, 'with how good a grace he sat his horse, how bravely he brake his lance.'

The devil Arrogancy is one that never speaks but he first wags his head twice or thrice like a wanton mare over her bit, and after he hath twinkled with his eyes, and chewed the words between his lips, to his servant he saith, 'My deminitive and defective slave, give me the coverture of my corpse to ensconce my person from frigidity'; and all this while he calls but for his cloak.

There is also Lying, that hath long been a traveller. If you talk with him of strange countries, he will hold you in prattle from morningsberry to candlelight. He will tell you of monsters that have faces in their breasts, and men that cover their bodies with their feet instead of a penthouse, and of many more incredible wonders.

And Sedition, the trouble-world: this devil, detected for some notable villainy in his country, or flying under colour of Religion beyond seas, is lately come over with seditious books, false intelligences, and defamatory libels to disgrace his Prince, detract her honourable Council, and seduce the common sort. This fellow in Paul's takes up all the malcontents, telling them wonders of the entertainment of good wits in other countries. In the country he storms and rails against inclosures, telling the husbandmen that the pleasure of their Lords eats the fat from their fingers, and these racked rents (which in good sooth authority might wisely look into) are the utter ruin of the yeomanry of England.

7th November. THE PREPARATIONS FOR DEFENCE.

Musters of the horse and foot are now commanded in all counties, so that there may be a view of the whole forces of the realm; armour and horses shall be taken from recusants and put into the hands of those of better trust. Such as spread false rumours of malicious purpose to stir up the minds of the people, which oftentimes happeneth in these troublous times, are to be committed to the common gaol. In the City 10,000 are to be furnished and had in readiness.

8th November. MR. SPENSER'S 'PROTHALAMION.'

To-day there was celebrated at Essex House the double marriage of the Lady Elizabeth and the Lady Katherine Somerset, the daughters of my Lord of Worcester, to Mr. Henry

Gifford and Mr. William Petre; in honour whereof Mr. Spenser hath written a sponsal verse entitled *Prothalamion.*

9th November. THE DEATH OF GEORGE PEELE.

George Peele that wrote *The Arraignment of Paris* after long illness is dead, 'tis said by the pox; and this day is buried in Clerkenwell.

14th November. A LAMENTATION FOR DRAKE.

There is a long poem called *Sir Francis Drake; His honourable life's commendation and his tragical death's lamentation*, published at Oxford, and written by Mr. Charles Fitzgeffrey. Herein is the fame of Drake extolled and commended to gods and men, his exploits related, and the great loss of his countrymen set forth.

> Spain clap thy hands, while we our hands do wring,
> And while we weep, laugh then at our distress,
> While we do sob and sigh, sit thou and sing,
> Smile then, while we lament with heaviness,
> While we our grief, do thou thy joy express:
> Since he who made us triumph and thee quake,
> Hath ceased to live; O, most victorious Drake.
>
> Proud Spain, although our dragon be bereft us,
> We rampant lions have enow for thee:
> Magnanimous Essex (heaven's delight) is left us,
> And O long may the heavens let him be!
> Great Cumberland and Howard yet have we;
> And O long may we have them and enjoy
> These worthies to our wealth, and thine annoy.
>
> These yet survive (O may they so for ever!)
> To make eternal thunder in thine ears
> With their heart-daunting names, and, like a fever,
> To make thee tremble all distraught with fears,
> When thou th' alarum of their trumpet hears:
> Eliza lives and while Eliza reigns
> Our England need not fear an hundred Spains.

18th November. A SPANISH STRATAGEM IN SCOTLAND.

The Spaniards in Scotland have a stratagem to make the Queen odious there. They have made a great number of ensigns with the picture of a headless lady, with an axe all bloody, and a shamble likewise bloody, with an inscription that the horror of this fact requireth a revenge from heaven and earth.

21st November. RECUSANTS TO BE COMMITTED.

About two years since divers recusant gentlemen of good hability and livelihood were restrained and committed, some to the palace of Ely, some to Banbury; but after bonds had been taken they were released. Now that the King of Spain is encouraged by the English fugitives beyond the sea that in his intended purposes he shall have the assistance of those that are backward in religion, it is thought meet that such recusants should again be restrained.

MR. DAVIES' 'ORCHESTRA.'

There is in the press that poem of dancing by Mr. John Davies entitled *Orchestra*, wherein Antinous wooeth Penelope, Ulysses' Queen, with a discourse of dancing, which, saith he, is a wondrous miracle devised by Love, and his proper exercise. Love shaped the world and the planets to dance, and the Moon to make her thirteen pavins in the year; and the winds also and the sea; only the Earth doth stand still for ever, for her rocks remove not. All things are ordered in dancing, as speech with grammar, rhetoric and poetry. To this the Queen maketh answer that Love's child must therefore be evil, but Antinous declareth that true Love danceth in all human actions.

DRAYTON'S POEMS.

There are entered three poetical fables by Mr. Michael Drayton, being the *Tragical Legend of Robert, Duke of Normandy*, the *Legend of Matilda the Chaste*, and the *Legend of Piers Gaveston*; of these the first being in the form of a dream seen by the poet, the last two related of themselves by the ghosts of the dead. Matilda, being approached by the messenger of King John, he tempteth her in these words:

> Wrong not thyself, nor yet the world deprive,
> Of that rare good which Nature freely lent,
> Think'st thou by such base nigardise to thrive,
> In sparing that which never will be spent?

And that is worst in age shall thee repent :
  Playing the churl, to hoard up beauty's pelf,
  And live, and die, and all unto thyself.

Fie on this lippish, lisping fond 'forsooth,'
This childish niceness, and these pettish 'noes,'
A graceful smile the wrinkling brow doth smooth,
Penance and Pleasure still are mortal foes,
Let springing youth rejourn old age's woes,
  Away with fasting, beggarly devotion,
  This is no way to climb unto promotion.

25th November. A THEATRE IN BLACKFRIARS.

James Burbage hath lately bought some rooms in the precinct of Blackfriars, near to the dwelling house of the Lord Chamberlain and the Lord Hunsdon, which he now altereth and would convert into a common playhouse. But the noblemen and gentlemen petition the Council that the rooms be converted to some other use, showing the annoyance and trouble that will be caused by the great resort of all manner of vagrant and lewd persons that under colour of resorting to the plays will come thither and work all manner of mischief; also to the pestering of the precinct, if it should please God to send any visitation of sickness, for the precinct is already grown very populous. Besides, the playhouse is so near the church that the noise of the drums and trumpets will greatly disturb and hinder the ministers and parishioners in time of divine service and sermons. It is alleged moreover that the players think now to plant themselves in the liberties because the Lord Mayor hath banished them from playing in the City because of the great inconveniences and ill rule that followeth them.

27th November. BEARD'S 'THEATRE OF GOD'S JUDGMENTS.'

Mr. Thomas Beard hath compiled a collection of histories out of sacred, ecclesiastical and profane authors concerning the admirable judgments of God upon the transgressors of His commandments, translated out of the French and augmented with more than three hundred examples. This book is dedicated to Sir Edward Wingfield and named *A Theatre of God's Judgments*, being composed in two books, the first of thirty-five chapters, the second of fifty-one.

Of Atheists giveth notable examples.

There was a certain blasphemous wretch that on a time being with his companions in a common inn carousing and making merry, asked them if they thought a man was possessed with a soul or no. Whereunto, when some replied that the souls of men were immortal, and that some of them after release from the body lived in Heaven, others in Hell, he answered and swore that he thought it nothing so, but rather that there was no soul in man to survive the body, but that Heaven and Hell were mere fables, and for himself he was ready to sell his soul to any that would buy it. Then one of his companions took up a cup of wine and said, 'Sell me thy soul for this cup of wine'; which he receiving bad him take his soul and drank up the wine. Now Satan himself was there in man's shape and bought it again of the other at the same price, and by and by bad him give him his soul; the whole company affirming it was meet he should have it, since he bought it, not perceiving the Devil. But the Devil thereupon laying hold of this foul seller carried him into the air before them all towards his own habitation, to the great astonishment and amazement of all beholders; and from that day to this he was never heard of, but tried to his own pain that men had souls; and that Hell was no fable according to his godless and profane opinion.

Holdeth that for the same sin our poet Marlowe was notably punished, his death being not only a manifest sign of God's judgment but also a horrible and fearful terror to all that beheld him.

Concludeth (as St. Augustine saith) that many sins are punished in this world that the providence of God might be more apparent; and many, yea most, reserved to be punished in the world to come that we might know that there is yet judgment behind.

28th November. THE FORCE SENT TO THE ISLE OF WIGHT.

In the late alarm the 900 men sent to the Isle of Wight were very ill chosen, being unable in their persons, apparelled very raggedly, and the furniture unmeet for service; which is a great marvel that so small regard should be used in the choice of men in a manner naked and without any provision at all for the defence of a place of that importance. Moreover the men arrived not at the Isle of Wight within nineteen days after the Council had given order for them to be sent.

1st December. THE EARL OF ESSEX DEFAMED.

It is noted of many that since his safe return the Earl of Essex, that was beforetimes given to carnal dalliance, hath sithence changed his former ways. But of late there are bruits that he infameth a nobleman's wife, and one near to her Majesty; whereat his friends marvel at a course so dishonourable and dangerous to himself. Being taxed therewith the Earl protesteth that the charge is false and unjust.

8th December. A DREADFUL SUDDEN TEMPEST AT WELLS.

At Wells last Sunday Dr. Rogers, being newly made priest by the Bishop of Wells, preached his first sermon in the Cathedral Church there before a very goodly auditory. In his sermon, according to a text which he had chosen, and having made no prayer, he began to discourse of spirits and their properties; and within a while after there entered in at the west window of the church a dark and unproportionable thing of the bigness of a football, and went along the wall on the pulpit side; and suddenly it seemed to break but with no less sound and terror than if an hundred cannons had been discharged at once; and therewithal came a most violent storm and tempest of lightning and thunder as if the church had been full of fire.

In this strange tempest all the people were sore amazed, many of them being stricken down to the ground, and the preacher himself being struck down in his pulpit. Many in the body of the church were marked in their garments, arms and bodies with the figures of stars and crosses, but there was no manner of mark upon any that was in the choir. This tempest brought with it a most terrible stench, and suddenly as it ceased, it brake down some stone work, melted the wires and irons of the clock but burned no timber. The storm being ended and the people beginning to come to themselves, the Bishop, being in the choir, spake cheerfully to them, inviting them to a sermon there in the afternoon, wherewith he recomforted them all.

10th December. THE SCOTTISH PRINCESS BAPTISED.

On Sunday, 28th November, the infant daughter of the Scottish King was baptised at Holyrood House, being carried and presented to the baptism by Mr. Robert Bowes, the English ambassador, supplying that office for her Majesty the only godmother. The child is named Elizabeth, the whole honour in the solemnisation of all the ceremonies being given alone to her Majesty, with good observation of all due compliments. It was very generally thought that the child should have been presented with some gift from her Majesty, but as Mr. Bowes had neither gift to deliver nor knowledge of the Queen's pleasure, he thought good to pass it over in the fairest and most indifferent terms he could for the best satisfaction of the King and Queen.

The Bailiffs and chief of Edinburgh have in the name of the whole town given to the Princess 10,000 marks; to be paid at her marriage. The grant and assurance for payment is written in golden letters, enclosed in a golden coffer, and delivered to the Queen for her daughter.

14th December. SEDITION IN OXFORDSHIRE.

In Oxfordshire there was lately a rising planned at Enslow Hill of 200 or 300 seditious people from various towns of the shire that met with design of raising a rebellion when most of the gentlemen of the shire were to appear in a law suit at the King's Bench. They would spoil the gentlemen's houses of arms and horses and go towards London where they expected that they should be joined by the apprentices. These men are chiefly young and unmarried, and not poor; three are now in safe keeping.

18th December. COOTE'S 'ENGLISH SCHOOLMASTER.'

There is entered a book called *The English Schoolmaster*, written by Mr. Edward Coote, schoolmaster, of teaching the reading of the English tongue by syllables; setteth down an order how the teacher shall direct the scholars to oppose one another, a short catechism, with sundry prayers and psalms in verse, concluding with a table of words difficult to be understood. Hath also a poem of the schoolmaster to his scholars, beginning:

> My child and scholar, take good heed
> Unto the words which here are set;
> And see you do accordingly,
> Or else be sure you shall be beat.

19th December. A Loyal Recusant.

Sir Thomas Cornwallis, who notwithstanding his difference of religion hath never been touched with any suspicion of disloyalty or ill affection towards her Majesty, is dispensed from the measures taken against recusants at this time.

A Strange Earth Moving.

In East Kent, at a place called Oakham Hill, there have been strange movings of the earth in divers places; the ground of two water pits, the one six foot deep, the other twelve at least, having sundry tusses of alders and ashes growing in the bottoms with a great rock of stone under them, was not only removed out of its place, but withal is mounted aloft and become hills, with the sedge, flags and black mud upon the tops of them, higher than the face of the water by nine foot. There were sundry other movings of the earth, the whole measure of the breaking ground being at least nine acres.

23rd December. Tyrone's Treachery.

Tyrone now giveth many apparent proofs of his bad meaning; he hath made public restraint of all victuals to be carried to Armagh, stopping the convoy and cutting off some of the soldiers that went with the victuals. Of late an attempt was made to surprise the place, wherein thirty-five of the garrison were slain, himself countenancing the matter in person. His kinsmen and followers make violent incursions into the Pale with open force up to the River of Boyne. He hath treacherously attempted to surprise the castle at Carlingford, where, missing his main purpose, there were carried away as prisoners in lamentable mannet two gentlewomen.

25th December. The Dearth.

The Council have written to the Lord Mayor putting him in mind of their orders last summer that all excess of fare might be avoided in public and private diet. And now because the greatest disorders are kept in tabling houses, taverns and inns, most strict order shall be taken that no persons have meat dressed in their houses at night on Wednesdays, Fridays or fast days; any that offend therein shall be committed to prison and their names certified to the Council. Moreover, in spite of her Majesty's proclamation, there are more gentlemen come out of the country and at this present about the City than in other years, for they come hither in this time of dearth to avoid housekeeping.

The Queen hath also caused the Archbishops to notify the Bishops to give strait order to all preachers that they exhort men especially at this time to abstinence and prayer, using all charitable devotion towards the relief of their poor neighbours, setting them on work, giving of alms and other charitable works. Further that especially at this time all persons be admonished not to give over housekeeping as many do, to live in good fellowship and discharge their servants to shift for themselves. Also the people shall be taught to endure this scarcity with patience and to beware how they give ear to any persuasions or practices of discontented and idle brains to move them to repine or swerve from the humble duties of good subjects, to the offence of God and displeasing of the Queen that hath so tender a care of their welfare.

26th December. CORN SHIPS TO BE STOPPED.

Owing to the great scarcity of corn, especially in Ireland, Sir Henry Palmer, Vice-admiral of the Narrow Seas, is expressly commanded to stay all shipping from the East Countries that shall pass by the Narrow Seas freighted with corn. This corn is to be sent to Waterford and Dublin, and for corn so seized Sir Henry shall give his bill and bind himself that, upon certificate from the place where the corn shall be unladen, there shall be good payment made to the owners or their assigns in London according to such prices as be thought reasonably worth, considering the place where it should be delivered. But if it manifestly appear that the corn was provided for Spain, it shall be seized as lawful prize. And for more assurance that these vessels with their corn sail immediately, to each of the ships shall be appointed one special man of trust and sufficient number of men to overcome the strangers if they should bend themselves to go to any other place. To waft these ships over to Ireland, the *Crane* is being sent out; and if the Vice-admiral think fit, the masters, factors and merchants of the strangers' ships shall be kept on board the *Crane* to prevent any practice against the Englishmen put on board, either of violence or carrying them to Spain against their wills.

OTHER BOOKS SET FORTH ANNO 1596.

THE BROWNISTS' CONFESSIONS.

The Brownists that are in exile beyond the seas have caused to be printed a little book called a 'true confession' of the faith that they hold; being led, as they declare, to publish this testimony by the 'rueful estate of our poor countrymen who remain yet fast locked in Egypt, that house of servants, in slavish subjection to strange Lords and laws, enforced to bear the burdens and intolerable yoke of their popish canons and decrees, being subject every day they rise to thirty-eight antichristian ecclesiastical offices, and many more Romish statutes and traditions almost without number: besides their high transgression daily in their vain will-worship of God by reading over a few prescribed prayers and collects which they have translated verbatim out of the Mass-book and which are yet tainted with many popish heretical errors and superstitions instead of true spiritual invocation upon the name of the Lord.' In this book are set down forty-five articles concerning the faith and duties of Christians, and very bitterly inveighing against the present state civil and ecclesiastical; as that Antichrist corrupted the offices and administrations of the Church and erected a strange, new forged ministry whereby all nations of the earth were forced to receive the Beast's mark and be brought into confusion and Babylonish bondage; that the Archbishops, deans, prebendaries and all others with the whole rabble of ecclesiastical courts are a strange and antichristian ministry and offices, and are not the ministry instituted in Christ's Testament, or allowed in or over his Church; that by God's commandment all that will be saved must with speed come forth of this Anti-Christian estate, leaving the suppression of it unto the magistrate to whom it belongeth.

A BOOK CONCERNING THE SPANISH SICKNESS.

A book by Dr. Peter Lowe, chirurgeon in ordinary to the French King, entitled *An easy, certain and perfect method to cure and prevent the Spanish sickness*, being dedicated to the Earl of

Essex, and treating of the causes, signs and cures of this disease. This disease was brought among Christians in the year 1492 by a Spaniard called Christopher Columbus with many Spaniards and some women who came from the new found Isles Occidental; afterward in 1493 when King Charles VIII. of France was besieging Naples with a puissant army, some of the Spaniards came to him, of which Columbus was chief, and spread this pernicious seed, terming it the 'Indian sickness,' which since hath its course not only among the Spaniards, who call it the 'Italian sickness,' but also among the Italians, who call it the 'malady of Naples,' for it began first to flourish in Naples. Amongst Frenchmen it is called the 'Spanish sickness'; in England the 'great pox'; in Scotland the 'Spanish fleas'; some call it the 'underfoot' because the infection often cometh by treading with the bare foot upon the spittle of the diseased. Some ignorant malicious people, saith he, call it the 'French disease,' without any cause or reason.

LAMBARD'S 'PERAMBULATION OF KENT.'

A new edition of the *Perambulation of Kent*, containing the description, history, and customs of that county. This book was first written in 1570 by Mr. William Lambarde, published in 1576, and now increased and altered after the author's own copy. There is added a new card of the beacons in Kent that was made by the direction of the late Lord Cobham, Lieutenant of the Shire, so that upon firing of the beacons a man with little labour might learn from the directory lines where the danger lies, and so confusions be avoided.

1597

1st January. BAD WEATHER.

There has been such great rain day and night that no one can travel on the roads either by coach or on horseback.

8th January. THE LATE INTENDED RISING.

Some of those charged with the late intended rising in Oxford being examined reveal that the matter arose concerning enclosures, for many in those parts have enclosed the common fields. One of them having complained to his fellow how hardly he maintained his wife and seven children with bread and water this hard year, the other made answer, 'Care not for work, for we shall have a merrier world shortly: there be lusty fellows abroad and I will get more, and I will work one day and play the other.' Saying also that there was once a rising at Enslow Hill when they were entreated to go down, and after hanged like dogs, but now would they never yield but go through with it. Servants were so held in and kept like dogs that they would be ready to cut their masters' throats. There was a mason in those parts who could make balls of wildfire and had a sling to fling the same whereby he could fire houses as occasion served. When they had risen they would go to my Lord Norris's in Ricott and get wine and beer, and take two of his brass ordnance and set them upon coach wheels and so proceed.

11th January. THE VICTUALS OF THE SOLDIERS IN IRELAND.

The soldier in Ireland when he is victualled from her Majesty's store hath in each week four flesh days and three fish days. On the former receiveth *per diem* loaf bread, 1½ lb.; beer, one pottle; beef, salt, 2 lb., or if it be fresh, 2½ lb., being without legs and necks. On fish days, loaf bread, 1½ lb.; beer, one pottle; butter, ½ lb., or instead thereof cheese, 1 lb., or 8 herrings *per diem*.

17th January. MR. NORDEN'S 'MIRROR OF HONOUR.'

Mr. Norden hath written a godly book entitled *The Mirror of Honour*, dedicated to the Earl of Essex ; wherein every professor of arms, from the general, chieftains and high commanders to the private officer and inferior soldier, may see the necessity of the fear of God, and the use of all divine virtues, both in commanding and obeying, practising and proceeding in the most honourable affairs of war ; a treatise most necessary, comfortable and expedient for all English subjects, whereby their duties to God, their Prince and their country, their assurance and safety, is lively set forth as in a glass before them.

Noteth the wicked assertion of a military man who affirmed that it is enough for the ministry to be masters of sin, and that it beseemeth soldiers to live like soldiers, to swear like soldiers, and to sin like soldiers.

23rd January. AN ITALIAN ARGOSY STAYED.

An Italian argosy of great burden, laden with grain and other provisions, that put into Portsmouth, is there stayed by the Lord Mountjoy. The Council order the grain to be unladen out of the ship and put in safe custody in the store houses at Portsmouth, and a perfect certificate made out of the quantity taken ; and that the master and others of the ship may not conceive amiss, as though any wrong was intended unto them, they shall be assured that the corn, being taken only for her Majesty's service, will be paid for in good sort at reasonable prices.

24th January. A GREAT VICTORY AT TURNHOUT.

From Sir Francis Vere is come news of a great victory of the Count Maurice over the Spaniards at Turnhout in Brabant on the 14th. The *rendezvous* being appointed for the 12th of the month at Gertrudenberg there arrived from all parts to the number of 5,000 foot and 800 horse. Next morning, by break of day, they began to march, drawing with them two demi-cannon and two large field pieces, and by the evening reached Ravel, one league from Turnhout. That night was spent in consultation, and in the end it was resolved to show themselves on the passage to Herentaulx, being the way of the enemy's retreat, with purpose if they left their quarter to be in the head of them ; if they abode it to plant the cannon and dislodge them.

At dawn they marched, and the vanguard hastened to get the passage of a narrow bridge half way betwixt the quarters ; which being gotten, and the troops put in order, some horse were sent into the enemy's quarter to know what they did ; who presently returned word that the enemy was marched to Herentaulx and that his rearguard was in sight. Hereupon all the horse advanced and they followed with the most speed they could. A musket shot from their quarter their rearguard stood to countenance some few of their men appointed to break down a bridge by which they had passed, and by which only they could be followed. With some few shot these were beaten back and the bridge taken, there remaining no more than to carry a man abreast.

When one hundred musqueteers were passed the bridge, our horse began to follow the enemy, and continued for near three hours with a very small number, the speed of the enemy and the badness of the passage making it impossible for our troops of foot to overtake the horse.

During all this time by many messengers the Count Maurice was advertised that, if he would send forward his horse, he might have a fair victory ; if not, the enemy would soon be in safety. At length he gave a good part of the horse to the Count Hollocke to go before, and himself followed with the rest. The enemy by this time were gotten into a heath and making great haste towards the entry of a strait at the end of it, which gotten they would be safe, being now not far from Herentaulx ; but now our horse began to appear on the heath. The enemy kept near the edge of the heath with their horse on the outside, marching in their battalions, not ranged in one front but in length, the Almains marching in front of the column, in the middle the Walloons, and last the Neapolitans who were the rearguard.

The Count Hollocke made the flank of them, and charged towards their horse, which fled. He pursued them not far but turned towards the flank of the Almains, at which time Sir Robert Sidney and Sir Francis Vere charging the Neopolitans, at one instant their vanguard and rearward were assailed and put in rout, and the mid battle kept them company. The Neapolitans keeping together were in a manner all slain on the place.

Of the rest there are escaped very few, for of 4,000 foot, by their own confession they acknowledge that 2,400 were left dead in the field, and 600 taken prisoners, amongst which are sixteen captains. Their commander, the Count of Varras (or La Verall), was killed in the charge, and all their ensigns taken to the number of thirty-nine. On our side twenty men were slain and less hurt.

That same night the troops returned to Turnhout, and the next day, after some few cannon shot, the castle was yielded by composition. From thence the army returned to Gertrudenberg, and every troop was sent to its garrison.

This blow will touch the Cardinal shrewdly, and, he being disappointed of those forces he kept of purpose in Brabant to make incursions, our men will be the safer, even though it should chance to freeze.

26th January. THE DEATH OF LADY CECIL.

On the death of Sir Robert Cecil's Lady many do write to console him in his great grief, and among them Sir Walter Ralegh to this effect :

'There is no man sorry for death itself but only for the time of death ; everyone knowing that it is a bond ever forfeited to God. If then we know the same to be certain and inevitable, we ought withal to take the time of his arrival in as good part as the knowledge ; and not to lament at the instant of every seeming adversity, which, we are assured, have been on their way towards us from the beginning. It appertaineth to every man of a wise and worthy spirit to draw together into suffrance the unknown future to the known present ; looking no less with the eyes of the mind than those of the body (the one beholding afar off, the other at hand) that those things of this world in which we live be not strange unto us when they approach, as to feebleness which is moved with novelties. But that like true men participating immortality and knowing our destinies to be of God, we do then make our estates and our wishes, our fortunes and our desires, all one.'

'I believe that sorrows are dangerous companions, converting bad into evil, and evil into worse, and do no other service than multiply harms. They are the treasons of weak hearts and of the foolish. The mind that entertaineth them is as the earth and dust whereon sorrows and adversities of the world do, as the beasts of the field, tread, trample and defile. The mind of man is that part of God which is in us, which, by how much it is subject to passion, by so much it is farther from Him that gave it us. Sorrows draw not the dead to life, but the living to death. And, if I were myself to advise myself in the like, I would never forget my patience till I saw all and the worst of evils, and so grieve for all at once; lest, lamenting for some one, another might not remain in the power of Destiny of greater discomfort.'

30th January. Mr. Bacon's 'Essays.'

Mr. Francis Bacon hath written a little book of *Essays*, being ten in number, *viz.*: of study; of discourse; of ceremonies and respects; of followers and friends; suitors; of expense; of regiment of health; of honour and reputation; of faction; of negotiating. There are added twelve Sacred Meditations in Latin, and a fragment 'Of the Colours of good and evil.'

Mr. Bacon's Essay of Studies.

'Studies serve for pastimes, for ornaments and abilities. Their chief use for pastimes, is in privateness and retiring; for ornament is in discourse, and for ability is in judgment. For expert men can execute, but learned ones are fittest to judge or censure.

¶ To spend too much time in them is sloth; to use them too much for ornament is affectation: to make judgment wholly by their rules is the humour of a scholar. ¶ They perfect Nature, and are perfected by experience. ¶ Crafty men contemn them, simple men admire them, wise men use them; for they teach not their own use, but that is a wisdom without them: and above them won by observation. ¶ Read not to contradict, nor to believe, but to weigh and consider. Some books are to be tasted, others to be swallowed, and some few to be chewed and disgested: That is, some books are to be read only in parts; others to be read, but cursorily; and some few to be read wholly and with diligence and attention. ¶ Reading maketh a full man, conference a ready man, and writing an exact man. And therefore if a man write little, he had need have a great memory; if he confer little, he had need have a present wit; and if he read little, he had need have much cunning, to seem to know that he doth not. ¶ Histories make men wise, Poets witty: the Mathematics subtle, natural Philosophy deep: Moral grave, Logic and Rhetoric able to contend.'

31st January. NEW PLAYS.

This month the Admiral's men have played two new plays, being *Alexander and Lodovick* and *Woman hard to please.*

2nd February. A DANGEROUS PERSON TAKEN.

There is lately apprehended one William Tomson, a very lewd and dangerous person, that is charged to have a purpose to burn her Majesty's ships or do some notable villainy. This man is to be examined concerning his devilish intents, and earnestly dealt with to declare by whom he hath been moved thereunto; wherein if by fair means and persuasions he be not moved to reveal the truth, then to be put to the manacles or the torture of the rack as in like cases is used.

5th February. A QUARREL AT COURT.

The Earl of Northumberland hath had a quarrel with the Earl of Southampton that was like to have proceeded to a combat, insomuch that my Lord of Southampton sent a gentleman with his rapier. Whereupon my Lord of Northumberland asked whether he brought a challenge; if so, he accepted it beforehand. The gentleman answered that he did not, only he brought his rapier. My Lord of Northumberland answered that he had not a novice in hand; he knew well when he was before or behind in points of honour, and therefore had nothing to say further unless he were challenged. But the affair came to nought, for by order of the Queen they were summoned to Court on bond of their allegiance and called before the Lords of the Council, who assured him, on their honours, that my Lord of Southampton had not spoken the words complained of, which afterward he affirmed himself. My Lord of Northumberland answered that he would rather believe their Lordships than any other; and the lie he had given was nothing. So my Lord Southampton hath revoked his challenge and they are made friends.

6th February. IRISH TRADE WITH SPAIN.

The Council have commanded that no ships either of traffic or of war from the ports of Waterford or Wexford in Ireland be permitted to go forth to the sea for the next six months unless very good bonds be given that they will not pass to any of the coasts of Spain or unto any of the King of Spain's dominions. This order is made because of the extraordinary preparations of the King of Spain, that in all likelihood are intended for Ireland, for which cause he stayeth and engageth in his service such serviceable mariners of other nations as do arrive there.

8th February. SPANISH DISASTERS.

An English pilot lately come from Ferrol declareth that he was pilot in the fleet of 90 ships, whereof 20 were men-of-war, that went out of Lisbon. Of these 45 were cast away between Lisbon and the Groin, one a great ship of 1,400 tons called the *Santiago*, with all the battery for the army; another the Admiral of the Levantiscos, with 1,200 men; 3 ships of 300 tons each, built by an Englishman called Lambart, with divers others all full of soldiers and provisions. In an Irish ship there were also cast away 14 Irishmen of name, capital rebels, and 200 common Irish soldiers. There now remain 70 ships of all sorts. They have great famine and sickness and daily look for provisions by sea from other parts of Spain. Their purpose was to go for Ireland, and they pretend so still.

THE BATTLE AT TURNHOUT.

In the late victory at Turnhout there were found about divers of the Spaniards which were slain certain inchantments and prayers in Latin, Englished thus:

'Whosoever shall carry about him this prayer hereunder written, let him not fear any enemy, neither can any weapon annoy him, neither darts nor other warlike instruments: neither the weapons of the inchanters, nor poisons, neither can the wicked spirit annoy him: he shall be safe at all times, and in all places. ✠✠✠

'*Barmasa* ✠ *leuitas* ✠ *buccella* ✠ *buicella* ✠ *agla* ✠ *agla* ✠ *tetra grammaton* ✠ *Adonai* ✠. Lord, great and admirable God, help Thy unworthy servant, N., from all danger of death of the body and soul, and from all the assaults of enemies, visible and invisible. ✠ There be ten names with which God is named, in whom ✠ they name God ✠ *Crux* ✠ *Ely* ✠ *Eloy* ✠ *Ela* ✠ *Adonai* ✠ *Corpus Christi cogi* ✠ *Sabaot* ✠ *Nomina Crux* ✠ the things are profitable to the servant of God, N., *hoc est enim corpus* ✠ *meum* ✠ *vt diligat me, Amen.*'

These and sundry others conjuring the weapons of the enemy not to hurt the bearer were found.

Since the battle little hath been done on either side. The Count Maurice sent the corpse of the Count of Varras to the Cardinal, who accepted it well, and yet was he buried without ceremony as one unworthy of any honour in that he had not better looked to his charge.

9th February. A NEW LOAN FOR THE QUEEN.

Her Majesty finding the charges sustained for preservation of the realm and subjects against their enemies so to increase thinketh it a reasonable purpose to require some present loan for the space of one year. The Lords Lieutenant are required to send for the collector of the last loan in their counties and by him and his books to understand the numbe and names of those that did lend sums of money to her Majesty in these later years; and if any be dead or departed out of the country to inquire who hath his lands and goods.

13th February. SUPERFLUOUS DIET AT THE ASSIZES.

The Justices, being about to go on their several circuits, are urged to make earnest admonishment to the Sheriffs to restrain their diets and entertainments at the Assizes, considering that these meetings were not ordained for feastings and prodigal expenses but for the administration of justice, and especially at this time of scarcity and dearth. They are reminded touching the abstinence from eating of flesh this time of Lent, that offenders against the orders should be punished; and also touching enclosures, whereby any highway is stopped, or villages or houses destroyed and dispeopled, or tillage greatly decayed; hereof they shall certify the Council.

COMPLAINTS FROM WILTSHIRE.

In Wiltshire it is declared that the soldiers despatched to the defence of the Isle of Wight last November were not sent back orderly so that their arms might be restored to the inhabitants that did set them forth; but very many of the soldiers being loosely dispersed ran away, and a great quantity of their arms and furniture (even to the number of 200) is either utterly lost or so broken and mangled as to be unserviceable. Moreover great abuses have been committed in the discharge of divers soldiers for sums of money. The Lord Chief Justice shall examine this matter very diligently, especially because, when like abuses have been committed before, the matter hath been so shifted from the county to those that had the government of the soldiers and from these again to the county, that it could hardly be found where the fault lay.

TROUBLES IN OXFORD.

The new Dean of Christchurch is much misliked of the students there who complain that like a new lord he maketh new laws, endeavouring an innovation that will enrich himself and undo the society. The cause of their complaint is that he seeketh to take away the allowance of commons enjoyed since the foundation of the college and to exchange for it an allowance of 2s. a week.

17th February. TROUBLES OF THE KEEPER AT WISBEACH.

The Keeper of the Jesuits at Wisbeach very earnestly craveth favour of Mr. Secretary because that two of his prisoners, both priests, are escaped from the castle by beating out the iron bars of their windows and letting themselves down by the bed cord. He would therefore have favour for three reasons; firstly, the prisoners escaped during his absence in London on a *subpoena*, wherefore his servants are to blame; secondly, because it was done in the night, when quiet rest is due to every man; thirdly, for that he is about to be married to a lady of sufficient ability, and if she should hear that he is in trouble, it might procure in her such an aversion that all his friends would hardly settle her again in any good affection.

21st February. COURT NEWS.

My Lord of Essex still keepeth his chamber, yet is he not believed to be sick. There is not a day passes that the Queen sends not often to see him, and himself goeth privately unto her. He giveth out very confidently that he will go into Wales, where his own land lies, to view it and see his friends. Sir Robert Cecil is now in greatest credit, the Queen passing the most part of the day in private and secret conference with him.

24th February. SIR THOMAS BASKERVILLE'S SOLDIERS.

The soldiers with Sir Thomas Baskerville are now at St. Valeries, their bands being weakened with the number fallen sick so that of late at a mustering there were found to be sick 300 and odd, but only fifty-seven missing. All their apparel is worn out, the bareness whereof in this wild, cold, and wasted country being a principal cause of their sickness.

25th February. THE LORD MAYOR REBUKED.

The Lord Mayor is rebuked for the great slackness in the execution of the orders for the restraint of killing and eating of flesh in Lent, and especially during this dearth ; which abuse is made known to the Council not only by the information of some few but almost every man in the City is an eyewitness to it.

4th March. COURT NEWS.

The Lord Treasurer is not well, and in this sharp weather keeps in. Sir Walter Ralegh hath been very often private with the Earl of Essex and is said to be a mediator of peace between him and Sir Robert Cecil, who likewise hath been private with him. Sir Walter allegeth that much good may grow by it ; her Majesty's continual unquietness will turn to contentment ; despatches for all matters of war and peace for the safety of the land will go forward to the hurt of the common enemies.

The Earl, wearied with not knowing how to please, is not unwilling to hearken to these motions made to him for the public good. He purposeth in three days' time, by her Majesty's leave, for some twenty days to go towards Wigmore Castle and so to Raglan.

9th March. A NOTABLE STRATAGEM AT THE CAPTURE OF AMIENS.

The Spaniards suddenly took Amiens by a stratagem on the 1st of the month, which is a shrewd loss to the King, for whole magazines of provisions for war are there with forty pieces of battery.

The capture was on this wise. The whole affair was under the conduct of the Governor of Dorlans, who had often been inside Amiens disguised, as the Bishop of Amiens confesseth. Hereby he perceived that the gate of the city which lieth on the further side of the Somme towards Dorlans was very carelessly guarded, especially at the hour of the sermon, to which all the good citizens went, leaving the gate in charge of mercenaries and common troops. He therefore chose out 700 picked men, sending on ahead fifteen or twenty of them, armed and with cuirasses, and carrying pistols and daggers, but disguised as peasants. Behind them came a waggon covered with straw, and conducted by the Governor himself, also disguised. The rest of the troops marched through the night and in such excellent order that by the hour appointed they were within a very short distance of the city.

About 8 o'clock in the morning, five or six of those in advance entered the gate, carrying sacks of nuts and apples as though they were peasants from the neighbouring villages going to market. These sat down within the gate, feigning to be weary, and waited until the waggon and the other men came up. Then the waggon, having come on to the bridge, stopped in such a way that half was under the arch of the gate where the portcullis would fall, and the other half still upon the bridge. Hereupon the men with the sacks, as though by mischance, spilt their nuts and apples, and the guard rushed after them; whereat the Governor cut the traces of the horses in the waggon so that it could not be moved, whilst his men with their harquebusses fired upon the guard and slew them. The men behind the waggon sprang in, and though the portcullis was lowered, it came down upon the waggon, leaving space enough for the soldiers to pass in and out. By this the main body came up, and having raised the portcullis and drawn out the waggon, they made themselves masters of the gate, and (which is more to be wondered at) they marched right through the city with their drums beating and flags flying.

At first they were in doubt what to do, as these few men had intended only to seize the gate, but seeing that no opposition was offered, they placed guards at the cross streets and in the square without anyone raising a finger. Then the commander sent the Spanish by companies of fifteen and twenty to traverse the streets, and when they saw any of the townsfolk on the roads or at the windows they fired on them so that not a man had the courage to stir.

And in this wise a great city of 50,000 persons, amongst whom were 10,000 soldiers, is taken by 700, with the loss of less than ten on both sides.

10th March. THE WARDENSHIP OF THE CINQUE PORTS.

Owing to the death of Lord Cobham, there is competition for the post of the Cinque Ports, the Earl of Essex very earnestly moving the Queen for Sir Robert Sidney, that is governor of Flushing. But she said he was too young for the office and Mr. Harry Brooke, the now Lord Cobham, should have it. Whereupon the Earl was resolved to leave the Court, and this morning, himself, his followers and horse being ready, about ten o'clock he went to speak with my Lord Treasurer; and being by Somerset House, Mr. Killigrew met him and willed him to come to the Queen. After some speech had privately with her, she hath made him Master of the Ordnance, which place he accepteth and is contented thereby.

11th March. THE OFFICE OF LORD PRESIDENT.

There is still no one appointed as Lord President in the north, and again the Archbishop of York hath written to the Lord Treasurer that someone be appointed. The cause of this delay is said to be the want of fit men, but is rather that the race of nobles whom the Queen found at the beginning of the reign having passed away, she by her wisdom and experience knoweth all the defects and infirmities of the nobility now growing up. Yet if the Queen could resolve on a man, her commission and instructions and the ordinary proceedings of the Court would sufficiently enable him. My Lord Huntingdon was very raw when he first came down, but having a resolute will to serve God and her Majesty grew to great experience.

12th March. THE LORD TREASURER'S GRIEF.

This morning died Sir William Hatton in Holborn, and the Lady Kildare, it is said, hath begged the wardenship of his daughters. The Lord Treasurer takes it very heavily and weeps pitifully, calling to remembrance the many late crosses he hath been afflicted withal by the death of his friends. Sir John Fortescue, going to Court, lighted at his house, but word was brought that his Lordship was not to be spoken with, and all are turned back that have any business with him by this accident of Sir William Hatton's death.

14th March. A WITCH HANGED AT LANCASTER.

At the Assizes holden at Lancaster on the 6th there was condemned and afterwards hanged one Edmond Hartley that had bewitched seven persons in the house of Mr. Nicholas Starkie, a gentleman dwelling at Cleworth.

About three years since the two children of this gentleman being taken ill very strangely he was at great charges of £200 for their cures; seeking remedy without due regard, first of a seminary priest, and then of this Hartley, that at first wrought some cure on the children, who remained well for almost a year and a half. During this time he would come to visit them; but at length feigned that he would go away into another county. Mr. Starkie therefore besought him to stay, and offered him a pension of 40s. a year; but after a time he would have more.

After this Mr. Starkie on a time going to his father's house, Hartley went with him. And being tormented all night long in bed, next morning he went into a little wood, not far off the house, where he made a circle, the compass of a yard and a half, with many crosses and partitions; which being finished he came back to call Mr. Starkie desiring him to tread it out, for he said he might not do it himself. This also being despatched, 'Well,' quoth he, 'now I shall trouble him that troubled me, and be meet with him that sought my death.'

When he perceived this and other bad qualities in him, Mr. Starkie began to be weary of the fellow, especially as his children grew no better but rather worse. He then sought, though secretly, for help of the physicians; after that to Dr. John Dee at Manchester, who wished him to crave the help and assistance of some godly preachers, with whom he should join in prayer and fasting for the help of his children. He procured also this Hartley to come before him, whom he so sharply reproved that the children had better rest for some three weeks after. But then they began to have their accustomed fits; first John Starkie, Mr. Starkie's son, then his daughter, and five other women of his household, three being children of 14, 12 and 10 years, and two women of 30 years and more.

It was noticed that when this Hartley meant them a mischief he would kiss them if he could, and therewith breathe the Devil into their bodies.

Amongst those afflicted was one Margaret Byrom, a kinswoman of Mistress Starkie, who would fall into fits when this Hartley came to see her. Hereupon some preachers, finding Hartley with her, asked him what he did with the maid. He said that he came to pray with her. 'Pray,' quoth one, 'why, man, thou canst not pray.' 'Yes, but I can,' quoth he. 'Say then the Lord's Prayer,' said the preacher; and he began to fumble about it very ill favouredly, but could not for his life say it to the end. They then thought him to be a witch, and caused him to be apprehended and brought before two Justices of the peace, by whom he was further examined and sent to Lancaster gaol.

When the assizes came, he was brought up, arraigned and convicted, Mr. Starkie having charged him with bewitching his children, which he proved sufficiently and made evident to the whole Bench. Howbeit for that they could find no law to hang him; whereupon Mr. Starkie called to mind the making of the circle, which being delivered on oath was received. Nevertheless Hartley stiffly denied it and stood out against him, and told him to his face that he should not hang him (for the Devil had promised him no halter should hang him); yet the jury cast him and the judge condemned him. When Hartley was hanged, the halter brake; whereupon he penitently confessed that he had deserved that punishment, and that all which Mr. Starkie had charged him with was true. And so he was hanged out the second time.

16th March. THE PRICE OF BEER.

These few days past divers brewers have appeared before the Council, some of them committed to prison and the rest bound to answer their contempt next term for selling beer at 10s. to 16s. the barrel, whereas no beer should be sold above 5s. the barrel for small beer, and 8s. the better sort. Nevertheless in answer to their petition that the price of malt is excessive, the Council will allow beer to be sold at 5s. for small beer and 10s. for the strongest.

THE EARL OF ESSEX'S PATENT.

The Earl of Essex cannot yet get his patent signed as Master of the Ordnance. Sir John Fortescue offered it twice to the Queen but she found some exceptions, and this afternoon the Earl took his Bill and presented it himself; but for all that it is not done, which moveth him greatly, especially as it is believed that the Lord Cobham's patent will be signed before or as soon as his. The Lord Cobham who, it is said, shall marry my Lord of Oxford's daughter, hearing how disdainfully my Lord of Essex speaks of him in public, doth likewise protest to hate the Earl as much.

19th March. A NEW PLAY.

There is a new play at the Rose called *Guido.*

20th March. FRENCH PIRATES.

Some short time since the *Bonham* of Poole being driven into Dartmouth by contrary winds met there with two ships of Dieppe, which continued in the port the space of two months; and they making forth to the seas a few days before the English ship and meeting with her shortly after, these two ships of Dieppe set upon the Englishmen, robbed and spoiled them of all their lading, goods and merchandise, with apparel, victuals, and other furniture, in most treacherous and barbarous sort, leaving them so destitute that they were like to perish.

25th March. SECTARIES TO GO TO CANYDA.

There are two merchant strangers, Abraham and Stephen van Harwick, and Charles Leigh, a merchant of London, that would undertake a voyage of discovery and fishing into the Bay of Canyda, and will plant themselves in an island called Ramea whence they hope to transport commodities of special use for the realm, and to establish a trade of fishing. These men have made suit to transport with them divers artificers and others noted to be sectaries, whereof four would go in this present voyage. This is allowed by the Council, provided that they shall not repair again into the realm unless they be contented to reform themselves and live in obedience to the laws established for matters of religion. Before their departure they shall swear oaths of true faith and obedience to her Majesty.

27th March. AN EXPLOSION IN DUBLIN.

From Dublin Sir John Norris reporteth a lamentable accident of the burning of six lasts of powder on the quay. The ruin of the town is exceeding great and by estimation twenty houses near adjoining are thrown to the ground, nor any house or church within the walls but is marvellously damaged in the tilings, glass and small timbers. Six score persons of all ages and sexes are known to be slain, but few English, besides sundry headless bodies and heads without bodies that were found. There is little appearance of this having happened by treachery, but it is guessed that some nail in the bark struck fire.

28th March. THE POSSESSED PERSONS IN LANCASHIRE.

The children of Mr. Starkie having still continued in their fits since the execution of the witch Edmond Hartley, the gentleman sent for Mr. Darrell, that wrought with the boy of Burton. At first Mr. Darrell was unwilling to come, but at the third sending he came on the 16th March to Cleworth, with Mr. George More, another preacher, and soon after their coming the children were thrown into their fits, and scorned the two preachers. For when they called for a Bible, the children fell a laughing at it and said, 'Reach them the bibble babble, bibble babble,' and continued with many other scornings and filthy speeches. The preachers determined therefore to fast and pray with the family. Having therefore the whole family together, and divers honest neighbours for the holding and tending of the possessed, they made entrance into the preparation, which was by way of exhortation, intreating the Lord to put the Devil to silence and that He would charge and command the spirits to hold their peace so that they might have good audience in praying and speaking the Word; which indeed came to pass at that time.

Morning being come, great preparation was made in the family to set all things in good order, and having a fair large parlour already trimmed, they brought in thither beds upon which they laid the seven sick possessed persons, all of them greatly vexed by their torments. It being now 7 o'clock they began the exercise of humbling their souls unto God, and continued with the exercise till 3 o'clock in the afternoon without much interruption; but then, as if Satan was much heated by fasting and prayer, they all brake out into exceeding loud cries, all seven roaring and belling in extreme and fearful manner. Then was there such struggling and striving between those praying and the devils, crying out so loud with such violence and extension of voice, labouring who should be loudest, till the preachers' voices were spent and no strength almost left in them. This battle continued very near the space of two hours, till they were exceedingly weakened; but at last it pleased God to weaken Satan's power, for the possessed were cast down suddenly and lay all along, stretched out as they had been dead; and every one of them afterwards declared that the spirit had passed out in the likeness of some ugly creature, as a crow's head, or an urchin (or hedgehog), or a foul ugly man with a bunch on his back.

In these possessions the children of Mr. Starkie have been very strangely afflicted, one of them, a girl of the age of thirteen years, being possessed, as it seemeth, with a spirit of pride that did most lively express both by words and gestures the proud women of our times, that cannot content themselves with any sober or modest attire. Whereupon she said, 'Come on, my lad,' (for so she called the spirit), 'come on and set my partlet on the one side as I do on the other.' And as she was setting of it, she said unto him, 'Thus, my lad, I will have a fine smock of silk, it shall be finer than thine. I will have a petticoat of silk, not red, but of the best silk that is; it shall be guarded and a foot high: it shall be laid on with gold lace; it shall have a French body, not of whalebone for that is not stiff enough, but of horn for that will hold it out; it shall come low before to keep in my belly. My lad, I will have a French fardingale, it shall be finer than thine; I will have it low before and high behind, and broad on either side, that I may lay my arms upon it. My lad, thy gown is crimson satin, but mine shall be of black wrought velvet, it shall be finer than thine. I will have my sleeves set out with wire, for sticks will break and are not stiff enough. I will have my periwinkle so fine, finer than thine. I will have my cap of black velvet with a feather in it, with flews of gold, and my hairs shall be set with pearls, finer than thine. I will have my partlet set with a rebater, and starched with blue starch; and pinned with a row or two of pins. My lad, I will have a busk of whalebone, it shall be tied with two silk points, and I will have a drawn wrought stomacher embossed with gold, finer than thine. I will have my hose of orange colour, this is in request, and my cork shoes of red Spanish leather, finer than thine. I will have a scarf of red silk, with a gold lace about the edge. I will have a fan with a silver steel and a glass set in it, finer than thine. My lad, thou must bring me a pair of gloves of the finest leather that may be, with two gold laces about the thumb, and a fringe on the top with flews and red silk underneath, that I may draw them through a gold ring, or else I will none of them.'

29th March. English Prisoners in Spain.

A poor mariner is lately returned to England escaped from St. Lucar. This man was one of the company of the *Little Exchange* whereof Captain John Cross was captain, that was taken by the Spaniards. Captain Cross and others were brought to Seville, where they had no allowances in their imprisonment but lived by the good help of the under-jailor who is an Englishman. There the English priests, Parsons, Thorne, and Walpole, that is head of the English college, came daily to persuade them to change their religion, and in the end so prevailed with the Cardinal of Seville that Captain Cross, Duffield, and Boyser, and eleven others were released and brought to the College, where all means were used to reconcile them to the Church of Rome, insomuch that they all reformed and received the sacrament; all but Captain Cross who was sent back to prison. While he was at Seville, seven persons were sent to England to be dispersed.

31st March. MENDOZA'S 'THEORIQUE AND PRACTISE OF WAR.'

The book of the *Theorique and practise of War*, written by Don Bernardino de Mendoza (that was Spanish ambassador here before '88) and published at Antwerp last year is now translated into English by Sir Edward Hoby. He counselleth that provisions or levies of men which are to be made for any manner of war, by sea or land, should be coloured with some different motive whereby no time may be given to the enemy to perceive it by preventing designs with the contrary. By no better means may this be effected than in sending upon such occasions ambassadors to those Kings who are most suspected would oppose, plotting with them treaties of new friendships and good correspondency according to the humour and disposition in which they shall find them, lulling them asleep with such offers as may hold in suspense and at the gaze the more part of the potentates.

'VIRGIDEMIARUM.'

There is entered a book called *Virgidemiarum*, to be in six books ; the first three books being toothless satires of matters poetical, academical and moral ; the other three not yet ready. Quoth the author :

> 'I first adventure with foolhardy might,
> To tread the steps of perilous despite :
> I first adventure ; follow me who list,
> And be the second English Satirist.'

2nd April. THE SOLDIERS IN FRANCE.

The great extremity that our troops endure by reason of the want of money hath caused Sir Thomas Baskerville to lay in pawn all his plate and all the other means that he hath to relieve them. Of late an enterprise was made to surprise Arras upon a vain hope and an uncertain French plot to blow open a port with a petard, assuring themselves by that to have entrance. But at their arrival there the strength of the place with little assistance from the town did frustrate their expectation. Our men had no loss but their toilsome march, though the French lost some few. In the camp the King is taxed for lechery, and Madame Gabrielle accounted cause of all ill-fortune, although every man seeth many nearer causes which cannot be remedied in that broken commonwealth.

5th April. 'CLITOPHON AND LEUCIPPE.'

A book called *The most delectable and pleasant history of Clitophon and Leucippe* is entered, written in Greek by Achilles Stacius an Alexandrian, and now newly translated into English by Mr. William Burton, being dedicated to the Earl of Southampton. Herein is related how Clitophon fell in love with Leucippe of Tyre, and how they fled from Tyre towards Alexandria, but being shipwrecked and separated both lovers endured many chances until they were strangely united in the Temple of Diana at Ephesus.

7th April. SEMINARIES TO BE BANISHED.

Her Majesty hath an intention to banish the seminary priests that are in divers prisons in the realm, and to this end the Attorney and Solicitor General and Mr. Francis Bacon are required to inform themselves what priests are in the prisons within and about the city of London and how far they are to be charged with any matter against the Queen or the State.

8th April. FORCES FOR IRELAND.

The forces that were levied for service in Ireland last October but afterward dismissed to their several counties are again to be viewed and mustered, and sent to the ports of embarkation by the last of this month, being in all 1,900 men, and in addition 560 men levied from the Midland Counties.

10th April. AN ENGLISH PIRACY.

One William Holliday hath behaved in very contemptuous manner towards Mr. Michael Leeman and certain merchant strangers of Holland and Zealand. Some four years since great spoil was made on the seas by a ship called the *Tiger*, whereof this Holliday was owner, and two or three others upon certain ships belonging to merchants of Holland. These spoilers going to the seas without commission carried the goods to Barbary and then sold them; they sank one of the ships, and threw divers of the mariners overboard. Upon complaint whereof to the States of the United Provinces there had arisen some tumult in such sort that, if special care had not been taken, the English merchants there had been in danger of the loss of their goods and lives. Whereupon for satisfaction of the merchants, order was given that such other prize goods as should be brought in by the malefactors and their ships should be stayed and the monies made thereof converted to the satisfaction of the damnified merchants. After this the *Tiger* brought into Plymouth a Spanish carvel laden with ginger, sugar, hides, and some pearl, which by order of the Lord Admiral was seized and Mr. Leeman appointed to repair to Plymouth with a sergeant-at-arms and letters of assistance from the Council. This was done, but the merchants that were spoiled received not above 2s. in the pound towards their losses. Since which time Holliday, in contempt of these proceedings, hath commenced an action of *trouver* against Mr. Leeman for the same goods, and by the deposition of some of the mariners, that then stood indicted for piracy and since are condemned to die, a verdict was passed against Leeman for most part of the goods. The Council have now written to the Lord Chief Justice to take order in this matter.

A Fray in St. Martin's.

This afternoon in the parish of St. Martin's-in-the-Fields two men, called Langton and Pinkney, exchanged insulting words and began to fight, Langton with a staff, and Pinkney with a rapier until Langton received a mortal wound in the upper part of his right arm and died of it a quarter of an hour after.

13th April. Two Ladies-in-Waiting punished.

The Queen hath of late used the fair Mistress Bridges with words and blows of anger, and she with Mistress Russell were put out of the Coffer Chambers. They lay three nights at the Lady Stafford's, but are now returned again to their wonted waiting. The cause of their displeasure is said to be their taking of physic, and one day going privately through the Privy Galleries to see the playing at *ballon*. Some days since the Earl of Essex kept his chamber three days with a great heat in the mouth which happened by overmuch exercise at *ballon*.

THE MARINERS TO BE STAYED.

The mariners that were appointed to be at Chatham by the 25th of this month are now to be stayed till the midst of May.

HOUNDS FOR THE FRENCH KING.

The servants of the Earl of Shrewsbury carry over to France fourteen or fifteen couple of hounds and certain greyhounds that are sent to the French King.

16th April. COURT NEWS.

There is news come out of Ireland that Tyrone hath yet put off the parley for fifteen days more. The two thousand foot are gone, and the Lord Burgh follows. This day he met Sir Oliver Lambart by the garden door within the Court; and asked him if he did not know him, and bid him put off his hat. The other said he owed him not that duty in respect of his usage of him. My Lord offered to pluck off his hat, which the other resisted and willed him to call to mind the place where he was. 'I do,' said my Lord, 'else would I have thrust a rapier through thee ere this'; and so they parted. About dinner time they met again at my Lord of Essex's, where my Lord Burgh secretly told him that he saw he braved him and bid him look to himself, for he would disgrace him. 'So I will,' said the other.

17th April. THE CLOTH TRADE.

The Merchants Adventurers complain that divers disordered persons, not free of the Company of Merchants Adventurers, trade with English cloths and other woollen goods to Hamburgh in Germany as well as to Flushing and Amsterdam in the Low Countries, contrary to the special privilege. Hereby in the markets of Stade and Middleburgh, being the established mart towns, there is great loss to the Merchants Adventurers and the abating and pulling down of price of cloths, a thing much prejudicial to the woolgrowers and clothmakers of the realm. The customers are now required to take bonds of every person shipping woollen commodity in other than the Adventurers' ships that they shall land the same at Stade or Middleburgh and not elsewhere.

THE NEW LORD CHAMBERLAIN.

This afternoon the Lord Hunsdon had the White Staff given him and thereby made Lord Chamberlain; and the Lords being in Council, her Majesty sent him to them, where he was sworn Councillor and signed many letters thereupon.

A Deceitful Practice.

One Ross, pretending himself to be servant to the Earl of Essex, with a counterfeit warrant in the names of the Council apprehended a certain Francis Barker in the county of Kent and brought him up to London, where he kept him certain days, shifting him up and down from place to place, and taking from him £47 in money and a gelding.

18th April. The Lord Burgh to be Deputy in Ireland.

The Lord Burgh, that was Governor in the Brille, is now to be Lord Deputy in Ireland to reform the many great abuses in that country. He shall inquire of the state of religion, for notorious negligence is reported, and even in the English Pale multitudes of parishes are destitute of incumbents and teachers, and in the great towns of assembly numbers not only forbear to come to the church but are willingly winked at to use all manner of Popish ceremonies. Many captains in remote parts have untruly informed the Muster Master of their full numbers. To reform this abuse he shall consult with such of the Council as have no interest in these abuses, and appoint commissioners to take monthly musters in all remote places; which will be a hard matter seeing the great corruption used herein.

19th April. The Earl of Essex and Sir R. Cecil.

Yesterday Sir Robert Cecil went in a coach with the Earl of Essex to his house, where Sir Walter Ralegh came and they dined together. After dinner they were very private, all three for two hours, where a treaty of peace was confirmed. Sir Walter hath taken upon him to provide victuals for three months for 6,000 men at an allowance of 9d. a man per diem. There is impressed unto him £3,000 a week for six weeks; he shall have Bridewell, Winchester House, and Durham House to be magazines for the victuals. He protesteth that he shall be loser by it, but few are of that opinion besides himself.

21st April. All Ships Stayed.

There is an order going forth for a general restraint throughout all the ports that no ship, hulk, or other vessel of what burden soever shall be suffered to depart until further notice.

23rd April. St. George's Day.

This day, the Court being at Whitehall, great solemnity for the Order of the Garter was observed. First, morning service in the chapel, with solemn music and voices, Dr. Bull playing; the Lords of the Order were present, who both in coming and retiring made three congées to the seat royal and so departed. Some hour after, they came again before her Majesty with all the officers of arms; and then came the Queen, with three ladies carrying her train, which were the Countess of Warwick, the Countess of Northumberland, and the Countess of Shrewsbury; the Earl of Bedford carrying the Sword before her, six pensioners carrying a rich canopy over her head. Then, after several congées there was short service, the clergy all being in their rich copes, with princely music of voices, organs, cornets, and sackbuts, with other ceremonies and music. Five new knights of the Order are made, being the Duke of Wirtenberg (that was formerly the Count Mompelgard), the Lord Hunsdon, the Lord Mountjoy, the Lord Thomas Howard and Sir Henry Lee. The Earl of Essex was exceeding earnest with his companions for Sir Henry, which he obtained. Then had he much ado to bring the Queen to give her consent to him.

28th April. The Stayed Ships.

The Merchant Adventurers have made humble suit that the ten ships ready laden might be permitted to go on their voyage, and will enter bond for their return by the end of May, unless hindered by contrariety of wind. This is allowed, seeing that there are ten ships with corn daily expected; also the five ships for Middleburg.

Deserters from the Irish Forces.

Of 47 men that were levied in Staffordshire for service in Ireland 10 are run away, and of the 47 men of Derbyshire 18, who are returned to their counties.

29th April. Dangers from France.

The Cardinal of Austria is now reported to have drawn great numbers of the forces out of the Low Countries towards the seaside and coast of Boulogne, a matter greatly to be regarded, which may breed great danger to the realm because it is uncertain what attempt he may make with this great preparation.

In Essex, therefore, Kent and Sussex, 600 are being mustered and trained to be ready on any occasion.

30th April. NEW PLAYS.

The new plays at the Rose Theatre this month are *Five Plays in One*, *A French Comedy* and *Uther Pendragon*.

1st May. A NOTABLE OUTRAGE ON A CORPSE.

In April last there died at Tonnerre in Burgundy one Monsieur de Lanne, a Doctor of Medicine, of the reformed religion, one that all right-minded men respected. Whereupon his widow asked of the Administrator of the Hospital that he might be buried in the burial ground there where several Protestants had already been buried. This was granted, but the Dean of the parish of Notre Dame protested, and for avoiding occasion of complaint the widow determined that the body should be buried by night. But when in the evening the friends of the dead man came together, news was brought that the monks of the Hospital would resist the burial by force, and that the Dean had assembled many lewd persons about the town to prevent it. It was agreed therefore by the widow that the body should be buried elsewhere, and so her friends departed, leaving only two women with the corpse in the house.

Being disappointed thereby, about midnight the Dean and his mob broke into the house, dragged the corpse into the market-place up to the pillory, broke open the coffin, wounded the body with pointed sticks, put cards in one hand and dice in the other, and would have set the body in the pillory had they not been prevented by some standers-by. They then took to insulting the body, threatening to throw it into the river.

In the morning the officers of the town, that had for the most part been of the faction of the League, had the body taken up by some peasants and buried without more ado in a dunghill, nor would they even allow it to be first returned into the coffin. Then they went back to the widow and demanded payment for their trouble, threatening that otherwise they would dig it up again and throw it to the dogs to eat. Nor would they allow any justice to be done to this woman without appealing to the King.

6th May. DISCONTENTS IN THE COUNTIES.

In the counties are many discontents by reason of this present scarcity. In the confines of Kent and Sussex divers have carried themselves in very tumultuous sort, inciting others with lewd words to commit outrage; wherefore it is purposed to renew the office of Marshal in the counties. In Norfolk, under pretence of need, some have entered into conspiracy to raise tumults and have begun with taking grain from the right owners by force and violence. In Sussex, Sir Thomas Palmer that was commanded a short while since to put in readiness 600 men was so slack and backward that the service was not executed, and is very sternly rebuked by the Council. At Hadley in Suffolk the Council have caused the Sheriffs to prohibit the officers of the town from making stage plays at the Whitsun holidays, for they doubt what inconveniences may follow thereon, especially at this time of scarcity when disordered people of the common sort are apt to misdemean themselves. Moreover the stage prepared is to be plucked down, and the officers informed that they are to obey this order as they will answer it at their perils.

9th May. MR. THOMAS ARUNDEL.

Mr. Thomas Arundel (that was made Count of the Empire) is again in close imprisonment for that of late he would have sent one Smallman, a soldier, to the Emperor's court that he might show his pedigree, whereby the Emperor should see that he had not bestowed that title of honour upon any base man. This Smallman is reported to be a dangerous man, one that hath been in Rome.

MUSTERS AGAINST INVASION.

The Commissioners for musters are ordered to have in readiness from the counties able men to the number of 6,000 to have special training to defend the realm and withstand the enemy that are now prepared to attempt some dangerous enterprise on the realm.

11th May. THE MAYOR OF CHESTER COMMENDED.

The Mayor of Chester is very highly commended by the Council for his diligence and discretion used in the transporting of soldiers to Ireland, for he so governed the matter of payment that he not only gave good satisfaction to all parties but yet saved some good part of her Majesty's charge. If others upon such occasions would use the like care, the Council would be less troubled in giving directions, and the Queen's service much better ordered than it is.

A Play of Humours.

To-day there is a new play of humours at the Rose, called *An Humorous Day's Mirth*, and written by Chapman. This play is of an old Count that hath a young Puritan to wife, who by a certain gallant is tempted to the Court and there mocked, so that she goeth back to her husband who would have hanged himself in jealous humour. There is a young gull who hath this humour in his manner of taking acquaintance, that he will speak to the very word of compliment after him of whom he takes acquaintance.

16th May. English Pirates.

There is a warrant for the arrest of a certain Captain Thomas Venables and his complices that in the ship *Dolphin* took by violence from the *John of Waterford* sundry parcels of goods and merchandises of good value belonging to the Earl of Ormond.

20th May. The Queen angry.

There hath been much ado between the Queen and the Lords of the Council about the preparation for sea; some of them urging the necessity of setting it forward for her safety, but she opposing it by no danger appearing towards her anywhere, and that she will not make wars but arm for defence, understanding how much of her treasure is spent already in victual only for ships and soldiers at land. She is extremely angry with them that make such haste in it, and at the Lord Treasurer for suffering it, seeing no greater occasion. Nor reason nor persuasion by some of the Lords could prevail but that she hath commanded order to be given to stay all proceeding, and sent Lord Thomas word that he should not go to sea.

23rd May. MacHugh slain.

News is come from Ireland that the traitor Feogh MacHugh is slain at Glynnes on the 8th, for our foot falling into that quarter where he lay, and coming several ways on him, he was so hardly followed that he was run out of breath and forced to take a cave where a sergeant to Captain Lee first lighted on him ; and the fury of the soldiers was so great that he could not be brought away alive. Thereupon the sergeant cut off MacHugh's head with his sword and presented it to the Deputy. His head and carcase are now brought in to Dublin, to the great comfort and joy of all that are in that province. Many of his followers have been slain. If this blow be as well followed as it is well given, the storm in Leinster will be calmed for a long time and the Ulster rebels, having lost so capital a confederate, will grow to better feeling of their own condition. Sir Calisthenes Brooke, Sir Thomas Maria Wingfield and Sir Richard Trevor are knighted for their services in this action.

THE QUEEN AND THE LADY MARY HOWARD.

The Queen hath of late much annoyance from the Lady Mary Howard, one of her ladies-in-waiting, for as much as she refused to bear her mantle at the hour when her Highness is wont to air in the garden, and on small rebuke did vent such unseemly answer as bred much choler in her Mistress. On other occasion she was not ready to carry the cup of grace during dinner in the Privy Chamber, nor was she attending at the hour of her Majesty's going to prayer. All which doth so much disquiet her Highness that she swore she would no more show her any countenance but out with all such ungracious, flouting wenches ; because forsooth she hath much favour and marks of love from the Earl of Essex, which is not so pleasing to the Queen, who doth still much exhort all her women to remain in virgin state, as much as may be. Moreover since the Irish affairs she seemeth more froward toward her women, nor doth she hold them in discourse with such familiar matter, but often chides for small neglects in such wise as to make these fair maids often cry and bewail in piteous sort.

The Lady Howard hath offended also in attiring her own person overfinely, which is rather to win my Lord of Essex than of good will to her Mistress. The lady is possessed with a rich border powdered with gold and pearl, and a velvet suit belonging thereto which hath moved many to envy ; nor hath it pleased the Queen who thought it exceeded her own. Wherefore the Queen sent privately and got the lady's rich vesture, which she put on herself and came among the ladies. The kirtle and border were far too short for her Majesty's height and she asked everyone how they liked her new fancied suit. At length she asked the Lady Mary herself if it was not made too short, and ill-becoming; to which the poor lady did consent. 'Why then,' quoth the Queen, 'if it become not me as being too short, I am minded it shall never become thee as being too fine; so it fitteth neither well.' By this sharp rebuke the Lady Howard is abashed and hath not adorned her herewith sithence.

26th May. A NEW PLAY.

The Admiral's men to-day played a new play called *The Life and Death of Henry the First.*

27th May. A DEBTOR'S CASE.

The Council have written to the Commissioners for such causes on behalf of one Francis Metcalfe, a prisoner in the Fleet. This man for a debt of £7 hath been detained in prison for the space of five years.

30th May. PREPARATION FOR AN EXPEDITION.

Of those men ordered to be specially trained for the Queen's service 4,000 are now to be set in readiness and shortly to be despatched to London, there being discovered a very urgent cause and fit opportunity to employ them.

2nd June. MR. ARUNDEL RELEASED.

Mr. Arundel is now released, since upon exact and careful examination he is not found guilty of any disloyalty, though this practising to contrive the justification of his vain title, contrary to his duty, is an act of great contempt. Nevertheless, the Queen, out of favour to Sir Matthew his father, hath remitted his punishment; but since his own house is haunted by massing priests he is committed to the care of Sir Matthew. It is not without cause for the State to be jealous of him, seeing by how strait an obligation he hath bound himself to a Prince so nearly allied to the Queen's chiefest enemy, and his own precious valuation of his title, which all other men do hold to be of little worth, doth give cause to believe that his own heart's love must be divided between the Queen and the Emperor.

SIR WALTER RALEGH RESTORED TO HIS PLACE.

Yesterday, the Earl of Essex being absent, Sir Walter Ralegh was brought to the Queen by Sir Robert Cecil. She used him very graciously and gave him authority to execute his place as Captain of the Guard, which he immediately undertook, and swore many men into the places void. In the evening he rode abroad with the Queen and had private conference with her; and now he comes boldly to the Privy Chamber as he was wont. Though this is done in the absence of the Earl yet is it known to be with his liking and furtherance. There is now love and kindness in all things between the Earl and the Lord Treasurer, and all furtherance given to his desires. About twelve days since the Lord Treasurer allowed the passing of a lease that by him was delayed these three years.

3rd June. LANGHAM'S 'GARDEN OF HEALTH.'

Mr. William Langham, practitioner in physic, hath by his long experience gathered together the sundry rare and hidden virtues of all kinds of herbs and plants into a book entitled *The Garden of Health*; all which simples, being plainly described in the book, can be gotten without any cost or labour, the most of them being such as grow in most places and are common among us. And for the better direction of the reader, the simples are set down in the order of the alphabet, with two general tables added, the one containing all the simples in order, the other setting down the names of the diseases and other operations needing these simples for any remedy for the same.

Noteth among many others, these remedies. A fig tied to a bull will make him tame though he be never so wild. The flowers of the bugloss comfort the brain, heart, memory and wit, ingender good blood, and void melancholy, madness and frenzy, and purge also the choler that cometh from heat. For chastity, commendeth *agnus castus*, docks, hemlocks, vervine, woodbine; but to provoke lust, anise, artichoke, carrots, garlick, ginger, mints, mustard, parsnips, radish and others. Briony is good for the rising or suffocating mother. For the hair; black and white helebore is good for worms in the head and falling hair, as also aloes, garlic, leeks, mustard, nettle, oak, walnuts, and others; milsoil maketh it to curl;

box, ivy, marigold, walnuts will cause it to be yellow. Barley, hemp and nettle cause hens to lay. These and many hundreds of others hath Mr. Langham set down.

4th June. ABUSES IN SOMERSET.

Great abuses have been committed in Somerset in the impresting of soldiers to be sent for the defence of Jersey and Guernsey, by the chopping and changing of the soldiers either by bribes or other partial respects, by the loss of arms and furniture, and by the loose dispersal and running away of men that after their implyoment should have been returned to their orderly trade and occupations.

8th June. MACHUGH'S HEAD.

The Council have written to the Lord Deputy of Ireland commending the service of Captain Lee in taking away that rebel Feogh MacHugh; but as for the sending over hither of the rebel's head (to make, as it is supposed, the fact of greater note or more acceptable to her Majesty), it would have pleased the Queen better that it should have been kept over there and bestowed among the fragments of heads and carcases of like rebels, for she would not have such ragged Robin Hoods to be regarded so honourably. Nevertheless because the meaning was good the error was less, and therefore the Council will send the head back again by the same messenger.

THE EARL OF ESSEX'S CLEMENCY.

One Chapman of Cunstall in Stafford was this day brought before the Council touching certain unreverend, lewd, scandalous speeches uttered of the Earl of Essex. Which words being proved, it was their Lordships' intention to have ordered him to be punished and to have appointed him to the pillory and to open whipping with loss of his ears had not the Earl prevented their resolution, who would not willingly have suffered the man to have been brought up had he known him to be so base and contemptible as he is. The Earl also signified his desire that the offence might pass for this time without the deserved punishment; and to this the Council assented seeing that Chapman made very humble submission, protesting that he uttered the speeches in great weakness and distemperature of mind after long sickness.

10th June. CALAIS.

A certain man newly come from Calais reporteth the place to be much fortified, a wall of earth and faggots made outside the ditch to the height of fifteen feet, but the old wall allowed to decay. There are 12,000 soldiers of all nations in twelve companies, but scarcity of victuals and mariners. The soldiers having only received a third of a month's pay since October are like to mutiny.

11th June. SIR THOMAS BASKERVILLE DEAD.

Sir Thomas Baskerville is dead in France. He lay sick not past five or six days and died raving; a man that loved not many to show them any extraordinary kindness, and is much taxed for covetousness; he is said to have detained a groat a week from every soldier upon pretence to have money to relieve them when they were sick.

Our troops are now before Amiens which the King besiegeth and in as great a lack of treasure as ever, some captains being five weeks unpaid, all four. The King hearing of their wants hath lent the companies now in the field 2,000 crowns and makes show to esteem better of them than at any time since their coming.

RUMOURS.

There is now great talk of these preparations for a sea voyage but it is not known where or how it shall be employed. The common sort talk of Calais, others of the Isles of the Azores, others that it is to set upon the King of Spain's navy wheresoever they can find it, or to meet with the Indian fleet. The whole number consists of fifteen of the Queen's ships, besides the two Spanish ships taken last year and now new fashioned after the English manner, twenty-two men-of-war of Holland, and twenty-four fly boats and hoys that serve for carriage of men and victuals. They have with them 4,000 pressed men, and 1,200 musketeers that come with Sir Francis Vere out of the Low Countries. The Earl of Essex is General both at sea and land, the Lord Thomas Howard Vice-Admiral and Sir Walter Ralegh Rear-Admiral. The Earl of Southampton, the Lord Mountjoy, and the Lord Rich go as adventurers; other noblemen pretend to go but it is thought they shall not get leave.

12th June. SIR ARTHUR SAVAGE TO COMMAND IN FRANCE.

Now that Sir Thomas Baskerville is dead, Sir Arthur Savage hath the principal charge of the 2,000 soldiers sent into France to aid the French King. He is to take order that as few Irish as possible be retained in his company, and those cassed as soon as may be, though those officers and others that have deserved well may be continued. The sick men shall be sent back forthwith, for it is a mere abuse that her Majesty should pay so many and have the service of so few. He shall not allow strangers to be passed in the musters, except it be two Frenchmen in a company that may be necessary to make any provision or otherwise to be employed on messages.

14th June. TIMOROUS GENTLEMEN.

Three gentlemen of the Isle of Wight recently left their livings there to dwell elsewhere; and, being rebuked for this desertion, they replied that they could dispose of their possessions as they pleased and make choice of their habitations where they listed. They are now very severely warned by the Council that if in a common danger they refuse to stand to the defence of their own and withdraw themselves for their private safety, her Majesty will enter into possession of it. Their ingratitude to her Majesty doth herein notably appear that it pleased her for their defence to send others thither that had no benefit by the Isle, yet they that have part of their possessions and living there would abandon the place and expose it to hazard: whereby they showed the weakness of their minds, unworthy of men fit to dwell in a commonwealth.

ABUSES OVER MUSTERS.

From the counties of Devon, Norfolk, Suffolk, Sussex, Somerset and Oxfordshire complaints of great abuses are reported, as of exacting or taking sums of money or other compositions of divers persons to keep them from being imprested, and in changing or dismissing others for bribes that were levied, also in defrauding the county of arms and furniture.

25th June. THE STATE OF IRELAND.

Ulster is now universally revolted; no part of it is free from hostility against her Majesty and adherence to the capital traitors of Tyrone. In Connaught not one of the six shires is free from revolt ; Sir Conyers Clifford with 21½ companies of foot is not strong enough to reduce the rebels to obedience, for his companies are weak and O'Donnell tyrannizeth over most of the people at his pleasure. In Munster two rebels followed by a rabble of loose people stand out, and several murders of English undertakers have been committed, but many of the murderers are cut off. Leinster by the late cutting off of Feogh MacHugh will grow to better terms of settling and conformity, though many of his followers remain.

30th June. NEW PLAYS.

At the Rose this month there are two new plays of *Frederick and Basilia* and *The life and death of Martin Swart.*

2nd July. THE 'WAT' RETURNS.

Sir Walter Ralegh's pinnace the *Wat* is come back safe to the Lizard. The company report well of the climate of Guiana, for though it standeth within the Tropic yet is it temperate enough, insomuch that they lost not a man upon the coast, and one that was sick before he came there was nothing sicker for being there but is come home safe. Of commodities there is great store ; whereof they bring examples, as a kind of long hemp, fine cotton wool wherewith the women make a fine thread that will make excellent good fustians or stockings ; great store of pitch, sweet gums, West Indian pepper, balsamum, parrots and monkeys. On their return divers whales playing about the pinnace, one of them crossed the stern and going under rubbed her back against the keel, but they sustained no loss thereby.

5th July. SIR ANTHONY SHIRLEY'S RETURN.

Sir Anthony Shirley, that left Plymouth at the end of May 1596 with five ships, is returned.

Not long after starting, being off Cape Verde, the General fell exceeding sick, and being hopeless of life and his company all dismayed and comfortless, he called his captains, masters and officers to him, and having his memory perfect made a very pithy and brief speech to them. He said that as they were Christians and all baptized and bred up under one and the true faith, so they should live together like Christians in the fear and service of God ; and as they were subjects of our most excellent

Sovereign and had vowed obedience unto her, so they should tend all their courses to the advancement of her dignity and the good of their country, and not to enter into any base or unfit actions. And because they came for his love into this action that for his sake they would so love together, as if he himself were still living with them, and that they would follow as their chief commander him whom under his own hand he would give commission to succeed him. All which with solemn protestation they granted to obey.

From this contagious filthy place they directed their course for S. Tome, but being by no means able to double the shoals of Madrabomba they were enforced to bear up and chose another course, for the men fell sick, and the water falling from heaven did stink and in six hours turned to maggots where it fell, either among their clothes or in wads of oakum. They departed therefore for the Isles of Cape Verde and landed upon the Isle of St. Iago, and here the General happily began to recover. And there they entered upon and captured the city of St. Iago, a very strong place, but being within they were so powerfully assaulted by the Portugals that they lost in the first assault eighty men; so that after two days they were forced to depart the town and make for the ships, having lost many men.

Thence they sailed to an isle called Fuego where there is a very high hill which continually burneth. Arriving at Dominica the 17th October with all the men sick and feeble they found two hot baths wherein the weak were greatly comforted, and in a month all made well again. From here they coasted until they came to the town of St. Martha where the Spaniards yielded to them, but could afford no ransom, only they took thence their ordnance and a prisoner lost there by Sir Francis Drake. Thence to Jamaica, a marvellous fertile island.

After other ill chances and in want of victuals, at last they shaped their course for Newfoundland, arriving there the 15th June, not having one hour's victuals to spare; and so after nine days they returned to England.

Mr. William Parker's Voyage.

With Sir Anthony is also come in Mr. William Parker, who at his own charges sailed from England in November last in the

Prudence, a tall ship of 120 tons, and a bark called the *Adventure*, with Captain Henn, having one hundred men in his company. In March he met with Sir Anthony Shirley at the Isle of Jamaica and went in his company till they reached Truxillo where they parted.

Mr. Parker then set his course for Cape de Cotoche on the East part of Yucatan, until he came to Cape Desconoscido. Here he put fifty-six of his men into a *periago* or Indian canoe, and leaving his ship six leagues from the town of Campeche, at 3 o'clock in the morning he landed hard by the monastery of San Francisco and took the town of Campeche, with the Captain and the *alcade*, finding therein 500 Spaniards; and in two towns close adjoining 8,000 Indians. The multitude of the Spaniards which had fled in the first assault by ten o'clock in the morning assembling together, renewed their strength and set furiously upon Mr. Parker and his men, insomuch that six were slain, and Mr. Parker himself was shot under the left breast with a bullet that yet lieth in the chine of his back.

Being thus put into shifts, they devised on a sudden a new stratagem; for having divers of the townsmen prisoners, they tied them arm in arm together and placed them instead of a barricado to defend them from the fury of the enemies' shot. And so with ensign displayed, taking with them their six dead men, they retired with more safety to the haven, where they took a frigate which rode ready fraught with the King's tribute in silver and other commodities, and brought it and the cannon to the *Prudence*. They took also a town of 300 or 400 Indians called Sebo, where they found champeche wood (good to dye withal), wax and honey. This done they left the coast and turned up to Cape de Cotoche again, but the *Adventure* with Captain Henn and thirteen of the men was taken by two frigates of war, whom the Spaniards afterward executed. After they had stayed five weeks upon that coast they shaped course for Havannah, and returning by the Isle of Bermuda, crossed over to the bank near Cape Race, and thence sailing for England fell in with Sir Anthony and reached Plymouth on the 3rd of this month.

6th July. A PROCLAMATION AGAINST INORDINATE APPAREL.

The great inconveniences that grow and daily increase in the realm by the ordinate excess in apparel have again caused her Majesty to make strait proclamation that the laws be duly executed. In this present time of difficulty the decay and lack of hospitality appears in the better sort in all counties, principally occasioned by the immeasurable charges and expenses which they are put to in superfluous apparelling their wives, children, and families; the confusion also of degrees in all places being great where the meanest are as richly apparelled as their betters, and the pride such inferior persons take in their garments, driving many for their maintenance to robbing and stealing by the highway. It is now laid down very exactly what stuffs may be worn by gentlemen and ladies in their several degrees.

SOLDIERS FOR PICARDY.

Seven hundred soldiers are to be sent as a supply for the forces in Picardy, to be gathered from the soldiers that were levied to serve in the voyage of the Earl of Essex but are now to be returned because that so many offer themselves voluntarily. The Lord Mayor is to make a privy search and to prest so many of the soldiers as he shall find new returned and such like vagrant persons of able body.

7th July. DELONEY'S 'JACK OF NEWBURY.'

There is a book called *The pleasant history of John Winchcomb in his younger years called Jack of Newbury*, the famous and worthy clothier of England that lived in the days of King Henry the Eighth, written by Deloney and dedicated to all famous cloth-workers of England. Herein is shown how Jack of Newbury was married to the widow of his master, and how she served him; how having become a man of great wealth after his dame's death he married one of his own servants; how he served King Henry; and how a draper in London that owed him money became bankrout, whom Jack found carrying a porter's basket, and set him up again so that he afterwards became an alderman of London.

8th July. THE COMPLAINTS OF THE COUNCIL OF WAR.

The Council of War of the fleet make great complaint that the ships are ill manned because of the monstrous abuse of the press-masters, who have furnished men of all occupations, of whom some did not know a rope and were never out at sea, while they let all the good men go at 20s. a piece. When they looked for a supply in the west, those of Dorsetshire sent not a man but all were either discharged underhand by the press-master or made a jest of the press.

10th July. THE FLEET ENTER PLYMOUTH.

The fleet are all come together safe to Plymouth, though as they were athwart the Bolt, three leagues short of Plymouth, a sudden storm overtook them with infinite lightning and thunder, and great wind, with the night exceeding dark save when the flashes of lightning came. Nevertheless God so blessed them that not so much as a boat miscarried.

12th July. THE FLEET SAILS.

The fleet sailed from Plymouth two days since with a fair wind.

VAGRANTS TO BE IMPRESTED.

The sheriffs and justices of Middlesex, Surrey and Kent are now bidden to aid the Lord Mayor to levy the 700 men for Picardy of the masterless men and such as have served in the wars, which will be a great ease and good to the country to be rid of those kind of people. And because they are more narrowly looked into by the provost marshals within the City than in the suburbs, the justices shall confer with the Lord Mayor that search may be made in the City, the suburbs and the counties at one time. Moreover standing watches shall be kept for the apprehending of masterless men, soldiers and vagrant persons, and as many as shall be taken shall be bestowed in Bridewell.

16th July. THE VAGRANTS.

Up to this time the Lord Mayor hath taken but eighty men, for the most part base persons and without apparel. It is not the intention of the Council that the City should be at charge to apparel them, but since the Lord Mayor may think it very unmeet to send men over to serve in the wars in such naked sort, they pray him to take order that the men may be furnished with such apparel as is necessary both in regard of the men and the honour of the realm, seeing they are to be sent over into a foreign country.

18th July. The Lord Mayor rebuked.

The Lord Mayor is rebuked by the Council because, when he received direction to take up masterless men, he, as it seems, would only apportion to the City to the number of 100, and so that there might be fewer of this kind of people found in the City, he published abroad the directions given him by the Council in order to drive them out of the City into the counties adjoining. These proceedings are misliked, and the Council again require him to make up the number of 250 or else he shall be required to answer his backwardness before them.

20th July. The Fleet driven back.

News is come that the fleet having been buffeted for four days continuously is driven back to port by the great and contrary tempests, but safe. My Lord of Essex is at Falmouth, Sir Walter Ralegh at Plymouth. So great was the storm that the beams, knees and stanching of Sir Walter's ship were shaken well nigh asunder, and on Saturday night they thought to yield themselves up to God, having no way to work that offered any hope, the men wasted with labour and watching, and the ship so open, her bulkhead rent, and her brick cook-room shaken to powder. Many of the gentlemen and the knights are returned extreme weak and dangerously sick, among them being Sir Ferdinando Gorges, the Sergeant Major, and Sir Carew Reynolds, captain of the *Foresight.* The ships are now repairing, but much of the victual is spoiled, and water lost by leaking of the casks; moreover the beer carried aboard the victual ships is found to be very unsavoury by the great abuse of the victuallers and London brewers, as well for their careless brewing as for the unseasonable stinking casks.

22nd July. The Earl of Essex at Plymouth.

The Lord General with his ships is now come to Plymouth and joined with Sir Walter Ralegh, being dismayed even to death by their mischances. My Lord was much aided in these distresses by the Admiral of the Low Countries.

23rd July. THE POLISH AMBASSADOR.

There lately arrived an ambassador from Poland, a gentleman of excellent fashion, wit, discourse, language and person, and the Queen was possessed that his negotiation tended to a proposition of peace. Her Majesty in respect that his father, the Duke of Finland, had so much honoured her, besides the liking she had of the gentleman's comeliness and qualities brought to her by report, resolved to receive him publicly in the Presence Chamber, where most of the Earls and noblemen about the Court attended, and made it a great day. He was brought in attired in a long robe of black velvet, well jewelled, and came to kiss her Majesty's hands where she stood under the state, whence he straight retired ten yards off her, and then with a strange countenance began his oration aloud in Latin.

The effect of his speech was that the King had sent him to put her Majesty in mind of the ancient confederacies between the Kings of Poland and England; that never a monarch in Europe did willingly neglect their friendship; that he had ever friendly received her merchants and subjects of all quality; that she had suffered his to be spoiled without restitution, not for lack of knowledge of the violence but out of mere injustice, not caring to minister remedy, notwithstanding many particular petitions and letters received. To confirm her disposition to avow these courses (violating both the law of nature and nations), because there were quarrels between her and the King of Spain, she took upon her by mandate to prohibit him and his countries, assuming to herself thereby a superiority not tolerable over other princes; which he was determined not to endure, but rather wished her to know that, if there were no more than the ancient amity between Spain and him, it was no reason why his subjects should be impeded, much less now when straight obligations of blood had so conjoined him with the illustrious house of Austria; and concluding that if her Majesty would not reform it, he would.

The Queen being much moved to be so challenged in public, especially so much against her expectation, after a short pause, answered him extempore in Latin. The words of her beginning were these: '*Expectavi Legationem, mihi vero querelam adduxisti*'; and continuing to this effect: 'Is this the business the King has sent you about? Surely I can hardly believe that if the King himself were present, he would have used such language; for if he should, I must have thought that being a King not of many years, and that *non de iure sanguinis sed iure electionis, immo noviter electus*, he may haply be uninformed of that course which his father and ancestors have taken with us, and which peradventure shall be observed by those that shall live to come after us. And as for you, although I perceive you have read many books to fortify your arguments in this case, yet I am apt to believe that you have not lighted upon the chapter that prescribes the form to be used between kings and princes; but were it not for the place you hold, to have so publicly an imputation thrown upon our justice, which as yet never failed, we would answer this audacity of yours in another style. And for the particulars of your negotiations, we will appoint some of our Council to confer with you, to see upon what ground this clamour of yours hath his foundation.'

24th July. THE POLISH AMBASSADOR.

The merchants that trade to Danzic or other parts in the East Countries forbear all offices of ceremony towards the Polish ambassador, as of visitation, sending presents or whatsoever of the like gratification, until it is resolved on the answer to be given him.

28th July. THE PLAYHOUSES ORDERED TO BE PLUCKED DOWN.

The Lord Mayor and Aldermen have again petitioned the Council for the present stay and final suppression of stage plays at the Theatre, Curtain, Bankside and all other places, alleging four reasons in particular.

Firstly, they corrupt youth, containing nothing but unchaste matters and ungodly practices which impress the very quality and corruption of manners which they represent, contrary to the rules and art prescribed for them even among the heathen, who used them seldom and at set times and not all the year long.

Secondly, they are the ordinary places for vagrant persons, masterless men, thieves, horse-stealers, whoremongers, coseners, connycatchers, contrivers of treason and other dangerous persons to meet together and to make their matches, which cannot be prevented when discovered by the governors of the City, for that they are out of the City's jurisdiction.

Thirdly, they maintain idleness in persons with no vocation and draw prentices and other servants from their ordinary work, and all sorts from resort to sermons and other Christian exercises, to the great hindrance of trades and profanation of religion.

Fourthly, in time of sickness many having sores and yet not heartsick take occasion to walk abroad and hear a play, whereby others are infected and themselves also many times miscarry.

In answer to this petition the Council direct that not only shall no plays be used in London during this summer, but that the Curtain and Theatre in Shoreditch and the playhouses on the Bankside shall be plucked down, and present order taken that no plays be used in any public place within three miles of the City till Allhallow tide. Likewise the magistrates shall send for the owners of the playhouses and enjoin them to pluck down quite the stages, galleries and rooms and so to deface them that they may not again be employed to such use.

A LEWD PLAY.

Much offence also is caused by a play called *The Isle of Dogs*, full of seditious and slanderous matter, written by Nashe and Jonson, and played by my Lord of Pembroke's men at the Swan. Nashe is fled away, but Spencer, Shaa and Jonson (who also acted in the play) are apprehended and committed to prison. Playing is now stayed.

29th July. TROUBLES ON THE BORDER AND IN IRELAND.

There is almost hourly complaint of devastation upon the Scottish Border, wherefore the Queen hath commanded that those principal gentlemen of the Border, as the Witheringtons, the Selbys and others, that are with the fleet at Plymouth shall be sent back.

In Ireland my Lord Burgh hath taken the fort at Blackwater on the 14th in a skirmish between some of the traitors' horse and foot; but his horse, led by Captain Turner, the Sergeant Major, engaged themselves too far into a wood so that he and nine others were slain. My Lord recovered the bodies, made good the place and killed 200 hard upon Tyrone's own camp, who hath 5,000 men near Duncannon. The place was well defended, as they had cast up sundry trenches and laid pikes in the ford, but my Lord led the vanguard himself and was the second man inside the fort.

2nd August. Lord Howard's Ships return.

The ships of Lord Thomas Howard are now returned safe to Plymouth, having been separated in the storm that drove back my Lord of Essex.

7th August. The Picardy Forces delayed.

The two hoys that were to transport 400 men under command of Captain Henry Poore have for some days been delayed by contrariety of winds.

13th August. A Proclamation concerning the Scottish Border.

A proclamation is published commanding those that live on the Border to live in peace and quietness and to offer no manner of incursion, stealth or injury, since the King of Scots is desirous to yield satisfaction for the injuries committed by his subjects. Nevertheless if any offence shall be offered by the opposites which shall not presently be satisfied according to the laws of the frontier, the Queen will not only leave her subjects to their liberty of just revenge, but will further enable them with extraordinary powers. The King of Scots proposeth likewise to inform his subjects of this determination of the Queen.

17th August. A Malicious Mayor.

Of late the Mayor of Wareham, under colour of a warrant from the Deputy Lieutenant for the impresting of certain soldiers, to serve a private grudge did imprest one Richard Berd, a man of 60 years old and one that hath borne office of Mayor in that town, and reputed a subsidy man.

19th August. The Fleet again sails.

Two days since the fleet again set forth from Plymouth, but much abated from the first assembly; for the former violent tempests much cooled and battered the courage of many of our young gentlemen, who, seeing that the winds and sea have affinity neither with London delicacy nor Court bravery, secretly retire themselves home, forgetting either to bid their friends farewell or to take leave of their General.

20th August. THE ALMSHOUSE AT STAMFORD.

The Lord Treasurer hath caused to be published the articles drawn up for the order and government of the hospital for a warden and twelve poor men that he hath founded at Stamford in Northampton; amongst which articles be these:

None to be named except those that have dwelt for seven years within seven miles of the Borough of Stamford, nor that is under 30 years of age, or hath a certainty of living of 53s. 4d. by the year, or is known to be diseased of any leprosy, or of the pox known as the French pox, or of any lunacy, or be a common drunkard, barretor, or infamous for theft, adultery, or the like. And any that after their choice shall fall into such infirmities of infectious diseases, or be infamed and convinced of such notable vices, shall be displaced. Nor shall any of these twelve poor men in alehouses or other places play at cards, dice or any unlawful game.

Everyone of them shall resort in their livery gowns to Common Prayer every Sunday, Wednesday, Friday and holy day to St. Martin's Church at morning and evening prayer; neither shall any be absent without just cause notified to the Vicar, and allowed by him; and for every default not excusable, the Parish Clerk shall have 6d. out of the wages allowed to the poor man.

There shall be paid to them every Sunday after evening prayer, to the Warden of the Hospital 3s., and to every other of the poor men 2s. 4d.

Upon the first Sunday of every quarter of the year, the Vicar shall assemble them together in the church before evening prayer, and severing them asunder shall hear them say the Lord's Prayer, and the Creed, and to answer to the Commandments. And he that shall not be able to say the same, after fourteen days' space given him to learn them, shall be avoided from his room. For this labour the Vicar to have 5s. every such Sunday, and the Parish Clerk 12d. for attending on the Vicar.

Upon this same Sunday, if the Lord of Burleigh or his lady keep house there, the poor men shall dine together at one table in the hall, and there receive two messes of meat, every mess being of two dishes, one with pottage and boiled meat, the other of roast; but if it be a fasting day then shall the messes be of white meat and fish. And if the Lord of Burleigh be absent, then each shall receive 4d.

For the maintenance of this almshouse, the Lord Burleigh giveth an annuity of £100 out of his lands called Cliff Park.

21st August. INGROSSERS.

Although Almighty God hath mercifully withdrawn His heavy hand wherewith we were deservedly punished by an universal scarcity through the unseasonable weather and now yieldeth us a change to the great comfort of all sorts of people, yet are there seen a number of wicked people, more like to wolves and cormorants than natural men, that most covetously seek to hold up the late great prices of corn and all other victuals by ingrossing the same into their private hands, bargaining beforehand for corn and in some part for grain growing, and for butter and cheese before it be brought to ordinary markets. The sheriffs shall therefore send up to the Council the names of all such; and for that in certain counties men of good livelihood and in estimation of worship enrich themselves by such ingrossings, the sheriffs shall seek to reform them, not only with sharp reprehensions but also certify their names, and thereby avoid the just offence of the inferior sort which cannot but be grieved to see such corruption of the better sort suffered without restraint.

22nd August. A BOOK ON CHEATING.

There is a book called *Mihil Mumchance, His discovery of the art of Cheating in false dice play and other unlawful games,* showing also divers new devices of cosenage practised at fairs and markets, with many deceitful practices used by bad and lewd women. At fairs and markets there are some who, attiring themselves in mean attire, will buy a piece of very fine lawn or holland, worth £5 or £6, bound up very handsomely, with another bundle bound up after the same manner but within stuffed with nothing but old rags and such trash. These bundles the cheater will carry till he meeteth with some simple countryman that seemeth to have store of crowns, to whom very secretly, as if he had gotten the lawn by stealth, he will proffer it at half its worth. The simple countryman being covetous of a good pennyworth bargains with him, and gives all the money in his purse, which is not above 40s. or 50s. Then the cheater having got the money pockets it up and bobs the poor man with the counterfeit bundle of rags, reserving the other bundle still to himself.

These cheaters have a treasurer, a very trusty secret friend, that whensoever there cometh any jewels or treasure to their share the present sale whereof might discover the matter, then he will take it in pawn and make out a bill of sale as if things were done in good order and dealing ; so that whensoever the cheater shall seek to make money of the pawn, if any question arise, he showeth a fair bill of sale for his discharge. Another help they have that of every purse which is cleanly conveyed, a rateable portion is duly delivered to the treasurer's hands, that whensoever by some misadventure any of them happen to be laid in prison this common stock may serve to satisfy the party grieved, thereby to save them from the gallows.

29th August. SHAKESPEARE'S 'RICHARD THE SECOND.'

Mr. William Shakespeare's play of *The Tragedy of Richard the Second* that was publicly acted by the Lord Chamberlain's men is being printed, but without that scene of the deposing of King Richard.

6th September. AN AMBASSADOR RECEIVED FROM DENMARK.

To-day Mr. Arnold Whitfield, Chancellor of the realm of Denmark, with his assistant, the Court being at Theobalds, had audience before the Queen, to whom they made certain requests which her Majesty answered without pause. The first, that the league and amity between the Queen and the late King should be continued to the new King, now newly adopted and crowned. The second was that it would please the Queen that the King his master might make a motion of peace between her Majesty and the King of Spain, and if he found the parties thereto addicted, to proceed further for the effecting thereof. To which her Majesty replied that she thought the King his master was too young to know the cause of the breach of the league between her and Spain, and as it was not broken by her consent, so it should not be sued nor sought by her, nor any in her behalf. 'For,' said she, 'know now, and be it known to the King your master, and all Kings, Christian or heathen, that the Queen of England hath no need to crave peace, for I assure you that I never endured one hour of fear since my first coming to my Kingdom and subjects.'

This being her Majesty's birthday the ambassador took occasion to say that sith it had pleased God on this day to glorify the world with so gracious a creature, he doubted not that the King should have an happy answer of his requests. 'I blame you not,' answered her Majesty, 'to expect a reasonable answer, and a sufficient; but you may think it a great miracle that a child born at four o'clock this morning should be able to answer so wise and learned a man as you are, sent from so great a Prince as you be, about so great and weighty affairs you speak of, and in an unknown tongue, by three o'clock in the afternoon.'

15th September. SLANDERS AGAINST THE LORD MAYOR.

A slanderous report is of late raised that the Lord Mayor hath caused the price of corn, that began to fall, to be enhanced to a higher rate, and that having brought into the Thames certain corn he kept up the market that he might sell his corn at a higher rate. The Queen being much offended at these reports now causeth a proclamation to be published, not only clearing the good name of the Lord Mayor, but showing that the grain was brought hither by his providence, whereof great numbers of poor people have been sustained in this time of dearth. Moreover, if any shall hereafter be found to disperse this or any other like untrue report, some severe punishment shall be inflicted on the offender, to the example of all others that for private malice and without just cause shall presume to defame any public person who shall be appointed under her Majesty for the good government of her people.

16th September. NEWS OF THE FLEET.

There is a gentleman come from my Lord of Essex with news that meeting with a stormy northerly wind as soon as they had doubled the South Cape, they were put off sixty or eighty leagues towards the Azores, and the wind so continuing, and fresh water lacking, they go for the Islands, to lie for the carracks and West Indian ships.

20th September. SIR JOHN NORRIS DEAD.

News is come that Sir John Norris is dead in Ireland, to the Queen's grief. He is succeeded as President of Munster by his brother Sir Thomas.

CONDEMNED PRISONERS.

There are at this time 28 persons lying in prisons condemned to be executed, 19 being men and 9 women; of these the Queen is pleased to pardon 8 men and 8 women.

22nd September. THE QUEEN'S LETTER TO THE LADY NORRIS.

Upon the news of Sir John Norris's death, the Queen wrote to the Lady Norris, his mother, in these terms: 'If it be true that society in sorrow works diminution, we do assure you, by this true messenger of our mind, that nature can have stirred no more dolorous affection in you as a mother for a dear son, than gratefulness and memory of his services past hath wrought in us his Sovereign apprehension of our miss of so worthy a servant. But now that nature's common work is done, and he that was born to die hath paid his tribute, let that Christian discretion stay the flux of your immoderate grieving, which hath instructed you both by example and knowledge that nothing of this kind hath happened but by God's divine Providence.' And at the top of the letter her Majesty wrote these words: 'Mine own Crow, harm not thyself for bootless help; but show a good example to comfort your dolorous yokefellow.'

23rd September. THE GOVERNOR OF DUNKIRK TAKEN.

Some of the garrison of Ostend have taken the Governor of Dunkirk and brought him prisoner to Sir Edward Norris. Sir Henry Palmer is now sent in person to bring the Governor over to England in all haste and to lodge him in Dover Castle.

24th September. MACHUGH'S HEAD.

Some days since two boys going to fetch their cattle from Enfield Chase found there a man's head. Hereupon, enquiry being made, Mr. John Dewrance, whose field it was, declareth that about a month since one John Lane brought this head to his house in Enfield, saying that it was the head of MacHugh, that arch traitor of Ireland, who was slain by Captain Thomas Lee and his company. Lane brought the head into England to the Earl of Essex, who referred him to Mr. Secretary for payment, but seeing that the head money had already been paid in Ireland Lane was told that he might bestow the head where he would ; and having it with him he made proffer to leave it with Mr. Dewrance, who would no wise permit it nor suffer it be buried in his garden. Lane therefore gave the head to his boy to bury in Enfield Chase, but the boy set it upon a tree.

27th September. A PROCLAMATION AGAINST PROVIDING THE SPANISH KING WITH MUNITION.

There is issued a proclamation warning those foreigners that send or carry with Spain or Portugal any manner of grain, or victuals, or any provisions for building of ships of war, or any kind of munitions, that her Majesty will not only authorise her own Admirals and Captains of her ships of war, but will also approve her subjects to impeach and arrest such ships.

29th September. THE SPANISH DANGER CEASES.

Now that the season is so far advanced there would appear to be no danger of an attempt of the enemy against the realm ; wherefore to save the charges the soldiers entertained for the defence of Guernsey and Jersey are to be withdrawn.

8th October. THE PLAYERS RELEASED.

Spencer, Shaa and Jonson, the players that were committed because of the play of *The Isle of Dogs*, are now to be released, from the Marshalsea.

9th October. A DISORDERLY ELECTION.

There hath been no small disorder in the election of those to serve in this forthcoming Parliament as Knights of the Shire for the county of York. On the 3rd October, about 8 o'clock, at the Castle at York the writ of summons for the election was duly read, also a letter sent from the Privy Council for the better direction of the election ; proclamation was also made by order of the Archbishop and the Council that no person thither assembled, except he were a freeholder of 40s. per annum above all charges and reprises, should presume to give voice in the election. Which things being done, first were nominated Sir John Stanhope, Sir Thomas Hoby, and Sir John Savile; whereat Sir John Savile caused the sheriff to read out to the freeholders certain statutes to the effect that none should be chosen to that place but such as were resident in the county at the head of the writ. Then Sir John cried out to the people, 'Will you have a Maleverer or a Fairfax?' meaning, as some said, to make knights at his own will or otherwise to distract the voices of the freeholders from the other two nominated.

Hereupon for the space of two hours and more the cries and voices of the people continued confused and diverse for Sir John Stanhope, Sir Thomas Hoby, Sir John Savile and Sir William Fairfax; but for some good space after the first cries, the number for Sir John Stanhope and Sir Thomas Hoby seemed to be more in show by some 600. Afterwards the greater number seemed doubtful, and it was agreed that some indifferent gentleman should be assigned to discern the companies and voices of each part, first by view, and then by trial of the polls for their freehold or residency. Whereupon the companies on each part being severed and divided, the undersheriff with the gentlemen went up into a chamber where they might see the companies and reasonably esteem of the great number of persons; with result that they did esteem those that stood on the hillside for Sir William Fairfax and Sir John Savile (being next the gate) to be more in number than the side for Sir John Stanhope and Sir Thomas Hoby by about 200 persons. But then some of the gentlemen did think that there were on that side citizens and inhabitants of York, women and children and other strangers, not having lawful voices, to the number of 500 or 600. It was therefore agreed that the companies should be further examined by pools upon their corporal oaths.

The undersheriff and the gentlemen triers then proceeded to the gate, whither the sheriff went also and took paper with him, the gentlemen having sticks to take the number of them by scotches or marks. It was further concluded that the company of Sir John Savile, being nearest the gate, should first be tried. The gentlemen and the undersheriff being thus come to the gate, it was agreed to shut the gate and no more to let any in on any side; then that two of the gentlemen triers on either side should nick every score, and that all should be sworn and examined against whom any exceptions should be taken, and that the undersheriff and his man were there for the purpose. So Mr. Wortley (who was of the part of Sir John Stanhope and Sir Thomas Hoby) took a knife and a stick to nick on the scores on his side.

Thereupon the undersheriff commanded the people back from out of the gatestead. Whereat came Sir John Savile on horseback, and called the undersheriff and demanded what he was about; who answered, to proceed to trial by poll according to agreement and law.

Sir John replied, 'Though they would make you an ass, they shall not make me a fool.' He would have no such trial; he would hold what he had; and, after other words, commanded the gate to be opened. The undersheriff replied that it might not be so, for he must do as the law required; to which Sir John answered, 'Open the door or break it open,' and himself pressed forward, so that the gentlemen triers shifted themselves away as well as they could, and two were in danger of their lives. Then also the undersheriff went out with Sir John without staying to proceed, whereby those who stayed behind knew not whether any election had been made or not.

After this, by the space of two hours or more, the knights, gentlemen and freeholders on the part of Sir John Stanhope continued in the castle hall and yard expecting the return of the sheriff; but he would not be found, being with Sir John Savile at dinner. Then Sir John Savile and Sir William Fairfax returned together with the undersheriff, who, first making proclamation of silence, immediately and without any further proceeding did pronounce Sir John Savile and Sir William Fairfax to be the knights lawfully elected; which thing was denied by the other part of Sir John Stanhope and Sir Thomas Hoby.

10th October. THE ART OF BRACHYGRAPHY.

There is a new edition published of *The Art of Brachygraphy*, that is to write as fast as a man speaketh treatably, writing but one letter for a word, including also the order of orthography, for the speedy writing of true English, and the key of caligraphy opening the ready way to write fair, invented by Mr. Peter Bales. This art serveth for an infinite number of uses; the memory is strengthened and as much can be written in one day as in a whole week by other writing; by it you may with speed write out any excellent written book or copy, never yet imprinted, to your private use and benefit; moreover the sermons, lectures and orations of excellent learned men shall hereby be kept, recorded and registered. The method of this brachygraphy is to denote words by single letters, to each letter being added a prick or tittle.

11th October. 'THE TRIMMING OF THOMAS NASHE.'

There is an answer to Nashe's Epistle to Richard Lichfield, the barber of Trinity College in Cambridge (that he wrote in *Have with you to Saffron Walden*), entitled *The Trimming of Thomas Nashe*. Herein Nashe is very straitly trimmed for his many ribaldries and lewd courses of life. Saith that there was a time when Nashe and his fellow Lusher lay in Coldharbour together when they had but one pair of breeches between them both, but not one penny to bless them with; so that by course Lusher wore the breeches one day and went conny-catching for victuals whilst Nashe lay in bed; and the next day Nashe wore the breeches to go and beg, for all the world like two buckets in one well. Taunteth him also with his *Isle of Dogs* for which he was proclaimed by the crier, and deserved the cropping of his ears. Saith that Nashe hath been cast into many prisons and hath polluted them all.

PLAYING RESUMED.

To-day began my Lord Admiral's and my Lord Pembroke's men to play at the Rose after the restraint, the play being *The Spanish Tragedy*.

THE ELECTION AT YORK.

The Council being informed of the contemptuous behaviour of Sir John Savile have required the Archbishop of York to commit him to prison, thereby to notify to the world, not that her Majesty's meaning nor the Council's is to mislike any man to use that freedom for his election which the law doth warrant and discretion requireth, yet, where authority is established as in such a nature the Archbishop and his Council hath, she will not suffer any precedency of contempt to go unpunished for warning to others.

12th October. A PROCLAMATION AGAINST ENGLISH MERCHANTS.

News is come out of Germany that the Emperor by proclamation hath commanded all English merchants to depart the Empire within three months, they and their goods, on pain of confiscation and imprisonment, so that the Merchant Adventurers must needs leave Stade.

14th October. 'POLITEUPHUIA, WIT'S COMMONWEALTH.'

Mr. N. Ling hath completed the book called *Politeuphuia : Wit's Commonwealth* which was compiled by Mr. John Bodenham. Herein are to be found many definitions beginning with that 'Of God' and ending 'Of Hell' and beneath each certain pithy sentences expanding the same ; as 'Of Generals in War,' defined thus : 'Generals are the heads and leaders of armies, and they ought to be great, magnanimous and constant in all their doings ; free from the defects of rashness and cowardice.' Which definition is followed by such sentences as these :

'Unless wise and valiant men be chosen Generals, the old chaos will return and virtue die at the feet of confusion.'

'He that will be a commander in armies, first let him be commanded in the same, for an ambitious soldier will never make a temperate conductor.'

'A General after a battle ended must have a circumspect care how he praiseth one captain more than another.'

There are eight conditions that a general ought to have ; to avoid unjust wrongs, to correct blasphemers, to succour innocents, to chastise quarrellers, to pay his soldiers, to defend his people, to provide things necessary, and to observe faith with his enemies.

16th October. HERRINGS TO BE STAYED.

The fishmongers of London making complaint of the dearth of white herrings by reason of the great quantity sent out of the realm to foreign parts, the Mayor of Yarmouth is bidden to stay those ships in the port which are now laden with herrings.

19th October. INGROSSERS AND BUILDERS PUNISHED.

To-day in the Star Chamber, one Francis Parker that hath been an ingrosser these sixteen years and every year carried corn to London in a boat without a licence is fined £500 to the Queen, imprisonment, £20 to the poor, to go to Westminster Hall with papers and to confess his fault. Others are fined £40 with imprisonment.

At the same time one Negoose and others for building cottages in London contrary to the proclamation are fined; one £100, one £40 and another £20; the houses to be destroyed for their base condition and the timber sold for the poor. If any be brothel houses, to burn them standing if it can be done without peril, otherwise to burn them in the fields; and those that are beautiful and spacious edifices to be converted into garners and storehouses.

DELONEY'S 'GENTLE CRAFT.'

Deloney hath written a book in praise of shoemakers called *The Gentle Craft*, showing what famous men have been shoemakers in time past in this land, with their worthy deeds and great hospitality. Relateth the pleasant history of St. Hugh (from whom cometh it that the shoemakers' tools are called St. Hugh's bones); the tale of Crispin and Crispianus; and lastly how Sir Simon Eyre, being first a shoemaker, became in the end Lord Mayor of London through the counsel of his wife, and how he builded Leadenhall.

20th October. 'RICHARD THE THIRD.'

There is to be printed that play acted by the Lord Chamberlain's men called *The Tragedy of King Richard the Third*, being written by Shakespeare, wherein Burbage played the King with great applause.

22nd October. THE LORD ADMIRAL TO BE ADVANCED.

It is said in Court that to-morrow the Lord Admiral shall be created Earl of Nottingham. The heralds have been with him; he hath borrowed my Lord of Pembroke's robes; his coronet is made and his patent is a drawing.

23rd October. THE LORD ADMIRAL ADVANCED.

As the Queen came from the Chapel this day, being Sunday, she created the Lord Admiral Earl of Nottingham. The Earl of Cumberland carried his sword, the Earl of Sussex his cap and coronet. He was brought in by the Earls of Shrewsbury and Worcester. Her Majesty made a speech unto him in acknowledgment of his services, and Mr. Secretary read the Letters Patent aloud, which are very honourable; all his great services *anno* '88 recited, and those lately at Cadiz. He is to take his place *vt Comes de Nottingham*, for so are the words in the patent. Hereby shall he take precedence over the Earl of Essex.

OSTEND THREATENED.

News is lately come of the approach of the enemy unto the town of Ostend, whereby it is supposed that some enterprise is intended. Four companies with Sir Arthur Savage are now to be sent from Picardy for the better security of the town.

24th October. THE PARLIAMENT ASSEMBLES.

This day the Parliament, being her Majesty's ninth Parliament, assembled at Westminster, where many of the knights of the shires, citizens of cities, burgesses of boroughs, and Barons of ports, having made their appearance before the Earl of Nottingham, Lord Steward of the Household, took the Oath of Supremacy seven or eight at a time before him and Sir William Knollys, Sir John Fortescue and Sir Robert Cecil. This done they passed into their own House to await her Majesty's pleasure.

The Queen being then come into the Upper House and set in her chair of estate, the Commons were summoned, and as many as conveniently could admitted. Then Sir Thomas Egerton, the Lord Keeper, by her Majesty's command, declared the cause of the summoning of this present Parliament, and having expressed his insufficiency for that task, spake to this effect:

'You are to enter into a due consideration of the laws, and where you find superfluity to prune and cut off; where defect to supply, and where ambiguity to explain; that they be not burdensome but profitable to the commonwealth. Yet as nothing is to be regarded if due mean be not taken to withstand the professed enemies which seek the destruction of the whole State, this before and above all is to be thought of; for in vain are laws if such prevail as go about to make a conquest of the

Kingdom. Wars heretofore were wont to be made either of ambition to enlarge dominions or of revenge to quit injuries; but this against us is not so. In this the Holy Religion of God is sought to be rooted out, the whole realm to be subdued, and the precious life of her Majesty to be taken away, which hitherto hath been preserved, maugre the Devil, the Pope and the Spanish Tyrant. Her Majesty hath not spared to disburse a mass of treasure and to sell her land for maintenance of her armies by sea and land, whereby, with such small helps as her subjects have yielded, she hath defended and kept safe her dominions from all such forcible attempts as have been made. Which though performed at infinite charge, her Majesty doth notwithstanding hear of nothing more unwillingly than of aids and subsidies from her people. The taxations at this day, howsoever they seem, are nothing so great as heretofore. In the time of Edward the Third, and of those before and after him, the payments of the Commons did far exceed any that have been made since her Majesty's reign; but never cause so great to employ great sums of money as now. To spare now is to spare for those which seek to devour all; and to give is to give to ourselves, her Majesty's part only being carefully to bestow what is delivered into her hands. This war is just; it is in defence of the Religion of God, of our most Gracious Sovereign, and of our natural country, of our wives, our children, our liberties, lands, lives, and whatsoever we have.'

Whereupon the Commons were dismissed to choose the Speaker, who shall be presented on Thursday next. The Commons therefore straightway repaired to their own House, and there being assembled and sitting some space of time very silent, at last Sir William Knollys, the Controller, stood up and spake:

'Necessity constraineth me to break off this silence and to give others cause for speech. According to the usual custom we are to choose our Speaker, and though I am least able and therefore unfit to speak in this place, yet better I deem it to discover my own imperfections than that her most Sacred Majesty's commandment to me delivered should not be fulfilled, or your expectation of this day's work by all our silences be frustrate.'

Having then spoken a little on the necessity for a Speaker, he saith, ' Now because that knowledge doth rest in certainty, I will with the more speed set afoot this motion, deliver my opinion unto you who is most fit for this place, being a member of this House, and those good abilities which I know to be in him '—here he made a little pause, and the House hawked and spat, and after silence made, he proceeded—' unto this place of dignity and calling in my opinion '—here he stayed a little—' Mr. Sergeant Yelverton '—looking upon him—' is the fittest man to be preferred '—at which words Mr. Yelverton blushed, put off his hat and sat bareheaded—' for I am assured that he is, yea, and I dare avow it, I know him to be, a man wise and learned, secret and circumspect, religious and faithful, no way disable but in every way able to supply this place. Wherefore in my judgment I deem him, though I will not say best worthy among us, yet sufficient enough to supply this place; and herein if any man think I err, I wish him to deliver his mind as freely as I have done; if not, that we all join together in giving general consent and approbation to this motion.'

So the whole House cried, ' Ay, ay, ay, let him be.' Then Sir William made a low reverence and sat down. After a little pause and silence Mr. Sergeant Yelverton rose up, and, after very humble reverence made, thus spake:

' Whence your unexpected choice of me to be your mouth or Speaker should proceed, I am utterly ignorant. If from my merits, strange it were that so few deserts should purchase suddenly so great an honour. Nor from my ability doth this your choice proceed; for well known is it to a great number in this place that my estate is nothing correspondent for the maintenance of this dignity; for my father dying left me a younger brother and nothing to me but my bare annuity. Then growing to man's estate and some small practice of the law, I took a wife by whom I have had many children, the keeping of us all being a great impoverishing to my estate, and the daily living of us all nothing but my daily industry. Neither from my person or nature doth this choice arise; for he that supplieth this place ought to be a man big and comely, stately and well spoken, his voice great, his carriage majestical, his nature haughty, and his purse plentiful and heavy; but contrarily, the stature of my body is small, myself not so well spoken, my voice low, my carriage lawyer-like and of the common fashion, my nature soft and bashful, my purse thin, light, and never plentiful. Where I now see the only cause of this choice is a gracious and favourable censure of your good and undeserved opinions of me. But I most humbly beseech you recall this your sudden election ; and therefore, because the more sudden, the sooner to be recalled. But if this cannot move your sudden choice yet let this one thing persuade you, that myself not being gracious in the eye of her Majesty, neither ever yet in account with great personages, shall deceive your expectation in those weighty matters and great affairs which should be committed unto me. For if Demosthenes being so learned and eloquent as he was, one whom none surpassed, trembled to speak before Phocion at Athens, how much more shall I, being unlearned and unskilful, supply this place of dignity, charge, and trouble to speak before so many Phocions as here be ? Yea, which is the greatest, before the unspeakable Majesty and Sacred Person of our dread and dear Sovereign, the terror of whose countenance will appal and abase even the stoutest heart ; yea, whose very name will pull down the greatest courage ? For how mightily doth the estate and name of a Prince deject the haughtiest stomach even of their greatest subjects ? I beseech you therefore again and again to proceed unto a new election, here being many better able and more sufficient and far more worthy than myself, both for the honour of this assembly and general good of the public state.'

After this speech, Sir John Fortescue, the Chancellor of the Exchequer, stood up, affirming all the former commendations of Sir William Knollys, and inferring further that he well perceived by Mr. Yelverton's speech, tending to the disabling of himself to this place, that he was thereby so much the more meet and sufficient ; and so for his part he also nominated Mr. Yelverton to be their Speaker, and moved the House for their liking and resolution therein, who all with one accord and consent yield unto this election.

Whereupon Mr. Controller and Mr. Chancellor rose up and placed Mr. Sergeant Yelverton in the Chair. Which done, Mr. Yelverton after some small pause stood up, and giving the whole House most hearty thanks for their good opinions and conceit of him, signified unto them nevertheless that by their good favours he will endeavour when he shall come before her Majesty, to be a humble suitor unto her Highness to be discharged of this place, if so he can.

After this the House immediately rose.

Divers people to-day pressing between Whitehall and the College Church to see the Queen and the nobility riding to the Parliament, Sir Thomas Gerrard the Knight Marshal and his men making way before them, were smothered and crushed to death.

26th October. A SUDDEN VERY GREAT ALARM.

To-day is come to Court a gentleman with news that he discovered the Spanish fleet, and finding one ship lagging took prisoner her captain, master and purser. The ship was rescued, but some letters taken in her show that they will make their rendezvous at Falmouth. Mayors and chief officers in the ports on the south shall now, as they regard the Queen's service and upon peril of their lives, send out as espials some of the best fisher boats to gain early intelligence of the designs of the enemy. The Picardy soldiers are to be landed in England with all possible expedition. Victuals and all kinds of provision are being collected in the West parts to replenish the fleet of the Earl of Essex which is looked for within a few days.

27th October. THE FORCES MUSTERING.

In Devon, Cornwall, Dorset, Hampshire, Berkshire, Kent, Sussex, Surrey, Wiltshire and Somerset the whole forces, both horsemen and footmen, are being put in readiness. All men that dwell anywhere near the sea are forbidden to leave their houses; and gentlemen of every county for the most part are commanded to go home for the defence of the sea coast. The Lord Chamberlain departeth at once for the western coast to command such forces as shall be fit for the resistance of the enemy if they land, and captains are appointed to attend him.

THE LORD BURGH DEAD.

The Lord Deputy, Lord Burgh, is dead in Ireland. Being on a journey to revictual the fort of Blackwater, he fell dangerously sick of an Irish ague at Armagh on the 6th, and being taken back in a litter to Newry died there on the 13th. His death comes very untimely, for there is not another fit man able to second the course already begun, all the money spent is lost, and besides there hangeth an imminent danger of a present and general revolt throughout that Kingdom.

THE SPEAKER PRESENTED.

To-day in Parliament, the House being set, Mr. Chancellor of the Exchequer moved and admonished that none of the House shall hereafter enter into the House with their spurs on for offending of others, and that none shall come in before they have paid the Sergeant's fees due to him according to the accustomed usage of the House.

This afternoon the Queen going by water repaired to the Upper House, accompanied with divers Lords spiritual and temporal, and the Commons having notice, Mr. Sergeant Yelverton was brought into the Upper House, and by the hands of Sir William Knollys and Sir John Fortescue, Chancellor of the Exchequer, presented.

Mr. Speaker in a speech full of gravity and moderation signified the election of the House of Commons, but, excusing himself by pretence of many disabilities and imperfections, and wishing earnestly he were of sufficiency to perform the duty of that place, made humble suit to her Majesty that he might be discharged and that the House of Commons might proceed to a new election. This excuse was not allowed by her Majesty, as the Lord Keeper delivered answer, who very well approved the choice of Mr. Yelverton and commended his sufficiency.

Mr. Speaker then proceeded in another speech, according to custom, to undertake this charge and to present her Majesty, in the behalf of the Commons, certain humble petitions, for access upon needful occasions, and for the using and enjoying of such liberties and privileges as in former times have been granted by her Majesty and her progenitors. Whereunto her Majesty, by the mouth of the Lord Keeper, yielded gracious assent, with admonition that these liberties should be discreetly and wisely used, as is meet.

The Parliament is adjourned until the 5th November.

PLAYING RESUMED.

To-day the Lord Admiral's players that have been absent for the last three months are now returned from the country and again begin to play at the Rose.

28th October. THE EARL OF ESSEX RETURNS.

This morning came letters to Court of the Earl of Essex's safe landing in Plymouth, that he hath unfortunately missed the King's own fleet with the treasure but fell upon the merchants' fleet. Four of them he hath taken and brought home safe, and sunk many more. The Earl of Southampton fought with one of the King's great men-of-war and sunk her. The Spanish fleet commanded by the Adelantado still hovers up and down upon the coast but as yet is not landed. The Earl of Essex put in to victual and to have fresh men, and with all possible speed to go to sea again; my Lord Mountjoy sailing to Plymouth was by three of the Spanish fleet chased in.

The King of Spain is said to be dead, who made his son swear by the Sacrament that he should never make peace with England till he revenged these disgraces. The Adelantado, by the young Prince's threatening to hang him if he put not to sea, is upon our coast and vows to land though he never return.

A mass of money is being sent down to the Earl of Essex for all wants and supplies needed to refurnish the fleet. My Lord's offers and ready disposition to adventure his life in this service are very graciously accepted by the Queen. The Earl of Pembroke also is bidden to furnish such further aid as shall be required of him both in men and supplies.

30th October. PREPARATIONS IN THE WEST.

A sum of £3,000 has been sent into the West for provisions to revictual the fleet, of which sum the Lord Thomas Howard, Lord Mountjoy and Sir Walter Ralegh may draw up to £2,000, and more will be sent if need require. The loans of money hitherto respited are to be brought in with all speed for the service.

31st October. OSTEND BESIEGED.

The Cardinal hath now besieged Ostend, lying on the west side of it, but 'tis not yet known whether for a bravado or whether he will remain there for some design. Meanwhile the

Lord Cobham stayeth all the hoys at Dover and Sandwich so that, if there be cause, they may carry over men and victuals. The forces of the shire are mustered and the castles being viewed.

A New Play.

To-day there was a new play at the Rose called *Friar Spendleton.*

2nd November. The Islands Voyage.

The accounts of the late voyage are now to hand. Soon after the fleet had set sail, it was again caught by another great tempest on St. Bartholomew's Day, and many of the ships scattered, thirty ships with Sir Walter Ralegh the Vice-admiral being separated from the rest; but most of the remainder staying with the Earl of Essex. It had been ordained that if any separation should happen, there should be three places of rendezvous, the first at the North Cape, the second at the Rock, and the third at the South Cape. To the Rock therefore came Sir Walter Ralegh, who had been delayed by the breaking of his main mast, and there joined him some thirty sail; and here they met with a small bark of England by whom they were told that the Adelantado was gone to the Islands to waft home the Indian fleet; which news was afterwards found to be false. Sir Walter therefore thinking it very requisite that the Admiral should be informed of this advertisement, sent one of his small ships to seek the fleet, which by good hap it found the next day, so that within two days after Sir Walter received two letters from the Earl of Essex requiring him to follow him to the Islands forthwith. Which was accordingly done and the Isle of Tercera reached on the 8th September; and on the 14th they met with the rest of the fleet at Flores to the great joy of the General, especially as many had buzzed doubts and jealousies in his ear concerning Sir Walter. Then a council was held whereat it was determined to take in some of the islands and an orderly course was set down, which was for the Admiral and Rear-admiral to undertake Fayal; the Lord Thomas Howard and Sir Francis Vere to undertake Gratiosa; the Lord Mountjoy and Sir Christopher Blount to St. Michael's; and the Netherland squadron was quartered to Pyke where is the greatest store of wines, and therefore, it was presumed, would not be taken in ill part of them.

Here the ships of Sir Walter purposed to water whilst the rest of the fleet plied up and down, looking for the Adelantado. But whilst the casks were being prepared, about midnight, being the 16th September, a message was brought that my Lord General was borne up for Fayal, and meant to take it straightway, and therefore willed Sir Walter to follow with all speed instantly; further that all wants of water and fresh victuals should be supplied at Fayal. The ships with Sir Walter accordingly weighed anchor and next morning making Fayal entered the road but found not the Lord General; whereat they greatly marvelled, because when he had sent for them, he was six leagues nearer to it than they. As soon as the fleet was seen, the inhabitants of the town began to pack away with bag and baggage all they could. The town, which is some four miles from the place were they were, was defended by two forts, one at the end, the other on the top of a high mountain near adjoining, very inaccessible by nature, and artificially fenced with flankers, rampiers, and a ditch, and with six pieces of great artillery, and 200 Spaniards for a garrison. There were also sent six companies to intrench themselves on the shore side to impeach the landing of our men.

Hereupon Sir Walter in his barge rode close aboard the high fort and all along the shore side towards the town to see what fit place there was to make a descent against the Lord General's coming. So Sir Walter held a council of many captains and officers to consult of taking the town if still the Lord General came not. Moreover the soldiers and mariners began to mutiny and rail on the Rear-admiral and all the commanders as not daring the taking of the town; and besides they were more eagerly set upon the spoil because they saw no great likelihood of any other benefit to be gotten from this voyage. At this council, some would by no means consent to the landing without the Lord General's knowledge, and especially Sir Gelly Merrick, but those of Sir Walter's own squadron were of the contrary opinion. They stayed therefore two days, and then a third, but on the fourth Sir Walter determined to land.

They made ready therefore a barge, a long boat, and a pinnace with sixty muskets and forty pike rather to guard the landing than to attempt any encounter. But no sooner were the men in the boats, than many companies of foot began to hasten down to possess themselves of the trenches where our men were to land. Sir Walter therefore rowed to Sir William Brooke's ship and Sir William Harvey's, and desired them to accompany him; to which they willingly assented, and there were made ready in addition with shot and pike 160 more men in the boats. Then the men from the Low Countries that belonged to my Lord of Essex's squadron cried out to be taken too, but Sir Walter durst not, not knowing for what service my Lord had intended them: but promised to send back his boats for them.

So the pinnaces hasted forward toward the landing place, but as the shot began to play thick upon them, the mariners would scarce come forwards, having the lesser liking to the business the nearer they came to it; and some of the leaders themselves stood blank so that Sir Walter did not spare to call upon them openly and rebuke aloud with disgraceful words. Sir Walter, seeing that it was both more disgrace and more dangerous for the mariners to make stay, with a loud voice commanded his watermen to row in full upon the rocks and bad as many as were not afraid to follow him. Hereupon some boats ran in, and so clambering over the rocks, and wading through the water they passed pell-mell with swords, shot and pikes upon the narrow entrance. Whereupon those that were at the defence, after some little resistance, began to shrink, and then suddenly retiring cast down their weapons, and fled away to the hills. The landing being thus gained with some few men lost, the boats were sent back for the men from the Low Countries, who, when they were come ashore, made up a force of 460 men, well armed and appointed, and of these thirty or forty were captains and gentlemen.

They therefore resolved to pass by the two forts and enter the town, and the next morning to attack these forts; which could not then be done, the day being far spent and the men overwearied with the last work, together with a long march and extreme hot weather, besides lack of victuals. So they set forward, the Rear-admiral with divers of the gentlemen going before the rest some twelve score paces in the manner of a vauntguard in a slow steady march, being shrewdly pelted by the muskets and great ordnance of the fort; but the main body that for a while marched in good order so soon as they began to find themselves within the mercy of the musket shot began to break their ranks, and from marching fell to flat running in straggling manner so that they were upon the heels of the vauntguard. Whereupon Sir Walter cried out on them for this shameful disorder and asked their captains if this was the manner of their old Low Country troops to show such base cowardice at the first sight of the enemy. To which they answered that these companies were men taken out of Flushing and Brille, and raw soldiers that ever lived in a safe garrison and seldom or never had seen the enemy. And indeed such as only serve to take pay, to walk rounds and guard ports in garrison towns, in the field will commonly be missing, or, if present, do little hurt for conscience' sake.

Then Sir Walter called for some to go out to survey the passage by the high fort, but the lieutenants and sergeants were very unwilling, so he said that he would go himself; 'notwithstanding,' quoth he, 'though I could enforce others to do it, they shall well perceive that I myself will do that which they dare not perform.' So with some few with him he went to discover the passage and to search out the strengths and ascents of the hill, being shrewdly troubled by the great artillery which beat upon the old walls as they passed, insomuch that two had their heads stricken clean from their bodies and divers others were hurt, and the Rear-admiral himself was shot through breeches and doublet. The passage being discovered, the rest of the troops were summoned to come on towards the town. But as they drew near the town, those in the other fort withdrew and fled up into the country; so that they entered the town peaceably, having lost some seven or eight slain and twenty-five hurt. Barricadoes were immediately made, good guards placed in divers places and a strong court of guard in the market place, and straggling forbidden on pain of death. That night they rested without further trouble than two false alarms.

Next morning, being 22nd September, the Lord General himself with his fleet bore into the road of Fayal, having all this while been looking about for the Adelantado and other adventures ; and hereupon the intent to attempt the high fort was frustrated. Meanwhile the proceedings in Fayal were by Sir Gelly Merrick related at large to the Lord General, and so aggravated and wrested into an evil sense by him, Sir Christopher Blount, Sir Anthony Shirley and others, by putting into my Lord of Essex's head that these parts were played by Sir Walter Ralegh only to steal honour and reputation from him, and to set his own frowardness to the view of the world. Which intimation of theirs was an exception that they knew my Lord of Essex is very apt of his own disposition to take hold of, being a man that affecteth nothing in the world so much as fame, and to be reputed matchless for magnanimity and undertaking, and can hardly endure any that shall obscure his glory in this kind, though otherwise he favour them never so much. It was besides alleged that the presumption and scorn to land such forces without my Lord's leave was not to be passed over without severe punishment, and a martial court fit to be called, to censure the offence and breach of order and discipline. These and such other bitter arguments were used to aggravate the General's wrath against all that were in this action, and especially against the Rear-admiral ; against whom they spared not so far to inveigh as that he was well worthy to lose his head for his labour. So well did they persuade the General that all the forenoon was spent in reprehending and displacing the land officers that went in the action.

Sir Walter was then sent for to answer before the Lord General in his ship, but before the messenger came for him was already gone in his barge to see my Lord, looking for great thanks at the General's hands. But when he was entered my Lord's cabin, after a faint welcome, my Lord began to challenge him of breach of order and articles, in that he had landed troops without the General's presence or his order. To which Sir Walter answered that there was an article that no captain should land anywhere without direction of the General or other principal commander ; but that he himself was a principal commander and therefore not subject to that article, nor under the power of the law martial, because a successive commander of the fleet under her Majesty's letters patent.

This dispute lasted some half hour and then the Lord General went ashore and rested himself in the Rear-admiral's lodging, being well enough satisfied at that time, this dispute having been brought to a quiet conclusion by the friendly mediation of Lord Thomas Howard. Thus the whole day was spent in reprehending and disciplining those with the Rear-admiral for their pains. That night the Spaniards in the high fort abandoned the place with all their baggage and fled into the country; and next morning, when it was too late, direction was given to guard the high fort. So when news was brought that they had abandoned the fort and carried all away, there was much murmuring, for if there had not been bestowed more labour in disciplining pretended faults than discretion in prosecuting the enemy who was at a disadvantage, then had not been lost the benefit of the prisoners' ransoms and the spoil which they had carried out of the town to that place for safety.

On the 26th September the whole fleet made towards Gratiosa, where the chief men of the Island submitted themselves to the Lord General, being required to yield some provisions of wine, fruits, and fresh victuals. Here the Lord General and some of the commanders would have stayed, but the Master of his ship, one Grove, was against that counsel, protesting that it would be dangerous for the whole fleet to anchor there. Wherefore they weighed anchor and made for St. Michael's Island, but as they came near two of the sternmost of the fleet shot off twice or thrice and bare up with all the sails they could pack on to the General's ship. These brought news of the Indian fleet, coming directly from the road of Gratiosa.

Upon this intelligence they cast about, and, within some three hours afterwards, they encountered and took three Spanish ships coming from Havannah, the greatest being of about 400 tons, and esteemed to be a very rich ship. To this Spaniard the *Wastspite*, being nearest, gave chase and caused her to strike and yield; but the Lord General, hasting after, would suffer none but his own boat to go aboard her, being full of good prisoners and pillage besides her lading, which was cochinella and other rich wares. This ship made relation of forty sail of Indiamen, whereof eight were freighted with the King's treasure, bound for Spain. Of these ships, some of ours fell in with sixteen, whereof they foundered one, and whilst they were busy seeking to take the spoil off her, the rest escaped and recovered Tercera. With all speed therefore our fleet followed them to Tercera, where they had entered some six hours before and had moored their ships under the town and fort.

Now there was a general council called aboard the Admiral what course to take herein, some of the colonels and captains offering with 1,500 men to take both island and forts but the sea commanders utterly against it, so that in the end it was deemed inconvenient and impossible to be effected as the forces then stood, and the time of year so far spent, with the winds and seas grown so tempestuous for landing in boats. The fleet therefore returned to St. Michael's and there anchored.

There it was consulted about landing and the taking of this good town, promising so many rewards to the victors. The General appointed that all companies should be made ready to land forthwith, but the Rear-admiral asked that he might first be permitted to view the place and to find out where the army might best make a descent. To this the Lord General at first yielded, but as Sir Walter was putting off, and scarce gone from the ship's side, my Lord, standing in his gallery with Sir Charles Blount, called him back again in great haste, and said that he would go himself and view it. Whereupon the Rear-admiral returned again, and my Lord went out of the ship into his barge, unarmed altogether but with his collar and sword, and without either shot or pike to wait on him. Sir Walter therefore called aloud to him, desiring him to take his casque and targetproof with him if he purposed to go near the shore, seeing there lay so many muskets on the rest there to receive him. Whereunto my Lord answered that he would none, because he disdained to take any advantage of the watermen that rowed with him.

The landing places being viewed afar off were not so well liked, so that upon another consultation being held it was agreed that the Rear-admiral, with all the strength of the fleet, should lie as near before the town of St. Michael as conveniently they could to hold them in expectation whilst my

Lord and the rest with 2,000 men should embark into the small barks and pinnaces and secretly in the night convey themselves about the point to land at a town called Villa Franca.

So the troops were shipped, and the Lord General also, and made haste to Villa Franca, where they arrived safe and were all landed by the next morning without any manner of resistance, while the ships under the command of the Rear-admiral all the night gave the enemy perpetual alarums with shot, drums and trumpets in such boats as were left, sometimes in one place, sometimes in another alongst the shore.

Next morning those with the Rear-admiral looked to see our troops marching over the hills and plains; but this good town of Villa Franca had so welcomed and entertained our men that the army was content there to ingarrison without any further pursuit of St. Michael's town; and there for six days they lay feasting, and carrying on board of oade, wheat, salt and other merchandise into certain private men's ships that followed the fleet for such a purpose.

While the fleet lay gaping for the coming of the army, which in all this time never sent word of their determination, there came a little Brazil man and let fall his anchor in the midst of our fleet, and a little after him a mighty huge carrack was discerned which made towards our fleet supposing it to be the Spanish armada, for indeed the King of Spain's men-of-war, when he makes fleets, are compounded of the shipping of divers nations, and besides with ours were not only Hollanders but the great Spanish galleon, the *St. Andrew*. Then by general commandment of the Rear-admiral, our ships took in all their flags, and directions were given that no man should weigh an anchor or shoot off a piece or put off a boat, but with leave and order. All this while she still bare in with all sails to the boat's end, when suddenly one of the Holland squadron weighed his anchors, hoisted his top sail and made towards the carrack. Whereupon discovering our ships to be enemy, she changed her course, and with the gale changing ran herself aground hard under the town and fort. Immediately there came out multitudes of boats, fetching away their men and best wares, and, that done, she was instantly set on fire in many places at once, so that though our men hasted all they could in all the boats that were left, they came all too late, for the broth was too hot for their supping. This vessel was judged to be of 1,800 tons, of infinite wealth, fraughted with the riches and wares both of the East and West, which was a loss as lamentable as inexcusable, for if the General and his troops had not lingered in Villa Franca, she had either fallen in their hands on shore or been taken at sea by the fleet.

After some days the fleet was summoned to Villa Franca, to the great joy of the inhabitants of St. Michael's. The wind and seas now beginning to rise and the opportunity being past of doing any damage to the enemy, preparations were now made for a return, and with all haste the soldiers were conveyed back to the boats with the help of the small pinnaces and boats, wherein my Lord twice was in very great danger of tumbling into the sea in overcharging his own boat with soldiers, amongst whom at such times it is very hard to keep any order or moderation. At this embarking the Spaniards and Portuguese made a brave skirmish, which being thoroughly answered, the General did make certain knights. At length on 9th October the fleet set sail for England.

5th November. OSTEND.

News is come from Sir Edward Norris, governor of Ostend, that there is no present danger. The enemy lie about the town and have divers times presented themselves before it; forces from the Low Countries have now been sent there.

THE QUEEN'S LETTER TO THE EMPEROR OF ETHIOPIA.

One Mr. Lawrence Aldersey, after many travels in foreign countries, being yet inflamed with a desire more thoroughly to survey and contemplate the world, now undertaketh a long and dangerous journey into the kingdom of the Emperor of Ethiopia. He beareth with him a letter from the Queen that he may enter that kingdom under the safeguard and protection of the Emperor's favour, and there remain safe and free from danger.

A MOTION IN PARLIAMENT AGAINST INCLOSURES.

To-day in the Parliament a Bill was read for the first time against forestallers, regrators and ingrossers. Whereupon

Mr. Francis Bacon spake first and made a motion against inclosures and depopulation of towns and houses of husbandry. He had perused, said he, the preambles of former statutes and by them did see the inconveniences of the matter, being then scarce out of the shell, to be now full ripened. It might be thought ill and very prejudicial to Lords that have inclosed great grounds, and pulled down even whole towns, and converted them to sheep pastures; yet considering the increase of people and benefit of the commonwealth, every man would deem the revival of former moth-eaten laws in this point a praiseworthy thing. 'I would be sorry,' quoth he, 'to see within this Kingdom that piece of Ovid's verse prove true, *iam seges ubi Troia fuit*, so in England, instead of a town full of people, nought but green fields, but a shepherd and a dog.'

After Mr. Bacon, Sir John Fortescue, the Chancellor of the Exchequer, in like manner showed his opinion, and so moving for a committee to consider of this motion, the House nominate all members of the Privy Council, being members of this House, all knights of the counties and all citizens of the cities returned to this present Parliament, together with Sir Edward Hoby, Mr. Francis Bacon, Mr. Nathaniel Bacon, Mr. Finch, Mr. Solicitor and divers others.

This concluded, Mr. Finch showing sundry great and horrible abuses of idle and vagrant persons, greatly offensive both to God and the world, and further the extreme and miserable estate of the godly and honest sort of the poor subjects of this realm, the matter is also referred to the same committee.

THE EARL OF ESSEX DISQUIETED.

The Earl of Essex is now returned to Court but is already disquieted, keeps in, and goes not to the Parliament. It is said that the Queen is not well pleased with him for his service at sea, wherein he might have done more than he did. Moreover his proceedings towards Sir Walter Ralegh in calling his actions to public question before a council of war where by a full court he was found guilty of death is greatly misliked. It is feared that the peace between the Earl of Essex and Sir Robert Cecil will burst out to terms of unkindness.

6th November. SPANISH PRISONERS AT LARGE.

Divers Spaniards that have of late been taken on the seas are allowed ordinarily to go up and down at their own liberty: but now the Lord Mayor shall inform himself of those that are within and without the City and see them committed to Bridewell, there to be safely kept with the diet of the house and set to work if they be not able to pay for their diet, and especially those lately taken by Newport; for it is against reason that any of the King of Spain's subjects should be suffered to enjoy their liberty here seeing the hard usage that is offered to our countrymen.

7th November. BARRET'S 'THEORICK AND PRACTICK OF MODERN WARS.'

Mr. Robert Barret hath written a book called *The Theorick and practick of modern wars*, discoursed dialogue-wise. Herein is declared the neglect of martial discipline and the inconvenience thereof; the imperfection of many training companies and its redress; the fittest weapons for our modern war, and their use; the part of a perfect soldier in general and in particular; the officers in degrees with their several duties; the embattling of men in forms now most in use, with figures and tables to the same; with sundry other martial points, comprehended in six books. Yet he would have captains trained by experience and not by book; for your reading captain when he is come into the field with an hundred men will rank them three and three, but at every third rank he must call to his boy, 'Holla sirrha, where is my book?' And having them all ranked, then marcheth he on fair, and far wider from his soldiers. Then cometh he to cast them into a ring, about, about, about, till he hath inclosed himself in the centre; now there is he puzzled—'Holla master, stand still until I have looked in my book.' Addeth to his book a table of the foreign words used by soldiers.

9th November. THE EARL OF ESSEX ABSENT FROM COURT.

To-day the Queen told my Lord Hunsdon that she much wondered at the absence of the Earl of Essex. He pleaded my Lord's want of health, the shooting in his temples upon cold or long speech, and yet his readiness to attend if she should be pleased to command his service. She accounted his duty and place sufficient to command him, and said that a prince was not to be contested withal by a subject. Nevertheless there is nothing but kindness and comfort to my Lord, if he will but turn about and take it.

The Privileges of the House.

Two days since Sir Thomas Knivett showing that since being a member of this Parliament he had been served with a *subpoena* to attend in the Chancery, the matter was referred to the committee for examination of such matters. Yesterday Mr. Brograve, Attorney of the Duchy, declared that the committee had met together and are of opinion that the serving of a *subpoena* is a manifest contempt committed against the whole House; for by reason of such process, a member so served must needs be withdrawn from the service of the House, both in his mind and person, by the mere necessity of following his own private business elsewhere. It was resolved therefore that two members should be sent to the Lord Keeper in the name of the whole House to require him to revoke the *subpoena*. Whereupon Sir Edward Hoby and Mr. Brograve went to the Lord Keeper and delivered the message of the House, to which the Lord Keeper asked whether they were appointed by any advised consideration of the House to deliver their message unto him with the word 'require.' They answered his Lordship, 'Yea.' Then his Lordship said that as he thought very reverently and honourably of the House and the liberties and privileges of the same, but so to revoke the *subpoena* in that sort is to restrain her Majesty in her greatest power, which is justice in the place wherein he serveth her. He saith that he will be advised further before giving his answer to the House.

Abuses in Bristol.

When Captain Docura, upon the recent alarm of the Spanish fleet, was sent into Bristol to see the trained bands which should have been in readiness and to train them to serve, the men were presented to him after many delays and altogether unarmed. Moreover he found very small care or feeling in the Mayor in these occasions, for he trusted to the situation of his town, being a great indraught in the land. This slender regard in these times of danger deserveth much to be blamed.

10th November. THE PARLIAMENT.

This day in the Parliament a Bill for taking away clergy from certain offenders was sent up to the Lords; committees were appointed touching the sundry enormities growing by patents of privilege and monopolies and the abuses of them; and a motion was made touching the abuses of licences for marriages granted by ecclesiastical persons.

14th November. THE KNIGHTS OF THE POST.

There is a book entered called *The discovery of the Knights of the Post*, written by one E. S. The knights of the post are those who will pretend themselves to be citizens of substance and so bail a man out of arrest for a reward. In term time they are most commonly to be found in Fleet Street, about St. John, or about Chancery Lane or in some of the pudding-pie houses in Westminster; but out of the term, then in Duke Humphrey's alley in Paul's, or at the Lion on the backside of St. Nicholas Shambles, or at the Rose in Pannier Alley, or the Dolphin at the end of Carter Lane, or the Woolsack.

INCESTUOUS MARRIAGES.

In the Parliament Sir John Fortescue declared that yesterday her Majesty called Mr. Secretary and himself unto her, and telling them that she had been informed of the horrible and great incestuous marriages discovered in the House, commanded them to take information of the grievances in particular of the members of the House that she might have certain notice thereof and thereupon give order for their due punishment and redress.

15th November. THE SUBSIDIES.

Mr. Chancellor, putting the House in remembrance of the Lord Keeper's speech on the first day of the Parliament touching the causes of the summoning of this Parliament, declared how great and excessive have been her Majesty's charges for the defence of her realm, amounting to more than treble the value of the last three subsidies and six fifteenths and tenths granted by the last Parliament. Then Mr. Secretary Cecil showed at large the purposes, practices and attempts of the King of Spain against her Majesty at sundry times, together with his great overthrows in the same by the mighty hand of God and of her Highness's forces, to his perpetual ignominy and great dishonour throughout the world. And so, after a large discourse most excellently delivered by him, concluded with a motion for proceeding to a committee ; which is agreed by the House.

16th November. MY LORD OF ESSEX'S ABSENCE.

There are many different censures about my Lord of Essex's absence from the Parliament, some earnestly expecting his advancement, others that daily make use of his absence confess his worth but wish him well only in words. Yet is my Lord for all his good parts least perfect in working his own good, for his patience continually giveth way to his crosses, and upon every discontentment he will absent himself from Court. Some there be that would say to him 'Let nothing draw thee from the Court ; sit in every Council, yet so that there may be nothing concluded but with thy good liking and privity. Thou hast 100,000 true hearts in this small isle that daily expect and wish thy settled content, and the fall of them that love thee not. What dignity is done to them, or indignity to thee, but in thy absence ? Thy enemies are thereby made strong and thou weak. And whereas thou retainest many in thy favour as true and secret friends, remember that Christ had but twelve and one proved a devil.'

18th November. THE EARL OF ESSEX ABSENT FROM PARLIAMENT.

Report was made by the Lord Keeper in the House of Lords that the Earl of Essex received not the writ of his summons till yesterday, through the negligence of the messenger, and now wanting health to give his attendance desireth to be excused of his absence, the Earls of Worcester and Southampton testifying his sickness.

19th November. THE SUBSIDIES.

Sir John Fortescue, Chancellor of the Exchequer, showed that at the committee of Parliament yesterday it was agreed to grant unto her Majesty three entire subsidies and six fifteenths and tenths. Whereupon, some members of the House being for delay in the payments of these subsidies, Sir Robert Cecil gave very many forcible reasons and causes of great importance for the speedy performance of the subsidies; which done, it was upon question resolved that the last payment of the subsidies shall be made in one year and at one entire payment in like sort as the two first of the same three subsidies are to be paid.

Then Mr. Davies, showing many corruptions in the Masters of Colleges in the Universities of Oxford and Cambridge in their abusing the possessions of Colleges contrary to the intents of founders, converting the same to their own private commodities, prayed the advice and assistance of the House for the better digesting of a Bill which he had drawn to the purpose. Herein Mr. Speaker referreth him to such members of the House as are of the Temple. Whereupon Sir Edward Hoby, liking very well of Mr. Davies' motion, moveth that the like consideration be had of Deans and Chapters.

Yesterday one Mr. Thomas Layton, one of the knights for the county of Salop, having been much visited with sickness since his coming up to this session of Parliament, is for better recovery of his health licensed by Mr. Speaker to depart home.

20th November. DISORDERS IN WALES.

During the late attempt of the Spaniards two of their ships were driven ashore in Wales; whereof one was forced into a creek in a place called Galtop. Hereupon Mr. Hugh Butler, that was in command of the trained bands in those parts, prepared six fisher boats to board the ship; but the Spaniards set out a play of truce and offered to send their cockboat ashore. This being perceived by one John Wogan, a gentleman of those parts, he with his brother and other associates to the number of twenty entered the ship before Mr. Butler, and not only withstood him by force but wounded him in three places, while his company rifled the ship of all her goods, money and things of value. At Caldey, the other Spanish ship in which there was treasure for Dunkirk is escaped through the disorderly behaviour of others.

THE SPANISH LOSSES.

There is news from Spain that forty-nine ships are arrived back on the coast, whereof twenty nine are the King's galleons; fifty of the fleet are missing. The *St. Peter* is leaky, the *St. Lucas* ran aground; they had to cast most of their horses and mules overboard. The fleet was within two days' sail of Land's End. One of the galleons with Don Pedro de Guevara, General of artillery, in her took fire and hath not since been seen; another ship, wherein were the materials for fortification and for firing our ships in harbour, attempting to aid her, took fire and was blown up, and a French ship with her, full of soldiers. There is now nothing but confusion, stories of misfortunes, yet brags of what they will do next spring; yet the defeat of an army so long in preparing hath been very sudden. Their plan was to have landed 8,000 in long-boats westward of Plymouth by peep of day while the ships occupied our forces west of Falmouth till the whole army was landed.

The Spanish King hath been very sick, and there are bonfires and processions for his recovery. He had a palsy and for two days was fed with liquor blown into his throat by the Infanta.

21st November. PRIVILEGE OF THE HOUSE.

Sir Edward Hoby moved the House for privilege for Sir John Tracy, being a member of the House and at that time at the Common Pleas to be put on a jury. Whereupon the Sergeant of the House was sent straightway with the Mace to call Sir John to his attendance in the House, and Sir John then returned to his place.

22nd November. A PETITION OF THE UNIVERSITIES.

Because of the speeches lately uttered by Mr. Davies in the Lower House of Parliament greatly tending to the utter discredit of the Governors and Heads of Colleges generally, the Vice-Chancellors both of Cambridge and Oxford have petitioned their Chancellors that Mr. Davies may be compelled to make such proof as he can of those scandalous matters, lest by colour of these scandalous defamations uttered in so public a place some new statute may pass to the general prejudice of both Universities.

23rd November. THE PARLIAMENT.

Mr. Walgrave delivering a Bill to the Speaker declareth that the transportation of a great number of herrings to Leghorn both occasioneth a very great scarcity of herrings in the realm, and is, saith he, a great means of spending much butter and cheese to the enhancing of the price thereof.

Mr. Attorney General and Mr. Doctor Stanhop having brought from the Lords an Act passed with their Lordships concerning the deprivation of divers bishops at the beginning of the reign, after their departure it was shortly found by Sir Edward Hoby that the Act was not duly and rightly endorsed by their Lordships; the endorsement being made above the Contents of the Act which ought to have been made under it. Whereupon the House being made privy thereto by the Speaker, Mr. Comptroller, with divers members, was sent to the Lords with the Act to signify the error and to pray amendment. Later Mr. Attorney and Dr. Stanhop came from the Lords with the Act endorsed according to the ancient former usage of Parliament, signifying to the House that the faulty endorsement of the Act in such manner before did grow only by an error in the Clerk of the Upper House, who had never exercised the place before the present Parliament; moreover their Lordships, liking very well of what the House had done touching this error, withal wish the House to continue all former good order and courses in all Parliament proceedings.

28th November. THE FRENCH AMBASSADOR RECEIVED.

To-day M. de Maisse, who is sent over by the French King, was received in audience by her Majesty. When he was conducted to the door of the Privy Chamber he made reverence to the Queen who was sitting by herself, and at some distance from the Lords and Ladies. As he entered she rose and came forward to the middle of the Chamber. M. de Maisse kissed the border of her garment, and she raised him with both hands and with a favourable countenance began to excuse herself that she had not given him audience sooner, saying that the day before she had been sick of an affliction on the right side of her face, and he would believe it if he looked at her eyes and countenance, for she did not remember when she had been so ill before. At this meeting the Ambassador spoke but in general terms, noting that as he spoke the Queen ofttimes raised herself from her chair and seemed to be impatient at his words. She complained of the fire that it hurt her eyes, although there was a great screen before it, and called for water to put it out.

30th November. A Prisoner released.

One Gilbert Layton that hath lain a prisoner in the Tower these six years is now to be released with condition that he shall at all times be forthcoming upon warning given him to be at a certain place in London, and also to behave himself as a good subject, and when her Majesty shall be at any of her houses in London not to repair to the Court. This man formerly confessed that he would kill the Queen.

An Accident at the Swan.

There was a prize played at the Swan on the Bankside where Turner and one Dunn playing the prizes, Turner thrust Dunn into the eye and so into the brains that he fell down dead without speaking any word.

1st December. Gerard's 'Herbal.'

Mr. John Gerard, Master in Chirurgery, hath written a great work called *The Herbal or general history of plants*, being dedicated to the Lord Burleigh. This work is in three books, whereof the first treateth of grasses, rushes, corn, bulbous or onion-rooted plants in 106 chapters. The second containeth the description, place, time, names, nature, and virtues of all sorts of herbs for meat, medicine or sweet smelling use, etc., and hath 511 chapters. The third of trees, shrubs, bushes, fruit-bearing plants, rosins, gums, roses, heath, mosses, some Indian and other rare plants, also mushrooms, coral and their several kinds, which book hath 167 chapters; and to all the chapters are there one or more cuts of the things described therein. Concludeth with a description of the goose-tree or barnacle, found in the north parts of Scotland.

On this tree do grow certain shellfishes of a white colour tending to russet wherein are contained little living creatures; which shells in time of maturity do open and of them grow those little living things, which falling into the water become the fowls which we call 'barnacles,' in the north of England brant geese, and in Lancashire tree geese. Mr. Gerard hath himself found similar between Dover and Romney, for causing the trunk of an old rotten tree to be drawn out of the water, there were growing on it many thousands of long crimson bladders, in shape like unto puddings newly filled befoıe they be sodden, very clear and shining. At the nether end did grow a shellfish, fashioned somewhat like a small mussel, but whiter. In these shells were found living things without form or shape; in others things that were very naked in shape like a bird; in others the birds covered with soft down, the shell half open and the bird ready to fall out.

3rd December. THE VENETIAN CORN SHIP.

There is still dispute concerning that Venetian ship the *St. Agatha Morisini* which was driven into Portsmouth last January laden with corn that was sold because of the then scarcity. Martin Frederico, a merchant of Venice, hath procuration from the Signiory to follow a cause, complaining that the corn was undervalued, sold at low prices, and a great part missing. Dr. Julius Caesar and others are appointed to examine the matter and to certify to the Council what fault they find in the dealing of the Commissioners, for her Majesty hath care that the Signiory should have all the satisfaction in these causes which in equity ought to be afforded them.

4th December. THE SERMON AT PAUL'S CROSS.

Mr. John Howson to-day preached the sermon at Paul's Cross on Matthew xxi., 12 and 13, showing how unlawful is the buying and selling of spiritual promotion. Saith that this buying and selling in the Church will make barren the two Universities; for those that be bred up in learning having in childhood suffered great and grievous affliction in the grammar schools, when they be come to the Universities live either of the College's allowance, needy of all things but hunger and fear, or being maintained by their own or their parents' cost, do expend in necessary maintenance, books, and degrees £500 or 1,000 marks before they be come to perfection. If they then cannot purchase a poor parsonage or vicarage of £40 or £50 a year unless they pay to the patron for the lease of their life either in annual pension or above the rate of a copyhold, what father will be so improvident to bring his son up at great charge? Concludeth that this buying and selling is indeed the sin of simony, an heresy intolerable, and one that will cause the Universities to be decayed, the Church supplied with ignorant pastors, hospitality removed from the clergy and the sign and forerunner of some evil to ensue to the Commonwealth.

8th December. A BOY POSSESSED AT NOTTINGHAM.

Some weeks since a boy called William Sommers of Nottingham began to be strangely tormented in body and gave great tokens that he was possessed by a wicked spirit; whereupon the Mayor and some of the Aldermen of Nottingham sent instantly for Mr. Darrell (who by prayer and fasting hath already restored eight or nine persons that have been vexed in like sort). At first Mr. Darrell was unwilling to come, but by their importunate letters and messengers at length he condescended to their desires, and came to Nottingham on the 5th November. The 7th was appointed for the exercise of prayer and fasting to the end that Sommers might be dispossessed; which at the prayers of Mr. Darrell and others to the number of a hundred and fifty is brought to pass. Hereupon Mr. Darrell is retained as preacher in Nottingham.

Sommers being dispossessed discovered certain witches, one whereof was called Doll Freeman, allied to one Freeman an Alderman of Nottingham. This Freeman offended that his kinswoman should be called in question threatened Sommers that he was himself a witch, and caused him to be committed to prison, where the Devil appeared unto him in the likeness of a mouse, threatening that if he would not let him re-enter and would not say that all he had done concerning his tormenting during his possession was but counterfeit, then he should be hanged; but if he would yield, the Devil would save him.

Thus a new stipulation being made between them, the Devil entered; and afterwards Sommers constantly declared that all which he had done before was only counterfeit. A general opinion being now conceived that Sommers hath counterfeited all his former proceeding, Mr. Darrell preacheth very bitterly against that conceit, persuading his auditory that

Satan will lurk sometimes about one out of whom he hath been cast, suffering the party to be well for a good space, but will not give him over until in the end he have repossessed him.

11th December. THE SUBSIDY.

The Bill for the granting of six fifteenths and tenths and three entire subsidies had a second reading to-day and was ordered to be ingrossed.

14th December. THE LORDS' PRIVILEGE ABUSED.

Six days since one William Cole, one of the Knight Marshal's men, that had arrested John York, the Archbishop's servant, was brought before the Lords by the Sergeant at Arms; and being found upon examination to have wilfully offended therein against the privilege of the House was committed to the Fleet; but to-day he is enlarged on paying only his fees.

THE ABUSE OF MONOPOLIES.

Mr. Francis Moore, one of the committees for consideration of the method and substance of the humble thanks to be yielded by Mr. Speaker unto her Majesty on behalf of the House for her care and favour in repressing sundry inconveniences and abuses practised by monopolies and patents of privilege, delivered a note of the meeting and travail of the committee therein. This being read by the Clerk was well liked of. Whereupon the Speaker moved the House that, albeit he was ready to perform their commandment according to the substance and effect of the note, yet they would not tie him to the strict and precise form of the words and terms; which is yielded unto accordingly.

14th December. MONSIEUR DE MAISSE.

M. de Maisse was again received by the Queen to-day, and saith that when he entered the Chamber one was playing the virginals, and she seemed to be so attentive to the music and as it were surprised by his entrance that he excused himself for interrupting her pastime. The Queen replied that she loveth music and every day playeth a pavan. She spoke several times of the King of Spain, his wishing to kill her. Whilst they conversed she would ofttimes make digression, as if she would gain time and not appear to be pressed by the ambassador's demands; which she would excuse saying, 'You will say, Master Ambassador, the tale I told you is mere trifling; see what it is to conduct affairs with old women such as I am.' She said also to him that she had long hands, both by nature and by power, for, quoth she, '*anne fas longas regibus esse manus*?' whereat she took off her gloves, showing her hands, longer than the ambassador's by three thick fingers.

17th December. TWO LONDON CRIMES.

The body of Mr. Richard Anger, a double reader of Gray's Inn, that hath been missed almost a month, was lately found floating in the Thames; and being viewed by certain skilful surgeons it is thought he was not drowned in the water but stifled or murthered, and after thrown into the Thames, which by other conjectures is greatly to be suspected. There are great presumptions against one of his sons, Richard Anger, and Edward Ingram, the porter of Gray's Inn. Forasmuch as the fact is so horrible that an ancient gentleman should be murdered in his chamber, these two are to be examined very strictly, and if they cannot be brought to confess the truth, then shall they be put to the manacles in Bridewell.

There is also one Richard Remchin, a gentleman, that hath long used the clipping of coin, and upon search there is found in a house of his in Fetter Lane a great quantity of clippings and coin clipped, to the sum of £20 in gold. This man's goods are to be seized and kept in the Tower until he hath been convicted, when they shall be converted to the Queen's use.

20th December. A DISPUTE CONCERNING PROCEDURE.

The Parliament stands adjourned over Christmas until the 11th January at 8 o'clock in the morning.

Some days since a Bill was sent up to the Lords and by them passed with amendment of one word and so sent down to the Lower House, where it was found that the amendment had been affiled to the Bill and ingrossed in parchment with the words '*soit baille aux Communes*' contrary to precedent. Wherefore the House caused the Bill to be returned to the Lords for amendment, saying that they had no warrant to take notice of that amendment because it was in parchment and not in paper. To-day the Lords answer that they do not expect an exception of such levity from the gravity of the House, taking it to be immaterial whether such amendments be written in parchment or in paper, either white paper, black paper or brown paper. Thereupon some members of the House charged the Clerk that by his default and error the House was charged with levity; to which he himself prayed that some of the ancient Parliament men of the House might examine the matter. After the Clerk had been heard and the matter blamed on the inexperience of the Clerk of the Upper House, it is determined by these ancientest Parliament men that all the members of the House, being Privy Councillors, together with the best sort of the rest of the members, accompanied with the Sergeants of the Law, shall straightway be sent to the Lords to signify in the name of the whole House that the House has not in any manner of sort erred in returning that Bill and amendments in parchment to have the same done in paper according to the ancient order of Parliament; and that the House doth take itself to be very hardly dealt with to be taxed by their Lordships with imputation of levity, and reproached by other unusual and unnecessary terms.

21st December. THE EARL OF ESSEX'S INDIGNATION.

'Tis said in Court that the Queen hath advanced the Earl of Essex to be Lord Marshal, whereby his precedency over the Lord Admiral is restored. My lord doth now show himself in more public sort and is purposed to have the patent of the new Earl of Nottingham altered. But he will have none of it, and yesterday in the afternoon he gave over his White Staff as Lord Steward, and to-day is gone to Chelsea where he purposeth, as 'tis said, to be sick, for the Queen by this long patience and suffering of his is grown to consider the wrong done unto him, which now she lays upon the Lord Treasurer and Sir Robert Cecil, though with infinite protestations they deny it. The Earl of Essex desires right to be done him, either by a commission to examine it, or by combat, either against the Earl of Nottingham himself or any of his sons or name that shall defend it; or that it will please her Majesty to see the wrongs done to him, and so will suffer himself to be commanded by her. There is such ado about it as troubles the place and all proceedings. Sir Walter Ralegh is employed to end this quarrel and make atonement between them. But the resolution of Lord Essex is not to yield but with altering the patent, which cannot be done by persuasion to bring the Earl of Nottingham to it.

THE QUEEN AND M. DE MAISSE.

The Queen gave audience to M. de Maisse to-day, and in their conference together she declared that she would do naught without her Council, for there is naught so dangerous in affairs of State as self-opinion; but no longer hath she such a Council as formerly, for she hath lost twenty or twenty-two of them. The Ambassador replied that she could always make others; but the Queen answered that they were young and not yet experienced in matters of state. The Queen spake also of the love of her people, saying that it is incredible, and she loveth them no less for it, and would die rather than lose any of it, to which the Ambassador answered that they are indeed happy to live under so good a Princess. The Queen said also that she was now come almost to the edge of her grave, and ought to bethink her of death; whereat suddenly she checked herself in her speech saying, 'I think not to die so soon, Master Ambassador; nor am I so old as they think.'

Nevertheless Monsieur de Maisse complaineth that nothing is resolved, for the Queen cannot assemble the Council because of the discontents of my Lord of Essex who will not sit with the rest, and she will resolve nothing without him. Twice my Lord hath left the Court not to return again, but each time he has been sent for the same day and come back again. Since the ambassador's coming there has been nothing spoken of in Court but this brabble.

24th December. THE PRICE OF PEPPER.

This Christmastide pepper is being sold in London at 8s. the pound, which is much noted because of the former restraint of the bringing in of pepper till all that captured in the Great Carrack, four years since, should be sold. Raisins this year are being sold at 6d. the pound, Gascon wines at 2s. 8d. the gallon, and sweet wines at 4s.

31st December. NEW PLAYS.

The Admiral's men have played four new plays this month, being *Valteger*, *Stukeley*, *Nabuchodonozor*, and *That will be shall be.*

OTHER BOOKS SET FORTH ANNO 1597.

Meres' 'God's Arithmetic.'

A little book called *God's Arithmetic* by Mr. Francis Meres, Master of Arts of both Universities, and student of Divinity. 'There be four parts of Arithmetic,' saith he, 'Addition, Multiplication, Substraction and Division, whereof the first two take their beginning from the right hand, and do multiply and increase: and these be God's numbers. The other two begin from the left and do substract and divide, and these be the Devil's.' Treateth of the advantage of marriage, and especially of ministers of religion. Saith that in old time Jacob served seven years for Rachel and bought his wife by his service, but now men must be hired to take wives, as if to take a wife were to take up a cross, and hence it ofttimes comes to pass that marriage is not good because the end of it is for goods and not for love.

Breton's 'Wits' Trenchmour.'

A witty book by Mr. Nicholas Breton entitled *Wits' Trenchmour* in form of a pleasant conference between an angler and a scholar.

Shakespeare's 'Romeo and Juliet.'

The tragedy of *Romeo and Juliet*, written by William Shakespeare, that hath been often played publicly with great applause by the servants of the Lord Hunsdon.

1598

1st January. TYRONE AGAIN SUBMITS.

The Earl of Tyrone again submitted in his own person to my Lord of Ormond, on the 22nd December. Hereby Tyrone hath promised upon his honour and credit to keep the peace for eight weeks during the truce. He will not upon any supposed wrong committed upon him enter into any revenge, but will cause the same to be informed, with proofs, to the Lord Justice or the Lieutenant General. He will not entertain any practice or intelligence with the King of Spain; and if he receive any letters he will acquaint the State withal. He will also deliver cattle into the fort at Blackwater, and send a safe conduct with the victuals and munitions now to be sent there.

2nd January. REFLECTIONS ON A PEACE WITH SPAIN.

Now that the French King proposeth a peace with the King of Spain there are divers considerations whether it be more profitable to continue the war or not. A peace assuredly obtained is better than any war. It shall be profitable, in that by making peace with Spain we shall have commodity to reduce Ireland to quietness, and thereby be spared the excessive charges of treasures, victuals, munition and men to be sent out of England; trade will be open for our merchants to all countries of Spain, Portugal, Barbary and the Levant, as also to the countries in the East, as Poland and Denmark, and the maritime towns of Germany. Hereby also shall the shipping and mariners increase, and decayed port towns be succoured, as Newcastle, Hull, Boston and Lynn northwards; Southampton, Poole, Weymouth, Bristol and Chester west and southwards. By peace also shall the insolency of the King of Scots be avoided, the borders strengthened and, by increase of trade, the customs increased.

Yet are there discommodities upon dissolving of soldiers. The soldiers spared out of Ireland will, if left there, make waste or be ready to provoke the Irish to new rebellion; such as return to England will live disorderly if they be not forced to return to their native counties and former trade: and the like discommodities from those that return from the Low Countries. Moreover the Queen shall lose all hope of Calais and be unassured of the great sums lent to the French King. In France also the restitution of the Catholic religion, though liberty be promised to Protestants, will breed division and civil war, whereby the Catholics getting the upper hand, will be ready to please the King by depriving all Protestants of their states and liberties.

3rd January. SIR JOHN SMYTHE RELEASED.

Sir John Smythe, who was committed to the Tower for his seditions in the summer of '96, having made submission to her Majesty in writing before the Council, is now to be set at liberty, to repair to his own house in Essex and not to depart thence within the compass of a mile.

4th January. THE FRENCH AMBASSADOR.

M. de Maisse hath now taken his leave and will set out for France to-morrow. The Queen hath resolved to send Mr. Secretary Cecil to France. Hereat in Court they say that this will be in good earnest, but others take it for a sign that peace is toward.

5th January. TYRONE AGAIN SUBMITS.

Three days before Christmas Tyrone again submitted himself, making a very humble and penitent submission, declaring upon the knees of his heart that he is most sorry for his late relapse and defection, promising also that if he be granted a truce for two months there shall be no impediment to the victualling of the fort at Blackwater.

10th January. COMPLAINTS CONCERNING THE FRENCH COURTS.

The Queen having resolved to send Sir Robert Cecil into France together with some other Commissioners for special affairs, some order will be taken for the continued complaints of the spoils committed by the French in the Narrow Seas; and to this end Dr. Compton goeth with the Secretary with remembrances and informations that appertain to these matters.

11th January. THE PARLIAMENT RENEWED.

To-day on the meeting of the House of Lords the Earl of Essex, being now created Earl Marshal, taketh his place next after the Earl of Oxford, Lord Chamberlain of England, and before the Earl of Nottingham, Lord Steward and Lord High Admiral.

13th January. THE STILLYARD TO BE SUPPRESSED.

The Queen hath commanded the Lord Mayor and Sheriffs to repair to the Stillyard and give those that reside there notice to depart out of the realm by the 28th of this month, and to all others of the Hanse Towns residing in the realm. This is done because of that mandate of the Emperor forbidding our English merchants of the company of Merchant Adventurers any traffic within the Empire, and commanding them to depart upon great pains, and to forbear all havens and landing places or any commerce. The Stillyard shall remain in the custody of the Lord Mayor until some more favourable course shall be heard of the Emperor for restitution of our merchants to their former lawful trade within the Empire.

14th January. THE MERCHANTS TO DEPART.

This afternoon the Lord Mayor entered the Stillyard and commanded the merchants to depart the realm by the 28th of this month; their number was about sixteen. They stood much upon the privileges of the Stillyard but they see that it serves small purpose.

THE COMMONS OFFENDED.

This morning Sir Walter Ralegh, with a number of members of the Lower House, having been sent to repair to the Upper House to move for a joint conference in the Bill for the erection of houses of correction, on their return declared that their Lordships, in giving answer to these members at the Bar, did not use their former and wonted courtesy of coming down towards the Bar, but all of them sitting still in their great estates very solemnly and all covered, the Lord Keeper also in like manner delivered the answer, to the great indignity of the House and contrary to all former usage. Whereupon this innovation being very much misliked of by sundry members, Mr. Controller,

Sir Walter Ralegh, Mr. Chancellor of the Exchequer, Sir Anthony Mildmay with many others are appointed to meet this afternoon at two o'clock in Sergeants-Inn in Chancery Lane for further resolution herein.

19th January. THE COMMONS' OFFENCE.

The persons selected by the House of Commons to receive satisfaction for the innovation disputed five days ago, being Sir William Knollys, Sir Edward Hoby, and others, to-day came before the Lords who considered their answer. Which being resolved, they signified to the Lower House that if they should send any of the House up to the Lords to receive an answer to their demands, answer should be given them. Whereupon the same members as before came into the Upper House and having placed themselves at the lower end of the room, the Lord Keeper moved them to come nearer to receive their answer; but when they perceived that the Lords were resolved not to come from their places to the Bar, they protested by Sir William Knollys that they had no commission to receive answer in that form and so departed.

20th January. A QUARREL AT COURT.

The Earl of Southampton is full of discontentments. Some days since he with Sir Walter Ralegh and Mr. Parker being at primero in the Presence Chamber, and the Queen being gone to bed, Mr. Ambrose Willoughby as Squire for the Body desired them to give over. Soon after he spake to them again that if they would not leave he would call in the guard to pull down the board, which Sir Walter seeing put up his money and went his ways. But my Lord Southampton took exceptions at him and told him he would remember it; and so finding him between the Tennis Court wall and the garden struck him, and Mr. Willoughby pulled off some of his locks. The Queen gave Mr. Willoughby thanks for what he did in the Presence, and told him he had done better if he had sent my Lord to the Porter's lodge to see who durst fetch him out.

THE COMMONS SATISFIED.

After conference held between the members of both Houses, it was shown by those that had been present in many Parliaments, and especially by the Lord Treasurer, the most ancient Parliament man, that the order and custom of the House is this: When any Bills or messages are brought from the House of Commons to be presented to the Upper House, then the Lord Keeper and the rest of the Lords are to arise from their places and to go down to the Bar, there to meet such as come from the Commons and to receive their messages; but, contrariwise, when any answer is to be delivered by the Lord Keeper in the name and on behalf of the Upper House, the knights and burgesses are to receive the same standing towards the lower end of the Upper House without the Bar, and the Lord Keeper is to deliver the same sitting in his place with his head covered, and all the Lords keeping their places. Their Lordships' answer to the Commons is therefore that in the delivery of their message to Sir Walter Ralegh and the others, they have not given them any just distaste or therein offered the House of Commons any indignity whatever. And herein the House of Commons is satisfied accordingly.

A BAWD CARTED.

To-day at the Sessions Prudence Crisp, otherwise known as Drury or Wingfield, is condemned to be carted. This woman hath a common brothel at Pickthatch where there have been many unlawful assemblies and atrocious riots.

26th January. THE STILLYARD.

News being received that our merchants at Stade have received longer time for their departure, the merchants of the Hanse Towns are now given until the end of February, or farther as our own merchants shall be used; they are charged on their peril not to depart in the mean season without satisfying their debts.

28th January. CASES OF PIRACY.

A certain Walter Artson, a Dutch merchant, hath complained and made proof in the High Court of the Admiralty that one Captain Elliot and his consorts in piratical manner took a ship called the *Neptune* with her lading of 120,000 of fish and two dry fats of linen cloth which they have disposed of in Dorsetshire and elsewhere.

On the coast of Cardigan a ship called the *Sea Cock* of Flushing, laden with goods to the value of £20,000, was by default of the pilot wrecked in her course from St. Lucar towards Middleburgh in Zealand. Whereupon the inhabitants of that county make an unconscionable spoil upon the utensils, apparel, munition, and furniture of the ship, together with a great part of the goods thrown upon the shore.

From Jersey also complaint is made that English pirates committed a spoil upon a ship named the *Judith*, laden with 20,000 of Newfoundland fish.

29th January. ABUSES IN THE NORTH.

A short while since the Council gave orders that those recusants in Lancashire who refused to pay the sums charged against them for the service in Ireland should be arrested, but though both the Bishop of Chester and the Sheriff used their best endeavours they missed of good success, because the recusants withdrew themselves from their abodes. The chiefest of them have now come to London to make friends to procure their release. There are still many disorders in the north. The prison at Lancaster is so ill kept that the recusants there have liberty to go when and whither they list, to hunt, hawk and go to horse races at their pleasure.

THE SPANISH PRISONERS.

The Spanish prisoners taken of late at sea are to be sent down to Plymouth and thence transported at her Majesty's great charges to Spain under the conveyance of Mr. Nicholas Owsley.

1st February. COURT NEWS.

The Earl of Southampton is now at Court again, having for a while absented himself by her Majesty's command. He is much troubled by her usage of him, for some have played unfriendly parts with him. Mr. Secretary hath procured him licence to travel, but his fair mistress doth wash her fairest face with too many tears; it is secretly said that he shall be married to her. The Lord Compton, Lord Cobham, Sir Walter Ralegh and my Lord Southampton severally feast Mr. Secretary before his departure, and have plays and banquets.

4th February. A RESTRAINT ON COCHINEAL.

There is such quantity of cochineal and indigo brought into the realm from prizes lately taken by the Earl of Essex that will serve this country for many years. The officers of the customs are now to forbear to receive any entry of cochineal for two years. If any be brought and the merchant be not content to carry it into some foreign port, it shall be laid up in the Custom-house till the two years be expired.

9th February. THE PARLIAMENT DISSOLVED.

The Parliament, having sat since 24th October and considered of many Bills almost daily, is this afternoon dissolved.

Her Majesty came to the Upper House somewhat after 3 o'clock, and being set with divers Lords spiritual and temporal, the members of the Lower House with the Speaker having waited a good while at the door were at length admitted to the Upper House, as many of them as could conveniently get in.

Then the Speaker having made three reverences to her Majesty began to speak. First he showed the happiness of a Commonwealth governed by laws by which subjects are held in due obedience; which her Majesty observing had now called a Parliament for the preservation of some laws, amending of others, cutting off of unnecessary statutes, and the making of new. And that her subjects in this Parliament, considering the strength of the realm to consist in the strength of the Prince and subjects, and their strength to stand first in the hands of God, and next in the provision of treasure, 'and therefore,' said he, 'your Majesty's most humble, dutiful and obedient subjects have by me their mouth and Speaker presented here a free gift of their free and loving hearts'—and so with that he kneeled down and delivered the Bill of Subsidy, which the Clerk of the Crown received and laid on a little table standing before the Speaker, betwixt two great wax candles on a plain green carpet—'the which I hope and think was granted without thought of "No," sure I am without word of "No."'

The second part of his speech showed a commandment laid on him by the House of Commons touching monopolies or patents of privilege, the which was a set and penned speech made at a committee. The third showed the thankfulness of the House of Commons for the pardon. The fourth and last showed the Speaker's own petition that if any faults had been committed in the House they might not now be revived; and if either he himself had spoken too much or not so much as in duty he ought to have done, he besought her Majesty's pardon.

This speech being ended, the Queen called Sir Thomas Egerton, the Lord Keeper, to whom, kneeling down before her, she spake in private; after which he went unto a place like a desk, made even with the cloth of estate on the right side, and there made answer to the Speaker's speech:

'Our most dread Sovereign, her Excellent Majesty, hath given me in charge to say unto you and the rest of her loving subjects that she doth thankfully accept of their free gift of subsidy, which she would not have required had not the puissance of the enemy required her thereunto. Secondly, touching the monopolies, her Majesty hopeth that her dutiful and loving subjects would not take away her prerogative, which is the chiefest flower in her garden, and the principal and head pearl in her crown and diadem; but they will rather leave that to her disposition. And as her Majesty hath proceeded to trial of them already, so she promiseth to continue that they shall all be examined to abide the trial and touchstone of the Law. Thirdly, touching her pardon, her Majesty's pleasure is that I show unto you that you do not so willingly accept it as she giveth it. Fourthly, for your pardon, Mr. Speaker, her Majesty saith that you have so learnedly and so eloquently defended yourself now, and painfully behaved yourself hitherto, as that your labour deserveth double her thanks. But in your petition I must also join with you in beseeching her most Excellent Majesty that if anything through want of experience or through mine own imperfections and ignorance have overslipped me it may be pardoned.'

These speeches being ended, the titles of all the Acts were read by Mr. Smith, the Clerk of the Upper House; of which her Majesty gave her royal assent to twenty-four public Acts or Statutes and nineteen private, but did refuse or quash forty-eight several Bills that have passed both Houses. Which done the Lord Keeper dissolved the Parliament in these words,

'*Dominus Custos Magni Sigilli ex mandato Dominæ Reginæ tunc dissoluit præsens Parliamentum.*'

An Outrage in the Middle Temple.

To-day a very notable outrage and great contempt was committed in the Hall of the Middle Temple by Mr. John Davies. While the Benchers and others of the Society were dining together in the Hall, Mr. Davies (who is himself a Bencher) came in wearing his cloak, his hat upon his head, and girt with his dagger; and accompanied with his servant and some stranger, both armed with swords. These two stayed at the lower end of the Hall, but Mr. Davies went up to the Benchers' table by the hearth and there drawing out a bastinado from under his cloak he struck Mr. Richard Martin over the head three or four times with such force that the cudgel was broken into pieces. This done he rushed through the Hall, and snatched a sword from his servant which he shook in the face of Mr. Martin. Then retiring out of the Hall, he drew his sword from the scabbard and repeatedly brandished it naked; after which he hastened to the Temple steps and betook himself off in a boat.

10th February. Sir Robert Cecil's Departure.

Mr. Secretary set off to-day for France, and Lord Thomas Howard, Sir Walter Ralegh and divers others go with him to Dover. Before his going Sir Robert moved the Queen to fix a privy seal for my Lord of Essex for £7,000 to be paid to him out of the cochinella as her Majesty's free gift.

A Note of the Chief Statutes enacted by the late Parliament.

An Act concerning the decay of towns and houses of husbandry because of late years more than in times past many towns, parishes, and houses of husbandry have been destroyed and become desolate. Hereby all houses that have been suffered to decay these seven years shall be repaired or again erected.

An Act for the maintenance of tillage and husbandry; for that the strength and flourishing estate of this kingdom hath always been and is upheld by the maintenance of the plough and tillage, being the occasion of the increase and multiplying of the people both for service in wars and in times of peace, being also a principal mean that they are set on work and thereby withdrawn from idleness, drunkenness, unlawful games and other lewd practices ; and by the same means the greater part of the subjects are preserved from extreme poverty in a competent state of maintenance, and the wealth of the realm kept and dispersed in many hands where it is more ready to answer all necessary charges for the service of the realm. In the Parliament of 1593, partly by reason of the great plenty of grain at that time, the law ordaining a certain proportion of land to be kept in tillage was suffered to lapse ; but since that time there have grown many more depopulations by turning tillage into pasture than ever before.

An Act for the relief of the poor, whereby the churchwardens of every parish and four substantial householders shall be made overseers of the poor, with power to set to work the children of all parents unable to maintain them ; to gather a convenient stock of flax, hemp, wool, thread, iron and other necessary ware to set the poor that have no means to maintain themselves on work ; to gather sums of money towards the necessary relief of the lame, impotent, old and blind ; and also for putting out of children to be apprentices.

An Act for repressing of rogues, vagabonds and sturdy beggars, repealing all other Acts. Hereby shall be deemed as rogues and beggars all persons, calling themselves scholars, begging for money ; seafaring men, pretending losses of their ships or goods ; all idle persons, begging or using any subtle craft or unlawful games or plays ; or feigning themselves to have knowledge in physiognomy, palmistry, or like crafty sciences, or pretending that they can tell destinies or fortunes, or such other like fantastical imaginations ; proctors, procurers, patent gatherers ; collectors for gaols, prisons, or hospitals ; all fencers, bearwards, common players of interludes and minstrels wandering abroad (other than players belonging to any Baron of the realm or other honourable person of greater note, to be authorised under the hand and seal of arms of such Baron) ; jugglers, tinkers, pedlars and petty chapmen ; labourers, able in body, loitering and refusing to work for such reasonable wages as are offered. And when such an one shall be taken, he shall be stripped naked from his middle upwards and shall be openly whipped until his or her body be bloody; and forthwith to be sent from parish to parish the next straight way to the parish where he was born, or, if that be not known, the parish where he last dwelt by the space of one year. Moreover, if a rogue shall appear to be dangerous to the inferior sort of people and will not be reformed, it shall be lawful for the Justices to commit him to a house of correction till the next Quarter Sessions, and thereafter to be banished out of the realm; and if any rogue so banished shall return without licence the punishment shall be death.

An Act for erecting hospitals or abiding and working houses for the poor by those charitably disposed, which may for the next twenty years be done by deed inrolled in the High Court of Chancery without necessity, as aforetime, of her Majesty's special licence.

Two Acts taking away of benefit of clergy; the one from those who shall force women with substance against their will, the other from those that rob houses in the day time.

An Act concerning labourers, whereby is amplified that Act passed in '63 which giveth to the Sheriffs, Justices of peace, Mayors and other officers the authority to rate the wages of labourers, weavers, spinsters, workmen or workwomen of every sort.

An Act against lewd and wandering persons pretending themselves to be soldiers or mariners; because that divers licentious persons, contemning both laws, magistrates and religion, of late days wander up and down in all parts of the realm, under the name of soldiers and mariners, abusing the title of that honourable profession to countenance their wicked ways, and do continually assemble themselves weaponed in the highways and elsewhere in troops to the great terror and astonishment of all true subjects, committing daily many heinous outrages, robberies, and horrible murders. It is enacted that all soldiers and mariners shall return to the place of their dwelling or birth and betake themselves to some lawful trade, on pain of being condemned as felons without benefit of clergy. But if, having so returned, no work can be found, then shall such soldier make complaint to two Justices of the peace, who shall take order for some honest work to be provided for him or else tax the whole hundred for his relief until sufficient work may be had.

The Act for the necessary relief of soldiers and mariners passed in '93 renewed, and greater penalties fixed for those that are remiss in their duty of making such provision.

12th February. THE MUSTERS.

Orders are again given this spring that all the forces within the counties shall be viewed and sufficient persons supplied in places of those found wanting by death or otherwise insufficient. They shall moreover be instructed in the discipline of war by the officers sent down as their trainers. The total number of men required at this time amounts to 45,800.

15th February. COURT NEWS.

It is said that before his departure Sir Robert Cecil was resolved not to stir a foot till the Earl of Essex assured him that nothing should pass here in his absence that might be a prejudice or offensive to him. The Earl of Essex is again fallen in love with his fairest B.; it cannot choose but come to the Queen's ears, and then he is undone and all they that depend on his favour. Yesternight Sir Gelly Merrick made a very great supper at Essex House; there were at it my Ladies Leicester, Northumberland, Bedford, Essex and Rich, and my Lords of Essex, Rutland, Mountjoy and others. They had two plays which kept them up till one o'clock after midnight.

16th February. A BAWD CARTED.

Elizabeth Holland being found guilty at the Sessions of keeping a brothel at Pickthatch, the Court adjudge that she shall be put into a cart at Newgate and be carted with a paper on her head showing her offence, and from thence to Smithfield, from thence to her house, thence to the Standard in Cheapside, and thence to Bridewell where she shall be punished; and all the way basins to be rung before her. Thence she shall be taken to Newgate, and there to remain until she have paid a fine of £40.

19th February. A COMPANY OF PLAYERS TO BE SUPPRESSED.

The third company of players now showing plays is to be suppressed, for only the companies of the Lord Admiral and the Lord Chamberlain are by licence allowed.

23rd February. Mr. Bodley's Munificence to the University of Oxford.

Mr. Thomas Bodley hath written to the Vice-Chancellor of the University of Oxford that he will take upon himself the charge and cost to reduce the Public Library again to its former use, and to make it fit and handsome with seats and shelves and desks and all that may be needful, to stir up other men's benevolence, to help to furnish it with books; all which he purposeth to begin as soon as timber can be gotten. Moreover, because the Library never had any lasting allowance for the augmentation of the number or supply of books decayed (whereby when those that were in being were either wasted or embezzled the whole foundation was brought to ruin), now shall the University be assured of a standing annual rent to be disbursed every year in buying of books, in officers' stipends and other pertinent occasions. Thus, perhaps in time to come it may prove a notable treasure for the multitude of volumes, an excellent benefit for the use and ease of students, and a singular ornament in the University.

25th February. The Lord Treasurer dangerously sick.

Yesternight upon a sudden the Lord Treasurer grew ill of a cough which put him to very great pain. The Queen sent very graciously to visit him; the Lord Cobham came to him, and so did the Lady Derby. He took his leave of her, charging her to be good and careful of her two sisters, and as his pain increased so did he think upon his end, calling upon God to receive his soul, and with little rest he passed over a tedious night. But this morning it pleased God for the good of this poor country to ease him of his pain and to give him some rest.

26th February. Shakespeare's 'Henry the Fourth.'

There is entered for printing the play of *The History of Henry the Fourth* that is played by the Lord Chamberlain's men and written by Mr. William Shakespeare. Herein is shown the battle of Shrewsbury, with Harry Hotspur of the North, together with the humorous conceits of the fat knight, Sir John Falstaffe. When the actors first played this play, they called the fat knight Sir John Oldcastle, which caused offence to a certain nobleman whose wife is descended from that Oldcastle who was executed as a Lollard in the time of King Henry the Fifth. Wherefore the name is now changed.

FLESH IN LENT.

The customary orders concerning the killing of flesh in Lent are issued. The prices also to be charged for meat are this year laid down, namely, for carcases of the best sort of mutton, at 15s. or under, for the second sort at 13s. 4d., for the third sort at 10s.; for lamb, at 4s. 8d., 4s., 3s. 4d.; for veal, at 15s., 13s., or 11s.; and of each by joints or pieces at the same rates.

MARLOWE'S 'HERO AND LEANDER.'

Mr. Edward Blunt hath printed that unfinished poem of *Hero and Leander* left by Christopher Marlowe, dedicating it to Sir Thomas Walsingham. 'We think not ourselves discharged,' saith Mr. Blunt, 'of the duty we owe to our friend when we have brought the breathless body for the earth; for albeit the eye there taketh his ever farewell of that beloved object, yet the impression of the man that hath been dear to us, living an after life in our memory then putteth us in mind of further obsequies due unto the deceased.' In this poem is set forth how that Leander, having espied Hero at the feast of Adonis, swam over the Hellespont to her tower in Sestos and then enjoyed her love; but the rest of the fable is wanting.

THE CAPRICIOUS NATURE OF LOVE.

It lies not in our power to love, or hate,
For will in us is overruled by Fate.
When two are stripped, long ere the course begin,
We wish that one should lose, the other win;
And one especially do we affect
Of two gold ingots, like in each respect.
The reason no man knows, let it suffice,
What we behold is censur'd by our eyes.
Where both deliberate, the love is slight;
Who ever lov'd, that lov'd not at first sight?

1st March. THE DISORDERS IN GOVERNMENT IN IRELAND.

Notwithstanding the great mass of treasure which is often sent to Ireland with special direction to be converted only to the defraying of the army, the companies still cry out for pay, and the counties and towns that have strained themselves above their powers to diet the soldiers and furnish beeves are not satisfied but continually complain. Out of this want of pay to the army and the towns groweth all the disorders among the soldiers, who break loose upon the country and havoc the inhabitants, and is a great mean to estrange and alter the hearts of the people.

At Newry was a mutiny of the soldiers, for when the money for their pay was sent according to the certificate of the Marshal, it was found that he had made no mention of the absent and sick soldiers, which in some bands were ten, in some sixteen more than had been certified. These, finding themselves left out of all reckoning for money, victuals and clothes, fell with the rest of the garrison into so extreme a mutiny, that the Marshal and all the captains were in great doubt what would become either of the town or themselves. In the end when the paymaster entered the town the soldiers so battered him with a fury of snowballs that he fell off his horse, and with such tempest and rage did they prosecute him that if the captains and officers had not come speedily to his rescue, he had died in that place. The next day when every soldier was to have his part of his captain, and no band there but presenting ten more at least than there was money allowed for, they fell again into fury against the Marshal; but at the last he, by his friends, pawned all the credit he had that if by a certain date they were not satisfied by the State they should have all he had amongst themselves.

2nd March. THE LADY LEICESTER RECONCILED TO THE QUEEN.

The Earl of Essex hath many times laboured to have his mother brought into the Presence, for since her marriage to the late Earl of Leicester she hath been out of her Majesty's favour. Leave was often granted, and she brought to the privy galleries, but the Queen found some occasion not to come. Last Monday (27th) she was persuaded to go to Mr. Controller's at the Tilt End and there was my Lady Leicester waiting with a fair jewel of £300. A great dinner was prepared by my Lady Shandos; the Queen's coach ready; and all the world expecting her Majesty's coming, when upon a sudden she resolved not to go and so sent word. The Earl of Essex, that kept his chamber the day before, in his nightgown went up to the Queen by the privy way, but all would not prevail. But yesterday my Lady Leicester was at Court, kissed the Queen's hand and her breast, and embraced her, and the Queen kissed her. The Earl of Essex is in exceeding great favour. He doth carefully attend her Majesty and her service, and very honourably takes the pains to see all matters dispatched as if the Secretary were here.

5th March. A NOTABLE FRAUD.

Dr. Stephen Laks, doctor in civil laws, hath been most notoriously abused by one John Dean, a scrivener of London. Dr. Laks entrusted the sum of £3,000 to this Dean to put out to use for him, whereupon Dean counterfeited the hands and seals of divers credible persons to thirty or forty bonds and assurances, and brought the counterfeit obligations to Dr. Laks, making him believe them to be good. Having thus cozened him of above £3,000 he hideth himself in secret and privileged places.

6th March. MR. BODLEY'S GIFT TO OXFORD.

Mr. Bodley's liberality to the University of Oxford has received very good acceptance and thanks by public letters. The matter is very generally approved of and many think how by some good book or other they may be written in the scroll of benefactors.

'THE COUNSELLOR.'

There is newly translated into English that work called *The Counsellor*, written in Latin by Laurentius Grimaldus, and consecrated to the honour of the Polonian Emperor. Herein is pleasantly and pithily discoursed the office of magistrates, the happy life of subjects, and the felicity of commonwealths.

8th March. THE EARL OF CUMBERLAND SAILS.

The Earl of Cumberland set sail from Portsmouth two days ago in his ship the *Scourge of Malice*, and a fleet of seventeen other ships and two barges. He hath with him many mariners, and soldiers of whom Sir John Berkeley is made Colonel General. This is the twelfth voyage that my Lord hath undertaken.

10th March. 'LOVE'S LABOURS LOST.'

Love's Labours Lost, a play by Mr. Shakespeare that he wrote some time since, and being newly corrected and augmented was presented before her Majesty this last Christmas, is being printed.

12th March. INSTRUCTIONS FOR THE MUSTERS.

Certain instructions have been drawn up for the training of the musters at this time that all may be trained alike.

A company shall be equally compounded of armed men and shot; the armed men to be pikes, except the officers; the shot to be half muskets and the rest with harquebuses. Of the men, the strongest and best to be pikes; the strongest and squarest fellows will be fit to carry muskets; and the least and nimblest shall be put to the harquebus.

Every company shall be divided into three corporalships or squadrons; and every squadron into as many files as the number will bear; and every file into fellowships or camaradoes. The corporal of every squadron shall be the chiefest file of that squadron; the lanspesado shall lead the others.

The company being thus divided, in training they shall be taught, firstly, carriage and use of arms; secondly, march and motions; thirdly, understanding of all sounds of the drum and words of direction. The carriage of arms must be comely and readiest for use. The use of pike is either in receiving or giving a charge, and is most in knowing how and when every man, and so every rank, shall give his push.

In teaching the use of shot the soldier must first learn to present his piece, and to take his level, and how and when to give his volley with those of his rank; which is the proper office of the sergeant. But in teaching to give volleys the ancient and vulgar manner of discipline is utterly to be condemned, which is that the whole volleys shall be given of all the shot in one battalion at one instant as well behind as before; for either the hindermost must venture to shoot their fellows before through the head, or will overshoot and so spend their shot unprofitably. Besides, the volley once given the enemy comes on without impeachment or annoyance. Instead, let the first rank only give their volley, and if the battalion march then that rank that hath given is to stand, and the second pass through and give their volley and so stand, and the third is to come up, and consequently all the ranks. But if the battalion stand, then the first rank having given their volley shall fall back and the second come in their room, and so the third and fourth, till the first rank become last, and the last first; all which is easily performed if you do but make all the shot to open their ranks.

In teaching the soldier to know the sound of the drum, he must not only observe what the drummer doth beat, but what time he keeps, for according unto that the soldier is to march slower or faster. All other motions are taught him by the voice; wherefore, to make them perfect in these motions, it is good to use them to certain words which being once learned shall serve always for direction. The words used in training at Plymouth were such as these:

'Leaders stand forward with your files. Ranks open forward paces 5. Faces to the right hand, to the left hand. Faces about. Open your files, feet 3. Close your files. Open your files to the right hand paces. Double your files to the right hand. Double your rank to the right hand. Close your files to the left hand. As you were. Ranks from behind close. Ranks open backward paces 5. Files to the right hand turn. Ranks to the right hand turn. Front pass through. Followers pass through. Front as you were. Files as you were.'

16th March. THE ENVOYS OF THE STATES.

The envoys from the States General of the United Provinces being received by her Majesty declared that they were confident she would, in the interests of the realm, her allies and the Protestant world prefer a war of righteousness to a peace of peril; for this pretended peace in France would lead to a civil war, there being many in France to force the King into war with those of the Reformed Religion. They beseech the Queen to support them, declaring that still less than with France would treaties be observed with her, a schismatic, with whom by the papists' law no faith should be kept. The King of Spain and the Pope bear perpetual hatred to her, and the King's chief aim is to break up our league, divide its forces, and crush them separately. Though the States are already overburdened by ordinary charges for their armies, the help given to the King of France, and for ships which had joined her Majesty, yet they will oblige themselves, even beyond their proper ability, till both are contented.

17th March. THE SCOTTISH KING'S 'DAEMONOLOGY.'

The Scottish King hath written a treatise of *Daemonology*, in form of a dialogue, and divided into three books, whereof the first treateth in general of magic and necromancy, the second of sorcery and witchcraft, and the third of those kinds of spirits that trouble men. The Devil, saith he, enticeth men and women on to witchcraft by three passions which are within ourselves, curiosity in ingenious minds, thirst of revenge, or greedy appetite of gear caused through great poverty. The first is the only enticement of magicians and necromancers, the other two of the sorcerers and witches.

Declareth that they meet oftest in churches where they convene for adoring the Devil, their master; at which time, every one of them proposeth unto him what wicked turn they have done, either for obtaining of riches or for avenging them upon any whom they have malice at. At such times the Devil teacheth them how to make pictures of wax or clay, that by roasting thereof the persons represented may be dried or melted away by continual sickness; to others he giveth such stones or powders as will help to cure or cast on diseases; to others he teacheth kinds of uncouth poisons which mediciners understand not. These witches can make folks to become mad or frantic, or spirits to follow or trouble persons or haunt houses. Noteth that in the time of papistry these unlawful arts were far rarer, and never so much heard of nor so rife as they are now; but more ghosts and spirits were seen nor tongue can tell, where now a man shall scarcely all his time hear once of these things.

His Majesty wrote this book because of the fearful abounding of witches in his country, to prove that such assaults of Satan are most commonly practised, and that the instruments thereof ought most severely to be punished, contrary to the opinions of Mr. Reginald Scot, put forth in his *Discovery of Witchcraft* some years since.

24th March. KEEPING OF DAIRIES.

From Nantwich in the county of Chester come complaints that certain gentlemen not only convert tillage to keeping of dairies but sell beforehand their butter and cheese to Londoners. Hereby there is both decay of tillage and that provision ingrossed that is often needed for victualling the forces in Ireland.

29th March. PARLEYS WITH TYRONE.

The Earl of Ormond, Lord Lieutenant of Ireland, hath again met Tyrone and held parley with him on the 15th of this month and the three following days; yet although some agreement was made between them there is still no certainty or assurance of Tyrone's conformity. He still continueth the sending of messengers into Spain, and now that he is grown strong by reason of his combinations in several parts is it to be doubted that he will not stoop until he have received some blow.

30th March. 'VIRGIDEMIARUM,' THE LAST PART.

The second part of *Virgidemiarum*, being three books of biting satires, is now entered, whereto is added a postscript, wherein the author maketh his defence against the censures of his former satires. To those who wrest the matter to their own spite, answereth he; 'Art thou guilty? Complain not, thou art not wronged. Art thou guiltless? Complain not, thou art not touched.' As for the style, he declareth that the English is not altogether so natural to a satire as the Latin; nevertheless he thinketh that his first satire doth somewhat resemble the sour and crabbed face of Juvenal, which endeavouring in that one, he did determinately omit in the rest.

Of satires thus, in the fifth book:

> 'The satire should be like the porcupine,
> That shoots sharp quills out in each angry line,
> And wounds the blushing cheek and fiery eye
> Of him that hears and readeth guiltily.
> Ye antique satires, how I bless your days,
> That brook'd your bolder style, their own dispraise,
> And well-near wish, yet joy my wish is vain,
> I had been then, nor were they now again:

For now our ears been of more brittle mould,
Than those dull earthen ears that were of old;
Sith those, like anvils, bore the hammer's head,
Our glass can never touch unshivered.'

1st April. THE BOY POSSESSED AT NOTTINGHAM.

The boy Sommers, from whom was cast an evil spirit last autumn, having again fallen into his fits, a commission was of late appointed from the Archbishop of York to search into the truth thereof.

Mr. Darrell having taken the names of threescore persons who were ready to be deposed touching the extraordinary handling of the boy, seventeen of them were sworn and examined before the commissioners. Then Sommers himself was called to be examined, whether he had counterfeited or not. He told them that all that he did was counterfeit. The high sheriff therefore exhorted him in the Name of God to tell the truth; whereat Sommers was violently cast into one of his fits before them all, wallowing up and down the chamber where they sat in a fearful manner. Pins were thrust deep into his hand and leg to try if he did counterfeit; but he was senseless, and no blood followed. At length being recovered as out of sleep, they asked what he had done. He said he could not tell. Being asked whether he had not been pricked with pins, he said yes; they asked where, and he showed the wrong hand. After some further questions he was conveyed away, and being absent he was worse tormented than before. They brought him back again to know if he would confess who had persuaded him to say he had counterfeited, and as he was coming up a pair of stairs through a gallery, he had cast himself over headlong to have broken his neck, if he had not been hindered.

When he was the second time brought before the commissioners he was more terribly handled than before, insomuch that the commissioners and all that were present were fully satisfied that he was corporally possessed and surceased to examine any more witnesses; even Mr. Walton, Archdeacon of Derby, being present and a principal enemy to Mr. Darrell, acknowledged that it was the finger of God upon this rare accident.

Herewith all that favoured Mr. Darrell began to rejoice and to run abroad into the town, telling their friends with great joy that Sommers was now found to be no dissembler. The rest that had held a contrary opinion were greatly checked, so that when some of them came out of the house where the commission sat they were rated at exceedingly, and at one of them a stone was cast. Thus for ten days Mr. Darrell and his friends triumphed.

But by direction of the Lord Chief Justice, Sommers is once again taken out of the hands of Mr. Darrell and his friends and confesseth, as before, the whole course of his dissimulation and why he had affirmed to the commissioners that his fits were counterfeit. With this alteration Mr. Darrell is greatly troubled; the parts taken on both sides begin to be more violent and the town is extraordinarily divided, one railing upon another at their meeting in the streets. The pulpits also ring of nothing but devils and witches, wherewith men, women and children are so frighted as many of them durst not stir in the night, nor so much as a servant go into his master's cellar about his business without company. Few grow to be sick or evil at ease but straightway they are deemed to be possessed. Such indeed are the stirs in Nottingham about this matter that it is feared the people will grow to further quarrels and mutinies or some greater inconvenience.

3rd April. BASTARD'S 'CHRESTOLEROS.'

Mr. Thomas Bastard hath written seven books of epigrams under the title of *Chrestoleros*, which are dedicated to Sir Charles Blount, Lord Mountjoy. Of my Lord of Essex, thus:

> Essex, the ends which men so fain would find,
> Riches, for which most are industrious,
> Honour, for which most men are virtuous,
> Are but beginnings to thy noble mind:
> Which thou as means doth frankly spend upon
> Thy country's good, by thy true honour won.

5th April. SEIZED BOOKS.

Of late there was a bark driven into Falmouth by tempest of weather and belonging to certain merchants of Wexford; herein were found papistical books, beads and other relics, not fit to be transported and brought into her Majesty's dominions.

All these are to be burnt in the market place of Perin, and he that first gave intelligence satisfied for his charges.

6th April. The Town of Twyford Burnt.

Twyford a town in Devon is consumed by fire. This fire began about one o'clock in the afternoon in a poor cottage where a woman was frying pancakes with straw for lack of other fuel; and in one hour and a half such was the rage of the fire that it consumed 409 houses, £150,000 in money, plate, merchandise, household stuff, and houses. Fifty persons are consumed, but an almshouse preserved with the poor men therein though in the midst of the flames. Nine thousand people were there maintained by the making of cloth. It is thought of many that this is a just punishment of God upon the town for the unmercifulness of the rich and small regard of the poor, which were daily seen to perish in the streets for lack of relief.

7th April. Sir Robert Cecil received by the French King.

Sir Robert Cecil did not reach the French King who was at Angers until the 17th March, having travelled more than 300 miles. Four days later he was received in audience of the King, and many nobles of great quality, when he delivered the Queen's letters, declaring further that it had pleased her Majesty to make election of him to communicate her secret and princely thoughts when it should please the King to discover his own disposition and judgment of this project of a general treaty. Mr. Secretary's intention was that this first audience should be but complimental where the King might make public acknowledgment of his obligation and respect towards her Majesty. Then he requested that the King would yield him some other access, beseeching him for this time only to permit him to present the Earl of Southampton who was come with deliberation to serve him. The King promised access the next day, and then very favourably embraced the Earl and the others presented to him. Then he suddenly took Sir Robert by the hand, saying that he would walk with him down into his garden *en qualité d'ami*, where for an hour and a half he entertained him with many pleasant and familiar discourses of his opinion of divers of his subjects and other particulars. The Commissioners from the States are now arrived.

9th April. CERTAIN LETTERS CAPTURED.

It is said that some days since certain fishermen fished up in the sea a packet of letters from the Cardinal of Austria to the King of Spain, wherein it appeareth that the French King will conclude peace without regard to her Majesty or to the States. Moreover the King of Spain requireth that if the French will have the English comprehended in the peace then shall the Catholic religion be free in England, and likewise with the Low Countries. Copies of these letters have been sent to Sir Robert Cecil.

10th April. MR. CHAPMAN TRANSLATETH HOMER'S 'ILIADES.'

Mr. George Chapman hath entered for the press *Seven Books of the Iliades of Homer, Prince of Poets*, translated according to the Greek, and dedicated 'To the most Honoured now living instance of the Achilleian virtues, eternized by divine Homer, the Earl of Essex, Earl Marshal, etc.' Writeth of my Lord in these terms: 'Most true Achilles (whom by sacred prophecy Homer did but prefigure in his admiral object) and in whose unmatched virtues shine the dignities of the soul, and the whole excellence of royal humanity, let not the peasant-common polities of the world that count all things servile and simple, that pamper not their own private sensualities, burying quick in their filthy sepulchres of earth the whole bodies and souls of honour, virtue and piety, stir your divine temper from perseverance in godlike pursuit of Eternity.'

APOLLO SENDETH THE PLAGUE.

Thus prayed he, and Apollo heard, who at the heart offended
Down from the topless brows of heaven, into the host descended,
His bow and quiver covered round, his golden shoulders wore,
His angry arrows, as he moved, did thunder on the shore;
So, like the lowring night he walked, and took his wreakful stand
Athwart the fleet: his silver bow, with his hard losing hand,

A dreadful sound did make; and first the mules and dogs he wounds,
And after with the breasts of men his mortal shafts confounds:
The funeral pyres did ever burn with heaps of men he slew;
Nine days together through the host his poisoned arrows flew;
The tenth a council through the camp Æcides designed,
Which Juno with the silver arms did put into his mind.

12th April. AN ATTEMPT TO POISON.

A very lewd fact is reported from the north where Mr. Barnabe Barnes, son to the late Bishop of Durham, attempted to poison John Brown, the Recorder of Berwick; but upon discovery he is fled and thought to have gone into Durham where the Bishop shall cause him to be apprehended and sent up to the Council in charge of some trusty person.

14th April. A SECOND PART TO 'HERO AND LEANDER.'

One Mr. Henry Petowe hath written *The Second Part of Hero and Leander*, containing their further fortunes, for that the history of *Hero and Leander*, penned by that admired poet Marlowe, but not finished, and resting like a head separated from the body with this harsh sentence '*Desunt nonnulla.*' Herein is shown how Leander was banished for his love to Hero, and she imprisoned for that the Duke Euristippus would have had her love; but that after long exile Leander came back and slew the Duke and was at length restored to Hero; and they living together in perfect love were at last transformed into two pine trees,

> Whose nature's such, the female pine will die
> Unless the male be ever planted by.

MR. PETOWE'S PRAISE OF MARLOWE.

Oh had that King of poets breathed longer,
Then had fair beauty's fort been much more stronger:
His golden pen had clos'd her so about
No bastard Æglet's quill the world throughout,
Had been of force to mar what he had made,
For why they were not expert in that trade:

What mortal soul with Marlowe might contend,
That could 'gainst reason force him stoop or bend ?
Whose silver charming tongue moved such delight,
That men would shun their sleep in still dark night,
To meditate upon his golden lines,
His rare conceits and sweet according rimes.
But Marlowe, still admired Marlowe's gone,
To live with beauty in Elizium ;
Immortal beauty, who desires to hear,
His sacred poesies sweet in every ear.
Marlowe must frame to Orpheus' melody,
Hymns all divine to make heaven harmony.
There ever live the Prince of Poetry
Live with the living in eternity.

16th April. THE NEGOTIATIONS WITH THE FRENCH KING BROKEN.

The negotiations between the French King are now broken, and Sir Robert Cecil and Dr. Herbert take their way homeward, for the King hath privately made agreement with the Spaniards which awaiteth only a commission sent out of Spain to conclude it. He excuseth himself by the delay which the Queen made, by the urgent necessity, and by the opportunity that was offered, referring Sir Robert Cecil and Monsieur Oldenbarnevelt, the ambassador from the States, to his Council.

To the Council Monsieur Oldenbarnevelt declared that the States, by God's mercy and the Queen's favour and assistance, are brought to that pass that they have not only been able to defend themselves, but also to assist France in her extremities, nor are they so to be neglected and slighted with whom the Kings both of France and England have thought fit to make strict leagues and alliances. After many other weighty reasons why they could not embrace peace with the Spaniard he concluded that some Kings to attain power and greatness have neglected and disregarded their leagues ; but for the most part sad hath been the consequence, for the state of Kings, unless it stand upon faith and fidelity, cannot stand upon power. He propounded therefore that if the King would listen no longer after peace but besiege Calais, they would at their own charges beleaguer at the same time some other place that the enemy's forces might be divided; and besides, towards the besieging of Calais, they would allow pay for 7,000 men and set forth 25 men-of-war, provided that he for the siege would find 3,000 horse, 6,000 foot and 6 pieces of ordnance.

To these things the Chancellor of France answered that all kindness should be showed to the States, but that the opportunity of peace offered to France, now languishing with long wars, was not only to be accepted of but also of urgent necessity to be catched at.

The States therefore utterly refusing peace, Sir Robert Cecil can proceed no further towards the general peace. Nevertheless he replied to the Chancellor, denying that the Queen had used any delay, but had with all speed sent into France to treat of peace, and declared that they made the necessity greater than could be believed. Moreover he desired them to put the King in mind with what vows he had bound and engaged himself before the Earl of Shrewsbury after the ratification of the league, and before by many letters signed with his own hand. The Queen, said he, hath not at all receded from the conditions of the league, yea, she hath performed more than she was obliged; but the King hath stuck to nothing; and with that he produced the draft of the league. He asked also that some course may be taken whereof those great sums formerly lent by the Queen may be repaid; for being now forsaken and left in the lurch, she hath learned too late to provide for her own state more carefully in time to come, and not to confer her benefits on those who so ill deserve them.

And so with fair and gentle answers the ambassadors are dismissed, in great discontent.

18*th April.* THE SPITAL SERMONS.

It hath long been accustomed at the sermons at the Spital in the Easter holidays to have a gathering for the redemption of such as are prisoners of the Turk or other heathens; but as there are few of late years taken by the Turk, and at this present divers poor mariners come hither out of Spain where they have been cruelly racked and endured great misery, it is proposed that a collection shall be made to relieve their present necessities and send them home into their counties.

21st April. ARISTOTLE'S 'POLITIQUES.'

Aristotle's *Politiques or Discourses of Government* are now for the first time Englished by one J. D. from the French of Loys le Roy, called Regius, being set forth with expositions taken out of the best authors, conferred together, illustrated by innumerable examples both new and old concerning the beginning, proceeding and excellency of civil government. As there is no philosopher can in depth of knowledge equal Aristotle, whose works may be justly termed 'The Treasury of human wisdom,' so these his discourses of Government have not the meanest relish thereof; especially where he handleth the changes and destructions of every commonwealth, with their causes, setting down several precepts for the upholding and preserving of each.

24th April. TYRONE RENEWETH THE TRUCE.

On the 10th of the month the Earl of Ormond again met Tyrone in parley, which continued four days, when peace was further agreed upon for six weeks, for due observation whereof he took his oath and subscribed with his own hand. Yet there is little likelihood the peace will be kept, for albeit Tyrone took a solemn oath at this conference that he had not combined with any in Leinster since the Lord Lieutenant had this charge delivered to him, yet by interception of some letters it appeared plainly that he had made a combination but last month with two in Leinster and had authorised others to draw confederates into his faction.

25th April. LORD BURLEIGH'S REBUKE.

My Lord of Essex stiffly maintaining that no peace could be made with the Spaniards but such as would be dishonourable and fraudulent on their side, the Lord Treasurer answered that he breathed forth nothing but war, slaughter and blood; and after a hot dispute in this matter, he drew forth a psalm book, and saying nothing, pointed him to this verse, 'Men of blood shall not live out half their days.'

30th April. ABUSES IN TENEMENT HOUSE.

There are complaints of abuses in Shoreditch, St. Giles-without-Cripplegate, Clerkenwell and other places in the suburbs that divers owners of small tenements, most of them erected within these few years, do let the same out by the week to base people and harbour thieves, rogues and vagabonds, whereby great mischiefs and lewd disorders are committed. Moreover by often removing of those persons from place to place, there can no certain knowledge be taken of them what they are and how they live and maintain themselves, an abuse most intolerable, and in no wise to be permitted in a Christian commonwealth. The justices are now charged to take the view of these cottages and base tenements, and those that inhabit in them, taking true notes of those that dwell in them, their names, out of what part they come, how long they have dwelt there, what trade they use, for what time they hire their lodgings, and what rent they pay, and in what sort. Of the owners also bonds shall be taken hereafter to let no houses by the week or month or any less time than a year, nor to let out (as many do) their chambers alone or some few rooms to poor persons that keep whole families in the same; nor to admit hereafter any that shall not bring a true certificate whence they come and of their good behaviour allowed by two justices of the peace at least.

There is also another abuse in these parishes when certain persons of wealth convert fair dwelling houses into tenements with raising of great rent for the same. Hereby, in place of those of good ability that used to live in these houses and pay all other charges with the rest of the parishioners, in their rooms are placed many poor persons that need relief from the parish where the landlords reap great rents and are subject to no charge.

1st May. SIR ROBERT CECIL'S RETURN.

Sir Robert Cecil and Dr. Herbert to-day reached London and came to Court, having left the French King on the 15th April and landed in England on the 29th.

3rd May. 'GREENE IN CONCEIPT.'

A book of the tragic history of fair Valeria of London called *Greene in conceipt* written by J. D., is entered, purporting to have been set down before him by the ghost of Greene. This Valeria, being by nature and the liberality of her parents a wanton, was wooed and wedded by an old man called Giraldo. But after some short time growing tired of her husband, she was led into wantonness by some of her light companions, and soon came so to like the game that henceforth she could never leave it. For a long while Giraldo knew nothing of his wife's faithlessness till he was brought to a sight of it by his boy Jockey, and pining thereat, he died of a broken heart. And thereafter Valeria was married by Arthemio, that loved her for her old husband's wealth, who soon began to treat her despitefully, consuming her goods and even entertaining his trulls before her face; so that within a brief space their movables were sold and they turned out into the streets penniless. And now Valeria having nowhere to go at length betook herself to Jockey, that had married a widow and kept a simple victualling house; thither she went and was received with all kindness. But at length, whether hoping for some better place or loath to trouble him continually, she fondly left him and thereby replunged into her former miseries, falling in the end to little better than open beggary, from which abject state she never recovered till death gave truce to her distresses.

6th May. THE CURES OF THE DISEASED IN REMOTE REGIONS.

There is a little book by G. W. of *The Cures of the Diseased in remote regions* to prevent mortality incident in foreign attempts of the English nation; which diseases are especially the *calenture* (or burning fever), the *tabardilla*, the *espinlas* (a pricking disease), the *cameras de sangre* (that is laxativeness or bloody flux), the *erizipila* and the *tinoso* (which we call the scurvy).

7th May. MR. GOSSON'S SERMON AT PAUL'S CROSS.

To-day Mr. Stephen Gosson, parson of Great Wigborough in Essex, preached at Paul's Cross from 2 Chronicles, chap. xx, verse 20, on the action of war. War, said he, was just in reason, in religion and in practice of the Church, and man himself provided for it by reason and hands instead of the horns, hoofs, teeth and talons given to brute beasts. Just and lawful wars are of several sorts; when one prince withholds that which is another's; or when the laws of nations are denied; or the fame and honour of a Prince be hurt; or disgrace or indignity offered to his ambassadors; or in defence of a Prince's friend; the last injury of all being invasion. Thence he passed to the war with the Spaniard.

9th May. AN ABUSE IN DARTMOUTH.

The magistrates in Emden make great complaint of an abuse committed last winter at Dartmouth. At that time a ship of Emden, called the *Fortune*, laden with corn and bound for Rochelle, was driven by contrary winds into Dartmouth. Wherefore because of the great dearth in the county, the Council gave direction that the same should be sold with the consent of the master. Hereupon the Mayor of Dartmouth sold the whole lading to certain rich men of the county by great quantities at far lower prices than corn of like goodness did then bear, and kept a good part thereof himself, so that the poor had no relief, the buyers made an unlawful gain, and the proprietaries thereof were damnified to the sum of £400.

10th May. THE QUEEN'S LETTERS TO THE FRENCH KING.

Since the return of the ambassadors the Queen hath by Sir Thomas Edmonds, Secretary for the French tongue, lovingly and freely admonished him to remember his faith given, and to have a regard to his conscience towards God and his reputation amongst men, lest he insnare himself by the counsels of corrupt and wicked men ; but amongst her grave admonitions are intermixed these nipping checks : 'If there be any sin in the world against the Holy Ghost it is ingratitude. If you get any reasonable terms at the Spaniard's hands, you may thank the English succours for it. Forsake not an old friend, for a new one will not be like him. The conscience and religion of a league and the faith of contracts are not used as nets to entrap, but only by wicked men. A bundle of rods bound together is not easily broken. There is no easier way to overthrow us both than by parting and disjoining us one from the other.'

14th May. THE VENETIAN ARGOSY.

The matter of the Venetian argosy, named the *St. Agatha Morisini* (that was stayed in January '97), is still in question, whereby the Council are greatly displeased to find themselves continually importuned with the complaints of the Venetian merchants and the business delayed, and charge those concerned to protract the time no longer but to make present satisfaction.

15th May. 'THE SERVINGMAN'S COMFORT.'

One J. M. hath written a book called *A health to the gentlemanly profession of servingmen or the Servingman's comfort,* wherein is set out the decay of good housekeeping from former days when the younger sons of gentlemen would be honest serving men; and the abuse of these times when to escape the service of the wars yeomen will send their sons to be gentlemen's servants, and maintain them at their own charges. Then must the country courtier be attired in the latest fashion with his venetians of the largest size (that will hold a bushel a breech at least), and his gait and gesture no longer of the plough but direct and upright, treading in time as though he would tell what paces are in a furlong. No longer can be seen the great chines of stalled beef, the great black-jack of noble beer, the long hall tables fully furnished with good victuals; these now be all changed into cates of less cost though dishes of rarer device, such as goose giblets, pigs' pettitoes, and other made dishes. Lamenteth how many misfortunes come by the decay of liberality, for when servingmen are turned away by their masters, then by necessity they be forced to rob passengers at Gadshill, Shootershill, Salisbury Plain or Newmarket Heath.

20th May. THE MONOPOLY IN STARCH.

The monopoly for importing starch that was formerly granted to Mr. Richard Young is now assigned to Sir John Pakington for eight years.

RUMOURS.

The talk in the City is now of Barnevelt, the agent and advocate of the States who is here and hath had audience these two days together, but no music will please us unless it be to the tune of peace. One of the chiefest reasons for it is a kind of disdain and envy at our neighbours' well doing, in that we, for their sake and defence entering into the war, and being barred from all commerce and intercourse of merchandise, they in the meantime thrust us out of all traffic to our utter undoing and their own advancement. Another motive to the peace is the troubles in Ireland which are like to put the Queen to exceeding charge, and withal there appears a black cloud in Scotland that threatens a storm.

21st May. Mr. Barnabe Barnes.

A week ago Mr. Barnabe Barnes was brought before the Council and commanded to give attendance before their lordships from time to time and not to depart until he shall be dismissed. The charge that Mr. Barnes attempted and put in practice to poison the Recorder of Berwick is to be examined by the Attorney-General, Mr. Francis Bacon, and Mr. William Waad; and if by the testimony of witnesses and other good means there appear proof or pregnant supposition that Mr. Barnes is any way culpable therein, then shall they take advice with the Lord Chief Justice what course is fit to be followed for the punishing of so foul and odious an offence.

The Sermon at Paul's Cross.

Mr. John Howson preached to-day at Paul's Cross, concluding that sermon upon the xxi. of Matthew, the 12 and 13 verses, which he began in December last. Concludeth that the sin of the Jews in making the Temple a den of thieves is committed by ourselves, who have added as great increases and strength to these sins as time hath added years and increase to the world.

25th May. Slanders against the Scottish King.

Some weeks since one Valentine Thomas (or Anderson), an Englishman, a lewd caitiff, being taken on the Border and brought to London, thereupon made certain declarations greatly to the dishonour of the Scottish King. He delivered without torture or menace divers informations of practices contrived between the King of Scots and himself for taking away the Queen's life, for which he was promised great reward by the King. Hereat the King taketh it hardly that the Queen should not have discovered the accusations, either to his ambassador or to himself to clear her mind and his honour. It is reported that the King will be quit by sound of trumpet and by challenge in what numbers soever, yea of a King to a King in case of need, if he is not cleared of the slander of the murder, protesting that for all the crowns in the world he would not be guilty even in thought.

27th May. THE 'METAMORPHOSIS OF PYGMALION'S IMAGE; AND CERTAIN SATIRES.'

There is a poem called *The Metamorphosis of Pygmalion's Image*, telling that story of Pygmalion who wrought an image of a woman in ivory, and he hotly wooing it she was suddenly transformed into a woman and returned his love. Hereto are adjoined five satires of the men of these times. This book is written by one calling himself W. K. and dedicated 'To the World's Mighty Monarch, Good Opinion.'

HIS DESCRIPTION OF A PURITAN.

Who would imagine yonder sober man,
That same devout meal-mouth'd precisian,
That cries 'Good brother,' 'Kind sister,' makes a duck
After the antique grace, can always pluck
A sacred book out of his civil hose,
And at th' op'ning and at our stomach's close,
Says with a turn'd-up eye a solemn grace
Of half an hour; then with silken face
Smiles on the holy crew, and then doth cry,
'O manners! O times of impurity!—'
Who thinks that this good man
Is a vile, sober, damned politician?
Not I, till with his bait of purity
He bit me sore in deepest usury.
No Jew, no Turk, would use a Christian
So inhumanely as this Puritan.
Dromedes' jades were not so bestial
As this same seeming saint—vile cannibal!
Take heed, O world! take heed avisedly
Of these same damned anthropophagi.
I had rather been within a harpy's claws
Than trust myself in their devouring jaws,
Who all confusion to the world would bring
Under the form of their new discipline.

30th May. A FRAY AT OXFORD.

Last Sunday at Oxford the Mayor suffered a company of 150 trained soldiers and other young men to go early in the morning to try their pieces, and to return into the city in battle array; but in returning they were stayed by Mr. Daniel, the proproctor, and some scholars, who took from them their drum and divers weapons, striking and beating some, and committing others to prison; insomuch that there was a great uproar and concourse, both of scholars and citizens, and if the citizens had not given way there would have been a bloody day and much slaughter. The Mayor complaineth to the Council that the scholars have not been punished and moreover they keep that which they took away. But the Vice-Chancellor declareth that the townsmen, with drum and shot and other weapons, and men attired in women's garments, brought into the town a woman bedecked with garlands and flowers, and named by them Queen of May. Moreover they had morrice-dances and other unseemly sports, and intended next Sunday to continue the same abuses; in which riotous proceedings seditious speeches were used. When the Vice-Chancellor sent to entreat the Mayor to meet him, the Mayor made a frivolous and dilatory answer, and in the meantime preferred an unjust and scandalous complaint against the University.

1st June. THE APOLOGY OF THE EARL OF ESSEX.

My Lord of Essex, being of so many taxed as the hinderer of the peace and quiet of his country at this time, hath written an apology of his present opinions in the form of a letter to Mr. Anthony Bacon. That generally he is affected to the men-of-war should not seem strange to any reasonable man; for every man doth love them of his own profession, and since the Queen hath used him yearly in her late actions he must reckon himself among the men of war. He would not now dissent from peace, if those who propose it would build upon any one true principle; but if they will promise themselves that they may have peace without ground, or think that peace shall be good for us without reason, or to leap blindfold into a Treaty without undue circumstance, then doth he not suspect too much, but they too little.

No peace can be had for the United Provinces, without a Spanish sovereign be acknowledged, and then will the Popish religion be either universally established or at least freely exercised in towns and provinces whence it is now banished.

Allow the first, and they banish God's true service to bring in idolatry; allow the second (a plurality of religions) which is less, and it is against the policy of all States; because where there is no unity in the Church there can be no unity or order in the State, yea, it is the manifest ruin of that State.

We can have no advantage of this peace; yet some will say it is better to have a patched peace than an unsupportable war, and yet at this time never hath this realm been stronger. 'We,' quoth he, 'thanks be to God, have a Queen who hath never been wasteful in her private expense, yet will she sell her plate and jewels in the Tower ere her people shall be undefended. We are a people that will turn our silk coats into iron jacks, and our silver plate into coats of plate, rather than our Sovereign shall be unserved.' Moreover, now that the King of Spain is weakest is the unfittest time to make peace; for if we make peace now, then, when his coffers are full of treasure and his fleet supplied with ships, he will be able not only to trouble kingdoms by war but to purchase them with money. Then will our men of war either be driven to seek new countries and new fortunes or consumed in a beggarly and miserable Irish war, and our nation be grown unwarlike, in love with the name and bewitched with the delights of peace.'

Being charged with publishing this *Apology*, my Lord protesteth that so far from giving copies of it, he ordered his man that kept his papers not to let any of his friends see it, but in his hand or at least in his presence. He suspecteth that it is come abroad by corruption of some of his servants that had access to his chamber, who might take and copy out his loose papers which lay ever sheet by sheet under the bed's head till he had leisure to finish the whole. He hath never sent any papers to the press or to a scrivener's shop.

2nd June. A LEWD SHOW AT BRUSSELS.

At Brussels of late was a dumb show representing the French King and the Cardinal, who after long wars fell to a treaty. While they are conferring, in cometh a lady and conveys herself behind the French King and prieth what they say, expressing much perturbation at it, sometimes fawning and sometimes flattering and plucking the French King by the sleeve. In the meantime one of the minions begins to chafe, enquiring what she is that presumes so near; where it is gestured she is the Queen of England. So they whisper and laugh at the conceipt. With that there come in four or five fellows dressed like boors, and begin to press to the place and interrupt the treaty. Whereupon the Cardinal enquires who they are, and they are described to be boors of Holland. Whereat the King laughs at the rudeness of the poor; but the Cardinal gestures that he will hang them all up so soon as he hath done with his great business. So are we mocked by them while we treat of peace.

5th June. A CASE OF PIRACY.

Mr. Nicholas Owsley, that lately transported the Spanish prisoners out of the realm to Lisbon in the *Unicorn* of Dansk and returned with such English prisoners as remained there, complaineth that in his course outward, he was set upon by a ship called the *Flying Dragon* of Bristol, and robbed of merchandise of good value.

7th June. TROUBLES AT PLYMOUTH.

During the last months there have been great differences between the Mayor of Plymouth and Sir Ferdinando Gorges commanding the fort in that place. The Council have therefore drawn up certain articles to be observed by both parties. The commander of the fort shall not meddle with the borough in matters of justice, nor shall he have anything to do with the Castle except at the time of some approach of the enemy. He shall not command any inhabitant to watch out of the town; nor shall he or his servants go on board to search any vessel except for her Majesty's special service, and then he shall acquaint the Mayor and take one of the Mayor's brethren and the searcher with him.

On the part of the town, it is commanded that if any townsman shall give occasion of offence unto any soldier, the officers of the town shall take order for just satisfaction unto the party grieved. At all times of approach of the enemy, the inhabitants shall be ready to obey the directions of Sir Ferdinando Gorges. No foreign prisoners shall be brought into the town but that notice shall be given to the commander of the Fort, and straight order taken that the prisoners be kept in safe custody and not suffered as heretofore to run up and down at their pleasure, whereby many inconveniences may ensue. If any passengers shall arrive from any foreign part, notice to be given to the commander that they may be examined upon points necessary to the furtherance of her Majesty's service.

In these troubles the two most blameworthy are the Town Clerk of Plymouth and Jennings, Sir Ferdinando Gorges' lieutenant. Both are to be put forth from their offices.

8th June. THE PEACE AT VERVINS.

Perpetual peace between the French King and the Spaniards was publicly proclaimed on the 26th May both at Paris and at Amiens in the presence of the Legate and the King's deputies. This peace was concluded and subscribed upon the 22nd April, but upon express condition that it should not be published till a month after, for the King of France wished the ambassadors of England and the States first to be gone from his Court. In this conference at Vervins the Spaniards have agreed to restore those towns which they hold in Picardy, Blavet in Brittany, and Calais. At first they would have kept Calais so long as the war lasteth with the States, giving the French an exchange in the meantime. The French stood to have Calais restored freely, and likewise Cambray; but they agreed, without much difficulty, that Calais shall be restored while the Spaniard keeps Cambray.

10th June. MURDERS IN IRELAND.

During this last truce, as at other times of cessation of arms, the rebels have taken great advantage and are grown to an exceeding great strength. The rebels in Leinster, by the granting of privileges to them, are grown to such strength and insolence that they have laid waste a great part of the county. Thence passing into the Queen's county they have so spoiled and utterly wasted it that the poor English gentlemen of the shire do scarcely dare to manure one foot of their land, or almost to look out of their castles; their tenants have joined the rebels, and this county which cost so much English blood and treasure to gain is almost lost.

After these murders and villainies this vile rabble of rebels drew into Wexford where, after many spoils and outrages committed upon the poor inhabitants of the county, they have lately slain the lieutenant, sergeant and six soldiers of Sir Henry Wallop's company; also 80 of two bands of Picardy soldiers, and besides these many of the gentlemen and inhabitants.

11th June. COMPLAINTS AGAINST THE EARL OF LINCOLN.

So many complaints have been made against the Earl of Lincoln by poor men's petitions and complaints that the Council have earnestly desired him to have some regard to satisfy them and prevent the occasion of any more. Now one Robert Blower declareth that, contrary to all law and conscience, certain disordered persons, by his Lordship's own appointment, have dispossessed him of a house and land in Oxfordshire. Whereupon the Council pray my Lord either to restore the poor man to the possession of his house or, if his complaint is unjust, to make it so sufficiently to appear that he shall be punished for false information or slander. Otherwise, if Blower receive no remedy, the Council must take some order for his relief.

15th June. JESUIT DEVICES.

Some priests in Lancashire have recently prevailed over divers persons to incline to papistry. They have a certain woman who pretendeth to be possessed with unclean spirits upon whom they have practised at some private places where for the novelty thereof sometimes as many as 500 persons would be drawn together, promising not to betray them. The party possessed being set in a chair maketh show to be most wonderfully writhen, and with very strange illusions; and thus daily they win many unto them. Now at least twenty persons are taken and sent to the Bishop of Chester for examination.

17th June. A CASE OF MANSLAUGHTER.

At the Sessions to-day Mr. Edward Harwood, a gentleman late of London, was arraigned for the murder of Mr. Adam Crosby whom he had slain in Bastian's Close in St. Giles-without-Cripplegate. Mr. Harwood put himself not guilty of murder but guilty of manslaughter, and asking for the book is branded with the letter T and released accordingly.

18th June. SOLDIERS FOR IRELAND.

For the service in Ireland there are now to be levied 2,000 men from the Principality of Wales and the counties near adjoining. Good and serviceable men are to be chosen, not admitting any rogues or vagabonds, and of them half shall be pikes, and half shot.

23rd June. NEWS FROM PARIS.

In the French Court it is declared that the towns will be given up under this treaty at the end of the month. A certain Dutchman, Sir Melchior Leven, that was knighted by my Lord of Essex at Cadiz, hath refused to fight Sir Charles Blount in Paris on the ground that the King hath forbidden duels, whereat all do mock him. Sir Charles who went with the Secretary on his embassage stayed behind on purpose to effect this challenge.

24th June. DISTRESS IN LINCOLNSHIRE.

The evil disposition of those who seek immoderate profit by ingrossing grain and transporting it out of the county is such that in the county of Lincoln there is great discontent of the people; insomuch that they were ready to break forth into great disorder but for the pains of the Bishop of Lincoln, Sir Henry Cromwell and Mr. Oliver Cromwell, who have committed to prison one notorious offender, by name William Baxter of Calcott. This Baxter is sent for by the Council.

28th June. THE TRUCE ENDED IN IRELAND.

The last truce with Tyrone expired on the 7th of the month, and within two days afterwards he made a division of his forces into three, whereof one part he sent to the Blackwater, which he now holdeth environed, swearing by his barbarous hand that he will not depart till he carry the fort; with another part he assaulteth the castle of the Cavan; the third part he hath laid ready to send into Leinster to strengthen his faction there. Such is the weakness of the forces in Ireland that nothing can be done to relieve the Blackwater; for the rest there is a strength of but 1,500 or 1,600 men until more troops arrive from England. Nevertheless the Lord Lieutenant hath not been idle. On the 13th of the month, hearing that some of the rebels were in the mountains near Dublin, he went after them stealthily with two companies, and would have slain many but for the rash overforwardness of certain gentlemen that galloped ahead and were engaged among the enemy ere they were aware, whereof four were slain. In these last weeks 434 of the rebels have been slain or executed by martial law.

2nd July. THE EARL OF ESSEX'S GREAT CONTEMPT.

The Earl of Essex is suddenly withdrawn from the Court, and it is said that yesterday there grew a smart debate between the Queen and my Lord, there being also present the Lord Admiral, Sir Robert Cecil and Mr. Windebank, Clerk of the Signet. Her Majesty thought Sir William Knollys the fittest man of any to be sent to Ireland; but the Earl of Essex obstinately insisted that Sir George Carew was fitter than he, and quite forgetting himself and neglecting his duty, he uncivilly turned his back upon the Queen as it were in contempt, and gave her a scornful look. She not enduring such contempt returned him a box on the ear and bade him get him gone and be hanged. Thereupon the Earl laid his hand on his sword, and the Lord Admiral stepping between, he swore a great oath that he neither would nor could put up with so great an affront and indignity, neither would he have taken it at King Henry the Eighth his hands, and in great passion withdrew himself forthwith from the Court.

6th July. THE GOVERNOR OF DUNKIRK.

Don Francisco D'Aquilla Alverado, the Governor of Dunkirk, that was taken in September last, and brought to England, is now to be sent back to Ostend where he will be nearer to his friends that speedier means may be wrought for the payment of his ransom.

7th July. STOW'S 'SURVEY OF LONDON.'

Mr. John Stow hath finished his *Survey of London*, containing the original, antiquity, increase, modern estate and description of the City, dedicating it to the Lord Mayor, the commonalty and citizens.

THE ANTIQUITY OF LONDON.

As Rome, the chief city of the world to glorify itself, drew her originals from the gods, goddesses and demy gods by the Trojan progeny, so this famous City of London for greater glory and in emulation of Rome deriveth itself from the very same original; for Brute, descended from the demy god Aeneas, the son of Venus, daughter of Juppiter, about the year of the world 2855 (the year before Christ's nativity 1108) builded a city near unto a river now called Thames, and named it Troynovant, or Trenovant, or Trinovantum as have some written copies. This afterwards being repaired by King Lud, he called it Caire-Lud or 'Lud's town,' and the strong gate which he builded in the west of the City, 'Ludgate.' Caesar in his *Commentaries* speaketh also of the City of the Trinobantes, which hath resemblance with Troynova or Trinobantum by no greater difference in the orthography than changing b into v.

Mr. Stow's Commendation of the City of London.

'Besides the commodities of the furtherance of religion and justice; the propagation of learning; the maintenance of arts; the increase of riches; and the defence of countries (all which are before showed to grow generally by cities, and be common to London with them), London bringeth singularly these things following.

'By advantage of the situation it disperseth foreign wares (as the stomach doth meat) to all the members most commodiously.

'By the benefit of the river of Thames, and great trade of merchandise, it is the chief maker of mariners, and nurse of our navy; and ships (as men know) be the wooden walls for defence of our Realm.

'It maintaineth in flourishing estate the counties of Norfolk, Suffolk, Essex, Kent and Sussex, which as they lie in the face of our most puissant neighbour, so ought they (above others) to be conserved in the greatest strength and riches; and these, as it is well known, stand not so much by the benefit of their own soil as by the neighbourhood and nearness which they have to London.

'It relieveth plentifully and with good policy not only her own poor people (a thing which scarcely any other town or shire doth) but also the poor that from each quarter of the realm do flock unto it, and it imparteth liberally to the necessity of the Universities besides. It is an ornament to the realm by the beauty thereof, and a terror to other countries by reason of the great wealth and frequency. It spreadeth the honour of our Country far abroad by her long navigations and maketh our power feared, even of barbarous Princes. It only is stowed with rich merchants, which sort only is tolerable ; for beggarly merchants do bite too near, and will do more harm than good to the Realm.

'It only of any place in the realm is able to furnish the sudden necessity with a strong army. It availeth the Prince in tonnage, poundage, and other customs, much more than all the rest of the Realm.

'It yieldeth a greater subsidy than any one part of the realm, I mean not for the proportion of the value of the goods only therein, but also for the faithful service there used, in making the assess ; for nowhere else be men taxed so near to their just value as in London ; yea, many are found there that for their countenance and credit sake refuse not to be rated above their ability, which thing never happened abroad in the country. I omit that in ancient time the inhabitants of London and other cities were accustomably taxed after the tenth of their goods when the country was assessed at the fifteenth, and rated at the eighth when the country was set at the twelfth, for that were to awake a sleeping dog, and I should be thought *dicenda tacenda locutus*, as the poet said.

'It only doth and is able to make the Prince a ready prest or loan of money.

'It only is found fit and able to entertain strangers honourably and to receive the Prince of the realm worthily.

'Almighty God (*qui nisi custodiat civitatem*, *frustra vigilat custos*) grant, that her Majesty evermore rightly esteem and rule this City, and He give grace that the citizens may answer duty as well towards God and her Majesty as towards this whole Realm and Country.'

10th July. A FENCER HANGED.

Nineteen persons were to-day hanged for felony at Tyburn and one pressed to death at Newgate. Also John Barrose, a Burgonian by nation and a fencer by profession, that lately came over and challenged all the fencers of England, was hanged all day long without Ludgate for killing an officer of the City which had arrested him for debt; such was his desperateness and bringeth such reward as may be example for others the like.

11th July. MR. BARNABE BARNES.

Mr. Barnabe Barnes that was committed to the Marshalsea is broken out of prison to avoid his trial and, as is supposed, fled away into the north.

12th July. DISORDERS IN IRELAND.

There is great disorder in Ireland since so many English soldiers disband themselves and run away, so that the country is at great charges both to fill up the decayed bands and further to strengthen the army. This abuse ariseth partly by the seducement of some lewd soldiers that convey themselves away so soon as they arrive, but chiefly through the negligence and lewd behaviour of some of the captains who for their own private gain dismiss the English and entertain the Irish. The Queen commandeth the captain shall be charged to take order for the apprehension of any that run away, and if he do not his duty for their apprehension then to be charged with the escape as consenting thereto. Likewise masters of ships shall be charged that they take no English soldiers into their ships if they be not maimed, hurt, or weakened with sickness and have sufficient passports.

16th July. THE QUEEN AND THE EARL OF ESSEX.

Yesterday the Queen was minded to have sent Mr. William Killigrew to the Earl of Essex as if of his own accord, but instructed by her; but being jealous that one of her chamber coming to the Earl might be thought by him to be commanded by her, she bad him stay.

A SAYING CONCERNING MY LORD OF ESSEX.

A certain great officer at Court when there was much talk of my Lord of Essex, his friends, and his enemies answered thus: 'I will tell you; I know but one friend and one enemy my Lord hath; and that one friend is the Queen, and that one enemy is himself.'

HORSE AND MEN REQUIRED FOR IRELAND.

Now that it is determined to subdue the rebels of Ireland to obedience by force, certain additional horse are required for the service. Of these the Bishops and clergy are required to furnish thirty; but because the last time like service was required of them the horse were so bad by reason of the long journey they made to the sea side, the negligence of the riders, and in part badly chosen, there shall now be sent in lieu £30 for the furnishing of each horseman with his horse. In like manner from the shires are required sixty-four horses. Recusant gentlemen also, to the number of twenty-six, each shall supply the cost of one horse apiece.

To Lough Foyle there is shortly to be sent a garrison of 2,000 men and 100 horse under the charge and conduct of Sir Samuel Bagnal: and for their furnishing and victuals is issued the sum of £8,000.

19th July. THE TROUBLES AT PLYMOUTH.

There are still disagreements at Plymouth, where the Mayor had a purpose to indict one John Hales, the sergeant of the band of Sir Ferdinando Gorges, for taking away the stocks in the town and some few deal boards, upon refusal of the Mayor to find firewood as he had indeed promised. Forasmuch as the matter was brought before the Council, who took order to compound the differences between the Mayor and Sir Ferdinando, this indictment is followed only upon spleen and stomach, and the Justices of Assize are ordered that, if the indictment is preferred against Hales at the Assize, it shall be forborne.

21st July. THE EARL OF ESSEX AND THE LORD GREY.

Of late the Earl of Essex, in doubt why the Lord Grey should be so well favoured at Court and especially by the Queen, forced him to declare himself either his only, or friend to the Secretary and so his enemy, protesting that there could be no neutrality. The Lord Grey answered that no base dependency should ever fashion his love or hate to the Earl's passions; and as for the Secretary he had diversely tasted of his favour and would never be dishonest or ungrateful. Whereupon the Earl of Essex answered that though he affected some parts in the Lord Grey, he loved not his person, neither should he be welcome to him, nor expect any advancement under him. Thereupon the Lord Grey complaineth greatly that the Queen will suffer one man to engross thus servilely all men of sword and derive the advancement of war only from his partial favour; for needs must the sovereignty of her princely authority be diminished, if not extinguished, if any save herself exercise these princely properties.

23rd July. ABUSES IN THE IRISH SERVICE.

It is said by those who have experience of this Irish service that it hath long been a general custom in Ireland for all sorts of people in all offices to make their most gain and private commodity, every man for himself, never regarding how wastefully or wilfully her Majesty's treasure was spent, how the poor subjects were spoiled, how the rebels increased, how well or ill her Majesty's service succeeded; but generally all men providing and caring only how to enrich themselves by their offices. Of the captains, most are so unconscionable that without pity or compassion they have kept from men of their own nation, even of their own blood, not only their imprest and diet money whiles they remained in garrison in extreme hunger and cold, but also have suffered them to make such havoc of the poor inhabitants of the land that the poor souls have nothing else to feed upon but roots, grass and boiled nettles. Yet will these captains swear most execrable oaths, stare and protest, as though heaven and earth came together, that their companies stood them in so many score pounds for so long a time to their utter undoing. Their abuse of her Majesty is such that it hath been usual in the time of musters for Irish soldiers to come from the rebels to make show at the musters with the English captains, and be passed away again without any further doings.

25th July. THE STILLYARD.

After these many delays to-day the Council desired the Lord Mayor to proceed to the seizing of the Stillyard, nevertheless to allow ten days wherein the goods may be removed.

25th July. MR. DARRELL BEFORE THE ECCLESIASTICAL COMMISSIONERS.

A few days since Mr. Darrell was called before the Commissioners for Causes Ecclesiastical at Lambeth, and from thence committed to prison by reason of his absurd and untrue, but yet very confident, assertions, giving just occasion thereby to suspect that he was but a counterfeit.

Moreover the boy Darling that was dispossessed at Burton two years ago was also brought to London, and he being closely examined also hath confessed that his possession was counterfeit, and wrote out a confession accordingly, which he signed. But being set at liberty he had conference with Mr. Darrell in the Gatehouse and thereupon wrote a letter to the Bishop of London affirming that he had been drawn on by subtleties to make this confession.

Hereafter he was called before the Archbishop of Canterbury, the Bishop of London, the Lord Chief Justices, and others, and the deposition against him heard in open court. Whereupon Mr. Darrell was by the full agreement of the whole court condemned for a counterfeit, and together with Mr. More, is committed to close prison till other order be taken for their further punishment.

At this Mr. Darrell's friends make great complaints on his behalf, as one whom God hath honoured to suffer for the testimony of His Holy Truth ; also that he was convicted before the Archbishop without hearing or examining. They say that his judges before any conviction exceedingly reviled him, becoming parties, pleaders and accusers ; and that there hath been running to court to forestall the Lords and Ladies of honour and others that would present a petition on his behalf. As for the boy Darling, he was kept in the Bishop of London's house, none of his friends suffered to come unto him. He was allured by promises, terrified by threatenings, as that he should be hanged as the Burgonian was, whom they showed unto him.

26th July. LORD BURLEIGH SICK.

The Lord Treasurer aileth greatly these last days. On the 24th he had no rest all the night, and yesterday attempting to rise out of his bed he was so weak that he could not sit up. To-day he would have one of the Queen's surgeons sent to him, and is much worse than he was after a very evil night, being still weaker and unable to read letters or sit up to do any business.

WANT OF ZEAL AT PLYMOUTH.

To the late demand for shipping to transport the soldiers for Ireland, the Mayor of Plymouth maketh answer that the quantity of shipping cannot be found there, and that the charge is too great for the town to furnish. Hereat the Council are displeased, noting the backwardness and indisposition of the Mayor, which is the more notable seeing the favour the town hath lately tasted in the cases brought before the Council. Bristol and Chester have performed the like service with great willingness and at very reasonable rates, and had present order for repayment of those sums that they laid out, as her Majesty always in most princely manner doth not delay the payment of any money disbursed for public service and promised by the Council's letters. Moreover the Mayor complaineth that the money disbursed for the charges of the Spaniards is not yet paid. To this the Council answer that the disbursement was of another nature and hath been very negligently solicited.

27th July. A WITCH CONDEMNED.

Josia Poley, a widow, was this day found guilty of practising witchcraft upon one Herbert Apshawe so that he languished for a space of thirty hours and then died. This was two and a half years since. About a fortnight since she practised witchcraft on a certain Margaret Burroughes who languished, but is still alive though in danger of her life.

29th July. GENERAL NEWS.

My Lord of Essex is not yet returned to the Court.

From Italy news is come of Sir Anthony Shirley, that went out of England the last winter giving out that he would serve the Emperor against the Turk, but now it appeareth that he doth serve the Turk against the Emperor; and so is he turned from a Christian to a Turk, which is most monstrous. No doubt if it be so the Lord will punish the same.

1st August. THE BLACKWATER FORT.

The fort of Blackwater is still held with great honour and resolution by Captain Williams who commandeth it, and although Tyrone lately bent his whole forces to surprise it, and hath left many men still who block them in on all sides of the fort, yet the worthy Captain doth still defend himself and the place;

and lately by some stratagem issued forth, and besides the killing of two or three of Tyrone's principal men hath gotten divers horses and mares of theirs into the fort.

4th August. THE DEATH OF LORD BURLEIGH.

This morning at 8 o'clock died Sir William Cecil, Lord Burleigh, Lord High Treasurer of England.

At 6 o'clock last night the physicians finding no distemper in his pulse or body affirmed that it was impossible he could be heart sick that had so good temper and so perfect pulse and senses, yet at 7 o'clock he fell into a convulsion like to the shaking of a cold ague. 'Now,' quoth he, 'the Lord be praised the time is come'; and calling for his children, blessed them and took his leave, commanding them to serve and fear God, and love one another. He prayed also for the Queen that she might live long and die in peace. Then he called for Thomas Bellot, his steward, one of his executors, and delivered him his will, saying, 'I have ever found thee true to me, and I now trust thee with all'; who like a godly honest man prayed his Lordship as he had lived religiously so now to remember his Saviour Christ, by Whose blood he was to have forgiveness of sins; with many the like speeches used by his chaplains; to whom he answered that it was done already, for he was assured God had forgiven his sins and would save his soul. Then he called his chaplains with all the company to say prayers for him, himself saying them after them all the time they prayed.

He continued languishing thus most patiently, still having memory perfect till 12 of the clock, lying praying to himself, saying the Lord's prayer in Latin; whereupon some inferred that he was papist, but it was not strange for him to pray in Latin because he never read any books or prayers but in Latin, French or Italian, very seldom in English. Now his speech began to fail him, and so languishing till 4 o'clock, sometimes wanting, sometimes having speech, he often said, 'O what a heart is this that will not let me die! Come Lord Jesus, one drop of death, Lord Jesus!' So he lay praying to himself softly; and at this time there were twenty in the chamber of his children, friends and servants, everyone praying and devising what to give him to hold the life in him if it were possible.

But when they strove to give him anything, he came to himself, saying, 'O ye torment me; for God's sake let me die quietly.' Then lying still the standers-by might hear him say softly to himself, 'Lord receive my spirit, Lord have mercy upon me'; which were the last words he was heard to speak.

So he continued speechless and senseless till 8 o'clock and then died; wherein one thing is observed most strange, that though many watched to see when he should die, he lay looking so sweetly and went away so mildly as in a sleep, that it could scarce be perceived when the breath went out of his body. Had he lived till the 15th September he should have been 77 years old.

The Character of Lord Burleigh.

He was rather meanly statured and well proportioned than tall, very straight and upright of body and legs, and, until age and his infirmity of the gout surprised him, very active and nimble of body, notably enduring travail and labour whereunto he used his body. Of visage very well favoured and of an excellent complexion, insomuch as even in his later days, when he was well and warm or had new dined or supped, he had as good colour in his face as most fair women; and altogether he was one of the sweetest and most well favoured, well mannered old men that hath been seen.

His natural disposition was ever gentle, temperate, merry, courteous, affable, slow to anger, ever shunning revenge, and never doing anything in fury or choler, neither yielding to passion, but always tempering his affections; insomuch as most part of his time he was noted to be most patient in hearing, so mild and ready in answering, as no man went away discontented, save that these last two or three years he was a little sharp in words sometimes. He was naturally merry and seldom sad, never moved with joyful or ill news. He could better cover his griefs than help it, and whatsoever was in his mind would never appear in his countenance or speech; he would of all things make great account of a little kindness. He was neither pompous nor proud, and yet loved to live honourably; being ever most charitable to the poor, whom he would better relieve in their parishes than in high ways or streets. He loved many times to be retired, to take air and recreation, and would then be as merry with his men as among his equals. In his business, most painful, careful, and watchful, never well till it was done.

THE LORD BURLEIGH'S PRECEPTS FOR HIS SON.

When Sir Robert Cecil was a young man the Lord Burleigh wrote out ten rules for the forming of his life, to this effect following:

1. Use great providence and circumspection in the choice of a wife, for from thence shall spring all thy future good or evil; and it is like a stratagem of war wherein a man can err but once. If thy estate be good, match near at home, and at leisure; if weak, far off, and quickly. Inquire diligently of her disposition, and how her parents were inclined in their youth. Let her not be poor how well born soever; for a man can buy nothing in the market with gentility. Neither choose a base and uncomely creature, nor a dwarf and fool; for by the one thou shalt beget a race of pigmies, and the other it will irk thee to hear her talk.

2. Bring up children in learning and obedience, yet without austerity; the foolish cockering of some parents and the over-stern carriage of others causeth more men and women to take ill courses than their own natural inclinations. Marry daughters in time, lest they marry themselves. Suffer not thy sons to pass the Alps: for they shall learn nothing there but pride, blasphemy and atheism. Neither train them up for the wars; for a soldier can hardly be an honest man or a good Christian; for every war is of itself unjust unless the cause make it just. Besides it is a science no longer in request than in use; soldiers in peace are like chimneys in summer.

3. Live not in the country without corn and cattle about thee; for he that puts his hand to purse for every household expense is like him that thinks to keep water in a sieve. Feed servants well and pay them with the most; and then thou mayest boldly require service and duty at their hands.

4. Let kindred and allies be welcome to thy table, but shake off parasites and sycophants that will fawn on thee in the summer of thy prosperity but in adverse storms will shelter thee no more than an arbour in winter.

5. Beware of suretiship for the best friends; for he that payeth another man's debts seeks his own decay. Neither borrow money of a friend, but of a stranger, where paying for it thou shalt hear of it no more; otherwise thou shalt eclipse thy credit, lose thy friend, and get pay as dear as to another. But in borrowing money be precious of thy word; for he that hath a care to keep days of payment is lord of other men's goods.

6. Attempt not law against a man before thou be thoroughly resolved that thou hast right on thy side; and then spare neither for money nor pains; for a cause or two so followed, and obtained, will free thee from suits a great part of thy life.

7. Be sure to keep some great man thy friend; but trouble him not for trifles. Present him with many yet small gifts and of little charge. And if thou have cause to bestow any great gratuity, let it be some such thing as may be daily in his sight. Otherwise in this ambitious age thou shalt remain as a hop without a pole living in obscurity, and be made a football for every insulting companion.

8. Towards thy superiors be humble yet generous; with thy equals familiar, yet respective; towards thy inferiors show much humility, and some familiarity; as to bow thy body, stretch forth thy hand, and uncover thy head, and such like compliments. The first prepares the way for thy advancement; the second makes thee known as a man well bred; the third gains a good report which once gotten is easily kept.

9. Trust not any with thy life, credit or estate; for it is mere folly for a man to entail himself to his friend.

10. Be not scurrilous in thy conversation nor satirical in thy jests; the one will make thee unwelcome in all company; and the other will pull on quarrels, and get thee hatred of thy best friends.

The Queen's Grief.

The Queen was certified of the Lord Treasurer's death this afternoon, which she seemed to take very grievously, shedding of tears and separating herself from all company. She hath sent my Lord of Buckhurst and Mr. Chancellor for the Seal and such things as concern her Majesty.

The absence of the Earl of Essex at this time is very unseasonable both for the common good and his own private; for the longer he persisteth in this careless humour towards her Majesty the more her heart will be hardened. If he should persist in contending with her in this manner it may breed such hatred in her as will never be reclaimed, so that though she may be forced to use his service, yet not having her Majesty's love therein he shall be subject to their tongues who will practise against him.

12th August. INSUFFICIENT SOLDIERS FROM RADNORSHIRE.

The men impressed in Radnorshire for the Irish service are said to have been very unserviceable, being taken out of the jails, rogues, and vagrant persons, evil armed and sent forth so naked and bare, without shoes or hose, as to be unfit for any service or to appear amongst men, besides of that lewd behaviour as they had like to have mutinied and made an uproar. The force for Lough Foyle is now in part embarked for Dublin.

14th August. VICTUALS FOR THE SOLDIERS.

The victuals appointed for the men to be sent to Lough Foyle:

Item		Quantity	Item		Quantity
Biscuit or wheat meal to make biscuit.	for each man per diem	1 lb.	Butter	to four men per diem	½ lb.
			Cheese		1¼ lb.
Sack		½ pint	Pease		1 quart
Aqua vitae		¼ pint			
Beer		1 quart	Oatmeal		1½ pint

Besides there is appointed for the men 4,000 lbs. of liquorice and 1,000 lbs. of aniseed to make beverage for those that be sick, or will drink it.

16th August. THE QUEEN AND THE EARL OF ESSEX.

The Queen sent Mr. William Killigrew with a message to the Earl of Essex that she looketh for a better answer from him of submission or else not to admit him again to her presence, but Sir William Knollys meeting him took him back to Court that he might let the Queen know that my Lord had a fit the night before and was ill with a cold and not yet freed from it. She blamed him for not going, to which he replied that my Lord's fit would have been imputed to her message; which she confessed, and concluded that he might stay until she heard from my Lord's physician. Her Majesty is now variable and distracted in herself.

22nd August. A GREAT DISASTER IN IRELAND.

The fort at Blackwater being reduced to great straits, it was resolved by Sir Henry Bagnal, the Marshal, to relieve it, alleging how greatly this service concerned her Majesty's honour. On the 14th August therefore the army, being by computation 3,500 foot and 300 horse, marched out of Armagh, leaving there all the victuals and some munition. Their form was in six regiments, marching severally at six or seven score paces between each regiment, the way being hard and the ground hilly, within caliver shot of wood and bog on both sides which was wholly possessed by the enemy, who played on them continually.

After marching thus for a mile, they approached a trench which the enemy had cast in front of their passage, a mile long, five foot deep, and four foot over, with a thorny hedge on the top, and in the middle of a bog. Over this ditch the vanguard passed, but the main battle stood for bringing up the saker, which stuck fast in a ford, and also for the rear which being hard set, had retired to Armagh. In the meantime the vanguard having passed were so distressed that they fell to run and were all in effect put to the sword. The Marshal, being chief commander, then came up to relieve them, but was shot dead in the head by a bullet; notwithstanding two other regiments passed over the trench. But as the battle came up two barrels of powder took fire amongst them, by which the men were disranked and routed, and in this confusion the two regiments that had passed the trench were for the most part put to the sword. Hereupon Sir Thomas Maria Wingfield, being now chief commander, commanded the retreat to Armagh, the battle being all in rout, but, with great resolution of the vanguard of horse, and the enemy's munition being well spent, recovered Armagh. Here the captains resolved to refresh their men with victuals and munition, and so to march directly to Newry. But in the meantime the enemy approached and fell round them on all sides with their force. Then the captains, finding the insufficiency both in mind and means of their men, concluded that the horse should venture to break forth through the enemy's quarter and so advertise the State, that present succour might be sent to fetch them off. This was done by the horsemen but with some loss. In this disaster are lost Sir Henry Bagnal and most of his regiment of 1, 000 slain; Captain Percy hurt, Captain Cosby slain and most of their regiment; Sir Calisthenes Brooke that led the horse was shot in the belly and is thought to be slain. In all about 2,000 footmen and fifteen captains.

23rd August. A Proclamation against Forestallers.

A proclamation is published straitly charging the justices and other officers that the orders against forestallers, ingrossers and regraters be strictly enforced, for that the price of grain is so increased by their unmerciful covetousness that many people are like to die of the dearth. Moreover it is forbidden from the 20th September next coming to employ upon the feeding of dogs any grain fit for the sustenance of men, or to make any starch.

The Lord Keeper's Letter to the Earl of Essex.

It is said that the Lord Keeper hath written to the Earl of Essex (who came yesterday to the Council but the second time since June) warning him of the dangers of his present courses. He is not yet so far gone but that he may well return. The return is safe, but the progress dangerous and desperate. For his enemies he doth that which they could never do for themselves, whilst his friends are left to open shame and contempt, his own fortune overthrown, and his honour and reputation ruinated. His best remedy is not to contend and strive but humbly to submit; even if cause of scandal be given him, yet policy, duty and religion enforce him to his sovereign, for God Himself requireth it as a principal bond of service to Himself.

The Irish Forces.

Upon the accident lately happened in Ireland the soldiers intended for Lough Foyle are now to be sent to Carlingford.

25th August. My Lord of Essex's Letter to the University of Cambridge.

On the death of the Lord Treasurer the University of Cambridge have chosen my Lord of Essex to be their Chancellor, which he accepting in a Latin letter declareth '*nec meditationem armorum strepitus, nec lectionem negotiantium frequentia permisere; ideoque acuendum esset ingenium iam obtusum; excolendus stilus iam plane barbarus; rediscenda mihi omnia Artium rudimenta iam essent, antequam uel Matri Academiae conceptus offerre, uel coram doctissimo uestro senatu uerba proferre satis confiderem.*' Nothing, quoth he, shall be more forward in his life than his love and care and watch in guarding their privileges and forwarding their affairs by his industry and constancy.

26th August. ESSEX'S REPLY TO THE LORD KEEPER.

The Earl of Essex hath answered the letter of the Lord Keeper, very vehemently protesting that the highest judge on earth hath imposed upon him, without trial or hearing, the most heavy judgment that ever hath been known. There is no tempest, saith he, to the passionate indignation of a prince; nor any time so unseasonable as when it lighteth upon those who might expect a harvest of their careful and painful labours. The indissoluble duty he oweth her Majesty is only the duty of allegiance; the duty of attendance is no indissoluble duty. He oweth her Majesty the duty of an Earl and of Lord Marshal of England; he hath been content to do her Majesty the service of a clerk, but can never serve her as a slave or a lackey. 'When,' saith he, 'the vilest of all indignities are done unto me, doth religion force me to sue? Or doth God require it? Is it impiety not to do it? What, cannot princes err? Cannot subjects receive wrong? Is an earthly power or authority infinite?' He saith further, 'As for me I have received wrong, and feel it. My cause is good, I know it; and whatsoever come, all the powers on earth can never show more strength and constancy in oppressing, than I can show in suffering whatsoever can or shall be imposed upon me.'

THE NEW MARSHAL IN IRELAND.

Sir Richard Bingham is appointed Marshal in Ireland in place of Sir Henry Bagnal that was slain.

27th August. NEW FORCES FOR IRELAND.

Soldiers to the number of 1,700 are required to strengthen the forces in Ireland. And because there hath been neglect used in choosing idle and loose people, so that it seemed the counties sought rather to disburden themselves of unprofitable people than to advance the Queen's service, the justices themselves shall repair to the villages and see good choice made of sufficient men, or cause them to be brought before them by the constables to be by them first viewed and allowed before they be presented to the general musters.

Two Patents.

The Council have directed warrants to all public officers on behalf of two that hold monopolies which have been repunged; the one being Sir Jerome Bowes that hath sole licence to make drinking glasses and to prevent the bringing in of glasses from any parts beyond seas. The other is Mr. John Spilman, the Queen's jeweller, that hath letters patent to gather rags for the making of writing paper, and forbidding the erection of any mill for making of paper without Mr. Spilman's consent.

29th August. The Defeat at the Blackwater.

The rebel Tyrone hath offered composition to the remnants of the army that were shut up in Armagh. First that they should surrender the Blackwater fort, leaving there the colours, drums and munition, the captains having left them only their rapiers and hackneys; the fort being delivered, the whole army with the men of the Blackwater to march away from Armagh with all their carriage and hurt men to Newry or Dundalk. These terms were accepted and the soldiers are now at Newry. Tyrone gave as his reason for this composition that he was at £500 charge by the day in keeping his forces together to attend our army, which he supposed had a month or six months' victual, in which time he knew that forces would land in Lough Foyle; and therefore he thought it better to save that charge, to gain the fort of the Blackwater, and to bend himself to hinder the landing of forces in Lough Foyle.

The Funeral of the Lord Treasurer.

To-day the Lord Treasurer's funeral was performed with all the rites belonging to so great a personage. First came two conductors in cloaks, then nigh on a hundred poor men; then the servants (a great company) of gentlemen, judges, knights, and noblemen ; then those of my Lord's own household ; the clerks and other officers of the offices of State ; the Bishop of London, the preacher ; the Heralds, the helm and crest borne by Rouge Dragon, the sword by Chester, the targe by Lancaster, the coat of arms by Norroy. Then came the body borne by eight gentlemen, with four assistants to carry the pall at each corner ; next the chief mourner, and after the Great Seal. Then followed the Earl of Essex, Earl Marshal, the Lord Keeper, the Lord Admiral, the Earl of Shrewsbury, the Earl of Worcester, and the Lord Chamberlain, all being on horseback with their footclothes of black cloth, in their mourning weeds according to their state. Then followed the Ancients of Gray's Inn, and all the rest after them, two and two ; then all yeomen in black coats ; and then all the people. The number of mourners, one and other, were above 500.

The funeral being honourably solemnised in the Abbey of Westminster, the corpse is now taken to Stamford to be interred.

It was noted that the Earl of Essex, whether it were upon consideration of the present occasion, or for his own disfavours, carried the heaviest countenance of the company. Presently after dinner he retired to Wanstead where they say he means to settle, seeing he cannot be received in Court, though he have relented much, and sought by divers means to recover his hold. But the Queen says he hath played long enough upon her, and that she means to play awhile upon him, and to stand as much upon her greatness as he doth upon stomach.

Upon Bartholemew day the Lord Cobham was installed Warden of the Cinque Ports at Canterbury at which solemnity were assembled almost 4000 horse. He kept the feast very magnificently, and spent 26 oxen with all other provision suitable.

Mistress Vernon, one of the ladies-in-waiting, hath been sent from Court and is at Essex House. Some say that she is with child, yet she complaineth not of foul play but says that the Earl of Southampton will justify it. It is bruited underhand that the Earl was in London four days in great secret of purpose to marry her and effected it accordingly.

31st August. RECUSANTS TO SUPPLY HORSES.

Certain recusants to the number of forty-six are required to provide £15 each towards the charges of furnishing light horse for Ireland.

5th September. LIGHTNING IN LONDON.

This afternoon there were two great cracks of lightning and thunder, whereby some men were smitten at the postern by the Tower, and one man slain at the bridgehouse in Southwark.

7th September. COURT NEWS.

The Earl of Southampton of late came over very secretly from France and married his Mistress Vernon. Yesterday the Queen was informed of the new Lady Southampton and her adventures, whereat her patience was so moved that she came not to the Chapel. The Queen has commanded that there shall be provided for her the sweetest and best appointed lodging in the Fleet; and the Earl is commanded, on his allegiance, to return with all speed to London, to advertise his arrival, but not to come to Court in person.

The Earl of Essex who was sick at Essex House is now gone in his litter towards Wanstead. The Queen hath sent her physician to attend him, and to-day he was visited by Mr. Killigrew, Mr. Greville and Lord Henry Howard from her.

MERES' 'PALLADIS TAMIA.'

There is a new book called *Palladis Tamia* by Mr. Francis Meres, being a collection of similitudes gathered from more than one hundred and fifty authors and set out under some two hundred and fifty diverse heads, whereof one is 'A Comparative discourse of our English poets with the Greek, Latin and Italian poets.' Saith that the English tongue is mightily enriched and gorgeously invested in rare ornaments by Sir Philip Sidney, Spenser, Daniel, Drayton, Warner, Shakespeare, Marlowe, and Chapman. Of lyric poets the best be Spenser (who excelleth in all kinds), Daniel, Drayton, Shakespeare, Breton. For the most passionate to bewail the perplexities of love, Henry Howard, Earl of Surrey, Sir Thomas Wyatt, Sir Francis Brian, Sir Philip Sidney, Sir Walter Ralegh, Sir Edward Dyer, Spenser, Daniel, Drayton, Shakespeare, Wheatstone, Gascoigne, Samuel Page, Churchyard, Breton.

The best for comedy be Edward, Earl of Oxford, Dr. Gager of Oxford, Mr. Rowley, Mr. Edwards, eloquent and witty John Lyly, Lodge, Gascoigne, Greene, Shakespeare, Thomas Nashe, Thomas Heywood, Anthony Munday (our best plotter), Chapman, Porter, Wilson, Hathaway and Henry Chettle. As tragic poets, the Lord Buckhurst, Dr. Legg, Dr. Edes, Mr. Edward Ferris, the author of the *Mirror for Magistrates*, Marlowe, Peele, Watson, Kyd, Shakespeare, Drayton, Chapman, Dekker, and Benjamin Jonson.

Moreover, saith he, 'as Plautus and Seneca are accounted the best for comedy and tragedy among the Latins, so Shakespeare among the English is the most excellent in both kinds for the stage: for comedy, witness his *Gentlemen of Verona*, his *Errors*, his *Love's Labours Lost*, his *Love's Labours Won*, his *Midsummer Night's Dream*, and his *Merchant of Venice*; for tragedy, his *Richard the Second*, *Richard the Third*, *Henry the Fourth*, *King John*, *Titus Andronicus* and his *Romeo and Juliet*.'

8th September. MARSTON'S 'SCOURGE OF VILLAINY.'

There is a book of ten Satires called the *Scourge of Villainy*, very invectively whipping the vices of these times, which the author dedicateth 'To his most esteemed and best beloved Self,' and beginning the first with this *proemium*—

I bear the scourge of just Rhamnusia,
Lashing the lewdness of Britannia.
Let others sing as their good Genius moves,
Of deep designs or else of clipping loves.
Fair fall them all that with wit's industry
Do clothe good subjects in true poesy.
But as for me, my vexed thoughtful soul,
Takes pleasure in displeasing sharp control.
Thou nursing Mother of fair wisdom's lore,
Ingenuous Melancholy, I implore
Thy grave assistance; take thy gloomy seat,
Inthrone thee in my blood. Let me intreat
Stay his quick jocund skips, and force him run
A sad pac'd course until my whips be done.
Daphne, unclip thine arms from my sad brow,
Black Cypress crown me whilst I do up plough

The hidden entrails of rank villainy ;
Quake guzzle dogs, that live on putrid slime,
Scud from the lashes of my yerking rime.

Concludeth with a satire of the Humours of our City gallants.

9th September. LAWLESSNESS NEAR LONDON.

Many grievous and extraordinary outrages are in these days committed by rogues, vagabonds and other licentious persons in places not far distant from London, who have taken such boldness that they assemble themselves together, armed even with petronels and pistols. These men do such mischief as the ordinary course of justice sufficeth not to keep them in awe. Moreover the officers appointed for conservation of the peace are terrified with their violence, and some of late slain and murdered. The Lord Mayor and justices of Middlesex, Surrey and Kent are required to make privy search in inns, alehouses, houses of victualling and lodging, stables, outhouses and the like, and all persons found to lurk suspiciously to be committed forthwith to strait prison to await trial at a special Sessions. A proclamation is now issued that a Provost Marshal shall be appointed, with authority to apprehend such as will not be corrected by the ordinary officers of justice and without delay to execute them upon the gallows by order of martial law.

10th September. SOME LEVIES DISCHARGED.

Of the levies, to the number of 1,700, that were to be ready at this time for service in Ireland many are now to be discharged, but in such wise that they may be assembled again and sent forth at ten days' warning ; but the rest, being 1,000, are to be set forth at once.

12th September. THE QUEEN'S LETTER TO THE COUNCIL OF IRELAND.

The Queen hath caused a letter to be written to the Council of Ireland informing them that Sir Richard Bingham is appointed Marshal, and showing her displeasure of the notorious errors in that government, but especially that she will not pass over their foul error to her dishonour when, after the late defeat, the Council framed such a letter to the traitor as was never the like read, either in form or substance for such baseness. This letter was not received by Tyrone, being stayed by accident. In it the Council had begged him to let the men in Armagh depart without doing them any further hurt, and especially, seeing his enemy the late Marshal was among the slain, they hoped that he would cease all further revenge against the rest.

15th September. THE EARL OF ESSEX RESTORED TO FAVOUR.

In the Court my Lord of Essex took his place in the Council five days ago and is now restored to the Queen's favour.

'SKIALETHEIA.'

There is a book entered called *Skialetheia, or a Shadow of Truth*, being a collection of certain epigrams and six satires on the follies of these times.

OF A LORD'S LIFE.

My Lord most court-like lies in bed till noon,
Then, all high-stomached, riseth to his dinner,
Falls straight to dice, before his meat be down,
Or to digest, walks to some female sinner.
Perhaps fore-tired he gets him to a play,
Comes home to supper, and then falls to dice,
There his devotion wakes till it be day,
And so to bed, where until noon he lies.
'This is a lord's life,' simple folk will sing.
A Lord's life? What, to trot so foul a ring?
Yet thus he lives, and what's the greatest grief,
Gnatho still swears he leads true virtue's life.

OF ONE THAT WOULD CRY 'OH RARE.'

As Caius walks the streets, if he but hear
A blackman grunt his note, he cries, 'Oh rare!'
He cries 'Oh rare' to hear the Irishmen
Cry 'Pip, fine pip,' with a shrill accent, when
He comes at Mercers' chapel; and 'Oh rare,'
At Ludgate at the prisoners' plainsong there:
'Oh rare' sings he, to hear a cobbler sing,
Or a wassail on Twelfth Night, or the ring
At cold St. Pancras Church; or anything:
He'll cry 'Oh rare,' and scratch the elbow too
To see two butchers' curs fight; the cuckoo

Will cry 'Oh rare' to see the champion bull;
Or the victorious mastiff with crown'd skull,
And garlanded with flowers, passing along
From Paris Garden; he renews his song,
To see my Lord Mayor's henchmen; or to see
(At an old Alderman's blest obsequy)
The Hospital boys in their blue equipage;
Or at a carted bawd, or whore in a cage.
He'll cry 'Oh rare' at a gong-farmer's cart;
'Oh rare,' to hear a ballad or a fart:
Briefly, so long he hath used to cry, 'Oh rare,'
That now that phrase is grown thin and threadbare,
But sure his wit will be more rare and thin,
If he continue as he doth begin.

16th September. JONSON'S 'EVERY MAN IN HIS HUMOUR.'

At the Curtain the Lord Chamberlain's men have a new play called *Every Man in his Humour*, written by Jonson, that displayeth the humours of our City gentlemen. A practice in it is to make a braggart captain, by name Bobadilla, boast much, but when it cometh to the proof to endure the bastinado, excusing himself that he was bound to the peace. Another is to make two gulls, one from the country and the other of the town, practise to each other this humour of melancholy, holding that 'tis the only best humour, for 'your true melancholy breeds your perfect fine wit.'

20th September. GENERAL NEWS.

In Ireland the Lord Ormond is hurt and since the great overthrow 400 more throats cut. Sir Francis Vere is coming towards the Low Countries, and Sir Alexander Ratcliffe and Sir Robert Drury with him. Honour pricks them on, and the world thinks that honour will quickly prick them off again. Sir Thomas Shirley has taken four hulks, Easterlings of Lubec, but it is hoped that the freight is Spanish. They are stayed and a commission granted to examine whether they are prize. The Court is now at Nonsuch, and last Sunday my Lord Chief Justice's expectation of being made a Councillor was disappointed. There was a French gentleman, a master of requests and resident of Lyons, brother to M. de Vicq, governor of Calais, a man honourably entertained by the Earl of Essex and greatly commended by the Queen for his speech and other carriage. There were divers Almains with him, whereof one lost 300 crowns at this new play of *Every Man in his Humour*.

22nd September. A PLAYER SLAIN.

Benjamin Jonson, the player that wrote the new play of Humours, whom they call the 'bricklayer,' to-day fought with Gabriel Spencer, one of the Admiral's players, in Shoreditch fields; Jonson is hurt in the arm, but Spencer being wounded in the right side is dead of it.

30th September. MR. SPENSER TO BE THE SHERIFF OF CORK.

The Council recommend Mr. Edmund Spenser to the Lords Justices of Ireland to be appointed Sheriff of Cork, he being well known for his good commendable parts, a man endowed with good knowledge in learning, and not without experience in the service of the wars.

2nd October. THE EARL OF CUMBERLAND'S RETURN.

My Lord of Cumberland is returned from his voyage, his losses in ships being two barges, the *Pegasus* and the old frigate; of the men, 600 died of the bloody flux and calenture at Porto Rico, 60 were slain in fight and 40 drowned in the two wrecks.

His first intention after leaving England was to go to Lisbon and there wait for five carracks and twenty-five ships that were laden for Brazil, but unluckily his fleet was espied by a carvel that gave the alarum and so the carracks came not forth. From thence therefore they went towards the Canaries to Lancerota, being informed that there dwelt a rich Marquis, worth £100,000 if he could be taken suddenly, but in this he was disappointed. Nevertheless my Lord thought it best to set his men on shore, for till this time he had never given them any training and many of them were very raw and unpractised to the service on land. Here they captured the town (which was most beggarly) and castle, but found nothing save a few pieces of ordnance and some little wine; which little was indeed too much, for the meaner sort were overthrown by it, and of the commanders, some were distempered with wine, some with pride of themselves or scorn of others, so that there were very few but that fell to most disorderly outrage one with another.

Thence they sailed on to Dominica and here my Lord made a speech to them all, rebuking them for the many gross faults committed amongst them since their coming to sea and warning them that his overpatient and forced sluggish humour was now shaken off, and that he would not for the future suffer to pass unpunished ill-deservers. At Dominica they stayed six days, watering the fleet and refreshing the sick men in a hot bath which was found near the sea as hot as either the Cross Bath or King's Bath in the City of Bath.

His Lordship now determined to attack the town of Porto Rico, and on the 6th June the soldiers were landed about three leagues from the town, towards which they marched along the sea shore till they met with a blackamoor whom they took to be their guide, and towards evening with much ado they came to the causeway that led out to the island. Wherefore the soldiers were led to a great lawn and there rested while a continual watch was kept to give immediate information of the ebb of the tide from the causeway. Early next morning the alarum was given very quietly and the companies quickly ranged; and after my Lord and Sir John Berkeley had somewhat disputed for the honour of leading the point, our men began the assault, which lasted for two hours, yet though they left noway unattempted they could not enter the gate. This causeway was so rugged that our men to keep on their feet made choice to wade in the water beside it. Here his Lordship was, by the stumbling of him that bore his target, overthrown even to the danger of drowning; for his armour so overburdened him that the Sergeant Major, that by chance was next him, had much ado at the first and second time to get him from under the water. When he was up he had received so much salt water that it drove him to so great extremity of present sickness that he was forced to lie down in that place upon the causeway.

In the fort the enemy had six pieces of great ordnance which were bent upon the causeway, and many musketeers, and at a port by the gate lay a fowler, which some call a murdering piece. For all this our soldiers came to the very gate, and began to hew at it with some two or three bills that they had; at the ports and loopholes they were at push of the pike, and having broken their own, with their naked hands took their enemies' pikes and perforce brake them. But the end was it could not then be taken; for the tide came in so fast that what was at their knees before was now come up to their middles. So the companies were withdrawn to the place where they had rested for the night.

Meanwhile my Lord went aboard, so sick that in truth he was to be feared for, with purpose to repose himself, but within a few hours he came ashore again and straightway put into execution a purpose which he had meantime digested. Wherefore he gave direction that one of the ships should bear close in, whatsoever it might cost, meanwhile musketeers should lie in the rocks and beat the enemy from his ordnance, so that 200 pike and shot might land between the fort and the town. This plot took such good effect that within a short space the enemy quitted the place. This fort having been made good, our men next marched towards a second fort, called the 'red fort'; but the enemy quitted that too. Next morning they began to march towards the town, which they found quitted of all able to make resistance, for besides women and men disabled for the wars the rest had taken themselves to their last hope, a fort called Mora.

When the town had been secured, his Lordship sent a drum to summon the fort to be delivered to him, which was refused by the Governor from within. After this summons his Lordship took exceeding great care for the taking of the fort with the least loss of men that possibly might be. He therefore took order to cut off all possible means of relief of victuals, and withal set up two platforms and several gabions that the wall might be beaten from two several places at once. For this purpose were brought from the *Scourge* two whole culverins, two demi-culverins, and four other pieces found about the town, whereof one was that very same which had slain Sir Nicholas Clifford. These were ready to batter on 17th June, being a Saturday, but my Lord would not have them begin on the Sabbath day, so that it was deferred till Monday.

In the meanwhile a martial court was called whereat two were condemned to death; the one, a soldier that had done violence to a Spaniard's wife, who was hanged in the market place; the other a sailor that for defacing some things in a church was thrice brought to the gallows, but at length his Lordship was intreated to grant him mercy.

On the Monday the battery began, and by evening it was seen that the *cavalero* flanking the gate being made of sandy earth was ready to fall at the next rain. Next day therefore they sent forth a drum from the fort to demand parley, the sum of their demands being that with colours flying, match in their cocks and bullets in their mouth, they should be set beyond the point at the Bridge to go whither they would; further that all the prisoners be delivered without ransom. My Lord utterly refused any such composition, but instead he offered them these articles written with his own hand:

'A resolution which you may trust to. I am content to give yourself and all your people their lives, yourself with your captains and officers to pass with your arms; all the rest of your soldiers with their rapiers and daggers only.

'You shall all stay here with me till I give you passage from the Island, which shall be within thirty days.

'Any one of you, which I shall choose, shall go with me into England, but shall not stay longer there than one month, but being well fitted for the purpose shall be safely sent home into Spain without ransom.'

It was doubted whether there were any in the fort that spake English, and therefore some were wishing the articles were translated into Spanish; but his Lordship peremptorily refused to seek their language but would have them find out his. Next morning the Spaniards accepted of these conditions, so that day the Governor and his company dined with my Lord, and after dinner the Governor went and brought out his companies (which of all sorts were near 400) and delivered the keys. The fort being occupied by our men, the fleet was commanded to come into the harbour, which all this time had rid without, for it is impossible that any ship should pass that point without sinking unless the fort grant her passage.

My Lord's intention now was to hold Porto Rico, for this is the very key of the West Indies which locketh and shutteth all the gold and silver in the continent of America and Brazilia.

But God otherwise disposed, for within a while many of our men fell sick. This sickness was an extreme looseness of the body which within a few days would grow into a flux of blood, sometimes in the beginning accompanied with hot agues, but always in the end attended by an extreme debility and waste of spirits. Towards the beginning of July there were not much above 200 dead, but by their departure on 13th August above 400, and as many so sick that most of them could not bring themselves on board. On their return to the Azores they were much distressed by grievous storms; and there they learnt that twenty-nine of the Spanish King's men-of-war, with five of them carracks, had passed that way a few days before. They set forth from Flores on 16th September. On Michaelmas day they sounded and the ground on the tallow assured them of being in the Sleeve, and the scollop shells confirmed their opinion that they were on the coast of France, though the Master judged otherwise; by whose judgment, if his Lordship had not contradicted out of his authority causing them to take a more northerly course, all had perished in all likelihood on the Ushant. Next morning they saw Normandy and are now come to shore.

3rd October. General News.

The Earl of Essex is now at Court on as good terms as ever he was, but there be no offices bestowed, nor no more show of bestowing them than the first day the Lord Treasurer died. One Stanley that came in sixteen days overland with letters out of Spain is lately committed to the Tower. He was very earnest to have private conference with her Majesty, pretending matters of great importance which he would by no means utter to anybody else. He affirms that the King of Spain was not dead at his coming away, but that he had retired himself and was coming on.

My Lord of Cumberland himself saith that he hath made a saving journey, but they that understand it better say that all he hath brought (whereof the greatest part is sugar and ginger) will not amount to above £15,000 or £16,000, which is not half the charge of setting out, besides the adventure and waste of his shipping and the loss of 600 men. Some find great fault and say his own wilfulness and want of direction overthrew the voyage, and that if he would have been advised, he might have done them all good, but he neglected present profit in hope of greater matters, and so forsook the substance for the shadow. By this and the rest the heat of our sea voyages is well allayed, which being no better conducted serve rather to fortify and confirm than hinder the enemy.

4th October. A MUTINY AMONGST THE LONDON SOLDIERS.

The soldiers that lately marched from London to the number of 300 have committed a notable outrage ; for when they came to Towchester and should have marched further the same day by the order of their conductor Captain Garrett Dillon, well near 200 of them fell into mutiny, refused to march, threatened their captain to kill him, and wounded some of his officers so grievously as it is doubtful whether they are living or dead. The chief movers of this mutiny are one Willoughby, whom the mutineers make their captain calling him 'Lord Willoughby,' a footman of the Earl of Derby, and a footman of the Lord Compton.

7th October. MR. HAKLUYT'S 'PRINCIPAL NAVIGATIONS.'

Mr. Richard Hakluyt hath now completed the first volume of a new edition of *The Principal navigations, voyages, traffics and discoveries of the English nation*, treating of the discoveries towards the north and north-east, also an account of the defeat of the Spanish huge armada in 1588 and the famous victory achieved at the city of Cadiz, 1596 ; and this he dedicateth to Lord Charles Howard, Lord High Admiral, whom Mr. Hakluyt would to settle and establish a Lecture of Navigation to be read in this City of London, for the banishing of our former gross ignorance in marine causes, and for the increase and multiplying of the sea-knowledge in this age, wherein God hath raised so general a desire in the youth of this Realm to discover all parts of the face of the earth.

9th October. SIR THOMAS SHIRLEY'S PRIZES.

The Mayor of Portsmouth, being commissioned to search any one of the Lubecers' ships that Sir Thomas Shirley should nominate, has performed the same, not forbearing to rip up the very ceiling of the ship ; nevertheless they have found neither treasure nor Spanish goods, but only salt and cork. The Lubec ships are therefore discharged and suffered to proceed on their voyage.

10th October. A TRAITOR TO BE SENT AWAY.

There is one Richard Zouch that hath served the King of Spain for many years who came over last summer and was committed to the Counter in Wood Street, where he hath remained these four months. Since none of his friends will relieve him and there is no reason her Majesty should be charged to maintain a fugitive and suspected person, the Council order that he shall be sent back again in some vessel bound for the Low Countries.

15th October. YARMOUTH HERRINGS.

It is allowed to the inhabitants of Great Yarmouth for one year to transport 600 lasts of herrings in strangers' bottoms to foreign parts, being in amity with her Majesty, in regard that in this troublesome time they cannot safely traffic in English ships.

28th October. FURTHER SOLDIERS FOR IRELAND.

Because of the spread of the rebellion to Munster there are now required a further levy of 2,000 soldiers to be sent to Ireland, these men being taken from Cornwall, Devon, Dorset, Southampton, Oxfordshire, Somerset and Wiltshire. They shall be ready by the 15th of next month.

4th November. THE DEATH OF THE SPANISH KING.

News is come that the King of Spain is dead, having been sick for many days of the gout, and numerous sores all over his body, so foul that one of his physicians fell ill of the very stench of them. In this last illness, he made himself very familiar not only with the thought of death but with the discussion thereof and all that should be done when he was gone, arranging each article of his funeral, and ordering the purchase of much black cloth to drape the Church of the Escurial. Also he caused them to bring to his bedside a shirt of lead wherewith, being dead, he should be wrapped, and the leaden coffin for his corpse. He examined them both, and, causing himself to be measured, gave order for their perfecting.

Some days before he died he summoned the Prince and the Infanta to his presence and gave them his blessing in words of affection, exhorting them to govern their subjects with love, to administer justice impartially, and to support and defend religion and the Catholic faith with all their might. He gave the Prince two sealed packets, instructing him to open them only after his death, and charging him to read, study and observe what was written therein as they would prove of the highest value to him. Also, that his wishes might be the more surely observed, the King placed in the Prince's service all his favourite ministers, causing the Prince himself to nominate them, thereby pledging himself not to dismiss them without necessary and good reason. During his illness he is said to have spent more than 700,000 crowns in gifts and in discharge of his conscience.

A few days later, in changing his bed, the King had such a sinking that for a while they thought him dead, but he recovered somewhat and they administered extreme unction. Though very feeble he had his memory perfect and asked for the cross which his father held when he was dying. Moreover he sent for the Prince and told him to remain that he might contemplate this example of earthly misery, exhorting him never to forget, when he had entered on his Kingdom, that he too must come to a like pass and must die. The Prince brake forth into weeping, but the King continued to speak calmly in most Christian spirit.

He died on 13th September at daybreak, having received all the sacraments of the Church with every sign of devoutness, piety, and religion, and to the apparent grief of all people, rich and poor. His death was announced that night, and thereupon began the funeral ceremonies, which were for nine days with continuous prayer and the tolling of bells that never ceased day nor night. He was buried the next day without any of the usual ceremonies and by his own orders without embalming. When the corpse had been laid in the leaden coffin the whole Council of State was summoned to witness; then the coffin was locked and the key taken to the King.

THE CHARACTER OF KING PHILIP II.

The King was seventy-one years old, having reigned forty-two years. He was a Prince that fought with gold rather than with steel, by his brain rather than by his arms, acquiring more by sitting still, by negotiation, by policy than his father did by armies and by war, so that he was one of the richest Princes that the world has ever seen, yet hath he left the revenues of his Kingdom and of the Crown burdened with about a million of debts. He was profoundly religious, displaying great calmness and professing himself unmoved alike in good or evil fortune. On great occasions, in the conduct of wars, or in the magnificence of his buildings he never counted the cost. He was no close reckoner, but lavished his gold without a thought, yet in small matters, in the government of his household, in his presents and rewards, more parsimonious than became his station. He held his desires in absolute control, showing an immutable and unalterable temper; feigning injuries, and feigning not to feel injuries, but never losing an opportunity to avenge them. No one ever saw him in a rage, being always patient, phlegmatic, temperate, melancholy.

The Prince that succeedeth is the King's only son, twenty years of age. He was educated by his father in great obedience and piety, but it cannot yet be said what his opinions may be, for he hath always kept them concealed out of respect for his father. Yet is he thought to be peacefully disposed, and hath shown himself satisfied with the new peace; if he hath an intention of taking up arms it is against infidels.

5th November. GREAT FLOODS.

In the counties of Lincoln, Northampton, Huntingdon, the Isle of Ely, Sussex, Surrey and elsewhere great hurt hath been sustained this autumn by reason of the waters that have of late overrun most part of their grounds, whereby these counties are reduced to great distress.

6th November. REBELLION SPREADING IN IRELAND.

There is now most barbarous and fearful rebellion raging in Munster. Most of the followers of noblemen and gentlemen of Munster have gone over to the enemy so that Sir Thomas Norris, the Governor, was unable either to encounter the rebels or to defend himself and so was forced to withdraw from his own house. These combinations and revolts have effected many execrable murders and cruelties upon the English in the counties of Limerick, Cork and Kerry and elsewhere; infants being taken from the nurses' breasts and dashed against the walls; the heart plucked out of the body of the husband in the view of the wife, who was forced to yield the use of her apron to wipe the blood from the murderers' fingers; an English gentleman in a town at midday cruelly murdered and his head cleft in divers pieces; divers sent into Youghal amongst the English, some with their throats cut but not killed, some with their tongues cut out of their heads, others with their noses cut off; by view whereof the English might the more bitterly lament the misery of their countrymen, and fear the like to befall themselves. And these execrable parts are performed by the Irish tenants and servants of the English; and those that but the last day were fed and nourished by the English are now the thieves that violently before their faces take from them their corn, cattle and other goods; and the party spoiled thinketh himself happy if he escape without loss of life or other shameful villainy to himself, his wife or children.

8th November. RUMOURS.

It is generally held that the Earl of Essex will go to Ireland towards the spring as Lieutenant-General, and the Lord Mountjoy as his Lord Deputy, with divers other young lords and noblemen, and that he shall be accompanied with the most part of those knights that be his creatures, for it is thought fit they should not come too easily by their honours but that in this case, as well as in many others, it should be granted for service done and to be done.

The new Countess of Southampton is brought abed of a daughter, and to mend her portion the Earl, her father, hath lately lost 1,800 crowns at tennis in Paris.

A JEST ON THE KING OF SPAIN.

It is reported about the Court that the King of Spain for all his striving to enlarge his possessions in his last days was eaten by lice while still living. Hereat one of the courtiers said to the Queen, 'God grant me no further ambition than to be eaten by worms when I am dead.'

9th November. THE CONSPIRACY OF EDWARD SQUIRE.

Edward Squire was arraigned this day in Westminster for his high treason in compassing the Queen's death, and being found guilty is condemned to be quartered.

This Squire dwelt in Greenwich divers years, and took upon him the practice of a scrivener and for some two years held an employment about the Queen's stable, as deputy to one Kaies, a purveyor of provisions. But being of a wit above his vocation, he disliked that condition of life and went to sea in the late voyage of Sir Francis Drake into the Indies; in which voyage sailing in the *Francis*, it was his hap to be taken by five Spanish frigates. Squire was thus brought prisoner into Spain, where soon after he was set at liberty.

Not long after his enlargement, he became known to Richard Walpole, the Jesuit, that is a kind of Vicar-General there to Parsons in his absence. This Walpole observed Squire, and finding him a man of more than ordinary sense and capacity for his quality and education, well advised and yet resolved, and not apprehensive at all of danger, perceived in him two conditions of especial advantage; the one that, coming into Spain a prisoner and not a fugitive, his return into England would be subject to less suspicion; the other that he understood Squire had some attendance about the Queen's stable.

Whereupon to prepare him for his purpose and to give colour that when Squire should return into England he was a man that had suffered in Spain for his conscience, Walpole subtlely compassed that upon a quarrel picked Squire was put into the Inquisition. By this means he got Squire's heart into his hands, mollified by distress, and became sure of him that he was a fixed and resolved Papist. After sufficient preparation, Walpole began to discourse of the miseries of the Catholics in England, and of the slanders of the government and upon how few persons' lives the State did stand. And Squire on the other side, wanting no wit to perceive which way he was led, after some time made vehement protestation of his mind and devotion to do service to the cause. Whereupon, Walpole saith: 'It were no doubt an action very meritorious to kill the Earl of Essex; but one thing is necessary.' And having kept him in suspense awhile, brake with him plainly and told him that he would put a service into his hands that he might accomplish without any evident peril of his life. And it was the empoisonment of the pommel of the Queen's saddle at such time as she should ride abroad, her Majesty being like to rest her hand thereupon for a good time together, and not unlike for her hand to come often about her face, mouth, and nostrils. Unto which accursed propositions, after that Squire had assented, then did the Friar use all diligence to confirm and bind him to resolution and performance, at sundry confessions taking his vow to be constant, and causing him to receive the sacrament upon it. And for a conclusion and final benediction of this most execrable plot, Squire kneeling before Walpole at confession, he lifted him up, hugged him about the neck with his left arm (such were Squire's own words) and crossing him with the other hand, after some words mumbled in Latin, said distinctly to him in English, 'God bless thee and give thee strength, my son; be of good courage: I pawn my soul for thine, and thou shalt have my prayers dead and alive.'

Then Walpole gave him full direction for the disposing of the poison, showing him that he should receive it in a double bladder, and when it should be used, he was to prick the bladder full of holes upon the upper part, and so carry it within the palm of his hand with a thick glove for safeguard of the hand. Then he should turn it in his hand upside down and so press it hard upon the pommel of the saddle.

Squire, therefore, being arrived in England about a fortnight before the Earl of Essex's setting forth towards the Islands, addressed himself to a Councillor of estate, both to avoid suspicion and to advise a means to go with the Earl in his ship; which indeed he did.

Now a se'nnight after he came out of Spain he understood that the horses were being made ready for the Queen's riding abroad. So he came into the stable yard where her Majesty's horse stood ready and in a familiar and cheerful manner, in the hearing of divers that stood by, he laid his hand upon the pommel of the saddle and said, 'God save the Queen'; and therewith bruised the poison as he was directed. But so it was that her Majesty's going abroad was stayed.

Within five or six days after this fact was committed, Squire went to sea in my Lord of Essex's own ship, taking the remainder of the same poison with him in a little pot in his portmantua, and when the Earl was at sea between Fayal and St. Michael, he bestowed it upon the pommels of a chair of wood, where the Earl used to dine and sup; but nothing came of it neither.

Squire now slept in security, for, although he had failed of success, yet he took himself to be out of danger, thinking that because it was carried between his confessor and him, it could never be revealed. But his confessor imparted it to some principal fugitives there which raised a great expectation of some effect to ensue. One of the more passionate of them began to inveigh bitterly against Squire and how he had undone the cause, and the better to be revenged on him, was content that one should give information against Squire by means of a letter which he pretended to have stolen out of one of their studies. Hereupon it was collected that this was but an engine against Squire, and that he was an honest man. Yet because it was a tender matter, Squire was sent for and examined. For a time he denied, but after gave it to be understood that there was somewhat true. Hold was taken of that; and thereupon Squire, not knowing how far his confessor had broken trust with him, by good persuasion and God's good working disclosed all without any rigour to the world.

10th November. AN ATTEMPT IN DUBLIN.

Ireland is now universally shaken with rebellion, and even the cities and port towns of the English Pale are not free from Tyrone's treasonable practices, who did very lately employ some of his instruments to surprise the Castle of Dublin, and to subvert the city, and consequently to commit to massacre all the English and their goods. This conspiracy was far advanced and very near the time of execution. It should have been performed by thirty resolute men set on by twenty-nine priests lying in Dublin and should have been assisted with 1,000 men of Tyrone's forces, beside the help of 1,000 more from the mountain rebels; but it was happily discovered by one of the conspirators.

14th November. THE QUEEN ROYALLY RECEIVED.

This evening the Queen came to Westminster by torch-light and was received most royally, by the commandment of the Council, by the Lord Mayor, the Aldermen and Sheriffs in scarlet, and a great number of the wealthy citizens in velvet coats and chains of gold, and all on horseback.

15th November. THE SOLDIERS IN IRELAND.

Sir Richard Bingham is now in Dublin and much complaineth of the new English soldiers ; for it is strange to see how suddenly they decay. Of the last thousand the fourth part are run away and many of the rest so poor and simple as to be utterly unserviceable ; which fault the Captains allege to be in the justices of the peace and their inferior magistrates rather than in the Lieutenants of the Shires.

16th November. BEACON WATCHES DISCONTINUED.

The beacon watches are now to be discontinued for the winter, except upon places where a descent of the enemy is likely, and to be renewed in the spring.

17th November. DETERMINATIONS FOR IRELAND.

The Queen, taking to heart that with the charge of nine or ten thousand men she is no place able to defend herself in her Kingdom of Ireland, is now pleased to bethink her of sending some great person whereunto the Earl of Essex is named as a nobleman that will be greatly followed and feared ; but there is not as yet any perfect conclusion of the matter.

20th November. THE EXECUTION OF LUKE HUTTON.

Luke Hutton, that notable highway robber, committing a robbery on St. Luke's Day (for his name's sake) was taken and is hanged at York of late, being charged and condemned on ninescore and seventeen indictments. This Hutton was formerly a scholar of Cambridge and, some say, son to the Archbishop of York, though others more certainly declare his father to be a prebendary of Durham.

28th November. MORE SOLDIERS REQUIRED.

Further levies to the number of 1,000 are now required for service in Ireland.

3rd December. THE DESPERATE STATE OF IRELAND.

The revolt and defection of the Irishry doth daily increase in every part, and of those who still seem to stand firm most are in effect gone in heart, so that there is no hope either to stay these dangers or preserve the Kingdom from losing unless new forces be immediately sent over. Rarely any week now passeth wherein there are not received advertisements either of the surprising of castles, burning of towns, or massacring the subjects and havocking their goods. Sir Thomas More, an Englishman by birth, was lately betrayed in his own house by the treachery of his watch, himself slain, and his wife and two daughters carried away by the traitors, who leaving his wife stripped in a bog she is dead since with the cold. Captain Gifford is slain in his own house, and his wife seeking to save her husband by prostrating herself upon him was in many places sore wounded.

Moreover, such is the nakedness of the soldiers for want of clothes, and their poverty for lack of lendings to buy them food, that many of them show like prisoners, half starved for want of cherishing, and like at any time to disband or break into some great mutiny; and if any of the companies should break and either run to the enemy or steal into England there would be small hope of the Kingdom.

PLAYS AT COURT.

Of late the Lord Chamberlain's players played four times at Court and the Earl of Nottingham's men twice, who played *The Downfall of Robin Hood*, and for this they are rewarded at the rate of £10 a play.

5th December. A LOAN IN THE CITY.

Because of the great charges of providing this army in Ireland her Majesty now seeketh a loan from the City, and lest it should be denied upon any just colour she is pleased to bind her own lands or give assignations of all customs. This loan is to be for six months at the rate of 10 in the 100. The strangers likewise that dwell in this country are required to lend 200,000 French crowns upon the same security.

11th December. AN ATTEMPT IN THE NORTH.

Six ships of Dunkirk were lately discovered on the coast of the North parts that did attempt to set some hundred men on land, but so good watch was kept that the beacons were fired, and, the country being ready to withstand them, they withdrew. Nevertheless it is thought likely that on their return they may make some attempt on the coast, either to surprise some gentlemen in their houses or set on fire some village or town near the coast, especially about Yarmouth.

15th December. SOLDIERS FOR IRELAND.

Orders are now given for 2,000 men from the garrisons in the Low Countries to be sent to Ireland, being better trained and hardened than any that can be levied at home; their places to be taken by others newly levied from London, Middlesex, Surrey, Essex, Kent and Sussex.

18th December. THE THAMES FROZEN.

These last days by reason of the great frosts the Thames hath been well-nigh frozen over at London Bridge, but now it beginneth to thaw.

20th December. A DECLARATION CONCERNING THE KING OF SCOTS.

Notwithstanding the satisfaction given to the King of Scots by the Queen's private letters, he remaineth still much grieved with the scandals imputed to him by Valentine Thomas, and hath earnestly moved the Queen to deliver some public testimony of her good opinion. Hereupon though in no way bound to yield account to any person on earth of her actions, more than in love and kindness, yet for further confirmation of her goodwill towards the King, she hath declared that she considereth him to be a Christian Prince of honour and religion, and that she giveth no credit to such things as Thomas hath affirmed against him.

24th December. THE LOAN IN THE CITY.

The money from the City comes in but slowly, so that the Queen's service is hampered. The Lord Mayor is required to use all expedition that the sum of £20,000 demanded be paid into the Receipt before the holidays. Some citizens of good ability have withdrawn themselves into the country, and they shall be sent for to appear before the Council to answer their careless behaviour.

THE REBELLION IN MUNSTER.

Mr. Edmund Spenser is come from Cork to the Court with letters from Sir Thomas Norris. There are 1,000 new soldiers arrived at Cork, 600 at Kinsale, and 400 at Waterford, men reasonably well chosen and furnished but very raw and inexpert, not having had any training before their arrival.

27th December. A SKIRMISH IN MUNSTER.

From Cork Sir Thomas Norris writeth that about a fortnight since he took in hand with thirteen of the new companies and four of the old to march to the relief of Kilmallock; but the traitors having notice of his setting forward, dislodged from the siege, burned their ladders and encountered him with skirmish. Nevertheless he entered Kilmallock and returned the next day, though the rebels began a new fight as soon as they were out of their quarters, and continued whilst they marched nine miles; in which time they gave many hot onsets, being so confident of the victory that they had in conceit divided the coats and arms of these new soldiers amongst themselves. But herein it pleased God so to assist our men that they only received in both fights the loss but of four men slain and some thirty hurt, and gave the enemy many repulses to their great loss and shame. Hereby hath grown to these new men such courage and boldness (being so far overmatched by the enemy in numbers) that they will be able to do her Majesty good service, if some speedy help may be sent to maintain them in their strength before they fall to weakness.

28th December. THE THAMES AGAIN FROZEN.

To-day there is a great fall of snow and the Thames again frozen over.

THE THEATRE PULLED DOWN.

There hath long been disputes between Mr. Giles Allen that owneth the land whereon the Theatre standeth and the Burbages concerning the renewing of the lease insomuch that the players these last months have left the Theatre and gone to the

Curtain. To-day Richard Burbage with one Peter Street, a carpenter, and some ten others, arming themselves with swords and other weapons, repair to the Theatre; and though Mr. Allen's people would prevent them, they break down the Theatre and take away the wood and timber to a place on the Bankside where, 'tis said, they would erect a new playhouse.

A Lewd Fellow.

Of late a certain Edward Francis of Melbury Osmond in Dorsetshire made very foul speeches of her Majesty. Wishing to persuade one Mistress Elizabeth Baylie to lead an incontinent life with him, and upon her refusing, he said that the best in England (meaning her Majesty) had done so, and had three bastards by noblemen of the Court, two sons and a daughter, and was herself base born; and that the land had been happy if she had been cut off twenty years since so that some noble prince might have reigned in her stead. When those who heard these words charged him with them he offered great gifts to stay his accusers, £40 each to four several men and £20 to the women; but they would not. But now seeing that he has to answer before the Council, he is stricken dead in conceit and is probably fled as he has forfeited £500 on a bond for not putting in a security.

29th December. Privileged Places in London.

During the late burdens and charges laid upon the City, the places privileged within the City have not only refused to furnish soldiers and to contribute themselves but retain those that have recourse thither to avoid the imprest. Moreover divers Doctors of Physic and others professing the law, besides many gentlemen, pretend themselves to be privileged and exempt from this charge because they are not free of the City. The Council order that the sums collected from the Liberties shall be proportionable to those levied in the City, and that any who have abode, house or dwelling in the City must contribute for the same.

30th December. A Play at Cambridge.

This last Christmas they have at Cambridge a play called *The Pilgrimage to Parnassus* wherein is shown the journey of two students, Philomusus and Studioso, to reach Helicon, and the temptations which they met in the way, as of Madido the drunkard, or Stupido the Puritan, or Amoretto by whom they are persuaded to lechery. At the last there meeteth them one Ingenioso who would turn them back from their journey, for, quoth he, 'come not there, seek for poverty no further; its too far to go to Parnassus to fetch repentance.'

31*st December*. NEW PLAYS THIS PAST YEAR AT THE ROSE.

During this past year my Lord of Nottingham's men have played these new plays at the Rose, namely, *Mother Redcap* (by Drayton and Munday), *Phaeton* (by Dekker), *The Downfall* and *The Death of Robert Earl of Huntingdon, called Robin Hood* (by Munday and Chettle), *A woman will have her will*, *The triplicity of Cuckolds* (by Dekker), *The famous wars of Henry the first and the Prince of Wales* (by Chettle, Dekker and Drayton), *Earl Godwin and his three sons*, in two parts (by Chettle, Dekker and Drayton), *King Arthur* (by Hathaway), *Black Bateman of the North*, in two parts (by Chettle, Dekker, Drayton and Wilson), *The Funeral of Richard Cordelion* (by Chettle, Drayton, Munday and Wilson), *The Isle of Women* (by Chapman), *The Madman's Morrice* (by Dekker, Drayton and Wilson), *Hannibal and Hermes or worse afeared than hurt* (by Dekker, Drayton and Wilson), *Valentine and Orson* (by Hathaway and Munday), *Pierce of Winchester* (by Dekker, Drayton and Wilson), *Brute* (by Day and Chettle), *Hot Anger soon cold* (by Porter), *Chance medley* (by Chettle, Dekker, Munday, Wilson and Drayton), *Catiline's Conspiracy* (by Chettle and Wilson), *Vayrode* (an old play remade by Chettle), *The Civil Wars of France*, in three parts (by Dekker and Drayton), *The fount of new fashions* (by Chapman), *Connan of Cornwall* (by Dekker and Drayton).

THESE BOOKS ALSO SET FORTH ANNO 1598.

MR. RICHARD BARNFIELD'S POEMS.

Mr. Richard Barnfield hath written these poems: *The Encomion of Lady Pecunia, or the praise of Money; The Complaint of Poetry for the death of Liberality; The Combat between Conscience and Covetousness in the mind of man*, and sundry short poems in divers humours; among these last being an epitaph upon the death of Sir Philip Sidney, an epitaph upon the death of his aunt, Mistress Elizabeth Skrymsher, together with a remembrance of some English poets:

> Live Spenser ever, in thy *Faery Queen*:
> Whose like, for deep conceit, was never seen.
> Crown'd mayest thou be, unto thy more renown,
> As King of Poets, with a laurel crown.
>
> And Daniel, praised for thy sweet chaste verse:
> Whose fame is grav'd on *Rosamond's* black herse.
> Still may'st thou live, and still be honoured
> For that rare work, *The White Rose and the Red.*
>
> And Drayton, whose well-written tragedies,
> And sweet epistles, soar thy fame to skies.
> Thy learned name is equal with the rest;
> Whose stately numbers are so well addressed.
>
> And Shakespeare thou, whose honey-flowing vein,
> Pleasing the world, thy praises doth obtain.
> Whose *Venus* and whose *Lucrece* (sweet and chaste)
> Thy name in fame's immortal book have plac'd.
> Live ever you, at least in fame live ever:
> Well may the body die, but fame dies never.

CHAPMAN'S ADDITIONS TO 'HERO AND LEANDER.'

A new edition of *Hero and Leander* wherein Mr. George Chapman concludeth the fable with three further sestiads of his own making, telling how Leander again swimming the Hellespont to visit his Hero was drowned and his body flung ashore; whereat Hero died straightway with the grief of it.

ACHILLES' SHIELD.

Mr. Chapman hath also translated into rimed decasyllabon verses that description of the Shield of Achilles from the 18th Book of Homer's *Iliades*; which work he undertook suddenly because, since the publication of the other books, comparison hath been made between Virgil and Homer, who, saith he, 'can be compared in nothing with more decisal and cutting of all arguments than in these two shields; and whosoever shall read Homer throughly and worthily will know the question comes from a superficial and too unripe a reader; for Homer's Poems were writ from a free fury, an absolute and full soul; Virgil's out of a courtly, laborious, and altogether imitatory spirit; not a simile he hath but what is Homer's; not an invention, person, or disposition but is wholly or originally builded upon Homerical foundations, and in many places hath the very words Homer useth.'

FLORIO'S 'WORLD OF WORDS.'

Signor John Florio hath compiled a most copious and exact dictionary in Italian and English, entitled *A world of words*, dedicated to the Earl of Rutland, the Earl of Southampton and the Countess of Bedford.

A BOOK OF PAINTING.

From Oxford *A tract containing the art of curious Painting, carving and building*, written first in Italian by John Paul Lomatius (or Lomazzo) and Englished by Richard Haydock, being dedicated to Mr. Thomas Bodley; which work is in seven books; the first of the Proportions of all things; the second of Actions and Gestures; the third of Colour; the fourth of Light; the fifth of perspectives; the sixth of practise; the seventh of history. To the third book addeth a discourse of the painting of women, which this author termeth 'painting upon the life,' noting the evil effects of those substances used by our dames, as of sublimate which the surgeons call corrosive; whereof such women as use it about their face have always black teeth, standing far out of their gums like a Spanish mule, an offensive breath, with a face half scorched, and an unclean complexion, whereby they hasten old age before time and give occasions to their husbands to seek strangers instead of their wives, with divers other inconveniences. Likewise much harm is wrought by all paintings and colourings made of iron, brass, lead, tin, ceruse (or white lead), camphire, juice of lemons, plume-alum, saltpeter, vitriol, and all manner of salts. Wherefore if there be no remedy but women will be meddling with this art of polishing, let them instead use such safe helps of beauty as these: cheerfulness and contentment, health, honesty, and wisdom, for even a hard favoured and brown woman being merry, pleasant and jocund will seem sufficient beautiful.

'THE COMEDY OF MUCEDORUS.'

A play called *A most pleasant comedy of Mucedorus, the King's son of Valentia, and Amadine, the King's daughter of Aragon, with the merry conceits of Mouse.* Herein is shown how Mucedorus being in disguise saved Amadine both from a bear and a wild man and in the end wedded her.

NORDEN'S 'SPECULUM BRITANNIÆ.'

Mr. John Norden continueth his Survey of England and hath now a further part of *Speculum Britanniæ* in the description of Hertfordshire, noting as in the former books the fairs, markets and great houses, and also an alphabetical table of the towns, parishes and hamlets, together with a map of the county. Mr. Norden much complaineth that he was drawn unto this work by honourable Councillors and promised sufficient allowance, and herein he hath spent above a thousand marks and five years' time.

A BOOK OF RIDDLES.

A book called *The Riddles of Heraclitus and Democritus*, whereof this is the 47th:

The Miller and the Miller's wife,
  That they might merry make,
Were set down with a dish of fruit,
  A cake and half a cake,
The parson of the town with them,
  His sister and no more:

Now have you heard of all the guests
  And of their bread the store;

Yet did they use the matter with
Such cunning, skill and art,
That everyone eat half a cake,
Before they did depart.

The answer: The miller's wife was the parson's sister, and so the division is not hard to make.

MR. TOFTE'S 'ALBA.'

Alba: the mouth's mind of a melancholy lover, divided into three parts and written by Mr. Robert Tofte, wherein the lover unsatisfied lamenteth his hard case.

'TYRO'S ROARING MEG.'

An idle book called *Tyro's Roaring Meg, planted against the walls of melancholy*, containing sundry epigrams in verse; also *Tyronis Epistolae siue mus rampant in agro aureo*; and *The mean in spending.*

TYRO'S EPISTLE OF LOVE.

Tyro by chance did read 'that Generation
Was the sole final cause of Augmentation.'
Eftsoons he shook the hand with single life,
And set his wit on tenters for a wife.
He took his quill and penn'd this dainty plaint,
Unto a mincing minion, fine and daint.
'O thou Eliptic line, wherein the sun
Of my felicity doth daily run;
Eye-pleasing object, honeysuckle sweet,
Tyro thy vassal tumbles at thy feet:
He a Leander, ready for thy sake,
To pass an Hellespont of pain and ache.
Be thou a Hero standing on the shore
With open arms and clasp him more and more.
Thou shalt perceive, 'so by thy love be won,
I am no snow to melt against the sun.
My bleared eyes shall steep themselves in tears,
Till some mild answer ventilate my fears.
Ah, dearest Nymph, some lightfoot lackey send
With white and black to give me life or end.

Roses are in thy lips, O hellish smart,
If angry nettles grow upon thy heart.
Farewell thou pretty Mop, and me remember ;
Written in haste the twentieth of December
About the dinner hour of eleven

1597

Tyro thy Delphic sword till crows be old,
Till Ister be lukewarm, and Ganges cold.’

MR. WENTWORTH'S ‘PITHY EXHORTATION.’

Mr. Peter Wentworth (that was sent to the Tower at the time of the Parliament in '93 for pressing upon her Majesty, contrary to her strict command, to name the successor to the Crown), left behind him two treatises which are now printed in Scotland, a year after his death. In the first, entitled *A pithy exhortation*, urgeth upon her Majesty to establish her successor to the Crown, showing the conveniences and answering the inconveniences that would come of it ; declareth that this would be the surest means to kill the hearts of all her enemies both here and in foreign countries, who are persuaded that if they could bereave the Queen of her life, then would her subjects have no one head to cleave and resort unto for succour, but should grow to civil war and unnatural division and be ready, every one of us, to cut each other's throats ; and then were we easily all overrun by our enemies. In the second treatise answereth that *Conference* of Doleman and holdeth that the King of Scots is the true successor.

ABBREVIATIONS

The following abbreviations have been used for sources frequently cited :

A.P.C. *Acts of the Privy Council,* edited by J. R. Dasent, 1900, etc.

A.R. *A Transcript of the Register of the Company of Stationers of London* ; 1554-1640. Edited by E. Arber, 5 vols., 1875-1894.

BIRCH'S HISTORICAL VIEW. *An Historical View of the Negotiations between the Courts of England, France and Brussels,* 1592-1617. By Thomas Birch, 1749.

BIRCH'S MEMOIRS. *Memoirs of the Reign of Queen Elizabeth . . . from the original papers of . . . Anthony Bacon and other manuscripts.* By Thomas Birch, 2 vols., 1754.

CAMDEN'S ELIZABETH. *The History of . . . Elizabeth, late Queen of England.* By William Camden. Translated into English, 1630, etc.

CAREW MSS. *Calendar of the Carew Manuscripts in the Archiepiscopal Library at Lambeth,* edited by J. S. Bullen and W. Bullen, 1869.

CHAMBERLAIN'S LETTERS. *Letters written by John Chamberlain during the reign of Queen Elizabeth.* Edited by Sarah Williams. Camden Society, 1861.

DEVEREUX. *Lives and Letters of the Devereux, Earls of Essex . . .* 1540-1646. By the Hon. W. B. Devereux, 2 vols., 1853.

D'EWES' JOURNALS. *A Compleat Journal of the Votes, Speeches and Debates both of the House of Lords and House of Commons throughout the whole Reign of Queen Elizabeth.* Collected by . . . Sir Simonds D'Ewes, 1693.

ELIZ. JOURNAL. *An Elizabethan Journal, being a record of those things most talked of during the years* 1591-1594. By G. B. Harrison, 1928.

ELIZABETHAN STAGE. *The Elizabethan Stage.* By E. K. Chambers. 4 vols. 1923.

HAKLUYT'S VOYAGES. *The Principal Navigations, Voyages, Traffiques and Discoveries of the English Nation.* By Richard Hakluyt. References to the edition in 8 vols. in The Everyman Library, 1907, etc.

HAWARDE. *Les Reportes del Cases in Camera Stellata,* 1593-1609. By William Hawarde. Edited by W. P. Baildon, 1894.

HENS. DIARY. *Henslowe's Diary.* Vol. i., The Text ; vol. ii., The Commentary. Edited by W. W. Greg, 1904-7.

m.e. Modern edition.

M.S.R. Malone Society Reprint.

ABBREVIATIONS

MIDDLESEX SESSIONS ROLLS. *Middlesex County Records.* Vol. i., *Indictments, Coroner's Inquests post mortem, and recognizances from 3 Edward VI. to the end of the reign of Queen Elizabeth.* Edited by J. C. Jeaffreson, 1886.

MURDIN'S STATE PAPERS. *A Collection of State Papers relating to foreign affairs . . . 1571 to 1596.* By William Murdin, 1759.

NUGAE ANTIQUAE. *Nugae Antiquae: being a miscellaneous collection of original papers* . . . by Sir John Harington, etc. Edited by T. Park, 2 vols., 1804.

PENSHURST PAPERS. *Papers of Lord D'Isle and Dudley at Penshurst Place.* Historical Manuscripts Commission. [In course of printing.]

PROCLAMATIONS. *A Book containing all such Proclamations as were published during the Reign of the late Queen Elizabeth. Collected together by the industry of Humphrey Dyson, of the City of London, Publique Notary,* 1618. This is an actual collection; references are to the manuscript pagination of the volume in the British Museum (G. 6463).

PURCHAS. *Hakluytus Posthumus, or Purchas his pilgrims,* 1625. References to the edition published by MacLehose and Co., 1907.

RYMER'S FŒDERA. *Fœdera, conventiones, literæ, et cuiuscumque generis Acta Publica inter Reges Angliæ et alios quosuis* . . . ex schedis Thomæ Rymer. Edited by Robert Sanderson, 2nd edition, 1727.

S.P. DOM. *State Papers Domestic* preserved in the Public Record Office Abstracted in the *Calendars of State Papers Domestic.*

S.P. IRELAND. *State Papers Ireland* preserved in the Public Record Office. Abstracted in the *Calendars of State Papers relating to Ireland in the reign of Queen Elizabeth.* Edited by E. G. Atkinson, 1893.

S.T.C. *A Short Title Catalogue of Books printed in England, Scotland and Ireland, and of English Books printed abroad.* Compiled by A. W. Pollard and G. R. Redgrave, 1926.

SALISBURY PAPERS. *Historical Manuscripts Commission.—Calendar of the Manuscripts of the Marquis of Salisbury, preserved at Hatfield House,* 1892, etc.

SIDNEY PAPERS. *Letters and Memorials of State . . . from the originals at Penshurst Place,* etc. By Arthur Collins. 2 vols. 1746.

SPEDDING. *The Life and Letters of Francis Bacon.* By James Spedding. 7 vols., 1861; [numbered vols. viii.-xiv. in the Spedding-Ellis edition of Bacon's Works].

STOW'S ANNALS. *Annales or a General Chronicle of England.* By John Stow; first printed in 1592. As there are several editions both of Stow and Camden and references are quite easy to find, particular editions or pages are not specified.

STRYPE, ANNALS. *Annals of the Reformation . . . during Queen Elizabeth's happy reign.* By John Strype, 4 vols., 1731, and 7 vols., 1824. [The later edition marks the pagination of the earlier; references are to the earlier.]

NOTES

1595

3rd January. THE REVELS AT GRAY'S INN. *Gesta Grayorum,* first printed 1688; m.e. in J. Nichols' *Progresses of Queen Elizabeth,* and *M.S.R.* Spedding claims that the speeches of the Councillors were written by Bacon, that on philosophy foreshadowing 'Solomon's House' in the *New Atlantis.* For the beginnings of the revels see *Eliz. Journal,* pp. 338-9, 342; also note on 4th February.

4th January. GRAY'S INN REVELS. *Gesta Grayorum.*

10th January. A NOTABLE CASE OF COSENAGE. *Salisbury Papers,* v. 82; see 2nd April.

13th January. GOSSON'S 'PLEASANT QUIPS.' *A.R.,* ii., 669; *S.T.C.,* 12096. This piece of Puritanical muck-raking is anonymous, but Gosson's name is written in a contemporary hand in the only surviving copy of the 1596 edition; m.e. privately 1847. Compare *Love's Labours Lost,* IV. ii. 128.

17th January. BARNFIELD'S 'CYNTHIA' AND 'CASSANDRA.' *A.R.,* ii. 669; *S.T.C.,* 1483; m.e. Roxburghe Club, 1816.

23rd January. COMPLAINTS AGAINST PATENTS. *Remembrancia,* ii. 82, 83, 84.

THE ESTATE OF THE ENGLISH FUGITIVES. *A.R.,* ii. 670; *S.T.C.,* 15562-5.

24th January. THE SCOTTISH AMBASSADOR GIVEN AUDIENCE. *Salisbury Papers,* v. 37.

25th January. THE IRISH REBELLION. *S.P. Ireland,* 178 : 10; letter from the Lord Deputy to Burleigh dated 15th January.

THE VACANT SOLICITORSHIP. Spedding's *Bacon,* i. 347-8.

27th January. HURAULT'S DISCOURSES. *S.T.C.,* 14000; dated in Epistle Dedicatory to Lord Cobham.

28th January. GRAY'S INN REVELS. *Gesta Grayorum*; see also pp. 1, 4, 11, 12.

31st January. THE JESUITS AT WISBEACH CASTLE. Strype, *Annals,* iv. 195. Wisbeach Castle was used as a place of internment for seminaries and recusants at this time.

1st February. THE GRAY'S INN REVELS. *Gesta Grayorum.*

3rd February. GRAY'S INN REVELS AT COURT. *Gesta Grayorum.*

4th February. SIR JOHN NORRIS'S RETURN. *S.P. Dom.,* 251 : 16. These were the troops who had been employed in the capture of Croyzon; see *Eliz. Journal,* pp. 329, 331.

THE GRAY'S INN REVELS ENDED. *Gesta Grayorum.* The Revels at Gray's Inn provide a most interesting revelation of the mentality of the bright young men of aristocratic and upper middle-class England. It seems extraordinary that this elaborate, and at times impudent, parody of State should not only have been tolerated but actively encouraged by the Council, the nobility, the City, and even by the Queen herself. *Gesta Grayorum* is a mirror of the mind of the younger generation—as brilliant as there has ever been in England—its wit, its tastes, amusements and aspirations. See also note on Chapman's *Humorous Day's Mirth*, 11th May, 1597.

7th February. AN ALARM AT OSTEND. *Salisbury Papers*, v. 104.

8th February. SIR WALTER RALEGH'S VOYAGE. Hakluyt's *Voyages*, vii. 280. See 27th September.

9th February. THE QUEEN'S LETTER TO THE GRAND SIGNIOR. *Salisbury Papers*, v. 105.

11th February. BISHOP FLETCHER'S MARRIAGE. *Salisbury Papers*, v. 106; *Nugae Antiquae*, ii. 46; Thomas Fuller's *Worthies* [Kent].

15th February. FLESH PROHIBITED IN LENT. *Proclamations*, 329. The regular opening formula of this annual order of the Council, repeated in 1595, 1596, 1597, 1598, reads a little hopelessly: 'First her Majesty's pleasure is, upon her understanding of the great disorders heretofore and *especially the last Lent* committed in killing and eating flesh in time of Lent . . .'

18th February. MOSSE'S 'ARRAIGNMENT AND CONVICTION OF USURY.' *A.R.*, ii. 671; *S.T.C.*, 18207. The Epistle Dedicatory is dated 1st January, 1595, the Epistle to the Reader 6th February, 1594[-5]; the book was entered 18th February (*i.e.* after printing).

20th February. THE TRIAL OF FR. SOUTHWELL. *Catholic Record Society*, v. 333; from an account by Thomas Leake, an eyewitness; see *Eliz. Journal*, pp. 140, 150.

21st February. NEW PLAYS AT THE ROSE. *Hens. Diary*, i. 21; ii. 174; neither play is known.

22nd February. THE EXECUTION OF FR. SOUTHWELL. See 20th February.

26th February. THE FORT AT BLACKWATER TAKEN. *S.P. Ireland*, 178 : 53.

4th March. A FATAL MISCHANCE. *Middlesex Sessions Rolls*, i. 220.

5th March. A NEW PLAY. *Hens. Diary*, i. 22; ii. 175. Dr. Greg suggests that the play may be Heywood's *Golden Age*.

6th March. THE WIDOW OF DR. LOPEZ. *S.P. Dom.*, 251 : 50. For the trial and execution of Dr. Lopez see *Eliz. Journal*, 289, 303, etc.

15th March. THE EARL OF CUMBERLAND'S SHIP. *Purchas*, xvi. 25. Approximate date. See *Eliz. Journal*, pp. 160, 317.

26th March. MR. CHAMPERNOUN'S CHOIRBOYS. *Salisbury Papers*, v. 155, 436.

1st April. NEWS OF SIR WALTER RALEGH. *Salisbury Papers*, v. 161; also *S.P. Dom.*, 256 : 100 (misdated 1596).

2nd April. THE LEWDNESS OF DOLL PHILLIPS. *A Quest of Enquiry by women to know, whether the Tripe-wife were trimmed by Doll yea or no,* by Oliver Oatmeal. This scandal is a continuation of 'A Notable Case of Cosenage' (10th January). Oliver's style is none of the clearest, but the case is here set down as near as may be ; for a note on 'Keep the Widow Waking' see the *Library* for June 1930. *S.T.C.*, 18758 ; m.e. in A. B. Grosart's *Elizabethan England in Gentle and Simple Life*, 1881.

4th April. A STRANGE MANNER OF DEATH. *Middlesex Sessions Rolls*, i. 221.

5th April. SOUTHWELL'S 'ST. PETER'S COMPLAINT.' *A.R.*, ii. 295 ; *S.T.C.*, 22956 ; published anonymously ; m.e. in *The Complete Poems of Robert Southwell*, by A. B. Grosart, 1872. Compare *A Midsummer Night's Dream*, V. i. 2-23 ; *Astrophel and Stella*, xxxix. ; *Macbeth*, II. ii. 36.

12th April. DRAYTON'S 'ENDYMION AND PHOEBE.' *A.R.*, ii. 296 ; *S.T.C.*, 7192 ; m.e. by J. W. Hebel, 1925. A work of some interest and importance, not only from its place in the *Venus and Adonis, Hero and Leander* group, but also because of the mythological, philosophical and metaphysical ideas which Drayton weaves into the poem, especially in the later pages.

SIR PHILIP SIDNEY'S 'DEFENCE OF POESY.' *A.R.*, ii. 666, and ii. 295 ; *S.T.C.*, 22534-5. The *Defence* was first entered on 29th November, 1594, by Ponsonby, presumably as a blocking entry ; *Astrophel and Stella* had been published in 1591, apparently against the wishes of the Sidney family, with a preface by Nashe. Olney entered a copy (called *The Apology for Poetry*) on 12th April and proceeded to print, but Ponsonby complained. Olney's entry was therefore cancelled, and it was agreed that Ponsonby should enjoy the copy. Olney's copy is usually preferred by editors, but Ponsonby's is the authorised edition ; *The Defence of Poesy* would therefore appear to be the true title ; m.e. by J. C. Collins, 1907, facsimile by Noel Douglas, 1927.

THE BENEFITS OF FAST DAYS. *A.R.*, ii. 296. *S.T.C.*, 9977. A reprint of a proclamation that had been issued in 1593.

15th April. DR. FLETCHER'S DISGRACE. *Salisbury Papers*, v. 171.

16th April. 'THE OLD WIVES' TALE.' *A.R.*, ii. 296 ; *S.T.C.*, 19545 ; m.e. by W. W. Greg, *M.S.R.*, 1908, etc.

17th April. SPANISH PREPARATIONS IN BRITTANY. *Salisbury Papers*, v. 171.

23rd April. THE FEAST OF ST. GEORGE. From a long and detailed account, given in the envoy's journal, printed in *Queen Elizabeth and some foreigners*, by V. von Klarwill, 1928, p. 375.

26th April. THE DUKE OF WIRTENBERG'S ENVOY. As for 23rd April ; p. 385.

30th April. TROOPS IN THE LOW COUNTRIES. *S.P. Dom.*, 251 : 126.

6th May. LODGE'S 'FIG FOR MOMUS.' *A.R.*, ii. 297 ; *S.T.C.*, 16658 ; m.e. in *The Complete Works of Thomas Lodge*, vol. iii., Hunterian Club, 1883. Entered 2nd April ; dated 6th May in the Epistle to the Gentlemen Readers. This collection is of some general interest. In the first Satire Lodge anticipates the manner of Hall and Marston, and can claim priority over both (see pp. 179, 266, and notes). The attack on alchemy is significant, but it concludes with a very obscure passage which is apparently an attempt to express that alchemy which occurs in the artist's mind as he turns to shapes the forms of things unknown.

8th May. A CATALOGUE OF ENGLISH PRINTED BOOKS. *A.R.*, ii. 297 ; *S.T.C.*, 17669.

9th May. THE EARL OF CUMBERLAND'S COMMISSION. Rymer's *Fœdera*, xvi. 274.

15th May. BANKS' HORSE. This date of the first appearance of Banks and Morocco is a guess, but the horse was certainly known before the end of the year (p. 66). There are several references to the performance, *e.g.*, *Love's Labours Lost*, I. ii. 58 ; Bastard's *Chrestoleros*, bk. 3, epig. 17 ; *Every Man in his Humour*, IV. iv. The completest Collection is by S. H. Atkins in *Notes and Queries*, 21st July, 1934.

22nd May. 'CERTAIN VERY PROPER SIMILES.' *A.R.*, ii. 296 ; *S.T.C.*, 11053 ; entered 12th April, dated 22nd May in Epistle Dedicatory to the Earl of Shrewsbury. See note on Bacon's *Essays*, 30th January, 1597.

23rd May. NEW PLAYS. *Hens. Diary*, i. 22 ; ii. 175. Dr. Greg identifies the first and second parts of this play as Heywood's *Silver* and *Bronze Age*.

25th May. THE NEGOTIATIONS WITH THE STATES. *Salisbury Papers*, v. 179 ; Camden's *Elizabeth* ; Birch's *Memoirs*, i. 244.

27th May. DR. DEE PROMOTED. *S.P. Dom.*, 252 : 35. This is Dee the celebrated alchemist ; see also p. 174.

'THE WORLD'S HYDROGRAPHICAL DESCRIPTION.' *A.R.*, ii. 299 ; *S.T.C.*, 6372. On the title-page is the uncommon inscription 'Published by I. Dauis of Sandrug by Dartmouth in the *Countie of Deuon. Gentleman.* Anno 1595. May 27.' The Epistle Dedicatory to the Lords of the Council bears the same date. It was entered on 1st June, 1595.

28th May. THE IRISH REBELLION. *S.P. Ireland*, 279 : 82 ; from a letter of the Lord Deputy to the Council.

THE CRUELTY OF THE TURKISH EMPEROR. *Salisbury Papers*, v. 189. This is the Emperor Amurath. Compare 'Not Amurath an Amurath succeeds, But Harry Harry.' *II. Henry IV.*, v. ii. 48-9.

30th May. MR. ROBERT DUDLEY'S RETURN. Hakluyt's *Voyages*, vi. 164.

3rd June. A NEW PLAY. *Hens. Diary*, i. 24 ; ii. 175. The play is lost.

5th June. A RIOT IN LONDON. *Salisbury Papers*, v. 249.

9th June. NEWS FROM LISBON. *S.P. Dom.*, 252 : 58. Captain Richard Hawkins was son of Sir John Hawkins.

10th June. A SKIRMISH WITH TYRONE. *Carew MSS.*, 154 ; *S.P. Ireland*, 179 : 95, 180 : 5, 6.

13th June. DISORDERS IN THE CITY. Stow's *Annals*. The exact date is given in *Salisbury Papers*, v. 249.

15th June. FURTHER RIOTING IN THE CITY. *Salisbury Papers*, v. 249.

16th June. THE RIOTOUS APPRENTICES. *Salisbury Papers*, v. 249, 250.

17th June. SLIGO TAKEN BY THE REBELS. *S.P. Ireland*, 180 : 16. Dated 7th June.

20th June. 'THE TRUMPET OF FAME.' *S.T.C.* 21088, where the poem is attributed to Henry Roberts; m.e. by T. Park, 1818. Approximate date.

23rd June. DISORDERS IN SOUTHWARK. *Remembrancia*, ii. 97.

27th June. RIOTOUS PRENTICES WHIPPED. Stow's *Annals*; see 13th June.

29th June. UNRULY YOUTHS ON TOWER HILL. Stow's *Annals*.

SIR JOHN HAWKINS' AGREEMENT WITH THE QUEEN. *S.P. Dom.*, 252 : 107.

A SEDITIOUS PAMPHLET. *Remembrancia*, ii. 98. This entry has a twofold interest; the incident in Deloney's career is apparently unrecorded; it is moreover almost the earliest instance on record of a printer's proof.

2nd July. A CASE IN THE STAR CHAMBER. Hawarde, p. 13.

4th July. A PROCLAMATION AGAINST UNLAWFUL ASSEMBLIES. *Proclamations*, 330.

ORDERS PRESCRIBED BY THE COUNCIL. *Proclamations*, 331.

THE CASE OF MR. EDWARD TALBOT CONCLUDED. Hawarde, p. 16. Hawarde notes that Essex and the Archbishop were afterwards checked by the Queen. Wood after long imprisonment confessed that he was 'the only deviser, procurer, acter & plotter in all this action, for the which he loste both his eares in the pillorye, was slitte in the nose, sealled in the foreheade, and censured to perpetual imprisonment.' Hawarde's own spelling of 'process' is 'proces.' See p. 64.

16th July. THE EXPEDITION FROM PLYMOUTH. *S.P. Dom.*, 253 : 19.

17th July. THREE NOTABLE OUTRAGES. *A.R.*, iii. 45; *S.T.C.*, 18289.

18th July. THE PROVOST-MARSHAL APPOINTED. Rymer's *Fœdera*, xvi. 279.

23rd July. AN ENGLISHMAN BURNT IN ROME. *Fugger News Letters*, edited by V. von Klarwill; translated by L. S. R. Byrne, 1926; pp. 527, 529, dated 17th, 24th June.

24th July. THE UNRULY YOUTHS CONDEMNED. Stow's *Annals*.

25th July. EXCESSIVE PRICES. Stow's *Annals*.

26th July. THE SPANIARDS LAND IN CORNWALL. *Salisbury Papers*, v. 290; Birch's *Memoirs*, i. 269; *S.P. Dom.*, 253 : 30.

27th July. THE IRISH REBELLION. *Carew MSS.*, 158; a long detailed account.

28th July. THE SPANISH LANDING. *S.P. Dom.*, 253 : 33.

7th August. A NEW SPANISH ARMADA. *Salisbury Papers*, v. 306.

11th August. THE SPANISH SHIPS. *Salisbury Papers*, v. 310.

13th August. IRISH NEWS. *S.P. Ireland*, 182 : 2, 5, 7; dated 1st-3rd August.

17th August. THE DEATH OF DON ANTONIO. *Calendar of State Papers Venetian*, ix. 365, 373.

22nd August. RUMOURS. *Sidney Papers*, i. 343.

23rd August. THE LANDING IN CORNWALL. *Salisbury Papers*, v. 322.

26th August. 'ORPHEUS HIS JOURNEY TO HELL.' *A.R.*, iii. 48; *S.T.C.*, 1060. Only one imperfect copy, in the British Museum, remains.

A BOOK OF MERRY TALES. *A.R.*, iii. 47; *S.T.C.*, 5738. Unlike most contemporary jest books this provides anecdotes which are quite witty, and some of them innocent enough for *Punch*.

MR. BARNES' 'DIVINE CENTURY.' *A.R.*, iii. 47; *S.T.C.*, 1467; m.e. by A. B. Grosart, 1875, and in Arber's *English Garner*. Barnes, though his work is not well known, is one of the best of the sonneteers, and some of the sonnets in this collection are noticeably full of feeling.

TWO TALES OF MR. BARNES. Nashe's *Have with you to Saffron Walden* (ed. by R. B. McKerrow, iii. 104, 109); see p. 146. Nashe, especially when malicious, is quite unreliable, but Barnes was certainly a notable character. See pp. 271, 279, 290.

29th August. A NEW PLAY. *Hens. Diary*, i. 24; ii. 176. This play, unless a revised version of Peele's *Edward the First* printed in 1593, is lost.

31st August. DRAKE AND HAWKINS SAIL. Hakluyt's *Voyages*, viii. 183.

5th September. THE EARL OF ESSEX'S ADVICE ON TRAVEL. Spedding's *Bacon*, ii. 1-20. Approximate date. Spedding points out that Bacon had a considerable share in the compilation of these letters, which were intended rather to display the wisdom of Essex than to benefit Rutland. They were well circulated; there are three copies in the Harleian Collection alone. The letters are dated January 1596, but they were presumably earlier, as Rutland set out at the end of September 1595 (*Sidney Papers*, i. 353), and was at the Hague on 5th November (Murdin, p. 697).

13th September. A PETITION AGAINST PLAYS. *Remembrancia*, ii. 103; reprinted in *Elizabethan Stage*, iv. 318.

14th September. ABUSES IN THE CITY. *Salisbury Papers*, v. 376.

CAPTAIN AMYAS PRESTON'S VOYAGE. Hakluyt's *Voyages*, vii. 172.

15th September. A GREAT FIRE AT WOBURN. T. Wilcocks, *A short narration of the fearful fire that fell in the town of Woburn*, etc., 1595. *S.T.C.*, 25629; entered 28th November. *A.R.*, iii. 54.

19th September. NEWS FROM IRELAND. *Sidney Papers*, i. 347.

BEGGING IN THE CITY. *Remembrancia*, ii. 102.

20th September. FRENCH NEWS. Birch's *Memoirs*, i. 296, 298, 300.

BRETON'S 'SOLEMN PASSION.' *S.T.C.*, 3696; m.e. in A. B. Grosart's edition of *The Complete Works of Nicholas Breton*, vol. i., 1879. Breton, though seldom great, is always interesting, and his religious poetry is sometimes inspired by an ecstasy which is rare at this time. To Breton the love of God is symbolised rather by a kiss than a rod.

MARKHAM'S 'MOST HONOURABLE TRAGEDY OF SIR RICHARD GRENVILLE.' *S.T.C.*, 17385; m.e. by E. Arber, 1869. For the last fight of the *Revenge* see *Eliz. Journal*, pp. 62-7.

22nd September. LYLY'S 'WOMAN IN THE MOON.' *S.T.C.*, 17090; m.e. by R. W. Bond in *The Complete Works of John Lyly*, vol. iii., 1902.

23rd September. THE EARL OF SOUTHAMPTON. *Sidney Papers*, i. 348.

27th September. THE FIGHT IN IRELAND. *Sidney Papers*, i. 351.

SIR WALTER RALEGH'S RETURN. Hakluyt's *Voyages*, vii. 183. The date of Ralegh's return is fixed by a letter of Rowland Whyte to Sir Robert Sidney in *Penshurst Papers*, ii. 160.

30th September. NEW PLAYS. *Hens. Diary*, i. 24, 25 ; ii. 176. Neither play is known.

2nd October. THE HIGH PRICE OF CORN. *A.P.C.*, xxv. 7. The original volume of *A.P.C.* covering the period 26th August, 1593, to October, 1595, is missing, but the record is complete for the rest of the period covered by the *Second Elizabethan Journal.*

6th October. THE SOLDIERS FURNISHED BY THE CLERGY. *A.P.C.*, xxv. 15.

TROUBLE OVER THE STARCH MONOPOLY. *A.P.C.*, xxv. 16.

9th October. M. LOMENIE'S STOUT SPEECHES. *Sidney Papers*, i. 354 ; Camden's *Elizabeth.*

14th October. WHEAT SPENT WEEKLY. *Remembrancia*, ii. 109.

15th October. MR. HUGH PLATT'S INVENTIONS. *S.T.C.*, 19988 ; approximate date ; reprinted in the *Harleian Miscellany.* For Platt's book of inventions see *Eliz. Journal*, p. 311. This is a very early example of the publicity pamphlet, or puff plausible.

SIR WALTER RALEGH. *Penshurst Papers*, ii. 173.

27th October. HIGH PRICES. *A.P.C.*, xxv. 25, 31.

29th October. AN ATTACK ON IRELAND FEARED. *A.P.C.*, xxv. 37, 47.

30th October. NEW PLAYS AT THE ROSE. *Hens. Diary*, i. 25 ; ii. 177.

1st November. THE ACCOUNT OF SIR WALTER RALEGH'S VOYAGE. *S.T.C.*, 20634-6, reprinted in Hakluyt's *Voyages*, vii. 272. Ralegh's admiration of the scenery is noteworthy, as genuine appreciation of natural beauties is not very commonly expressed in Elizabethan literature.

5th November. COURT NEWS. *Sidney Papers*, i. 357. The book is summarised, I fear prematurely, in *Eliz. Journal*, p. 340. Essex's sicknesses were not entirely politic. He was apparently 'a bundle of nerves,' and when thwarted or rebuked he would quickly worry himself into a state of acute melancholy or actual illness ; his nervous energy was another symptom of this lack of balance.

6th November. MR. BACON DISAPPOINTED OF THE SOLICITORSHIP. Spedding's *Bacon*, i. 370-3. The details are taken from Bacon's *Apology*, which is naturally biassed ; but it is apparent from a letter to Essex (*ibid.* i. 373) that he was careful not to commit himself. The obligation was not all on Bacon's side in the relationship between Bacon and Essex ; and the notion of Bacon as the subtle viper who bit the hand that fed it, though picturesque, is somewhat fantastic. See also pp. 60 and 139 and notes.

MR. DARCY'S PATENT. *Remembrancia*, ii. 119.

9th November. A TRUCE WITH TYRONE. *Carew MSS.*, 172, 173, 174.

12th November. THE EARL OF HERTFORD COMMITTED. *Sidney Papers*, i. 356, 358, 360. Collins' *Peerage*, ed. E. Brydges, 1812, vol. i. 172.

EXTRAORDINARY MEASURES AGAINST INVASION. *A.P.C.*, xxv. 64. The orders to the counties are detailed and elaborate. Numbers are laid down (*a*) that each county should provide for its own safety, (*b*) that it should despatch to aid its neighbour. The total of 61,800 is reached by adding up the maxima of the county quotas, which are taken from Cornwall, Devon, Dorset, Wiltshire, Southampton, Berkshire, Sussex, Surrey, Kent, London, Essex, Hertford, Suffolk, Cambridge, Huntingdon, Lincoln and Norfolk.

AN IMPUDENT COOK. *Remembrancia*, ii. 122.

17th November. THE QUEEN'S ACCESSION DAY. Stow's *Annals*; *Sidney Papers*, i. 362. Spedding (*Bacon*, i. 377-92) showed that Bacon was responsible for the devices for which Essex received credit. The speeches in full are printed by Spedding and in Nicoll's *Progresses of Queen Elizabeth*. The festivals this year were particularly brilliant; they evoked three ballads.

20th November. SOUTHWELL'S 'TRIUMPHS OVER DEATH.' *A.R.*, iii. 53; *S.T.C.*, 22971; m.e. in E. Brydge's *Archaica*, 1815, vol. i. It is a sign of the great respect felt for Southwell that, so soon after his death, the printer should acknowledge the author's name and justify the publication in a poem 'To the Reader.' Compare *Hamlet*, III. i. 80.

22nd November. COURT NEWS. *Penshurst Papers*, ii. 189.

23rd November. IRISH NEWS. *Sidney Papers*, i. 362, 363.

26th November. AN INQUISITION CONCERNING RECUSANTS. *A.P.C.*, xxv. 85.

30th November. NEW PLAYS. *Hens. Diary*, i. 27; ii. 177. *Harry the Fifth* is presumably *The Famous Victories of Henry V.*

1st December. FRENCH OPINIONS. Birch's *Memoirs*, i. 328; from a letter of Edmondes to Essex dated 24th November.

5th December. THE LIEUTENANT OF THE TOWER COMMITTED. *Sidney Papers*, i. 372. For other papers in the case see Strype's *Annals*, iv. 238.

6th December. WOOD IN THE PILLORY. *Penshurst Papers*, ii. 195. See pp. 32, 34.

7th December. THE QUEEN'S LETTER TO THE KING. Birch's *Historical View*, p. 28. Camden's *Elizabeth*.

12th December. THE QUEEN DINES WITH THE LORD KEEPER. *Sidney Papers*, i. 376.

13th December. THE NAVY TO BE SET OUT. *A.P.C.*, xxv. 98.

THE DEATH OF SIR ROGER WILLIAMS. *Sidney Papers*, i. 377. This genuinely religious strain in Essex is notable; it explains the respect which the Puritans felt for him. The later exploits in Sir Roger Williams' career will be found in many places in *Eliz. Journal* (*e.g.*, p. 33).

14th December. MR. DARCY'S GRANT. *A.P.C.*, xxv. 106. For previous trouble over Mr. Darcy's patent, see *Eliz. Journal*, p. 215; also pp. 7, 58, 65 herein.

17th December. 'MAROCCUS EXTATICUS.' *A.R.*, iii. 55; *S.T.C.*, 6225.

19th December. THE LORD PRESIDENT OF THE NORTH DEAD. *Sidney Papers*, i. 380, 382.

21st December. PRIVATE SHIPS FOR THE NAVY. *A.P.C.*, xxv. 122.

SIR HENRY UNTON SENT TO THE FRENCH KING. *Sidney Papers*, i. 378, 396. With Unton Essex sent a secret memorandum on the way in which he should be received in France in order that the Queen might be forced to send reinforcements (Birch's *Memoirs*, i. 353-4). Essex was not over-scrupulous in furthering his own schemes.

THE INVASION IN CORNWALL. *A.P.C.*, xxv. 129.

25th December. NEWS OF SIR FRANCIS DRAKE. *S.P. Dom.*, 255 : 17. Letter from the Mayor of Plymouth to Lord Burleigh dated 23rd. For Drake's last voyage, see p. 94.

28th December. SMUGGLING OF CORN. *A.P.C.*, xxv. 137.

OTHER BOOKS ALSO SET FORTH ANNO 1595.

Under this heading are grouped some of the more interesting books that appeared during the year which cannot be more accurately dated.

CHURCHYARD'S 'CHARITY' AND 'A PRAISE OF POETRY.' *S.T.C.*, 5245 ; m.e. in A. Boswell's *Frondes Caducae*, 1817. Churchyard was now aged about 75 ; he continued to write until his death in 1604. He comments in the margin of the stanza quoted : 'Want of charitie hath made me loose my pattent. My pattent shows that.'

HUNNIS' 'RECREATIONS.' *S.T.C.*, 13973 ; entered 4th December, 1587 ; *A.R.*, ii. 481.

'POLIMANTEIA.' *S.T.C.*, 5883. It was written by W. Covell, and perhaps dates from the first quarter of 1596 ; m.e. in A. B. Grosart's *Elizabethan England in Gentle and Simple Life*, 1881. The book is apparently inspired by the genuine anxiety felt because on 5th September, 1595, the Queen had entered on her Grand Climacteric (*i.e.*, the ninth of the fatal astrological periods of seven years). It is an important revelation of the anxious thoughts of intelligent minds in this year of alarm. See also pp. 71, 85, 86.

'PLUTARCH'S LIVES.' *S.T.C.*, 20067 ; m.e. in *The Temple Classics* edited by H. D. Rouse.

1596

3rd January. THE LADY HUNTINGDON. *Sidney Papers*, i. 386.

8th January. 'THE BLACK DOG OF NEWGATE.' *S.T.C.*, 14029; for Hutton see p. 323; m.e. by A. V. Judges in *The Elizabethan Underworld*, 1930, p. 266.

18th January. VICTUALS FOR THE NAVY. *A.P.C.*, xxv. 108, 138, 161, 164, etc.

19th January. 'A WATCHWORD FOR WAR.' *A.R.*, iii. 57; *S.T.C.*, 11492. A valuable comment on the general alarm at the beginning of the year. Thomas Nun, in *A Comfort against the Spaniard*, 1596, begins his preface, 'Is it true that the Spaniards will come this spring? And is it not true that we are ready to receive them? Hath this land at any time had either better provision or more soldiers? Braver captains to lead them, or sounder divines to encourage them?' See also *Polimanteia* (p. 69 and note); and compare the closing words of Shakespeare's *King John*, written, I believe, a few months later.

20th January. 'THE SECOND PART OF THE FAERY QUEEN.' *S.T.C.*, 23082; m.e. by J. C. Smith and E. de Selincourt, 1912, etc. *A.R.*, iii. 57.

23rd January. COPLEY'S 'FIG FOR FORTUNE.' *A.R.*, iii. 57; *S.T.C.*, 5737; m.e. for the Spenser Society, 1883.

24th January. SIR HENRY UNTON AND THE FRENCH KING. Murdin's *State Papers*, p. 701. Murdin prints in full Unton's own interesting accounts of this and the subsequent negotiations.

MR. DARCY'S PATENT IS ANNULLED. *Remembrancia*, ii. 142.

25th January. CONDEMNED PRISONERS TO BE PARDONED. *A.P.C.*, xxv. 182.

26th January. NEWS FROM FRANCE. Murdin's *State Papers*, pp. 706, 707, 710.

30th January. A SECOND VOYAGE TO GUIANA. Hakluyt's *Voyages*, vii. 362. See p. 111.

31st January. NEW PLAYS BY THE LORD ADMIRAL'S MEN. *Hens. Diary*, i. 27, 28; ii. 178.

THE MILD WEATHER. T. Bastard, *Chrestoleros*, bk. ii., epig. 6.

1st February. FLESH PROHIBITED DURING LENT. *Proclamations*, 332.

2nd February. PROCEEDINGS WITH TYRONE. *Carew MSS.*, 184, 204.

3rd February. CONTRIBUTIONS TO THE FLEET. *A.P.C.*, xxv. 198. The collection of ship money caused the Council to dictate many letters at this time.

4th February. FRENCH NEWS. Murdin's *State Papers*, pp. 712, 715.

5th February. NEWS OF DRAKE. *S.P. Dom.*, 256 : 37.

7th February. MR. THOMAS ARUNDEL'S RETURN. *Salisbury Papers*, vi. 43, 49. See pp. 82, 90, 186, 189. Acceptance of honours from foreign

Princes was regarded by the Queen as an act of disloyalty. A few months before Sir Anthony Shirley and Sir Nicholas Clifford were punished for a similar offence; see *Eliz. Journal*, pp. 298, 300.

11th February. FORGERS SENTENCED. Hawarde, p. 37.

12th February. 'THE BLIND BEGGAR OF ALEXANDRIA.' *Hens. Diary*, i. 28; ii. 179; *S.T.C.*, 4965; entered 15th August, 1598; m.e. by W. W. Greg, *M.S.R.*, 1928, and in *The Comedies of George Chapman*, ed. by T. M. Parrott, 1913. Count Hermes is the first of the important 'humorous' characters and a good deal of play is made with his black patch and pistol. *The Blind Beggar* was the most fantastic of all the Rose plays, the chief part presumably being written for Alleyn, who had a fine opportunity of showing the range of his skill as a quick-change artist in a succession of very different parts.

13th February. FRENCH NEWS. Murdin's *State Papers*, p. 723.

COLSE'S 'PENELOPE'S COMPLAINT.' *A.R.*, iii. 59; *S.T.C.*, 5582; m.e. by A. B. Grosart, 1880. For *Willobie His Avisa* and its connection with *Penelope's Complaint* see *Eliz. Journal*, p. 319, and my edition in the *Bodley Head Quartos*, vol. xv., pp. 184, 234-5.

14th February. THE FRENCH KING AND HER MAJESTY'S PICTURE. Murdin's *State Papers*, p. 717. From a letter of Unton to the Queen dated 3rd February. Unton tactfully makes unfavourable comment on the King's mistress as 'attyred in a playne Sattayne Gowne, with a Velvet Hood all over her Head (to keape away the Weather from her) which became her verie ill; and, in my Opinion, she is altered verie much for the worse in her Complection and Favor, yeat verie grosselye painted.'

23rd February. THE SUBURBS. *A.P.C.*, xxv. 230. This problem was perennial; see for instance *Eliz. Journal*, p. 334.

25th February. THE CONDEMNED PRISONERS. *A.P.C.*, xxv. 233; see p. 73.

28th *February.* MASTERLESS MEN TO BE TAKEN UP. *A.P.C.*, xxv., 250.

RELUCTANT SEAMEN. *A.P.C.*, xxv. 253.

1st March. A HORRIBLE MURDER. *S.T.C.*, 17748.

4th March. SOLDIERS FOR IRELAND. *A.P.C.*, xxv. 262, 264, 281.

8th March. THE SOLDIERS' COATS. *A.P.C.*, xxv. 278.

11th March. TYRONE'S GRIEVANCES. *Carew MSS.*, 233, 234.

ABUSES IN PLAY. *A.P.C.*, xxv. 289.

13th March. THE QUEEN AND LORD BURLEIGH. Birch's *Memoirs*, i. 448.

THE LATE EARL OF HUNTINGDON *Salisbury Papers*, vi. 93. From letters from the Council of the North and the Archbishop of York dated 10th March, The Earl had now been dead three months; See pp. 66 and 70.

17th March. A SPANISH RAID NEAR PLYMOUTH. *S.P. Dom.*, 256 : 89.

20th March. MR. THOMAS ARUNDEL. *Salisbury Papers*, vi. 105.

21st March. EVASION OF COMMON CHARGES. *A.P.C.*, xxv. 293, 296-301.

25th March. SIR HENRY UNTON SICK. Murdin's *State Papers*, p. 730.

27th March. THE DEATH OF SIR JOHN HAWKINS REPORTED. *S.P. Dom.*, 256 : 111 ; see p. 94 for the account of the voyage.

28th March. COUNTERFEITING OF PASSPORTS. *A.P.C.*, xxv. 320.

A SCARCITY OF GAME. *A.P.C.*, xxv. 322.

29th March. CALVIN'S 'APHORISMS.' *A.R.*, iii. 62 ; *S.T.C.*, 4374 ; entered 29th March, Epistle Dedicatory dated 18th May.

30th March. A BOOK OF SURGERY. *A.R.*, iii. 62 ; *S.T.C.*, 5442 ; an interesting work. In Chapter 27 is given the contents of the chest which the young surgeon should take with him to the wars by land or sea. The surgeon's tools are also illustrated.

2nd April. CALAIS ASSAULTED. Stow's *Annals*.

4th April. THE ATTACK ON CALAIS. Devereux, i. 355. *S.P. Dom.*, 257 : 4. In the preparations made at Dover, Essex showed the utmost energy, never sparing himself, and writing sometimes three letters a day to the Court to expedite succours from London.

5th April. CALAIS. *S.P. Dom.*, 257 : 10.

SIR HENRY UNTON DEAD. *Salisbury Papers*, vi. 122.

MR. NORDEN'S 'CHRISTIAN COMFORT.' *A.R.*, iii. 62 ; *S.T.C.*, 18604. Another example of the general alarm in this year ; compare *King John*, IV. ii. 141 and 185.

6th April. CALAIS. *S.P. Dom.*, 257 : 12.

7th April. A MUTINY AT CHESTER. *A.P.C.*, xxv. 331.

9th April. THE BISHOP OF ST. DAVID'S UNHAPPY SERMON. *Nugae Antiquae*, ii. 215 ; *Salisbury Papers*, vi. 139. According to Fuller (*Church History*, book x.) the Bishop had previously made so favourable an impression on the Queen by honest plain speaking in his sermons that she promised him the reversion of the Archbishopric of Canterbury ; hereafter the offer was withdrawn. See Corrigenda, p. vi.

SUDDEN LEVIES CALLED FOR. *A.P.C.*, xxv. 338 ; Stow's *Annals*.

10th April. THE LEVIES DISMISSED. *A.P.C.*, xxv. 338.

THE QUEEN AND THE BISHOP OF ST. DAVID'S. *Nugae Antiquae*, ii. 218.

11th April. THE LEVIES AGAIN REQUIRED. *A.P.C.*, xxv. 340 ; Stow's *Annals*.

THE SERVICE OF POSTS. *Proclamations*, 333.

13th April. THE EARL OF ESSEX'S COMMISSION FOR CALAIS. *S.P. Dom.*, 257 : 22, 24.

14th April. THE QUEEN'S LETTER TO THE EARL OF ESSEX. *S.P. Dom.*, 257 : 32.

CALAIS. *S.P. Dom.*, 257 : 27.

15th April. Mr. Arundel released. *Salisbury Papers*, vi. 145.

A Murder at Oxford. *A.P.C.*, xxv. 350.

16th April. Calais taken. *S.P. Dom.*, 257 : 30, 35.

17th April. The Troops for Calais dismissed. *A.P.C.*, xxv. 353.

18th April. The French Treachery. Stow's *Annals*.

20th April. Another Order concerning Post-horses. *Proclamations*, 333.

22nd April. A Declaration of the Causes of the Present Navy. *S.T.C.*, 9203. According to Stow the *Declaration* was printed at this time.

24th April. Instructions for the Fleet. *S.P. Dom.*, 257 : 45.

25th April. Sir Anthony Shirley's Voyage. Hakluyt's *Voyages*, vii. 213 ; see also pp. 100, 102, 194.

26th April. The Return of Drake's Fleet. *A.P.C.*, xxv. 365, 367.

27th April. The Death of Drake and Hawkins. *S.P. Dom.*, 257 : 48, 50.

29th April. One condemned for spreading False Rumours. Hawarde, p. 39.

A New Play. *Hens. Diary*, i. 30 ; ii. 180. Nothing is known of the play.

1st May. Recusants in Sussex. Strype, *Annals*, iv. 289 ; appròximate date.

Drake's Fleet return. Hakluyt's *Voyages*, vii. 183. The expedition had sailed on 31st August, 1595.

2nd May. Sir Anthony Shirley's Voyage. Hakluyt's *Voyages*, vii. 213.

3rd May. A Proclamation against Counterfeit Messengers. *Proclamations*, 334.

11th May. Sir Thomas Egerton made Lord Keeper. Stow's *Annals*.

16th May. The Dispute between Yarmouth and Lowestoft. *A.P.C.*, xxv. 401.

18th May. A Mischance at London Bridge. Birch's *Memoirs*, ii. 6.

19th May. A New Play. *Hens. Diary*, i. 30 ; ii. 180. Nothing is known of the play.

23rd May. Sir Anthony Shirley's Voyage. Hakluyt's *Voyages*, vii. 213. See p. 194.

31st May. Certain Mayors commended. *A.P.C.*, xxv. 421-4.

1st June. The Army at Plymouth. Birch's *Memoirs*, ii. 14, 15, 17 ;. *The Commentaries of Sir Francis Vere* (m.e. in *Stuart Tracts*, 1603-1693, ed. Sir Charles Firth, 1903). Vere's minute of the duties of the several officers in an army survives in the *Harleian MSS.* (168, f. 119).

3rd June. The Fleet sails. Stow's *Annals*.

The State of the Middle Marches. *A.P.C.*, xxv. 430.

5th June. THE FLEET. Stow's *Annals.*

6th June. SUPERFLUOUS ALEHOUSES. *A.P.C.*, xxv. 438.

DEFENCE OF THE REALM. *A.P.C.*, xxv. 439, 442.

7th June. A SCOTTISH LORD'S INVENTIONS. Birch's *Memoirs,* ii. 28. This paper (dated 7th June) occurring among the *Bacon Papers* was presumably sent to the Earl of Essex. Lord Napier was thus one of the early projectors both of the submarine and the tank. Poison gas was among the inventions of the ingenious Mr. Platt ; in Thomas Arundel's chamber was found a note of various military devices, including the words, 'Learn of Mr. Platt his way to poison air and so to infect a whole camp' (*Salisbury Papers,* vii. 167). Lord Napier was also the inventor of logarithms ; see *D.N.B.*

11th June. SIR JOHN SMYTHE'S MISDEMEANOUR. *S.P. Dom.*, 259 : 16, 21.

13th June. SIR JOHN SMYTHE. *A.P.C.*, xxv. 450.

15th June. THE DEATH OF DR. FLETCHER. *Nugae Antiquae,* ii. 45 ; Fuller's *Worthies of Kent* ; Camden's *Elizabeth.* The two councillors were presumably Sir Robert Cecil and the Earl of Essex. The Bishop left several children, of whom the eldest was John Fletcher, afterwards the dramatist, at this time aged 17. A slightly different version of the epitaph is preserved in the *Farmer Chetham MS.* (Chetham Society, 1873, part ii., p. 183).

SIR JOHN SMYTHE BEFORE THE COUNCIL. *A.P.C.*, xxv. 459. See also pp. 107, 108, 109, 248. The lawyer's name appears variously 'Ridgeley,' 'Ridley' and 'Ruggeley.'

16th June. THE TREATMENT OF SPANISH PRISONERS. *A.P.C.*, xxv. 468.

20th June. AN ALIEN BANISHED. *A.P.C.*, xxv. 479. Another instance of seditious books brought from overseas is reported in *A.P.C.*, xxvi. 10.

22nd June. A NEW PLAY. *Hens. Diary,* i. 42 ; ii. 180. Nothing is known of the play.

27th June. THE CASE OF SIR JOHN SMYTHE. *A.P.C.*, xxv. 501, 506. In the letter to the Attorney-General, Burleigh added this postscript : 'I praie you to forbeare to examine him of anie part of his false reportes of me.'

4th July. SERVICE WITHOUT THE REALM. *A.P.C.*, xxvi. 3.

5th July. SIR ROBERT CECIL MADE SECRETARY. *A.P.C.*, xxvi. 7 ; Camden's *Elizabeth.*

11th July. BLACKAMOORS IN LONDON. *A.P.C.*, xxvi. 16.

15th July. THE EARL OF NORTHUMBERLAND NAMED AS AMBASSADOR. *Salisbury Papers,* vi. 260.

17th July. IRISH NEWS. *S.P. Ireland,* 191 : 6 (xix.), 9, 10.

18th July. NEW PLAYS. *Hens. Diary,* i. 42 ; ii. 180-1. Neither play is known.

ROGUES IN MIDDLESEX. *A.P.C.*, xxvi. 23.

BLACKAMOORS IN ENGLAND. *A.P.C.*, xxvi., 20.

19th July. GREAT GOOD NEWS FROM SPAIN. *S.P. Dom.*, 259 : 71.

22nd July. PLAYING INHIBITED. *A.P.C.*, xxvi. 38.

25th July. THE SECOND VOYAGE TO GUIANA. Hakluyt's *Voyages*, vii. 358. The pamphlet was entered 11th October. This date of Keymis's return is approximate.

26th July. THE DUNKIRK PIRATES. *A.P.C.*, xxvi. 61.

A PRESUMPTUOUS BALLAD. From a letter of Sir Stephen Slany, Lord Mayor, to Burleigh, printed in Thomas Wright's *Queen Elizabeth and her Times*, 1838, ii. 462. The ballad has not survived. See also p. 32.

27th July. THE POSSESSION OF THOMAS DARLING. *The most wonderful and true storie of a certain witch named Alse Gooderidge of Stapenhill*, 1597; entered 6th June, 1597. The pamphlet gives a long and detailed account of the boy's sufferings, compiled from the notes of Jesse Bee. Both in this narrative, and that of the Warboys case (see *Eliz. Journal*, p. 224 and note), the significant details are most carefully recorded : the Elizabethan eye-witness receives too little credit for the skill and accuracy of his reports of observed phenomena. Samuel Harsnett notes (in *A Discovery of the Fraudelent practises of John Darrel*, 1599, p. 2) that the book ' being penned by one *Iesse Bee* a Sadler in *Burton*, the same was first contracted by one *M. Denison* a minister in that countrey : and then after it had beene seene and allowed by *M. Darrell*, & *M. Hildersham*, it was published in print : and was commonly sold and called for, by this title, vz. *The booke of the dispossessing of the boy of Burton*.' The date of the Derby Assizes is fixed by a letter of Sir Edmund Anderson written from Derby on 25th July (*Rutland MSS. Hist. MSS. Com.*, XII., Ap. iv., p. 332). Sir Humphrey Ferrers was a man of some importance in the neighbourhood. Darling subsequently admitted that the whole affair was a fraud. For further adventures of Mr. Darell, see pp. 176, 241, 267, 292. Falstaffe, hastily disguised as the old woman of Brainford, also wore a broad thrummed hat (*Merry Wives*, IV. ii. 82).

28th July. THE SPANISH PRISONERS. *A.P.C.*, xxvi. 64. See 14th June.

30th July. THE QUEEN'S PICTURE. *A.P.C.*, xxvi. 69.

31st July. A PROCLAMATION FOR THE DEARTH OF CORN. *Proclamations*, p. 338.

1st August. NEWS FROM THE FLEET. Birch's *Memoirs*, ii. 95.

2nd August. PREPARATIONS FOR THE RETURN OF THE FLEET. *S.P. Dom.*, 259 : 88.

4th August. ' THE METAMORPHOSIS OF AJAX.' *S.T.C.*, 12779 ; m.e. by P. Warlock and J. Lindsay, 1927, wherein are printed a number of the epigrams called forth by this famous Rabelaisian tract. I have suggested (in a note on Jaques in the edition of *The Scourge of Villainy*, Bodley Head Quartos, vol. xiii.) that Shakespeare's melancholy philosopher may owe his name to this book ; on which unsavoury subject it may be noted that 'jakes' in the First Quarto of *Lear* is spelt ' jaques.' See also E. I. Fripp's *Shakespeare Studies*, 1930, p. 154.

5th August. CHURCHYARD'S POEM ON SIR F. KNOLLYS. *S.T.C.*, 5254 ; m.e. by T. Parks in *Heliconia*, vol. ii., 1815. Approximate date.

8th August. A DAY OF TRIUMPH and THE TAKING OF CADIZ. Stow's *Annals*. There are a number of different accounts of the taking of Cadiz apart from incidental details in various Collections of State Papers ; see, for instance, Sir Francis Vere's *Commentaries*, and especially the *Monson Tracts*, edited by M. Oppenheim for the Navy Records Society, 1902, which should be consulted for the more important naval events of these years.

THE SCARCITY OF CORN. *A.P.C.*, xxvi. 81, 95-8.

LADY UNTON. *S.P. Dom.*, 259 : 93.

9th August. THE CADIZ FORCES. *A.P.C.*, xxvi. 102.

11th August. THE CADIZ VOYAGE. *A.P.C.*, xxvi. 109.

12th August. THE EARL OF ESSEX AT COURT. Birch's *Memoirs*, ii. 103, 95, 96 ; *Calendar of State Papers Venetian*, ix. 505.

14th August. AN ITALIAN GENTLEMAN PRESENTED AT COURT. *Calendar of State Papers Venetian*, ix. 505. Approximate date. From Signor Gradenigo's letter to the Venetian Ambassador in France ; a short but interesting description of England, which impressed the writer as 'so opulent, fat, and abounding with all things that it may with truth be said that poverty hath no place there.'

16th August. THE FALL OF A HOUSE. Stow's *Annals*.

18th August. THE QUEEN'S TOUCH. *Calendar of State Papers Venetian*, ix. 505. From Signor Gradenigo's letter ; approximate date.

19th August. THE CADIZ PLUNDER. *A.P.C.*, xxvi. 120.

THE ADVANTAGES OF THE CADIZ EXPEDITION. *S.P. Dom.*, 260 : 46.

20th August. DISORDER ON THE BORDERS. *Proclamations*, 339.

22nd August. CAPTIVES IN ALGIERS. *A.P.C.*, xxvi. 126 ; for the adventures of Captain Glemham, see *Eliz. Journal*, pp. 18, 118, 132, 311.

23rd August. MR. PLATT'S SUNDRY REMEDIES AGAINST THE FAMINE. *A.R.*, iii. 69 ; *S.T.C.*, 19996. The book gives a number of nauseous substitutes (of the kind familiar during the later months of the Great War) for common food and drink.

29th August. THE TREATY WITH FRANCE SWORN. Camden's *Elizabeth*.

30th August. TWO NEW PRIVY COUNCILLORS. *A.P.C.*, xxvi. 135.

THE QUEEN'S EXPENSES ON BEHALF OF THE FRENCH KING. *S.P. Dom.*, 257 : 76 (dated 6th May) and 259 : 127.

1st September. SPENSER'S 'FOUR HYMNS.' *S.T.C.*, 23086 ; m.e. by W. L. Renwick, 1929, etc. The book was not entered, but is dated in the Epistle Dedicatory 'Greenwich this first of September, 1596.'

5th September. VOLUNTEERS FOR THE LOW COUNTRIES. *A.P.C.*, xvi. 140.

10th September. SOLDIERS FOR IRELAND. *A.P.C.*, xxvi. 161.

12th September. COMPLAINTS AGAINST LORD CHIEF JUSTICE ANDERSON. Strype, *Annals*, iv. 264 ; approximate date. For the portrait of Anderson and further harsh proceedings see *Eliz. Journal*, pp. 144, 220.

13th September. A PETITION AGAINST PLAYS. *Remembrancia*, ii. 103 ; quoted in *Elizabethan Stage*, iv. 318.

16th September. THE DEPARTURE OF THE EARL OF SHREWSBURY. Stow's *Annals*.

19th September. NEWS FROM IRELAND. *Sidney Papers*, i. 347.

22nd September. THE QUEEN DISPLEASED WITH THE LORD TREASURER. Devereux, i. 389; from a somewhat humble letter written by Burleigh to Essex, who answered politely next day. This letter evidently gave great elation to Essex's own circle. Anthony Bacon, writing to Dr. Hawkins, commented that the renewed favour of the Earl 'hath made the old fox to crouch and whine, and to insinuate himself by a very submiss letter to my Lord of Essex, subscribed in these terms, *Your lordship's, if you will, at commandment*'—an indication that neither Essex nor his followers were discreet in dealing with confidential matters. See Birch's *Memoirs*, ii. 153. Compare *I. Henry IV.*, I. iii. 29.

MONSIEUR DE REAULX'S UNFORTUNATE BREATH. *Penshurst Papers*, ii. 217.

23rd September. AN AID TO THE FRENCH KING. *A.P.C.*, xxvi. 192.

25th September. ROGUES IN SOMERSETSHIRE. Strype, *Annals*, iv. 290, 291.

28th September. SIR RICHARD BINGHAM'S FLIGHT. *S.P. Ireland*, 193: 28, 46, 51. Sir Richard's chief offence seems to have been honesty. See 26th August, 1598.

29th September. THE SCHEDULE OF DAILY PAY FOR THE SOLDIERS IN FRANCE. *A.P.C.*, xxvi. 216. These rates of pay were extremely generous compared with the incomes of some professional men; parsons and schoolmasters for instance.

30th September. 'ULYSSES UPON AJAX.' *S.T.C.*, 12782; approximate date. The answer lacks the wit, but none of the scurrility, of the *Metamorphosis*; it entirely misses the serious purpose behind Harington's book. It does, however, illuminate Elizabethan sanitary arrangements.

3rd October. HIGHWAY ROBBERIES. *Middlesex Sessions Rolls*, i. 229. Cases where the accused refused to plead and were sentenced to *peine forte et dure* are not uncommon. Of this penalty William Harrison in his *Description of England* says, 'Such felons as stand mute and speak not at their arraignment, are pressed to death by huge weights laid upon a board, that lieth over their breast, and a sharp stone under their backs; these commonly held their peace, thereby to save their goods unto their wives and children, which, if they were condemned, should be confiscated to the Prince.'

4th October. ADVICE FOR MY LORD ESSEX. Spedding's *Bacon*, ii. 40-45. This entry is based on Bacon's famous letter of advice to Essex. It is not likely that the letter was circulated, but most probable that his faults were discussed by his true friends, who realised as clearly as Bacon what should be done, and avoided. This letter shows Bacon's immense practical wisdom; it explains, and justifies, his desertion of Essex. But Essex would never listen to sober advice; as De Maisse observed, '*Il est tout son conseil luy mesmes.*' Compare *Richard II.*, I. iv. 25, for Bolingbroke's 'popular courses'; also *I. Henry IV.*, III. i. 176.

6th October. RYE FROM THE EAST COUNTRIES. *A.P.C.*, xxvi. 223.

7th October. MY LORD OF LINCOLN'S RETURN. *A.R.*, iii. 73. E. Monings, *The Landgrave of Hessen, his princely receiving of Her Majesty's ambassador*, 1596; *S.T.C.*, 18013; Birch's *Memoirs*, ii. 178. 'Turks' are horses.

9th October. MR. MORLEY'S 'INTRODUCTION TO PRACTICAL MUSIC.' *A.R.*, iii. 72; *S.T.C.*, 18133.

10th October. THE FRENCH KING'S ENTRY INTO ROUEN. Stow's *Annals*; from the account by William Seager, Somerset Herald, who was present.

13th October. SIR THOMAS BASKERVILLE'S INSTRUCTIONS. *A.P.C.*, xxvi. 244.

14th October. A THIRD VOYAGE TO GUIANA. Hakluyt's *Voyages*, viii. 1; see also p. 194.

15th October. THE LEAGUE WITH FRANCE. Stow's *Annals*.

17th October. THE FORCES FOR FRANCE STAYED. *A.P.C.*, xxvi. 255.

18th October. THE FORCES TO BE SENT TO FRANCE. *A.P.C.*, xxvi. 257.

20th October. THE CONTRIBUTIONS TOWARDS SHIPPING. *A.P.C.*, xxvi. 260, 265, 266. As is shown by many entries in *A.P.C.*, the Council found great difficulty in persuading neighbouring towns to contribute to the expenses of the port towns in the Cadiz expedition.

23rd October. NASHE'S 'HAVE WITH YOU TO SAFFRON WALDEN.' Approximate date. *S.T.C.*, 18369; m.e. in *The Complete Works of Thomas Nashe*, by R. B. McKerrow, vol. iii., 1910; for an excellent account of the Harvey-Nashe quarrel see vol. v. p. 65. After a somewhat slow start, Nashe produced one of the best pieces of abuse in the language. The book is full of scurrilous and amusing gossip about Harvey's friends, such as Barnes (for which see p. 43).

28th October. A GREAT ALARM FROM SPAIN. *A.P.C.*, xxvi. 279.

31st October. GREAT PREPARATIONS FOR DEFENCE. *A.P.C.*, xxvi. 262-290.

CORN SHIPS IN LONDON. *A.P.C.*, xxvi. 281.

2nd November. THE EARL OF SHREWSBURY RETURNS. Stow's *Annals*.

A PROCLAMATION CONCERNING THE DEARTH. *Proclamations*, 340.

4th November. VARIOUS OPINIONS CONCERNING THE SPANISH DANGER. *S.P. Dom.*, 260: 82, 87, 93.

5th November. LODGE'S 'WITS' MISERY.' Dated 5th November in the Epistle. *S.T.C.*, 16677; m.e. in *The Complete Works of Thomas Lodge*, Hunterian Club, 1883. Lodge owes the pattern of the work to *Piers Penniless*, as in part he acknowledges. The book is a mixture of rather heavy allegorical satire and odd book learning, with a foretaste both of the 'Humours' and the 'Character.' The devil Adulation is an acknowledged borrowing from 'The Flatterer' of Theophrastus—this being apparently the first instance of an English writer using the 'Characters' of Theophrastus—but instead of isolating his characters in separate essays, he blends them into the general scheme. *Wits' Misery* is best known for the oft-quoted allusion to 'the Visard of ye ghost, which cried so miserably at ye Theater like an oister wife, *Hamlet, revenge*.'

7th November. THE PREPARATIONS FOR DEFENCE. *A.P.C.*, xxvi. 292-302.

8th November. MR. SPENSER'S 'PROTHALAMION.' *S.T.C.*, 23088; m.e. by W. L. Renwick, 1929, etc.

9th November. The Death of George Peele. *Elizabethan Stage*, iii. 459.

14th November. A Lamentation for Drake. *S.T.C.*, 10943 ; a most interesting poem. The author's theology is classical throughout and he writes with catching enthusiasm ; to many of the poets (as to Milton later) the gods of Rome were quite as real as the persons of Christian theology.

18th November. A Spanish Stratagem in Scotland. Birch's *Memoirs*, ii. 196.

21st November. Recusants to be committed. *A.P.C.*, xxvi. 322.

Mr. Davies' 'Orchestra.' *A.R.*, iii. 74 ; *S.T.C.*, 6360 ; m.e. in *The Complete Poems of Sir John Davies*, edited by A. B. Grosart, 1876, vol. i. *Orchestra* was entered first on 5th June, 1594, and again on 21st November, 1596 ; the first was probably a 'blocking entry.' Several of the works of gentlemen authors were thus entered some time before an edition appeared ; *e.g.*, Sidney's *Defence of Poesy* (p. 20 and note) and Florio's translation of Montaigne's *Essays*, entered 20th October, 1595, and 4th June, 1600, but not published till 1603 (*A.R.*, iii. 50 and iii. 162).

Drayton's Poems. *A.R.*, iii. 74 ; *S.T.C.*, 7232. This is another specimen of the autobiographical lament, fashionable at this time, being admittedly a rival to *Shore's Wife*, *Rosamond*, *Lucrece* and *Elstred* (see *Eliz. Journal*, pp. 246, 262, 271, 330, 322).

25th November. A Theatre in Blackfriars. *S.P. Dom.*, 260 : 116 ; printed in *Elizabethan Stage*, iv. 319, 320 : approximate date. This enterprise, though unfortunate, was another of James Burbage's strokes of genius. As he had been the first to realise the possibilities of the permanent theatre twenty years before, so now he first saw that the gentleman spectator was taking a serious interest in the drama of the professional companies, and would pay a high price for the privacy and comfort of the indoor theatre : but it was nearly twelve years before his son's company were able to occupy the Blackfriars building ; see also note on Chapman's *Humorous Day's Mirth*, 11th May, 1597.

27th November. Beard's 'Theatre of God's Judgments.' *A.R.*, iii. 75 ; *S.T.C.*, 1659. A magnificent repertory of scandalous tales of the wicked, compiled with the highest of motives. As Beard prints very few contemporary examples, it is clear that Marlowe's death was notorious ; see *Eliz. Journal*, p. 244, and authorities therein quoted.

28th November. The Force sent to the Isle of Wight. *A.P.C.*, xxvi. 336, 337.

1st December. The Earl of Essex defamed. Birch's *Memoirs*, ii 218, 220.

8th December. A dreadful sudden Tempest at Wales. Stow's *Annals*. A similar phenomenon at Manchester was thus reported in the *Times* of 30th July, 1930 : '" I saw a ball of fire coming through the air. It was about the size of a football," said an eye-witness. " There was a terrific roar when the bolt struck the spire of the church. It appeared to rip it all the way down. Slates fell in every direction." '

10th December. The Scottish Princess baptised. Rymer's *Fœdera*, xvi. 304. This is the romantic Princess Elizabeth who married the Elector

Palatine in 1612. I have not discovered whether the post-dated cheque was ever honoured.

14th December. SEDITION IN OXFORDSHIRE. *S.P. Dom.*, 261 : 10.

18th December. COOTE'S 'ENGLISH SCHOOLMASTER.' *A.R.*, iii. 77; *S.T.C.*, 5711. This book reached a 42nd edition in 1684, and a copy printed in 1692 survives.

19th December. A LOYAL RECUSANT. *A.P.C.*, xxvi. 375.

A STRANGE EARTH MOVING. Stow's *Annals*.

23rd December. TYRONE'S TREACHERY. *Carew MSS.*, 257.

25th December. THE DEARTH. *A.P.C.*, xxvi. 380, 383 : see p. 127.

26th December. CORN SHIPS TO BE STOPPED. *A.P.C.*, xxvi. 393-7.

OTHER BOOKS SET FORTH ANNO 1596.

THE BROWNISTS' CONFESSIONS. *S.T.C.*, 237. This pamphlet largely confirms the opinions held by the authorities of the seditious nature of Brownism (see *Eliz. Journal*, p. 208); it appears to have been printed in Amsterdam.

A BOOK CONCERNING THE SPANISH SICKNESS. *S.T.C.*, 16872.

LAMBARD'S 'PERAMBULATION OF KENT.' *S.T.C.*, 15176.

1597

1st January. BAD WEATHER. *Fugger News Letters*, 585.

8th January. THE LATE INTENDED RISING. *S.P. Dom.*, 262 : 4.

11th January. THE VICTUALS OF THE SOLDIERS IN IRELAND. *Carew MSS.*, 259.

17th January. MR. NORDEN'S 'MIRROR OF HONOUR.' *A.R.*, iii. 78 ; *S.T.C.*, 18614. A conventional, pious book, but readable in parts.

23rd January. AN ITALIAN ARGOSY STAYED. *A.P.C.*, xxvi. 445.

24th January. A GREAT VICTORY AT TURNHOUT. *Salisbury Papers*, vii. 24-5, 26, 30. This account is taken chiefly from Vere's letter to Essex, dated 17*th*.

26th January. THE DEATH OF LADY CECIL. Letter printed in E. Edwards' *The Life of Sir Walter Ralegh*, 1868, ii. 161. Compare *Hamlet*, v. ii. 236 : 'Since no man has aught of what he leaves, what is't to leave betimes' ; also *All's Well*, I. i. 65 : 'Moderate lamentation is the right of the dead, excessive grief the enemy to the living.'

30th January. MR. BACON'S 'ESSAYS.' *A.R.*, iii. 79 ; *S.T.C.*, 1137 ; m.e. in the Hazlewood Books, edited by F. E. Etchells and H. Macdonald, 1924. Dated 30th January, 1597, in the Epistle Dedicatory to Anthony Bacon ; entered 5th February. This is the first edition of the *Essays* which reached their final form in 1624 ; other editions were published in 1598, 1606, 1612 (2), 1613 (3), 1614, 1624, 1625 (2), 1629, 1632, 1639. The essay 'Of Studies' is here reproduced complete in its original form ; at this time the essay is rather a collection of *sententiae* than a formal composition ; see also *Politeuphia*, p. 213 and note. Note also that Bacon dates his preface 1597 and *not* 1596 ; the method of beginning the new year on 1st January was coming to be the practice with certain authors and publishers.

31st January. NEW PLAYS. *Hens. Diary*, i. 50-1 ; ii. 182.

2nd February. A DANGEROUS PERSON TAKEN. *A.P.C.*, xxvi. 457.

5th February. A QUARREL AT COURT. Birch's *Memoirs*, ii. 274.

6th February. IRISH TRADE WITH SPAIN. *A.P.C.*, xxvi. 467.

8th February. SPANISH DISASTER. *S.P. Dom.*, 262 : 37.

THE BATTLE AT TURNHOUT. *A discourse of the late overthrow given to the King of Spain's army at Turnhout, etc., translated from the French*, 1597. *Salisbury Papers*, vii. 43.

9th February. A NEW LOAN FOR THE QUEEN. *A.P.C.*, xxvi. 468.

13th February. SUPERFLUOUS DIET AT THE ASSIZES. *A.P.C.*, xxvi. 481.

COMPLAINTS FROM WILTSHIRE. *A.P.C.*, xxvi. 487.

TROUBLES IN OXFORD. *S.P. Dom.*, 262 : 40. From a letter of Dudley Carleton to John Chamberlain.

17th February. TROUBLES OF THE KEEPER AT WISBEACH. *S.P. Dom.*, 262 : 42.

21st February. COURT NEWS. *Sidney Papers*, ii. 16, 17, 18.

24th February. SIR THOMAS BASKERVILLE'S SOLDIERS. *Salisbury Papers*, vii. 69.

25th February. THE LORD MAYOR REBUKED. *A.P.C.*, xxvi. 520.

4th March. COURT NEWS. *Sidney Papers*, ii. 24.

9th March. A NOTABLE STRATAGEM AT THE CAPTURE OF AMIENS. *Salisbury Papers*, vii., 88 ; *Calendar of State Papers Venetian*, ix. 558.

10th March. THE WARDENSHIP OF THE CINQUE PORTS. *Sidney Papers*, ii. 27.

11th March. THE OFFICE OF LORD PRESIDENT. *S.P. Dom.*, 262 : 64. The Earl of Huntingdon died on 14th December, 1595 (p. 66).

12th March. THE LORD TREASURER'S GRIEF. *Sidney Papers*, ii. 27.

14th March. A WITCH HANGED AT LANCASTER. George More, *A True Discourse concerning the certain possession and dispossession of 7 persons in one family in Lancashire*, etc., 1600. In 1598 Darrell and More were committed to the Clink, where this book was written to confute the Jesuits who declared that the Lancashire exorcisms were frauds perpetrated by the preachers ; though the Jesuits themselves made capital out of one of the possessed women (see p. 285). The assizes, according to More, were held on 6th March ; Hartley was probably executed about two days later ; he was dead some days before the 16th. The law did not condemn a man to death for witchcraft but for murder by witchcraft ; conjuration of evil spirits was however a capital offence; see C. L'Estrange Ewen, *Witch Hunting and Witch Trials*, 1929, and E. W. Notestein, *History of Witchcraft in England from 1558-1718* ; my edition of *The Trial of the Lancashire Witches* in 1612, and authorities therein quoted. Lancashire was a hotbed of witchcraft at this time.

16th March. THE PRICE OF BEER. *A.P.C.*, xxvi. 543.

THE EARL OF ESSEX'S PATENT. *Sidney Papers*, ii. 30.

19th March. A NEW PLAY. *Hens. Diary*, i. 51 ; ii. 183.

20th March. FRENCH PIRATES. *A.P.C.*, xxvi. 561.

25th March. SECTARIES TO GO TO CANYDA. *A.P.C.*, xxvii. 6.

27th March. AN EXPLOSION IN DUBLIN. *S.P. Ireland*, 198 : 21.

28th March. THE POSSESSED PERSONS IN LANCASHIRE. For authorities, see 14th March. The 'madness' and 'exorcism' of the Puritan Malvolio would be highly appreciated in 1600-1 when the pamphlet war, engendered by the efforts of Messrs. Darrell and More, was at its hottest. Malvolio's 'vain bibble-babble' and his fashionable yellow stockings show that he too was suffering from possession by the evil spirit of pride.

29th March. ENGLISH PRISONERS IN SPAIN. *S.P. Dom.*, 262 : 86.

31st March. MENDOZA'S 'THEORIQUE AND PRACTISE OF WAR.' *S.T.C.*, 17819 ; the book is commended at the end by a 'Censure' written by Don Francisco Arias de Bobadilla, who is apparently immortalised in Jonson's *Every Man in his Humour* (p. 309) ; Bobadil in the First Quarto of the play appears as Bobadilla.

'VIRGIDEMIARUM.' *A.R.*, iii. 82; *S.T.C.*, 12716. There is some difficulty about the issues of the 1st and 2nd parts. The book was entered on 31st March, 1597, and three satires were published in 1597, though the title-page of this edition reads, 'Virgidemiarum, Sixe Bookes.' The second part—'Virgidemiarum. The three last bookes *of byting Satyres*'—is dated 1598; it is a separate issue and was entered on 30th March, 1598. Presumably the title 'Virgidemiarum, Sixe Bookes' was printed for use with copies of the first series which were bound with copies of the last three books. The first publication was anonymous.

2nd April. THE SOLDIERS IN FRANCE. *Salisbury Papers*, vii. 125, 129, 130.

5th April. 'CLITOPHON AND LEUCIPPE.' *A.R.*, iii. 82; *S.T.C.*, 90; m.e. by S. Gaselee and H. F. B. Brett Smith, 1923. The translator was elder brother of Burton the Melancholick. The Earl of Southampton had a taste for this kind of book.

7th April. SEMINARIES TO BE BANISHED. *A.P.C.*, xxvii., 21.

8th April. FORCES FOR IRELAND. *A.P.C.*, xxvii. 21-6, 26-8.

10th April. AN ENGLISH PIRACY. *A.P.C.*, xxvii. 31. There are several instances of piracy committed by English mariners during this year.

A FRAY IN ST. MARTIN'S. *Middlesex Sessions Rolls*, i. 227. One of several fatal frays. At his trial Pinkney escaped by benefit of clergy.

13th April. TWO LADIES-IN-WAITING PUNISHED. *Sidney Papers*, ii. 38, 34.

THE MARINERS TO BE STAYED. *A.P.C.*, xxvii. 37.

HOUNDS FOR THE FRENCH KING. *A.P.C.*, xxvii. 38.

16th April. COURT NEWS. *Sidney Papers*, ii. 40.

17th April. THE CLOTH TRADE. *A.P.C.*, xxvii. 5.

THE NEW LORD CHAMBERLAIN. *Sidney Papers*, ii. 41.

A DECEITFUL PRACTICE. *A.P.C.*, xxvii. 54.

18th April. THE LORD BURGH TO BE DEPUTY IN IRELAND. *Carew MSS.*, 267.

19th April. THE EARL OF ESSEX AND SIR R. CECIL. *Sidney Papers*, ii. 42.

21st April. ALL SHIPS STAYED. *A.P.C.*, xxvii. 60.

23rd April. ST. GEORGE'S DAY. Hawarde, p. 74; *Sidney Papers*, ii. 45

28th April. THE STAYED SHIPS. *A.P.C.*, xxvii. 74.

DESERTERS FROM THE IRISH FORCES. *A.P.C.*, xxvii. 75; and xxvi. 164.

29th April. DANGERS FROM FRANCE. *A.P.C.*, xxvii. 80, 93.

30th April. NEW PLAYS. *Hens. Diary*, i. 52; ii. 183. On the identity of these plays see Dr. Greg's notes.

1st May. A NOTABLE OUTRAGE ON A CORPSE. *Salisbury Papers*, vii. 165; undated, but the doctor died on 19th April.

6th May. DISCONTENTS IN THE COUNTIES. *A.P.C.*, xxvii. 56, 88, 92, 96, 97.

9th May. Mr. Thomas Arundel. *Salisbury Papers*, vii. 193, 195. See pp. 76, 82, 90.

Musters against invasion. *A.P.C.*, xxvii. 101-7.

11th May. The Mayor of Chester commended. *A.P.C.*, xxvii. 115.

A Play of Humours. *Hens. Diary*, i. 52; ii. 184. *S.T.C.*, 4987; m.e. in *The Comedies of George Chapman*, edited by T. M. Parrott, 1914. This is the first surviving play in the new mode, of which Jonson's *Every Man in his Humour* is the most successful and famous example. The play is significant of several changes in the playgoing public: it is a society comedy, of special interest to the gentleman spectator who was now beginning to invade the theatre; it substitutes society wit for the usual clowning and romance which had hitherto been served up as comedy; and, in an elementary form, it presents a problem proper to comedy—whether Florilla is more Puritan than woman. Although the 'humours' of the characters are not labelled in big letters, the *Humorous Day's Mirth* certainly belongs to the type, for the essential of a Humour play is a practical joke (usually in bad taste), designed to place the 'humorous' person in a ridiculous situation where his particular humour can be displayed at its most foolish. Jonson was notably skilful in managing such plots because he could balance so many of these situations in one play. From this time onward the younger generation begins to be noticeable. Young people of independent means who belonged neither to immediate Court circles nor to the professions had not been much in evidence for some years; henceforward actors depend for support more on gentlemen of leisure and culture than on the old-fashioned patron or the crowd. Moreover, the gentlemen themselves not only write poetry, but a few months later begin to write plays, to produce them in private theatres, and to print them.

16th May. English Pirates. *A.P.C.*, xxvii. 116. Another case of piracy; see p. 180.

20th May. The Queen angry. *Sidney Papers*, ii. 52.

23rd May. MacHugh slain. *Carew MSS.*, *Russell's Journal*, p. 259; *S.P. Ireland*, 199: 25, 28.

The Queen and the Lady Mary Howard. *Nugae Antiquae*, i. 232-4, 361.

26th May. A New Play. *Hens. Diary*, i. 52; ii. 185. Nothing is known of the play.

27th May. A Debtor's Case. *A.P.C.*, xxvii. 143.

30th May. Preparations for an Expedition. *A.P.C.*, xxvii. 160-164.

2nd June. Mr. Arundel released. *Salisbury Papers*, vii. 229; see 9th May.

Sir Walter Ralegh restored to his place. *Sidney Papers*, ii. 54. It was now five years since Ralegh had been thrown into the Tower for the scandal of his marriage; see *Eliz. Journal*, p. 134.

3rd June. Langham's 'Garden of Health.' *A.R.*, iii. 85; *S.T.C.*, 15195. The title-page is misdated 1579. This is a most important book for the understanding of Elizabethan homely medicine, and well worth the attention of Shakespearean students.

4th June. Abuses in Somerset. *A.P.C.*, xxvii. 167.

8th June. MACHUGH'S HEAD. *A.P.C.*, xxvii. 185; *S.P. Ireland*, 199 : 86. For further adventures of MacHugh's head see 24th September.

THE EARL OF ESSEX'S CLEMENCY. *A.P.C.*, xxvii. 181.

10th June. CALAIS. *S.P. Dom.*, 263 : 97.

11th June. SIR THOMAS BASKERVILLE DEAD. *Salisbury Papers*, vii. 232, 242, 256, 200, 286.

RUMOURS. Chamberlain's *Letters*, p. 4.

12th June. SIR ARTHUR SAVAGE TO COMMAND IN FRANCE. *A.P.C.*, xxvii. 203.

14th June. TIMOROUS GENTLEMEN. *A.P.C.*, xxvii. 193.

ABUSES OVER MUSTERS. A.P.C., xxvii. 197.

25th June. THE STATE OF IRELAND. *Carew MSS.*, 268. This 'Summary Collection' of the state of Ireland is calendared 'April 1597' but must be later than the death of MacHugh.

30th June. NEW PLAYS. *Hens. Diary*, i. 53; ii. 185. Neither play survives but the 'plot' of *Frederick and Basilia* is reprinted by Dr. Greg in *Henslowe Papers*, p. 135, from the original in the British Museum.

2nd July. THE 'WAT' RETURNS. Hakluyt's *Voyages*, viii. 1. See 14th October, 1596.

5th July. SIR ANTHONY SHIRLEY'S RETURN. Hakluyt's *Voyages*, vii. 213. See 25th April, 2nd and 23rd May, 1596.

MR. WILLIAM PARKER'S VOYAGE. Hakluyt's *Voyages*, vii. 222.

6th July. A PROCLAMATION AGAINST INORDINATE APPAREL. *Proclamations*, 343. The detailed list of the stuffs permitted to the several ranks occupies 3½ pages.

SOLDIERS FOR PICARDY. *A.P.C.*, xxvii. 283.

7th July. DELONEY'S 'JACK OF NEWBURY.' *A.R.*, iii. 87; *S.T.C.*, 6559—the earliest extant copy 'now the tenth time imprinted,' dated 1626; m.e. in *The Works of Thomas Deloney*, edited by F. O. Mann, 1912. The book was first entered to Millington on 7th March, who assigned it to Lowndes on 25th May; both entries include the condition that it be lawfully authorised—a reasonable precaution after the previous association of Deloney and Millington (see p. 32). A ballad on the subject, entered 8th July, probably gives the date of publication.

8th July. THE COMPLAINTS OF THE COUNCIL OF WAR. *S.P. Dom.*, 264 : 12.

10th July. THE FLEET ENTER PLYMOUTH. Devereux, i. 421.

12th July. THE FLEET SAILS. *S.P. Dom.*, 264 : 21.

VAGRANTS TO BE IMPRESTED. *A.P.C.*, xxvii. 290. Dogberry, mindful of a similar order, charges his watch, 'You shall comprehend all vagrom men' (*Much Ado*, III. iii. 25).

16th July. THE VAGRANTS. *A.P.C.*, xxvii. 292.

18th July. THE LORD MAYOR REBUKED. *A.P.C.*, xxvii. 298.

20th July. THE FLEET DRIVEN BACK. Purchas, xx. 41; *S.P. Dom.*, 264 : 32, 34.

22nd July. THE EARL OF ESSEX AT PLYMOUTH. *S.P. Dom.*, 264 : 40, 41.

23rd July. THE POLISH AMBASSADOR. *S.P. Dom.*, 264 : 57. This account is taken from a letter written by Sir R. Cecil to Essex on the 26th; the full text of both speeches is given in Stow's *Annals*.

24th July. THE POLISH AMBASSADOR. *A.P.C.*, xxvii. 307.

28th July. THE PLAYHOUSES ORDERED TO BE PLUCKED DOWN and A LEWD PLAY. *Remembrancia*, ii. 171; *A.P.C.*, xxvii. 313 (both reprinted in *Elizabethan Stage*, iv. 321), 338; *Hens. Diary*, i. 54; *Elizabethan Stage*, iii. 454; McKerrow's *Nashe*, v. 29. Apparently the Lord Mayor had been reading Sidney's *Defence of Poesy*, but his immediate desire to reform the stage was more probably due to the quite real danger that the players might incite the mob at this uneasy time. Playing ceased until October (see pp. 209, 212), but the playhouses, as usual, survived intact.

29th July. TROUBLES ON THE BORDER AND IN IRELAND. *S.P. Ireland*, 200 : 24, 25, 27; and *S.P. Dom.*, 264 : 61—from a letter of Cecil to Essex.

2nd August. LORD HOWARD'S SHIPS RETURN. *S.P. Dom.*, 264 : 64.

7th August. THE PICARDY FORCES DELAYED. *A.P.C.*, xxvii. 324.

13th August. A PROCLAMATION CONCERNING THE SCOTTISH BORDER. *Proclamations*, 349.

17th August. A MALICIOUS MAYOR. *A.P.C.*, xxvii. 346.

19th August. THE FLEET AGAIN SAILS. Purchas, xx. 44.

20th August. THE ALMSHOUSE AT STAMFORD. *Proclamations*, 349b.

21st August. INGROSSERS. *A.P.C.*, xxvii. 359.

22nd August. A BOOK ON CHEATING. *A.R.*, iii. 89; *S.T.C.*, 17916.

29th August. SHAKESPEARE'S 'RICHARD THE SECOND.' *A.R.*, iii. 89; *S.T.C.*, 22307; facsimile edited by W. Griggs and P. A. Daniel, 1890. This was a most popular book and went quickly into three editions; the first is anonymous, but Shakespeare's name appears on both editions of 1598. There was no further edition until 1608 which first included the Deposition Scene; presumably after the troubles of Sir John Hayward (who was imprisoned in 1599 for injudiciously dedicating *The first part of the reign of King Henry IIII.* to Essex) it was thought inadvisable to continue publication.

6th September. AN AMBASSADOR RECEIVED FROM DENMARK. Stow's *Annals*.

15th September. SLANDERS AGAINST THE LORD MAYOR. *Proclamations*, 350.

16th September. NEWS OF THE FLEET. *S.P. Dom.*, 264 : 110.

20th September. SIR JOHN NORRIS DEAD. *S.P. Ireland*, 200 : 130.

CONDEMNED PRISONERS, *A.P.C.*, xxviii. 8.

22nd September. THE QUEEN'S LETTER TO THE LADY NORRIS. Printed in full in J. Nichols' *Progresses of Queen Elizabeth*, 1805, vol. iii.

23rd September. THE GOVERNOR OF DUNKIRK TAKEN. *A.P.C.*, xxviii. 10.

24th September. MACHUGH'S HEAD. *Salisbury Papers*, vii. 395. See 8th June.

27th September. A PROCLAMATION AGAINST PROVIDING THE SPANISH KING WITH MUNITION. *Proclamations*, 351.

29th September. THE SPANISH DANGER CEASES. *A.P.C.*, xxviii. 27.

8th October. THE PLAYERS RELEASED. *A.P.C.*, xxviii. 33. See 28th July.

9th October. A DISORDERLY ELECTION. *Salisbury Papers*, vii. 411-415. The matter was reported to the Council by the Archbishop of York, who blamed Sir John Savile.

10th October. THE ART OF BRACHYGRAPHY. *S.T.C.*, 1311; dated on title-page. The book was the work of an Oxford man and is sponsored by a number of dedicatory verses. Bales' system is very general and could not be used for anything more elaborate than note taking. Entered 10th November, 1599 (*A.R.*, iii. 150).

11th October. 'THE TRIMMING OF THOMAS NASHE.' *A.R.*, iii. 92; *S.T.C.*, 12906; m.e. in *The Works of Gabriel Harvey*, edited by A. B. Grosart, 1885, vol. iii. Dr. McKerrow points out (*Nashe*, v. 107) that as the *Trimming* is concerned only with Nashe's Epistle to the barber and not with his quarrel with Harvey, it is not likely to be Harvey's work, nor does it resemble Harvey's style. I suspect that it was written by some Cambridge man, possibly with the approval of the barber, who may well have resented Nashe's unsolicited advertisement. With this book the Harvey-Nashe 'flyting' ceased.

PLAYING RESUMED. *Hens. Diary*, i. 54; ii. 186.

THE ELECTION AT YORK. *Salisbury Papers*, vii. 426.

12th October. A PROCLAMATION AGAINST ENGLISH MERCHANTS. *S.P. Dom.*, 264 : 143; *Salisbury Papers*, vii. 429; F. Peck's *Desideria Curiosa*, bk. v., p. 21.

14th October. 'POLITEUPHIA, WIT'S COMMONWEALTH.' *A.R.*, iii. 93; *S.T.C.*, 15685. This was a most popular book; the 17th edition appeared in 1655 and copies exist dated 1663, 1669, 1671, 1674, 1688, 1699. *Wit's Commonwealth* in design is not dissimilar to the first version of Bacon's *Essays* (see 30th January), being a large collection of apt remarks and quotations, and one of the many commonplace books so much in favour at this time; compare also Meres' *Paladis Tamia*, p. 305.

16th October. HERRINGS TO BE STAYED. *A.P.C.*, xxviii. 40.

19th October. INGROSSERS AND BUILDERS PUNISHED. Hawarde, p. 78.

DELONEY'S 'GENTLE CRAFT.' *A.R.*, iii. 93; *S.T.C.*, 6555. This is the 1st part, the 2nd being published some months later; m.e. in *The Works of Deloney* by F. O. Mann, 1912. The earliest extant edition is dated 1648. Dekker in 1599 dramatised the last section in *The Shoemakers' Holiday*.

20th October. 'RICHARD THE THIRD.' *A.R.*, iii. 93; *S.T.C.*, 22314; facsimile by W. Griggs and P. A. Daniel. The play was very popular, being reprinted in 1598, 1602, 1605, 1612, 1622, 1629, 1634.

22nd October. THE LORD ADMIRAL TO BE ADVANCED. *Sidney Papers*, ii. 69.

23rd October. The Lord Admiral advanced. *Sidney Papers*, ii. 70.

Ostend threatened. *A.P.C.*, xxviii. 48.

24th October. The Parliament assembles. D'Ewes' *Journals*, pp. 548, 524. Stow's *Annals*. For the opening of the Parliament of 1593 see *Eliz. Journal*, 195, etc.

26th October. A Sudden very Great Alarm. *Sidney Papers*, ii. 71; *A.P.C.*, xxviii. 50-56.

27th October. The Forces mustering. *A.P.C.*, xxviii. 57-61; *Sidney Papers*, ii. 72.

The Lord Burgh dead. *S.P. Ireland*, 201 : 17, 14.

The Speaker presented. D'Ewes' *Journals*, pp. 550, 526.

Playing resumed. *Hens. Diary*, i. 49; *Elizabethan Stage*, ii. 141.

28th October. The Earl of Essex returns. *Sidney Papers*, ii. 72; *A.P.C.*, xxviii. 62, 63. The report of King Philip's death was premature, though expected.

30th October. Preparations in the West. *A.P.C.*, xxviii. 67.

31st October. Ostend besieged. *S.P. Dom.*, 264 : 163, 164.

A New Play. *Hens. Diary*, i. 54; ii. 187. After 5th November the daily record of performances in the *Diary* ceases, and in its place Henslowe notes payments made on behalf of the companies.

2nd November. The Islands Voyage. Purchas, vol. xx. This account is based on the narrative of Sir Arthur Gorges, who was an enemy of the Essex faction and therefore not impartial, but other writers are even more condemnatory; Monson, who was Essex's own captain, wrote: 'No man can receive blame hereby; all is to be attributed to the want of experience in my Lord, and his flexible nature to be overruled.' With the return of the expedition Essex's reputation amongst the intelligent observers began to wane as it was more generally realised that he was not only an incompetent commander but acutely jealous of other and abler leaders than himself; he was, moreover, attracting the devotion of the more desperate and reckless adventurers. From this time onward Essex begins to be a definite menace to the commonwealth. For the best modern commentary on the expedition see *The Naval Tracts of Sir William Monson*, edited by M. Oppenheim, 1902, for *The Navy Records Society* (vols. xxii.-xxiii.).

5th November. Ostend. *S.P. Dom.*, 265 : 3.

The Queen's Letter to the Emperor of Ethiopia. Hakluyt's *Voyages*, v. 77.

A Motion in Parliament against Inclosures. D'Ewes' *Journals*, p. 551.

6th November. Spanish Prisoners at large. *A.P.C.*, xxviii. 102.

7th November. Barret's 'Theorick and Practick of Modern Wars.' *A.R.*, iii. 95; *S.T.C.*, 1500; one of the most interesting and best written of the military text-books of the period. Michael Cassio, in Iago's estimation, was another of your reading captains, a bookish theoric.

9th November. The Earl of Essex absent from Court. *S.P. Dom.*, 265 : 7. From a letter of Hunsdon to Essex.

THE PRIVILEGES OF THE HOUSE. D'Ewes' *Journals*, p. 553. The answer is not recorded.

ABUSES IN BRISTOL. *A.P.C.*, xxviii. 111.

10th November. THE PARLIAMENT. D'Ewes' *Journals*, p. 555.

14th November. THE KNIGHTS OF THE POST. *A.R.*, iii. 96 ; *S.T.C.*, 214 : 89. A lively little book written in the form of conversations on the Plymouth road.

INCESTUOUS MARRIAGES. D'Ewes' *Journals*, p. 556.

15th November. THE SUBSIDIES. D'Ewes' *Journals*, p. 557. For the subsidies granted by the previous Parliament, see *Eliz. Journal*, pp. 203-4, 205, 210, 213-4, 228.

16th November. MY LORD OF ESSEX'S ABSENCE. *S.P. Dom.*, 265 : 10. From a long letter to Essex from 'thy true servant not daring to subscribe.' Compare Bacon's advice noted on p. 139. The register of attendances in *A.P.C.* shows that Essex was absent from Council meetings from 3rd November to 22nd December.

18th November. THE EARL OF ESSEX ABSENT FROM PARLIAMENT. D'Ewes' *Journals*, p. 529.

19th November. THE SUBSIDIES. D'Ewes' *Journals*, p. 559.

20th November. DISORDERS IN WALES. *A.P.C.*, xxviii. 119, 121.

THE SPANISH LOSSES. *S.P. Dom.*, 264 : 148 ; letter from a spy dated 19th October.

21st November. PRIVILEGE OF THE HOUSE. D'Ewes' *Journal*, p. 560.

22nd November. A PETITION OF THE UNIVERSITIES. *MSS. Addit.*, 5843, f. 449.

23rd November. THE PARLIAMENT. D'Ewes' *Journals*, pp. 562-3.

28th November. THE FRENCH AMBASSADOR RECEIVED. *Baschet Transcripts*, 30, f. 205. This and the other entries concerning De Maisse are taken from his Journal, of which a transcript is kept in the Public Record Office. A translation is in preparation to be published by the Nonesuch Press.

30th November. A PRISONER RELEASED. *A.P.C.*, xxviii. 156. See *Eliz. Journal*, p. 207.

AN ACCIDENT AT THE SWAN. *Letters of Philip Gawdy*, edited by I. H. Jeayes, Roxburghe Club, 1906, p. 93 ; approximate date.

1st December. GERARD'S 'HERBAL.' *A.R.*, iii. 85 ; *S.T.C.*, 11750 ; entered 6th June ; Epistle to the Reader dated 1st December.

3rd December. THE VENETIAN CORN SHIP. *A.P.C.*, xxviii. 167 ; see pp. 162, 277.

4th December. THE SERMON AT PAUL'S CROSS. Entered 9th January, 1598. *A.R.*, iii. 100 ; *S.T.C.*, 13881 ; there were two editions. The sermon was concluded on 28th May, 1598. Mr. Howson's estimate of £500-£666 in Elizabethan money seems excessive ; his argument, expressed in different terms, is that parents pay for a University career because it ensures for their children an income of £40-£50 per annum for life ; it is not surprising that so many parsons in the Church of England were second-rate men.

8th December. A BOY POSSESSED AT NOTTINGHAM. Approximate date; for authorities see note on 28th July, 1598.

11th December. THE SUBSIDY. D'Ewes' *Journals*, p. 571.

14th December. THE LORDS' PRIVILEGE ABUSED. D'Ewes' *Journals*, pp. 532, 533.

THE ABUSE OF MONOPOLIES. D'Ewes' *Journals*, p. 573.

MONSIEUR DE MAISSE. *Baschet Transcripts*, 30, ff. 218-220.

17th December. TWO LONDON CRIMES. *A.P.C.*, xxviii. 187, 188, 219.

20th December. A DISPUTE CONCERNING PROCEDURE. D'Ewes' *Journals*, pp. 573-4, 575-7.

21st December. THE EARL OF ESSEX'S INDIGNATION. *Sidney Papers*, ii. 77.

THE QUEEN AND M. DE MAISSE. *Baschet Transcripts*, 30, ff. 227 v.-231; 29, f. 161.

24th December. THE PRICE OF PEPPER. Stow's *Annals*. For the Great Carrack and the pepper, see *Eliz. Journal*, pp. 195, 267.

31st December. NEW PLAYS. *Hens. Diary*, i. 50; ii. 181. Dr. Greg notes that *The famous history of the life and death of Captain Thomas Stukeley* was entered on 11th August, 1600, and printed in 1605; the printed version, however, has probably been cut down and altered. It is reprinted in R. Simpson's *School of Shakspere*, 1878.

OTHER BOOKS SET FORTH ANNO 1597

MERES' 'GOD'S ARITHMETIC.' *S.T.C.*, 17833; except for occasional gems of phrasing this is a dull little book. For *Palladis Tamia* see p. 305.

BRETON'S 'WIT'S TRENCHMOUR.' *S.T.C.*, 3713; m.e. in *The Works of Nicholas Breton*, edited by A. B. Grosart. This is the kind of book which Beatrice and Benedick read; in style it is somewhat between *Euphues* and a 'metaphysical' poem.

SHAKESPEARE'S 'ROMEO AND JULIET.' *S.T.C.*, 22322. This is the pirated First Quarto; facsimile by C. Praetorius, 1886; a parallel text of the two quartos was edited by P. A. Daniel for the New Shakespere Society in 1874.

1598

1st January. TYRONE AGAIN SUBMITS. *Carew MSS.*, 278-281.

2nd January. REFLECTIONS ON A PEACE WITH SPAIN. *S.P. Dom.*, 266 : 3 ; from Burleigh's manuscript, 'Reflections upon the proposal of the French King to her Majesty.'

3rd January. SIR JOHN SMYTHE RELEASED. *S.P. Dom.*, 266 : 4. See pp. 105-6, etc.

4th January. THE FRENCH AMBASSADOR. *Baschet Transcripts*, 30, ff. 244 v-245.

5th January. TYRONE AGAIN SUBMITS. *Carew MSS.*, 278.

10th January. COMPLAINTS CONCERNING THE FRENCH COURTS. *A.P.C.*, xxviii. 234.

11th January. THE PARLIAMENT RENEWED. D'Ewes' *Journals*, p. 535.

13th January. THE STILLYARD TO BE SUPPRESSED. *S.P. Dom.*, 266 : 14.

14th January. THE MERCHANTS TO DEPART. *Sidney Papers*, ii. 81.

THE COMMONS OFFENDED. D'Ewes' *Journals*, p. 580.

19th January. THE COMMONS' OFFENCE. D'Ewes' *Journals*, p. 540.

20th January. A QUARREL AT COURT. *Sidney Papers*, ii. 82, 83.

THE COMMONS SATISFIED. D'Ewes' *Journals*, pp. 539-40, 584-5.

A BAWD CARTED. *Middlesex Sessions Rolls*, i. 235. Her sentence was the same as that of Elizabeth Holland (see p. 258).

26th January. THE STILLYARD. *S.P. Dom.*, 266 : 29.

28th January. CASES OF PIRACY. *A.P.C.*, xxviii., 283, 284, 285.

29th January. ABUSES IN THE NORTH. *S.P. Dom.*, 266 : 18, 32. Religion in the North was perpetually in a parlous state, hence the prevalence of witchcraft : see also *Eliz. Journal*, pp. 117, 141.

THE SPANISH PRISONERS. *A.P.C.*, xxviii. 287.

1st February. COURT NEWS. *Sidney Papers*, ii. 86, 87, 88.

4th February. A RESTRAINT ON COCHINEAL. *S.P. Dom.*, 266 : 43.

9th February. THE PARLIAMENT DISSOLVED. D'Ewes' *Journals*, pp. 546-7, 595-6.

AN OUTRAGE IN THE MIDDLE TEMPLE. *Archaeologia*, xxi. 107. For this display of temper Davies was ejected from the Middle Temple '*nunquam in posterum restituendus*' ; he was restored in October 1601.

10th February. SIR ROBERT CECIL'S DEPARTURE. *Sidney Papers*, ii. 89.

A NOTE OF THE CHIEF STATUTES ENACTED BY THE LATE PARLIAMENT. *S.T.C.*, 9493, etc.

12th February. THE MUSTERS. *A.P.C.*, xxviii. 303-307.

15th February. COURT NEWS. *Sidney Papers*, ii. 89, 90, 91.

16th February. A BAWD CARTED. *Middlesex Sessions Rolls*, i. 235. I met with a survival of this custom of ringing basins in a Lincolnshire village in the summer of 1919. The sergeant in charge of some German prisoners working for farmers in those parts was discovered one night in another's bed; whereupon all the village youth turned out armed with cans which they beat to the refrain of 'Ran, tan; he's a very bad man,' until dispersed by the village policeman.

19th February. A COMPANY OF PLAYERS TO BE SUPPRESSED. *A.P.C.*, xxviii. 327.

23rd February. MR. BODLEY'S MUNIFICENCE TO THE UNIVERSITY OF OXFORD. From *Letters of Thomas Bodley to the University of Oxford*, 1598-1611, edited by G. W. Wheeler, 1927, p. 4.

25th February. THE LORD TREASURER DANGEROUSLY ILL. *Sidney Papers*, ii. 92.

26th February. SHAKESPEARE'S 'HENRY THE FOURTH.' *A.R.*, iii. 105; *S.T.C.*, 22280; facsimile by W. Griggs and H. Evans, 1881. There is no direct contemporary evidence for the change of name, but the indirect evidence (for which see the introduction to this play in the Arden Shakespeare), together with the passages in Fuller's *Worthies* [Warwickshire] and Rowe's *Life of Shakespeare*, seems to be ample. Falstaffe, to judge by the number of references in the *Shakspere Allusion Book*, was the most popular of all Shakespeare's characters; he is the supreme comic figure of the Great War of 1588-1604. The Quarto of *I. Henry IV.* was reprinted in 1599, 1604, 1608, 1613, 1622, 1632, 1639.

FLESH IN LENT. *Proclamations*, 353.

MARLOWE'S 'HERO AND LEANDER.' *S.T.C.*, 17413; m.e. in *The Works of Christopher Marlowe*, edited by C. F. Tucker Brooke, 1910. The date is approximate, but Blunt's edition of the first part of *Hero and Leander* must have been issued early in 1598, for Henry Petowe had finished his sequel by 14th April (p. 271). On 2nd March Blunt assigned his rights to Linley, who published a second edition with Chapman's sequel later in the year (p. 329). Presumably Linley, possessing the rights in Chapman's addition, bought the copyright from Blunt to enable him to issue the whole poem. *Hero and Leander* was first entered to Wolfe on 28th September, 1593, but there is no trace of an edition earlier than 1598.

1st March. THE DISORDERS IN GOVERNMENT IN IRELAND. *S.P. Ireland*, 202 : part i., 53, 54; letters dated 19th February.

2nd March. THE LADY LEICESTER RECONCILED TO THE QUEEN. *Sidney Papers*, ii. 92, 93. The Lady at this time was the wife of Sir Christopher Blount.

5th March. A NOTABLE FRAUD. *A.P.C.*, xxviii. 351.

6th March. MR. BODLEY'S GIFT TO OXFORD. *S.P. Dom.*, 266 : 87.

'THE COUNSELLOR.' *A.R.*, iii. 106; *S.T.C.*, 12372. The late Sir Israel Gollancz (in *A Book of Homage to Shakespeare*, 1916, p. 173) maintained that Shakespeare took the name of Polonius, which in the First Quarto of *Hamlet* is Corambis, from this treatise.

8th March. THE EARL OF CUMBERLAND SAILS. Purchas, xvi. 28.

10th March. 'LOVE'S LABOURS LOST.' *S.T.C.*, 22294; facsimile by W. Griggs and F. J. Furnivall; m.e. by Sir A. T. Quiller Couch and J.

Dover Wilson, 1923. The play was probably first performed in 1593; see *Eliz. Journal*, p. 398.

12th March. INSTRUCTIONS FOR THE MUSTERS. *S.P. Dom.*, 266 : 100, endorsed 'March 1595'; see 12th February.

16th March. THE ENVOYS OF THE STATES. *Salisbury MSS.*, viii. 84.

17th March. THE SCOTTISH KING'S 'DAEMONOLOGY.' *A.R.*, iii. 106; *S.T.C.*, 14364; m.e. in *The Bodley Head Quartos*, vol. ix., 1924. The book was entered on this date, but no English edition is known earlier than 1603. Contrary to the opinion held by those who have not read it, *Daemonology* is concise, well written, and the best contemporary account of the full belief in witchcraft.

24th March. KEEPING OF DAIRIES. *A.P.C.*, xxviii. 372.

29th March. PARLEYS WITH TYRONE. *S.P. Ireland*, 202 : pt. i., 89.

30th March. 'VIRGIDEMIARUM,' THE LAST PART. *A.R.*, iii. 109; *S.T.C.*, 12716; see note on 31st March, 1597. The satires in the second book are more obscure and general than in the first; but at times Hall achieves some perfect eighteenth-century couplets, which was presumably the reason why Warton praised him so highly. Compare Jaques' similar apology for the satirist (*As You Like It*, II. vii. 70).

1st April. THE BOY POSSESSED AT NOTTINGHAM. For authorities see note on 28th July.

3rd April. BASTARD'S 'CHRESTOLEROS.' *A.R.*, iii. 110; *S.T.C.*, 1559; m.e. by E. V. Otterson, 1842.

5th April. SEIZED BOOKS. *A.P.C.*, xxviii. 387.

6th April. THE TOWN OF TWYFORD BURNT. Stow's *Annals*.

7th April. SIR ROBERT CECIL RECEIVED BY THE FRENCH KING. Birch's *Historical View*, p. 105; *Salisbury Papers*, viii. 90.

9th April. CERTAIN LETTERS INTERCEPTED. Birch's *Historical View*, p. 140; *Sidney Papers*, ii. 100.

10th April. MR. CHAPMAN TRANSLATETH HOMER'S 'ILIADES.' *A.R.*, iii. 110; *S.T.C.*, 13632. Contemporaries could hardly have failed to see an intentional likeness between Achilles in Shakespeare's *Troilus and Cressida* and the 'now living instance of the Achilleian virtues.' It should be noted that Shakespeare founded the Achilles episodes on this translation, his play presumably being privately staged either in the late summer of 1598 or during Essex's retirement in 1600.

12th April. AN ATTEMPT TO POISON. *A.P.C.*, xxviii. 393; see also pp. 42-3, 279, 290.

14th April. A SECOND PART TO 'HERO AND LEANDER.' *A.R.*, iii. 111; *S.T.C.*, 19807. This continuation of Marlowe's narrative is of no literary importance, though the praise of Marlowe is significant; about half is here quoted.

16th April. THE NEGOTIATIONS WITH THE FRENCH KING BROKEN. Camden's *Elizabeth*. Cecil's full and detailed account of the negotiations is given in Birch's *Historical Memoirs*.

18th April. THE SPITAL SERMONS. *A.P.C.*, xxviii. 408.

21st April. ARISTOTLE'S 'POLITIQUES.' *A.R.*, iii. 112 ; *S.T.C.*, 760 ; an important and beautifully printed volume.

24th April. TYRONE RENEWETH THE TRUCE. *S.P. Ireland*, 202 : pt. ii., 9.

25th April. LORD BURLEIGH'S REBUKE. Camden's *Elizabeth*. Approximate date.

30th April. ABUSES IN TENEMENT HOUSES. *A.P.C.*, xxviii. 427, 435.

1st May. SIR ROBERT CECIL'S RETURN. Stow's *Annals* ; Birch's *Historical View*, p. 161.

3rd May. 'GREENE IN CONCEIPT.' *A.R.*, iii. 114 ; *S.T.C.*, 6819 ; m.e. by A. B. Grosart, 1878. J. D[ickenson] imitates Greene's earlier euphuistic manner, as he acknowledges in the title ; his story of Valeria reads as if it were true with but a minimum of transmutation. More of the Euphuistic novels may be founded on fact than would at first sight appear.

6th May. THE CURES OF THE DISEASED IN REMOTE REGIONS. *A.R.*, iii. 114 ; *S.T.C.*, 25106 ; m.e. in facsimile by Charles Singer, 1915, who identifies *calenture* as heatstroke or sunstroke, *tabardilla* as yellow fever or typhus, *espinlas* as 'prickly heat,' *cameras de sangre* as dysentery.

7th May. MR. GOSSON'S SERMON AT PAUL'S CROSS. *A.R.*, iii. 116 ; *S.T.C.*, 12099. This Gosson was the author of *The School of Abuse*, 1579, which Sidney answered in *The Defence of Poesy* ; see p. 6.

9th May. AN ABUSE IN DARTMOUTH. *A.P.C.*, xxviii. 438.

10th May. THE QUEEN'S LETTERS TO THE FRENCH KING. Camden's *Elizabeth*. Approximate date.

14th May. THE VENETIAN ARGOSY. *A.P.C.*, xxviii. 440 ; see also pp. 162, 240.

15th May. 'THE SERVINGMAN'S COMFORT.' *A.R.*, iii. 115 ; *S.T.C.*, 17140. For the social student this is a most important book, of which Shakespeare probably owned a marked copy. This work and the mockery of the country 'gentleman' (such as Mr. Stephen, Sogliardo, Sir Andrew Aguecheek) on the stage seem to reflect a prevalent discussion on the 'new gentry' to which Hamlet refers (? autumn 1601) in "By the Lord, Horatio, these three years I have taken note of it ; the age is grown so picked that the toe of the peasant comes so near the heel of the courtier, he galls his kibe' ; see especially *Every Man out of His Humour*, Fungoso's letter to his father Sordido (III. ii.). Similarly the 'new rich,' or war profiteers, were especially a topic of comment at the end of the Great War ; for which see *Punch*, 1918-22, *passim*.

20th May. THE MONOPOLY IN STARCH. *Proclamations*, 3546.

RUMOURS. Chamberlain's *Letters*, p. 11. Over a century later Swift makes a similar complaint of the Dutch in *The Conduct of the Allies*.

21st May. MR. BARNABE BARNES. *A.P.C.*, xxviii. 441, 456 ; see also pp. 279, 290.

THE SERMON AT PAUL'S CROSS. *S.T.C.*, 12099 ; see p. 240.

25th May. SLANDERS AGAINST THE SCOTTISH KING. *Calendar of Border Papers*, ii. 537 ; *S.P. Dom.*, 269 : 20.

27th May. 'The Metamorphosis of Pygmalion's Image; and Certain Satires.' *A.R.*, iii. 116; *S.T.C.*, 17482; m.e. in *The Works of John Marston*, by A. H. Bullen, 1887, vol. 3.

30th May. A Fray at Oxford. *Salisbury Papers*, viii. 191, 201, 202.

1st June. The Apology of the Earl of Essex. *S.T.C.*, 6788; *Salisbury Papers*, viii. 545. Essex's *Apology* (said to have been written by Anthony Bacon) was published in 1603, after the Queen's death, though in manuscript circulation at this time.

2nd June. A Lewd Show at Brussels. *Salisbury Papers*, viii. 190.

5th June. A Case of Piracy. *A.P.C.*, xxviii. 456.

7th June. Troubles at Plymouth. *A.P.C.*, xxviii. 500, 517.

8th June. The Peace at Vervins. *Salisbury Papers*, viii. 193; *The History of the Civil Wars of France*, by H. C. D'Avila, 1678, p. 732.

10th June. Murders in Ireland. *S.P. Ireland*, 202 : pt. ii., 56.

11th June. Complaints against the Earl of Lincoln. *A.P.C.*, xxviii. 506.

15th June. Jesuit Devices. *Salisbury Papers*, viii. 213, 293. This affair is a sequel to the efforts of Mr. Darrell at Cleworth in March 1597, the woman being one of the seven possessed in the Starkie household (p. 173).

17th June. A Case of Manslaughter. *Middlesex Sessions Rolls*, i. 237.

18th June. Soldiers for Ireland. *A.P.C.*, xxviii. 524, 527.

23rd June. News from Paris. *Salisbury Papers*, viii. 219 (where the story is that 'the German whom the Earl knighted refuses to fight a Frenchman'), and pp. 224-31 where a long account of the challenge is given; see also Chamberlain's *Letters*, pp. 10 and 14, where he says 'the news I wrote of Sir Charles Blount must be recalled, for it was a mistaking of a combat between a Frenchman and a Dutch baron.' All the same, Sir Melchior did refuse Sir Charles' challenge on the grounds stated. It is perhaps more than a coincidence that Jonson, who was finishing off *Every Man in His Humour* at this time, should cause Captain Bobadilla to offer a similar excuse to the blunt squire Giulliano (*alias* Downright).

24th June. Distress in Lincolnshire. *A.P.C.*, xxviii. 537.

28th June. The Truce ended in Ireland. *S.P. Ireland*, 200 : pt. ii., 62, 74; dated 10th and 18th June.

2nd July. The Earl of Essex's Great Contempt. The only direct authority for this famous incident is Camden's *Elizabeth*, which gives no date; but the date can be deduced from *A.P.C.*, wherein attendances at the Council Board are recorded. Essex had been present on 25th, 26th, 29th, 30th June; he next attended on 8th August; he was then absent until 22nd August, when he sat in the morning but was absent in the afternoon; his next appearance was on 10th September, and thereafter he attended regularly. The great offence therefore was committed on 30th June or 1st July. On 22nd August he attended the Council by request to advise on the Irish situation; his behaviour on this occasion—sulky, curious and defiant—probably provoked Egerton's letter (see pp. 301, 302). In early copies the letter is dated 15th October, but this seems too late; it might however have been written on the 9th or 10th August. See Corrigenda, p. vi.

6th July. THE GOVERNOR OF DUNKIRK. *A.P.C.*, xxviii. 563; see p. 208.

7th July. STOW'S 'SURVEY OF LONDON.' *A.R.*, iii. 121; *S.T.C.*, 23341; other editions appeared in 1599 and 1603, and, after Stow's death in 1605, in 1608 and 1633; m.e. by C. L. Kingsford in 1908.

10th July. A FENCER HANGED. Stow's *Annals*.

11th July. MR. BARNABE BARNES. *A.P.C.*, xxviii. 568.

12th July. DISORDERS IN IRELAND. *A.P.C.*, xxviii. 572.

16th July. THE QUEEN AND THE EARL OF ESSEX. Birch's *Memoirs*, ii. 389.

A SAYING CONCERNING MY LORD OF ESSEX. Quoted from Bacon's *Apothegms* in Spedding's *Bacon*, ii. 91.

HORSE AND MEN REQUIRED FOR IRELAND. *A.P.C.*, xxviii. 567, 586, 588, 590, 591.

19th July. THE TROUBLES AT PLYMOUTH. *A.P.C.*, xxviii. 598.

21st July. THE EARL OF ESSEX AND THE LORD GREY. *Salisbury Papers*, viii. 269.

23rd July. ABUSES IN THE IRISH SERVICE. *S.P. Ireland*, 202 : pt. ii., 108.

25th July. THE STILLYARD. *A.P.C.*, xxviii. 613.

MR. DARRELL BEFORE THE ECCLESIASTICAL COMMISSIONERS. The affairs of John Darrell gave rise to a small pamphlet war between 1598 and 1603. In 1598 there was printed abroad the pro-Darrell *Brief narration of the possession, dispossession, and repossession of William Somers*, etc.; this was answered in 1599 by Samuel Harsnet, chaplain to the Bishop of London, in *A discovery of the fraudulent practises of John Darrell*, etc., which gives a long and detailed commentary on the whole series of exorcisms. The present account (pp. 241, 267) is based on both sources. For other books connected with the case and a general account of the controversy, see *A History of Witchcraft in England from* 1558 *to* 1718, by Wallace Notestein, 1911, chap. iv.

26th July. LORD BURLEIGH SICK. *Salisbury Papers*, viii. 276, 277.

WANT OF ZEAL AT PLYMOUTH. *A.P.C.*, xxviii. 622.

27th July. A WITCH CONDEMNED. *Middlesex Sessions Rolls*, i. 225.

29th July. GENERAL NEWS. *Stowe MSS.*, 55, f. 114. From a letter of Sir Thomas Ferrers to Sir Humphrey Ferrers.

1st August. THE BLACKWATER FORT. *S.P.* Ireland, 202 : pt. ii., 105.

4th August. THE DEATH OF LORD BURLEIGH. *The Life of that great statesman William Cecil, Lord Burghley. . . . Published from the original manuscript wrote soon after his Lordship's death; now in the Library of the right honourable Brownlow, Earl of Exeter*, etc., edited by Arthur Collis, 1732.

THE LORD BURLEIGH'S PRECEPTS FOR HIS SON. *S.T.C.*, 4897; reprinted in Strype's *Annals*, iv. 340. These observations were not printed until 1617, but such gifts were not meant to lie hid, and it is reasonably probable that they would be discussed at this time. Moreover, there is a 'damnable iteration' about Polonius' 'few precepts.'

THE QUEEN'S GRIEF. Birch's *Memoirs*, ii. 390; from a letter to Essex from Sir William Knollys.

12th August. INSUFFICIENT SOLDIERS FROM RADNORSHIRE. *A.P.C.*, xxix. 43.

14th August. VICTUALS FOR THE SOLDIERS. *A.P.C.*, xxix. 49.

16th August. THE QUEEN AND THE EARL OF ESSEX. Birch's *Memoirs*, ii. 390; approximate date.

22nd August. A GREAT DISASTER IN IRELAND. *S.P. Ireland*, 202: pt. iii., 3, 19, 20, 20 (i), 28 (ii). This was the greatest defeat suffered by English troops during the reign.

23rd August. A PROCLAMATION AGAINST FORESTALLERS. *Proclamations*, 355.

THE LORD KEEPER'S LETTER TO THE EARL OF ESSEX. Printed in Birch's *Memoirs*, ii. 385, where it is dated 15th October; see note on 2nd July.

THE IRISH FORCES. *A.P.C.*, xxix. 79.

25th August. MY LORD OF ESSEX'S LETTER TO THE UNIVERSITY OF CAMBRIDGE. *MSS. Addit.*, 5843, f. 450.

26th August. ESSEX'S REPLY TO THE LORD KEEPER. Printed in Birch's *Memoirs*, ii. 386, with the date 18th October. There are several copies in various collections, *e.g.*, *S.P. Dom.*, 268: 43. According to Fynes Moryson (*Itinerary*, MacLehose edition, ii. 316), Bacon, in detailing the charges against Essex at his appearance before the Commissioners on 5th June, 1600, made a special point of this letter, 'which letter he also said was published by the Earles own friends.' From this it would appear likely that both letters were much discussed by the friends—and enemies—of Essex.

THE NEW MARSHAL IN IRELAND. *A.P.C.*, xxix. 104.

27th August. NEW FORCES FOR IRELAND. *A.P.C.*, xxix. 94. On a similar occasion Justice Shallow at least tried to do his duty.

TWO PATENTS. *A.P.C.*, xxix. 101, 106.

29th August. THE DEFEAT AT THE BLACKWATER. *S.P. Ireland*, 202: pt. iii., 34.

THE FUNERAL OF THE LORD TREASURER. *S.P. Dom.*, 268: 32; Chamberlain's *Letters*, p. 18.

31st August. RECUSANTS TO SUPPLY HORSES. *A.P.C.*, xxix. 116.

5th September. LIGHTNING IN LONDON. Stow's *Annals*. In Richard Smith's little Diary—*Rerum vulgatorum notae* (Sloane MSS., 414)—the thunder is recorded on 4th and 5th of November.

7th September. COURT NEWS. *S.P.Dom.*, 268: 47, 50.

MERES' 'PALLADIS TAMIA.' *A.R.*, iii. 125; *S.T.C.*, 17834; a good specimen of literary ragbag which shows the range of Meres' reading. The English authorities quoted are *The Chronicles of England*, Dr. Playfair, Hugh Broughton, Fox, Lyly, Harington, Capgrave, Pettie, Hakluyt, Greene, Sidney and Warner.

8th September. MARSTON'S 'SCOURGE OF VILLAINY.' *A.R.*, iii. 125; *S.T.C.*, 17485. It was reissued in 1599 with an additional satire (*Stultorum plena sunt omnia*), and included in the bonfire of disreputable books on 4th June, 1599; m.e. in *The Bodley Head Quartos*, vol. xiii. 1925. I have tried to suggest the importance of Marston as a melancholic in an *Essay on Elizabethan Melancholy* appended to my edition of Breton's *Melancholic Humours*, 1929.

9th September. LAWLESSNESS NEAR LONDON. *A.P.C.*, xxix. 128, 140; *Proclamations*, 386.

10th September. SOME LEVIES DISCHARGED. *A.P.C.*, xxix. 155, 157.

12th September. THE QUEEN'S LETTER TO THE COUNCIL OF IRELAND. *S.P. Ireland*, 202 : pt. iii., 20 (ii) and 64.

15th September. THE EARL OF ESSEX RESTORED TO FAVOUR. *A.P.C.*, xxix. 154-7; *S.P. Dom.*, 268 : 56; from a letter to Dudley Carleton from Toby Matthew.

'SKIALETHEIA.' *A.R.*, iii. 126; *S.T.C.*, 12504; m.e. by J. P. Collins, 1870, and A. B. Grosart, 1878. The author is identified as E. Guilpin (of whom nothing is known) by passages quoted in *England's Parnassus*. It is an important book for the student, being full of personalities and intimate details, including several references to the theatres.

16th September. JONSON'S 'EVERY MAN IN HIS HUMOUR.' *S.P. Dom.*, 268 : 61; approximate date, fixed by Toby Matthews' letter (see 20th September). First published in Quarto in 1601 (*S.T.C.*, 14756); this edition is of the play as first presented in 1598; m.e. in *The Oxford Ben Jonson*, edited by C. H. Herford and P. Simpson, 1927, vol. iii. The version of the play usually printed is that revised by Jonson for his Folio of 1616. See note on Chapman's *Humorous Day's Mirth*, 11th May, 1597.

20th September. GENERAL NEWS. *S.P. Dom.*, 268 : 61; from Toby Matthews' letter (above). Compare 'Honour pricks me on. Yea, but how if honour prick me off when I come on, how then?' (*I. Henry IV.*, v. i. 131). Shakespeare may have invented this jest, but it is as likely that he was making use of a current phrase (as 'If you knows of a better 'ole, go to it'); after the Islands Voyage military glory began to grow somewhat fusty.

22nd September. A PLAYER SLAIN. A translation of the indictment is given in F. G. Fleay's *Chronicle of the English Drama*, i. 343; the original is reproduced in *The Oxford Ben Jonson*, by C. H. Herford and P. Simpson, 1925, i. 219. In the *Conversations*, Jonson's version of the affair is that 'since his coming to England being appealed to the fields he had killed his adversarie, which hurt him jn the arme & whose sword was 10 Inches longer than his, for the which he was Emprisoned and almost at the Gallowes. Then took he his Religion by trust of a priest who Visited him jn Prison' (*ibid.* i. 139). For the 'bricklayer' see *Henslowe Papers*, edited by W. W. Greg, p. 48.

30th September. MR. SPENSER TO BE SHERIFF OF CORK. *A.P.C.*, xxix. 204.

2nd October. THE EARL OF CUMBERLAND'S RETURN. Purchas, xvi. 29.

8th October. GENERAL NEWS. Chamberlain's *Letters*, p. 20.

4th October. A MUTINY AMONGST THE LONDON SOLDIERS. *A.P.C.*, xxix. 214.

7th October. MR. HAKLUYT'S 'PRINCIPAL NAVIGATIONS.' *S.T.C.*, 12626; dated in Epistle Dedicatory; m.e. published MacLehose, 1903, reprinted in *The Everyman Library*, 8 vols., 1907, etc.

9th October. SIR THOMAS SHIRLEY'S PRIZES. *Salisbury Papers*, viii. 385.

10th October. A TRAITOR TO BE SENT AWAY. *A.P.C.*, xxix. 224.

15th October. YARMOUTH HERRINGS. *A.P.C.*, xxix. 230, 245.

28th October. FURTHER SOLDIERS FOR IRELAND. *A.P.C.*, xxix. 239.

4th November. THE DEATH OF THE SPANISH KING. *Calendar of State Papers Venetian*, ix. 727, 731, 732, 737, 738, from the despatches of the Venetian Ambassador in Spain to the Doge. In Richard Smith's Diary (Sloan MSS., 414) the death of the King of Spain is noted between 4th and 12th November; the news apparently did not reach London before this time.

5th November. GREAT FLOODS. *A.P.C.*, xxix. 264.

6th November. REBELLION SPREADING IN IRELAND. *S.P. Ireland*, 202 : pt. iii., 3, 127. From a letter to Cecil from the Lord Chief Justice of Munster, dated 26th October.

8th November. RUMOURS. Chamberlain's *Letters*, p. 26.

A JEST ON THE KING OF SPAIN. *Nugae Antiquae*, i. 175, 244.

9th November. THE CONSPIRACY OF EDWARD SQUIRE. Stow's *Annals* and *A letter written out of England to a gentleman at Padua*, 1599; reprinted in Spedding's *Bacon*, ii. 110. Spedding on good grounds attributes the 'letter' to Bacon, who took part in the examinations. The original depositions are preserved in *S.P. Dom.*, 268 : 83, 86, 89; of which the official account is a fair summary.

10th November. AN ATTEMPT IN DUBLIN. *S.P. Ireland*, 202 : pt. iii., 135. From a letter from the Council of Ireland dated 31st October.

14th November. THE QUEEN ROYALLY RECEIVED. Stow's *Annals*.

15th November. THE SOLDIERS IN IRELAND. *S.P. Ireland*, 202 : pt. iii., 149.

16th November. BEACON WATCHES DISCONTINUED. *A.P.C.*, xxix. 288.

17th November. DETERMINATIONS FOR IRELAND. *S.P. Ireland*, 202 : pt. iii., 162.

20th November. THE EXECUTION OF LUKE HUTTON. Approximate date, from the ballad *Luke Hutton's Lamentation* (m.e. by A. V. Judges in *The Elizabethan Underworld*, 1930, p. 292); *Nugae Antiquae*, ii. 253, and Fuller's *Church History* therein cited. See also p. 70.

28th November. MORE SOLDIERS REQUIRED. *A.P.C.*, xxix. 312.

3rd December. THE DESPERATE STATE OF IRELAND. *S.P. Ireland*, 202 : pt. iii., 168, 167.

PLAYS AT COURT. *A.P.C.*, xxix. 324; *Hens. Diary*, i. 98; ii. 190.

5th December. A LOAN IN THE CITY. *A.P.C.*, xxix. 336, 339.

11th December. AN ATTEMPT IN THE NORTH. *A.P.C.*, xxix. 356.

15th December. SOLDIERS FOR IRELAND. *S.P. Dom.*, 269 : 12, 16; *A.P.C.*, xxix. 358, 388.

18th December. THE THAMES FROZEN. Stow's *Annals*. The brick piles of Old London Bridge were so thick that the flow of the water was considerably retarded. Hence the freezing of the Thames was not infrequent in severe winters, and liable to be an embarrassment, as the force of flow was used to give power to the City corn mills. See *Eliz. Journal*, p. 324.

20*th December*. A DECLARATION CONCERNING THE KING OF SCOTS. *S.P. Dom.*, 269 : 20.

24*th December*. THE LOAN IN THE CITY. *A.P.C.*, xxix. 382, 401.

THE REBELLION IN MUNSTER. *S.P. Ireland*, 202 : pt. iv., 15.

27*th December*. A SKIRMISH IN MUNSTER. *S.P. Ireland*, 202 : pt. iv., 36.

28*th December*. THE THAMES AGAIN FROZEN. Stow's *Annals*.

THE THEATRE PULLED DOWN. The original complaint is quoted in J. O. Halliwell Phillipps' *Outlines of the Life of Shakespeare*, i. 360 ; see also *Elizabethan Stage*, ii. 398. There is some difference of opinion whether the Burbages removed all the timber on this occasion or completed the work on 20th January, 1599.

A LEWD FELLOW. *S.P. Dom.*, 269 : 22.

29*th December*. PRIVILEGED PLACES IN LONDON. *A.P.C.*, xxix. 414.

30*th December*. A PLAY AT CAMBRIDGE. *The Pilgrimage to Parnassus*, etc., edited from MSS. by W. D. Macray, 1886. This play, and more especially the two sequels—*The Return from Parnassus*, parts i. and ii.—are important expressions of the general discontent of university men that their studies neither satisfied the intellect nor led to preferment. Macray misdated the play 1597 ; references to Marston's *Satires* and Bastard's *Chrestoleros* show it to belong to 1598.

31*st December*. NEW PLAYS THIS PAST YEAR AT THE ROSE. This list is taken from Dr. Greg's catalogue of the plays mentioned in *Henslowe's Diary* (ii. 187-199), and is roughly chronological. As it is not possible to deduce from the entries of payments to dramatists and others the date of the first performance of a new play, I thought it best to group the list together. Of the plays mentioned, there only survive in print the two parts of *Robert, Earl of Huntingdon*, *Two angry women of Abingdon*, and *A woman will have her will*.

THESE BOOKS ALSO SET FORTH ANNO 1598.

MR. RICHARD BARNFIELD'S POEMS. *S.T.C.*, 1488 ; m.e. by the Roxburghe Club, 1816.

CHAPMAN'S ADDITIONS TO 'HERO AND LEANDER.' *S.T.C.*, 17414 ; m.e. in *The Works of Christopher Marlowe*, edited by C. F. Tucker Brooke 1910.

ACHILLES' SHIELD. *S.T.C.*, 13632.

FLORIO'S 'WORLD OF WORDS.' *S.T.C.*, 11098.

A BOOK OF PAINTING. *S.T.C.*, 16698. This is an important book for the study of the Elizabethan mind with its adherence to symmetrical systems of thought ; it is a good example of the 'Idols of the Theatre.' It details also the theory and practice of sensual appeal—a subject on which much curious observation was made.

'The Comedy of Mucedorus. *S.T.C.*, 18230. This ridiculous (though quite serious) romantic play is almost a burlesque in anticipation of tragi-comedy of the Beaumont and Fletcher kind. It was most popular with the citizens of London, 17 different editions in Quarto printed before 1670 survive; m.e. in *The Shakespeare Apocrypha*, edited by C. F. Tucker Brooke, 1908.

Norden's 'Speculum Britanniæ.' *S.T.C.*, 18637.

A Book of Riddles. *S.T.C.*, 13174. This is not apparently a first edition, though no earlier is known. It may have been Master Slender's aid to social accomplishment. (*Merry Wives*, I. i. 209)

Mr. Tofte's 'Alba.' *S.T.C.*, 24096. This very long lament is chiefly notable for the well-known reference to *Love's Labours Lost*; m.e. by A. B. Grosart, 1880.

Tyro's Roaring Meg. *S.T.C.*, 24477. A piece of undergraduate exuberance which owes something to Marston.

Mr. Wentworth's 'Pithy Exhortation.' *S.T.C.*, 25245. For Wentworth's offence see *Eliz. Journal*, pp. 201, 202, 243.

ADDENDA AND CORRIGENDA

26th July, 1595. The Spaniards Land in Cornwall. A long account of the raid is given in Richard Carew's *Survey of Cornwall*, 1603. See iii, *Eliz. Journal*, p. 262.

9th April, 1596. The Bishop of St. David's Unhappy Sermon. This entry is eleven days too late, for the sermon was preached on 28th March. It was published after the Queen's death in 1603 (S.T.C., 21432).

10th December, 1596. The Scottish Princess Baptized. The promise was handsomely honoured. In a letter to Dudley Carleton at the time of Princess Elizabeth's marriage in 1612 it is noted that Scotland has very unexpectedly sent her £20,000 for a wedding present (*Calendar of S.P. Dom.*, James I., 1611–18, No. 64, p. 161).

30th November, 1597. An Accident at the Swan. This entry should be deleted. The event is again recorded in its proper place in iii, *Eliz. Journal*, p. 315.

23rd August, 1598. The Lord Keeper's Letter to the Earl of Essex. In John Speed's *History of Great Britain* both letters are printed, the first being dated 18th July, which is probably correct.

APPENDIX

A TABLE OF AGES

It may be an aid to the reader's imagination in visualising the Elizabethan age to note the ages of some of the more interesting men at the date when the *Second Elizabethan Journal* begins. The dates of birth are taken for the most part from the *Dictionary of National Biography*; dates in *italic numerals* are approximate.

OVER SEVENTY

William Cecil, Lord Burleigh, Lord High Treasurer (1520); Thomas Churchyard (*1520*); John Stow (*1525*).

OVER SIXTY

John Whitgift, Archbishop of Canterbury (*1530*); Sir John Hawkins (1532); QUEEN ELIZABETH (1533); Mr. Sergeant Yelverton, Speaker of the House in 1597-8 (*1535*).

OVER FIFTY

Lord Charles Howard, Lord High Admiral (1536); William Byrd (*1538*); Sir Thomas Egerton, Lord Keeper in 1596 (*1540*); Sir Francis Drake (*1540*); The Earl of Tyrone (*1540*); Thomas Deloney (*1543*); Nicholas Breton (*1545*); Thomas Bodley (*1545*).

OVER FORTY

George Carey, Lord Hunsdon, Lord Chamberlain in 1597 (1547); Sir John Norris (*1547*); Sir Walter Ralegh (*1552*); Richard Hakluyt (*1552*); Edmund Spenser (*1552*); Sir Edward Coke, Attorney-General (1552); John Lyly (*1554*); Richard Hooker (1554); Lancelot Andrews (1555).

IN THE THIRTIES

George Clifford, Earl of Cumberland (1558); Thomas Lodge (*1558*); George Peele (*1558*); George Chapman (*1559*); Sir Francis Vere (1560); Francis Bacon (1561); Lord Thomas Howard (1561); John Harington (1561); Robert Southwell (*1561*); Samuel Daniel (1562); Michael Drayton (1563); Charles Blount, Lord Mountjoy (1563); Sir Robert Cecil, Principal Secretary (*1563*); Henry Percy, Earl of Northumberland (1564); William Shakespeare (1564); Sir Anthony Shirley (1565).

IN THE TWENTIES

King James VI. (1566); Robert Devereux, Earl of Essex (*1566*); Edward Alleyne (1566); Thomas Nashe (1567); Richard Burbage

(*1567*); Barnabe Barnes (*1569*); John Davies (1569); Thomas Dekker (*1570*); Henry Wriothesley, Earl of Southampton (1573); John Donne (1573); Benjamin Jonson (*1573*); Joseph Hall (1574); John Marston (1574).

UNDER TWENTY

Roger Manners, Earl of Rutland (1576); Robert Burton (1577); John Fletcher (1579); John Webster (1580); Francis Beaumont (1584); George Wither (1588); Robert Herrick (1591); Prince Henry, afterwards Prince of Wales (1594).

INDEX

E

I

Printed in Great Britain
by Amazon